British public policy
1776–1939

British public policy
1776–1939

An economic, social and political perspective

SYDNEY CHECKLAND

Professor of Economic History, University of Glasgow

CAMBRIDGE UNIVERSITY PRESS

Cambridge

London   *New York*   *New Rochelle*
Melbourne   *Sydney*

Published by the Press Syndicate of the University of Cambridge
The Pitt Building, Trumpington Street, Cambridge CB2 1RP
32 East 57th Street, New York, NY 10022, USA
296 Beaconsfield Parade, Middle Park, Melbourne 3206, Australia

First published 1983

Printed in Great Britain at
the University Press, Cambridge

Library of Congress catalogue card number: 82-9552

British Library Cataloguing in Publication Data
Checkland, Sydney
British public policy 1776–1939.
1. Great Britain – Politics and government –
18th century 2. Great Britain – Politics and
government – 19th century 3. Great Britain –
Politics and government – 20th century.
I. Title
354.4107′2   DA470
ISBN 0 521 24596 6

BO

For
Sydney Clare
Our daughter, the engineer

'What to think, what to say, what to do?'
Franz Lehar, *The Merry Widow*, 1905

Contents

Preface

Over the considerable period of preparation of the book I have drawn heavily upon the help of colleagues at Glasgow University. They include Kay Carmichael, Neil Charlesworth, Anne Crowther, David Donnison, Tom Hart, James Kellas, Joseph Melling, Michael Moss, Charles Munn, Forbes Munro, Keith Robbins, Robert Silver, Andrew Skinner and Anthony Slaven. For library support I am especially indebted to Janie Ferguson and Jean Robertson. Conversations with our Chancellor, Sir Alec Cairncross, have been characteristically stimulating. Of non-Glaswegians I wish to thank Roger Davidson, Malcolm Falkus, Peter Payne, Sidney Pollard and Richard Sayers. A visiting fellowship at the Australian National University made it possible to draw upon Kenneth Inglis, Oliver MacDonagh and Barry Smith; at Monash University there was John McCarty and Keith Trace. The typing of successive revisions has been done by Isabel Burnside with assistance from her husband Bill. To this indispensable and much valued service they have added the holding of the home fort during absences. Blythe O'Driscoll as departmental secretary has eased the teaching and administrative side of life. The index has been prepared by Aileen Forbes Ballantyne. Olive Checkland has shared the enterprise from its beginning, by continuous discussion, by criticism that has combined the sobering and the encouraging as occasion demanded and by reading and commenting on the manuscript in its successive forms as it struggled into shape.

S.G.C.
Number 5, The University,
Glasgow.

Introduction

It is necessary from time to time to remind one generation of the experience
which led a former generation to important legislative actions.

W. S. Jevons, *The State in Relation to Labour*, 1882.

This book discusses the main aspects of the evolution and actions of
the British state from the late eighteenth century to the outbreak of
the second world war. It has three principal objectives. It is intended
as a particular point of entry into the general history of Britain,
namely the decisions made by governments over the generations.
Secondly, it is an introduction to the study of public policy as such,
especially at the university and college level. Finally, there is the
hope that the book will provide perspectives for those who are
currently involved or interested in policy making.

For those who wish to concentrate on a part of the period an effort
has been made in the text to facilitate this through the division of the
books into five time-spans. Similarly the book can be used the-
matically: each of the principal items of the policy agenda can be
selectively followed over the full period. The literature listed has
been generated largely in the 1960s and 1970s.

The discussion involves thinking at two levels. There is first the
need to see each area of state action as a problem in its own limited
terms, capable in some degree of being isolated from the others.
Each has its own complex history; each asserted itself in its own time
and in its own manner. The economic and social policy agenda as it
had evolved by 1939 consisted of eight principal groups of elements,
as outlined in chapter 22, section 2.

The second aspect is the integrative one: it involves making some
sort of pattern of the interactions between these separate policy
responses. This is necessary because the degree of separateness
between them was never absolute, and progressively diminished

1

with time as the functions of the state increased and converged, impacting on each other. As this happened the role of the state as an ad hoc responder to discrete challenges began to change; the state was being pressed into a set of initiatives that were gradually being forced into some kind of system. At the same time the growth of state·actions progressively limited the choices of many individuals and groups (the latter becoming ever larger and more complex, themselves often awarded legal definition by the state). Reciprocally, such groups, especially large-scale business and the trade unions, sought to impose limitations on the actions of the state as affecting themselves.

The difference between Britain and most European states must be borne in mind. On the continent, in France, Prussia, Austria and elsewhere, the tradition of state action and surveillance was strong and was never abandoned. By contrast, Britain had broken with centralism in the seventeenth century, and though there were plenty of mercantilist devices in operation in the later eighteenth century, especially as affecting international trade, there was no strong interventionist government at the centre, and only the most rudimentary of bureaucracies, until most of the nineteenth century had passed. In Britain these things had to be brought into being, largely as an aftermath of industrialisation.

The essence of the British state, for the present purposes, was parliament and the central bureaucracy. To these must be added the local authorities and their administrators. The judiciary provided a third element, interpreting statute and generating the common law. The state therefore has here no metaphysical meaning – it consisted of the organs of power, implementation and interpretation, as they evolved and as the contest for their control proceeded. The elected and hereditary elements at the centre, comprising parliament, were sovereign. Parliament could operate at will both upon the bureaucracy and the judiciary. But its actions were often much affected by the bureaucracy, both in terms of policy formation and its implementation. The judiciary, though responsible for the interpretation of statutes as they stood, had considerable scope for enforcing the law in terms that derived from its own view of society.

The state as a source of policy has two aspects. Firstly, it represents the presiding will. Whether active or passive, and whether justified or not, it is the ultimate repository of power. But the ability of the government of the day to contain pressures or to coerce is always limited; there is no truly absolute state, nor can there be, short of a state-induced societal hypnosis, though some states have approached the absolute more closely than others. Secondly, the state embodies, to a greater or lesser degree, in its politicians and civil servants, a supervising intelligence, in the form of a continuous attempt to understand the choices that confront it, in order to choose between them. The objectives of this intelligence may be wholly self-serving or class-serving, in conformity with the Marxist model, or government may be illuminated by some concept of the general good or even under certain conditions be dominated by it. The ultimate elements of power at the service of government for the enforcement of its will are the military, the police and the penal system.

State will and intelligence do not spring forth complete and articulated in a moment of time; they too are products of the historical process. All this is true of Great Britain, as of other societies. There was a dynamic shifting of power between groups, together with a continuous reforming of such groups, generating new opportunities for some, and new frustrations and resentments for others. Indeed the most powerful group at any given time was itself almost always a moving coalition, subject to complex patterns of time-lag.

There was an element of society whose members did indeed try to rise above the approach deriving from selfishness, faction or class, and attempted objective observation and thought concerning the working of the human system within which they found themselves, and who pondered the problems of power and legitimacy and the available theories concerning them. Some of this kind of speculation arose from intellectual curiosity, especially the urge to see if the methods of the physical sciences could be applied to social behaviour. But much of it was ameliorative. Some of it was evangelical, springing from the redemptive passion of those driven by their religion. Some of it derived from rationalism, resting on the hope, inspired by the eighteenth-century Enlightenment, that men, by construing their own condition, could improve it. Most of those who created such thought systems came from a particular range of society, namely the middle classes; these evangelical improvers and amateur social scientists were culture-bound within the value system of their class. They were thus objects of suspicion by the working

3

classes. There was no reciprocity: the middle classes, by and large, were not aware of any body of thought coming in the opposite direction, from the working classes, at least until late in the nineteenth century.

The story is further complicated, and given additional drama, by the fact that Britain was not one nation, but four. Wales and Scotland, with some qualifications, were assimilated to a larger system, dominated by England, without too much difficulty. But Ireland was a different case. It was an underdeveloped country within the system of the leading industrial nation. It was the scene of two interrelated resentments, each bitterly reinforcing the other, namely peasant deprivation blamed upon an alien landlord class, and the denial of civil liberties and of personal and national dignity. Where not otherwise specified, it is the English or British case that is being discussed; Scottish or Irish differences are indicated.

Here the extension of the British story must stop; the empire with its host of tempting policy problems, can be given only an occasional reference. But it cannot be wholly left out of account. There is always a logic that links the internal dynamics of a society (and thus the functioning of its state) to the external impact or vulnerability of that society. Throughout the period under consideration Britain was a great imperial power, more precariously so by 1939, but still in this role. There is a case for arguing that imperialism is an inherent phenomenon, almost inevitably generated in societies that have, by the mysterious processes of history, achieved a high level of autonomy and coherence, and hence of potency, but not equilibrium. Such societies are impelled to impact outward upon other societies that have failed to achieve a matching status. In so doing they alter themselves, assuming structures, attitudes and outlooks derived from their imperial role, and imposing a kind of reciprocal of these upon the societies they have come to dominate.

There is, too, the question of societal scale. The population of Great Britain (England, Wales and Scotland) increased by more than four times between 1801 and 1931, from about 10.5 million to 44.8 million. Ireland's population, on the other hand, decreased absolutely, from 5.2 million in 1801 to 4.3 million in 1921; proportionally, from having a population roughly half of that of Britain in 1801 Ireland had less than one tenth by 1921. There were thus dramatic changes both in the overall size of British society, and in the relative size of its components. On this the state could not directly operate, except by the control of migration in and out, and to the extent that the poor law system had demographic implications. In general the size of society was no affair of the state; it changed according to dynamics in which the state had no significant part. But from the 1880s governments were concerned with the quality of the general population, so far as this could be affected by various forms of welfare provision.

The complexity of the treatment increases with the passage of time. This is, of course, a direct reflection of the growth of state intervention in the market and the property-owning systems. As we approach 1939 the discussion of social welfare bulks large. This is because of the enormous range and diversity of legislation and administration that welfare objectives had generated by this time.

The greater the agreement or tolerance between the constituent social groups, the less will be the state's role; conversely the greater the tensions in society, the more active the state will necessarily be in its efforts to contain them, and the more determined the struggle between groups for its control. The extent and nature of these tensions will depend upon the form and rate of change, arising ultimately from the adoption of new technology or new organisational forms: these will determine which interest groups are obsolescent and hence conservative, and those whose day has come. But the state itself can either impair or encourage the new technology. Moreover the state can be either the means of easing or resolving group conflicts, or it can be the means of enforcement of a particular group interest. The rights or interests of each group will be projected in terms of its own self-rationalisation, heightened by various techniques of consciousness-raising, including ingrained historical myths concerning itself and its relationship with the rest of society.

The degree of freedom permitted by the state to the mass of men will depend upon these group relationships: if the differences between groups are relatively slight, Rousseau's general will, or something approaching it, will be present; if they are not, there will be conflict. It is often forgotten how narrow are the bounds and how historically rare are the circumstances of society in which men and women are permitted to speak their minds without fear, free of the choice between staying mute, or lining up with one or other irreconcilable faction. Anything approaching full political participation is even rarer: British democracy is not, as is sometimes claimed, a principle of hundreds of years standing: working-class males gained their first and very partial entry into the franchise in 1867 and females in 1918.

While the industrial system sophisticated itself through the adoption of science-based technology, two new demands arose. There was a claim for greater popular participation in decision making. This was accompanied by the requirement that the state eliminate economic and social suffering, at the same time promoting greater equity by undertaking a redistribution of incomes and wealth. The demand to be released from the old harsh discipline of low incomes, unemployment and social suffering implied the removal from the system by the state of the traditional social and political discipline of fear.

What was the relationship between social groups or classes as industrialisation spread? Two theses are possible. It is argued by some that the tensions between industrial employers and the workers must, by the inherent working of the relationship involved, become progressively worse until the system breaks down, producing a confrontational society, culminating in revolutionary change: this latter consummation failed to appear in Britain between 1776 and 1939. The alternative view is that the working classes, with the aid of upper- and middle-class allies, exerted a continuous pressure for social amelioration. This was accompanied by the structuring of the labour force by the trade union movement and by political action by the Labour Party. The pressure for spreading the gains of industrialisation thus became irresistible, because of an ameliorative drive, together with the increasing vulnerability of the system to labour pressures. To these factors must be added the unprecedented growth of output and the need to find mass consumers for it. But at the same time the system was highly unstable, going through decennial cycles of prosperity and depression and, according to some scholars, generating longer-term oscillations covering a generation or so. On this general interpretation the problem for those in charge of the state was to make concessions to the aspirations of the working classes in the right form and at the right place. But this had to be done in the light of an estimate of the structure of the economy and of the state actions necessary for the improvement of its short- and longer-term performance.

To assess the effects of state actions on the general mass of the population it is necessary to take account of the changing involvement of the state with the family, with general morality and behaviour, and with those who broke the rules and were subjected to the final sanctions of imprisonment, physical punishment and even death.

Four great transitions took place in Britain between 1776 and 1939. The first had to do with the structure of society; it concerned the change from the landed rule of the eighteenth century, to the dominance by the middle classes in the Victorian age, to an uneasy tension between middle and working classes in the 1920s and 30s. The second carried economic policy from the British form of mercantilism, prevalent until well into the nineteenth century, through a period of state abdication unique among industrial nations, to a sudden and elaborate system of macro-controls in the 1930s. The third moved social policy from a provision that was minimal and local as embodied in the poor law, with strong overtones of moral sanctions, via a set of struggles over particular issues, to a far-reaching state commitment to welfare. The fourth was the elaboration of a system of implementation and control such that policy making came to be shared between parliament and the senior members of the bureaucracy. The circumstances governing these four concurrent changes, and the relationships between them, provide our outline agenda.

PART I

Industrialisation and war, 1776–1815

1

The state and the proto-industrial economy of Britain

1. Political and industrial revolutions

The domestic economy over which the British parliament presided after 1776 was being remade from within by the atomistic decision of individuals and groups of individuals who, secure in the state's defence of property rights and equality before the law, were busy creating new productive and trading enterprises, embodying a new range of technology and inducing a new set of economic and social relationships. Governments had little to do with this great renovation. Paradoxically, the British state was intensely concerned with the effects of political revolution abroad, in North America and France, but scarcely at all with the industrial revolution at home.

It is perhaps not surprising that those who operated the British state had no real comprehension of the processes of industrialisation or concern with them. The political settlement consolidated in England by 1688 was conceived in terms of the control of central power and its subjection to the will of parliament. The landowners, in constructing defences for their property against the arbitrary will of the state in the form of the Stuart monarchs, created a system that could become, though somewhat inadvertently, a defence of the liberties of all. This it did through the enforcement of the supremacy of parliament, the rule of law, the independence of the judiciary and of juries, the requirement of due process and a relatively free press. Though the King still chose his ministers, they needed a majority in parliament in order to govern. Britain in the security of her insularity had no Kant, no Hegel to reify the state; indeed she had Locke who had so largely minimised its claims. Nor had Britain any great standing army or state bureaucracy as in France or Prussia; there was no military–bureaucratic caste.

Yet Britain, in spite of the relative simplicity of her state apparatus,

11

was highly effective in war. War at sea was more capital intensive than on land; the vast labour force and bureaucratic organisation necessary for land armies was not called for in Britain; capital for war was readily accessible because of the high standing of the government as a borrower on the London money market.

Parliament had wrested the weapon of taxation from the monarchy in order to protect property from it. Indeed, the protection of private property was one of the primary functions of the British state.

2. The dominant landed interest; the aspiring capitalists; the impotent majority

The state was largely in the hands of the landed interest. It consisted of the aristocracy and gentry, men whose concern lay with agriculture rather than industry and commerce. They dominated parliament, the civil service, the army and navy, the church, the educational system and local government in the shires. In this land-ruled society the voting franchise was small in England and tiny in Scotland, though there was nothing comparable to it on the continent, except perhaps in Holland and Sweden. As late as 1831 the electorate of England was less than half a million in a population of about 14 million; in Scotland there were less than 5,000 voters out of 2.7 million. On this basic pattern electoral management operated. Burke in the later eighteenth century considered that the 'general public' in Britain (those concerned with and informed about public affairs) numbered some 400,000 people. The landed interest of England and Scotland had a powerful extension in the Anglo-Irish landlords who owned most of the soil of Ireland and who constituted the Irish parliament in Dublin.[1]

It is true, of course, that there were contests between Whigs and Tories, but these were within a single land-owning class. To a large degree such divisions were in terms of familial and factional interests, sustained by tradition and habit. The most important general issues between the groups derived from the settlement of 1688. The Whigs were the party of the Crown until the accession of George III in 1760 when the Tories assumed that role. The Whigs

1. See chapter 2, sections 4 and 5 below.

then took to stressing the 'balanced Constitution', in which the Crown and its ministers should act with the consent of parliament. After 1789 an important element among the Whigs, led by Charles James Fox (1749–1806), showed sympathy with revolutionary France and opposed the war against it in the name of liberty and freedom from central authority.

The late eighteenth- and early nineteenth-century polity was one of weak central control. The impact of government on people's lives was largely at the parish level. There were in England some 15,000 of these petty instruments of administration. In the shires local government was dominated by the nobility and squires, the latter ruling the Quarter Sessions as Justices of the Peace. In the cities and towns power lay with the unreformed corporations and parish vestries, in both of which self-perpetuating oligarchy was powerful. When a new and serious problem arose ad hoc bodies would be created, by Act of Parliament, as for example Improvement Commissioners for a given town or part of it. This meant that new functions were discharged, but they were accompanied by growing incoherence. At both national and local levels the system worked on the basis of patronage, privilege and perquisites. This contributed both to the corruption and cost of government, and to the general suspicion that surrounded it.

But though the landed men dominated politics and the state, the commercial and financial interests were far from being excluded from state power. Trade and finance had generated a class of men who were capitalists in the sense of unifying a world economy by buying and selling, borrowing and lending. From the reigns of William III (1695–1702) and Anne (1702–14) there had occurred what might reasonably be called a financial revolution: quite suddenly the extension of commercial instruments had increased the volume and complexity of credit, so that the men of business and of money now had in their control a much wider range of mobile property, not only goods and money, but the web of promises to pay. These were the men to whom the state had to go for credit to meet its exigencies, especially those of war. London was rapidly becoming the capital of world capitalism. The men responsible for this could not be restrained by the traditional landed holders of power, but could aspire both to become landowners and to participation in the state. They formed associations in order to regulate their markets

13

among themselves or to exercise group pressures on the state, especially over tariff protection and the relationship with other states, as well as to fight the workers.

The greatest pre-industrial capitalist centre was the City of London with its money market and its guilds, with the Courts of the Bank of England and the East India Company representing the inner circle of commercial power. But there was of course no unanimity. Conflicts of interest between business groups produced divisions so that an elaborate, internal politics took place, changing as the business situation changed. In general terms the struggles took the form of challenges made by those excluded from monopoly rights, urging that either the state should destroy them, or should cause them to be shared. Over much of this the state did indeed preside, especially by the award of charter privileges.

The mass of the people, labouring on the land, had no direct say whatever in the workings of the state; they did not decide, decisions were made about them. This non-participation was, of course, inherent in traditional agrarian society. It was possible because the long course of history, with its relatively static technological base, had given rise to no expectation on the part of working men that they should share in the state. And yet there had been no unfree men in England or Wales since Tudor times. All were entitled in principle to equal treatment before the law, a concept absent in most parts of Europe and indeed the world. How far the law in fact dealt with an even hand as between classes is a different matter.

There was little overt use of the central state in imposing and enforcing sanctions, partly because the functions performed by the state, as they directly affected daily life, were relatively few and were long accepted. There was a considerable survival of the old moral economy based upon rural paternalism (though the extent of this is much debated); this could help to reconcile the labourer to a social and political structure in which he had no say. Moreover a prolonged war against the traditional enemy, France, had generated in a large part of the population sentiments of national unity, especially from 1803 when the war was resumed, this time not against a regime ostensibly dedicated to a new liberty, but against Napoleon's expansionism which threatened to make him master of Europe and so a threat to Britain.

These then were the components of society and the state at the

14

national and regional level before which the challenges of an industrialising society were deploying themselves.

3. The public sector; the state and the infrastructure

The state, of course, owned the army and naval establishments – barracks, armories, ships and dockyards. These were the largest component of the public sector. The dockyards were models of large-scale administration. Defence needs were also largely responsible for the Ordnance Survey, the Admiralty Charts and the astronomical and tide-tables. There were also the public buildings, under state administration since the fourteenth century, and the Mint. But the total of such state-owned capital assets was small. Nor did the state's demand for armaments apparently lead to striking new developments in manufacturing technology (apart from pulley block-making in the naval dockyards), or in large-scale administration, of the kind that took place in the United States. The only state-provided public utility service was the Post Office, in effect a public corporation since the reign of Charles I. It was an object of admiration: 'a wonderful establishment', enthused a character in Jane Austen's *Emma* of 1816, 'The regularity and dispatch of it!' Beyond this the British state had no desire to own or operate; even the Bank of England was a private corporation, run by business men.

But the British state could and did use market control in order to sponsor improvement of the infrastructure. The first of the London docks to be built, namely the West India Dock, was made possible by the West India Dock Act of 1799. It compelled all vessels coming from or going to the West Indies to use the new dock over a period of twenty-one years. The same principle was used to promote the West India Docks (completed 1805) and the East India Docks (1806). These state-awarded monopolies were the basis upon which the Port of London surpassed Amsterdam.

Though the public sector was minimal, the state was not without a role in economic development. Parliament was the great authoriser and constitutor of canal companies and turnpike trusts, awarding every such venture its birth certificate in the form of its Act of Parliament. Local weights and measures were finally abolished by statute in 1834, the state then imposing a set standard.

In two further respects the importance of the state to the working of the economy must not be overlooked. Through the highly developed legal system it was the enforcer of business contracts, and by its maintenance of the civil peace and its protection of property it provided necessary conditions for business confidence. The British state was able to mobilise and deploy resources for war in a highly effective manner, outdoing most if not all continental states.[1] The excise system as a source of revenue required a professional cadre. In spite of patronages, British governments had available bureaucratic organisation of a high order.

4. Mercantilism and the state

Adam Smith (1723–90) made of his *Wealth of Nations* of 1776 not only a grand analytical treatise, but a polemical tract against the British state in its immediate economic manifestations. He provided a devastating critique of the mercantilist 'system', a set of devices for the manipulation of the economy, much of which dated from the Tudors, and indeed from late medieval times. Mercantilism rested on the antagonistic philosophy of the zero-sum game – that there was a fixed quantum of gain from trade, and that what one country gained another must lose. To this Smith posed the opposite view – that with free and open exchange of goods within and between countries a vastly increased quantum of gain could be generated to the benefit of all. The state thus had a duty to remove 'impertinent obstructions', which, Smith believed, were the result of a merchants' conspiracy against the nation.

Nevertheless Smith insisted that the state had important and indeed essential functions. The most obvious of these were the protection of the nation from foreign attack (Smith approved the Navigation Acts confining British trade to British ships in principle because he believed that 'defence is prior to opulence'), together with the preservation of civil society by the protection of each citizen against the rest. The latter duty of the state involved the protection both of persons and property. The rich had to be kept secure from the poor, otherwise there would be no incentive for men to improve their material condition, and hence that of society as a whole. Indeed men, through the state, should create barriers against

1. See section 7 below.

their own greed and passions. But some of the protections for property had been abused, impairing the working of market forces. Smith believed that the state should reform the legal system as it affected land, altering the laws of succession and entail so that wealthy families could not so easily protect their estates against their own inefficiency and wasteful consumption. Moreover Smith argued that the state had a responsibility to educate the workers, partly in order to compensate for the alienation induced in them by the division of labour, and partly in order to produce an informed populace consistent with the dignity of man. But Smith's ideas had to overcome both the self-preservative behaviour of landlords, and the merchants' philosophy of mercantilism and the vested interests it embodied.

The state had also assumed a responsibility to encourage inventors by giving them the protection of the patent laws. But these could be a two-edged weapon. It has been charged that James Watt, having patented the separate condenser for the steam engine, a principle crucial for any future development, became an obstructionist by the inhibitive enforcement of his patent, delaying both the improvement and dissemination of mechanical power.

The mercantilist panoply was an extensive one.[1] The Navigation Acts, dating from 1651, were an attempt to make of the British Atlantic empire a closed trading system or, at the least, to admit foreigners to participation only on relatively disadvantageous terms. In the seventeenth century they were aimed at the Dutch, with their enormously efficient merchant fleet, and in the eighteenth century against the French, the great continental enemy and imperial rival. Before the British–French commercial treaty of 1786 protectionist legislation had kept almost all French manufactures out of Britain for over a century, except what came in by the busy activity of smugglers. The colonial trade was confined to British ships and crews (which, however, included those of her colonies); certain profitable 'enumerated articles', namely sugar, tobacco, indigo and cotton, could not be carried directly from British colonial possessions to any other country, but had to pass through a British port. Yet all British subjects were free to participate in the Atlantic economy. The Atlantic empire was thus an area of freedom of trade, bound together by imperial preferences.

1. For mercantilism as regional policy see chapter 2, section 3 on Scotland below.

British commerce east of the Cape of Good Hope had no such free-trade aspect: it was a straightforward monopoly sanctioned by the state through recurrent charter renewals. Beyond the Cape, to the Persian Gulf, India, the South-Eastern Archipelago and to China, only the East India Company could trade. Though the monopoly to India was ended in 1813, the Company continued to be enormously powerful. It was a state-chartered multi-national both in terms of the areas it covered and in its political potency. It continued as a quasi-state, governing British India even when its trading monopoly to that sub-continent had gone. It was a dominant element in the London money market and was powerful in the policies of the City of London and of Westminster.

There was a complex and inhibitive range of tariffs and prohibitions, the rationale of many of which had long since been forgotten. For example the export of coal was effectively prohibited by a duty of 70%; wool exports were illegal. The export of machinery was forbidden in order to protect the newly mechanised textile industries. There were tariffs on foreign timber and sugar, with preferences for the British colonies. But the most important element in the protective system, and the most politically sensitive, was the corn law, imposing a tax on imported cereals. It was basic to the position of the landed interest, but it could also by the same token keep the price of bread for labourers' families higher than it might have been. Moreover by 1815 the corn law could act as a kind of bulkhead in the economy, protecting the agricultural sector against the increasing assertiveness of the industrial. But the relevance of the corn law depended upon the comparative price of corn at home and abroad. British agricultural productivity, under the impetus of the enclosure movement, was improving rapidly, especially as the eighteenth century yielded to the nineteenth, so that the case for the protection of British cereal farming by the state was weakening.

The state struck one trade dead by statute and by naval enforcement: the commerce in slaves was prohibited from 1807. What had formerly been a free right of British subjects was summarily ended. Contrary to the dictates of economic interest, the British state forbade the trade to British nationals, and embarked upon a campaign to end it throughout the world.

18

Slaves were not the only people subject to state restraint on movement: the elite of workers were not allowed, without permission, to emigrate, carrying their skills abroad to rival nations. Internal migration was also restricted by law.[1] Consistent with the control on skilled emigrants, the export of machinery was also prohibited, except when licensed. Most European countries had similar constraints on the movement of men and machines.

Some of the circumstances responsible for mercantilism lay in the political development of Britain. The corn law represented protection of the basic activity of cereal agriculture and the classes who dominated it in a proto-industrial society. The Navigation Laws were an attempt to maintain a trading system in the Atlantic closed against commercial enemies; the East India Company's monopoly provided a means of administering an informal empire in the East. The regulation of the labour market was an uneasy compromise of long-standing between the felt need for a responsive labour supply and the fear of the outcome if labour was permitted to bargain too strongly or move too freely.

There was no economic strategy integrated in thought or action, but rather a set of provisions inherited from earlier generations and perpetuated by continuing power positions. But there was an intuitive feeling that one's own country must come first in a world of rival nations that felt and acted according to the same rule. This sense of solidarity exposed the state to particular economic interests which could carry the government because of their concentration of effort and effectiveness of political placing; the state by acceding to the pressures of commercial men caused trade to become even less competitive in the provision of goods and services.

Because trade was a kind of surrogate for war, there was little sense, except perhaps among the intellectuals of the Enlightenment and the politicians affected by their ideas, of the possibility of an open trade between nations, regulated either by market forces or agreement. It is true that Pitt sought to liberate European commerce in the 1780s, but renewed conflict with the French defeated his efforts. British economic development, therefore, took place in spite of a protective and encumbering state.

1. See section 10 below.

5. *The emerging counter-ideology: laissez-faire*

Nevertheless, the general trend of economic ideas and policy in Britain in the decade or so down to the outbreak of war with revolutionary France in 1793 was in the direction of a freer system, in which the market mechanism could be given greater scope within which to promote Adam Smith's 'system of natural liberty'. William Pitt (1759–1806), who was not yet twenty-five when he became Prime Minister in 1783, was deeply affected by Smith's ideas. The most striking evidence of this new view was the negotiation under Pitt of the Eden Treaty of 1786, lowering the trade barriers between Britain and France. The correct programme for Britain, as proposed by Adam Smith, was clear. Let the state withdraw from meddling in such matters; let nations enjoy the benefits of free inter-change and of specialising on those lines of production in which they have the greatest comparative advantage or least disadvantage. From all this would flow the additional benefit that freedom for the individual could be maximised and the restrictions, inefficiencies and corruptions of the state could be minimised.

But there were powerful groups in Britain that no government could provoke beyond a certain point. The chief of these was the landed interest with its agricultural protection, together with those established men of commerce who benefited from the restrictions on trade and who, as Adam Smith argued, were responsible for their perpetuation. Most powerful of all in terms of strategic position was the monied interest of the City of London, centred upon the Bank of England, the East India Company and the West Indian planters and traders: these men represented the furthest development of capitalism, with its strong monopoly elements. Moreover they were the great holders of liquid assets to whom the state had to turn for ready resources; they managed and held much of the national debt, expanding rapidly as the war against revolutionary and Napoleonic France proceeded.

6. *The monetary and banking system*

Concern with the monetary and fiscal systems, those two great aggregative elements which no government of an advanced commercial society could ignore, was always present. But parliamentary treatment of them was highly asymmetrical. The state imposed a legal limit on the rate of interest at 5% through the usury laws; this meant that bidding for money in terms of price above that level was illegal. But there were various devices and fictions for circumventing the law, of which governments themselves could make use when pressed for money. The British state had established no monetary institution of its own and had meddled but minimally with the money market except for the usury laws. Such matters, apart from the chartering and re-chartering of the Bank of England and the three Scottish public banks, were left within the private sector. The fiscal system, on the other hand, was elaborate and interventionist, in the mercantilist tradition, especially in the form of tariffs.

The banking systems of England and Scotland were the freest in Europe. This was so partly because the legislation governing banking in Britain reflected the ideas of the Enlightenment. Partly, too, this was because Britain's rulers, the condition of their rule being set by the Revolutionary Settlement of 1688–9, were parlimentarians and not monarchs (as in France or Prussia), so that the cameralist tradition of Europe, with its insistence that the money supply be a state responsibility, had no place in Britain. Moreover, Britain had never suffered a monetary collapse like that of the Mississippi scheme in France in 1720, such as to induce in governments a dread of freely issued paper money; the South Sea Bubble crisis of 1720 in London and the Ayr Bank failure of 1772 in Scotland, in spite of their severity, did not generate a fear of paper money outside the control of the state. The British parliament could, therefore, abdicate from the monetary sphere, and very largely did so. The result was a system that had evolved in terms of business needs and behaviour and was regulated by them. To this there was one exception: the government had in 1709 conceded a monopoly of large-scale banking in England to the Bank of England under the rule which forbade any English banking concern to have more than six partners, thus precluding the establishment of joint-stock banking in England on the Scottish scale, and ensuring that the Bank of England was central to the system, without significant rival.

The governing principle of the monetary system was that of the convertibility of bank notes (whether issued by the Bank of England or by other banks) into gold at a fixed parity on demand. Demand deposits had also to be instantaneously redeemable in gold. The gold

21

supply within the country was thus the grand, though often imprecise and lagged, control on the supply of money and credit. Gold flowed easily in and out of the country in response to the balance of payments or international lending, and in and out of monetary use within the country. The domestic operations of the economy, especially investment and employment, were thus expanded or contracted according to the movement of gold internationally, and to its movements domestically in and out of the banking system. It was the privately owned Bank of England that regulated the system. It did so largely by varying its willingness to re-discount bills of exchange held by other bankers, and by altering its rate of interest within the 5% limit set by the usury laws. One principal guide in this was the state of the foreign exchanges; the Bank contracted credit if the exchanges moved adversely to sterling, signalling an efflux of gold, and expanded credit when the reverse condition applied. Insofar as there was an official rationale to all this, it was provided by the Scotsman David Hume (1711–76), perhaps the first great international monetarist: he argued that over any given period there is a pattern of national cost levels and exchange rates which, if allowed to assert itself in the form of a gold standard system in which the state had no part, would constitute a true equilibrium between trading nations.

But though the system seemed so simple in abstract terms, the Bank of England did not find it easy to learn its role within it. The relevant indicators were often difficult to read; even more fundamental was the multi-variable nature of the situations in which the Bank had to operate, a complexity that was largely veiled by gold standard theory. Moreover the Bank's actions in extending credit to the business community could be political in the sense of conflicting with the borrowing needs of the state. In terms of the business world the Bank's actions in contraction damaged particular interests as it forced liquidations and generated unemployment, and so provoked criticism and hostility. Much as the theorists might argue for the 'neutrality' of a gold-flow system, its operation was subject to many pressures in practice: there was and could be no wholly 'neutral' monetary policy.

Under the pressure of war with France the system was radically changed in 1797. No government fighting a major war could conform to the classic gold standard criteria. Under the threat of

22

French invasion in Pembrokeshire in South Wales, there was an internal drain of gold – people demanded it from the bankers, thus adding to the pressures on the system. The Bank of England had no option but to suspend payments of gold; the Scottish chartered banks did the same. Throughout the rest of the long war, and indeed until 1819, the system contained no automatic mechanism to guide those who presided over it. With the system thus released from the control of gold, the Bank of England and the country banks could extend credit as demanded by the government in its switching of the economy from peace to war. Inflation inevitably followed. The Bullion Report of 1810 is a classic document, the first great official inquiry into these matters. In it came the first appearance under state aegis of the quantity theory of money and of the Humean theory of the foreign exchanges as mechanisms for equilibrating international price levels.

7. *The fiscal system: debt and taxation*

The national debt was enlarged by the war against revolutionary and Napoleonic France on a scale and in a manner frightening to many contemporaries, creating a most serious problem when peace came. It had stood at £243 million in 1793; by 1815 it was £745 million. Interest charges stood at £30 million, representing well over a quarter of government expenditure. Since Walpole's time as Prime Minister (1721–42) the credit of the British government had stood high among capitalists so that the state could borrow conveniently and cheaply to promote its objectives. It was thus made free, for a time at least, of the limitations of its income derived from taxation. The most costly of its objectives was war and preparations for war, especially against the French. The Seven Years' War (1756–63) was financed without serious difficulty, making it possible for Britain to expel France from India and North America and greatly to weaken her in the West Indies. The link between finance and empire was thus one of empathy, each promoting the other. The Navigation System and the East India Company's monopoly were both given greater scope by the victories made possible by financiers willing to lend to the British state. But borrowing had obvious limitations, both in terms of the willingness of the owners of funds to lend, and in terms of the cumulative burdens incurred by the state through the need to pay interest on the public debt, an obligation that could consume an ever-rising proportion of current tax income.

Before the introduction of the income tax in 1799 the taxation system had two general components. Indirect taxes were the basis of public revenue, used for meeting the ordinary expenditures of the state. They were taxes on consumption: the excise (on home-produced goods) and the customs duties (on imports). Both were regressive in the sense of bearing more heavily on the poor than on the rich, involving levies on such wage goods as tea, sugar, tobacco, beer, spirits, salt and vinegar. The excise was especially unpopular, and likely to lead to civil disturbances if raised. The tax system thus bore heavily upon the labouring classes. Its potential was limited by the incomes of labourers, and by the disposition of the working classes, if pressed hard enough, to riot.

Direct taxes were levied on the incomes of the middle and upper classes: they were used mainly for emergencies, especially war. Indeed, it was the cost of the war that caused the tax question to intrude into the relations between the wealth-possessing classes and the state. As with indirect taxes, there were two elements. These were the land tax, and what was known as the assessed taxes. The land tax as regulated by the Act of 1692 was intended to include all forms of property and income. But though land, being visible, was relatively easy to assess, 'personality' or 'movables' (viz. non-landed property) was extraordinarily difficult. The result was that these fell out of the assessment, leaving land only to bear the burden. This naturally caused landowners to complain against the monied men. The assessed taxes were a miscellaneous lot, each one of which was thought, in a general way, to reflect relative wealth: there were taxes on houses, windows, horses, carriages, dogs, plate, servants, guns and so on: successive governments tinkered with this list.

With the renewal of war with France in 1793 Pitt raised the assessed taxes to new levels. But this was not enough. It was necessary to implement the intention of the Act of 1692 and tax incomes from all sources. The British income tax began in 1799, at a flat rate of 2s in the pound (10%) on all incomes of £200 and upward. The system was reorganised by Addington (1757–1844) in 1803, when the five schedules specifying the categories of income that still operate were introduced. The tax was at a flat rate; though there were advocates of the progressive principle, it was not adopted. The taxpayer was obliged to declare his income in a most exhaustive manner, one of the most serious of encroachments upon the liberty of the subject, acceptable only in the extremity of war. Though the new income tax did not bear the main burden of the war (supplying 18.5% of total gross income), it marked the beginning of a new fiscal age.

The tax system continued to be a matter to be settled among the better-off; the *demos* had no say in a debate that lay between the landed, the commercial and the industrial classes. There was no question of subvention from central to local government; the localities had to meet their own charges for the poor law, cleaning, lighting, drainage and the like.

8. The landed interest, enclosure and the protection of cereal agriculture

Through the corn law the British state was committed to the perpetuation of the pattern of economic and political power typical of pre-industrial society, with the landlords (who dominated government) in a self-secured position. Under it the farmers and the labourers also enjoyed more stable and sustained incomes, or at least this was the intention. There was, too, the question of national security: no pre-industrial government was prepared to see Britain become a net importer of its basic food on any scale. Hence on the grounds both of internal stability and external security, the corn laws seemed universally justified. Against this policy there was not yet any sufficiently powerful countervailing view, resting on an industrial urban interest, that could provide an effective challenge.

The mechanics of the corn law were somewhat complicated, regulating both imports and exports of wheat, and being changed from time to time. In particular there was the problem of establishing the price of wheat at the ports, which determined (under the rules as they stood at any particular time) whether wheat would be allowed in or out, and on what terms. The 1804 Corn Law raised and varied the schedule of prices, but was rarely operative because of wartime inflation. In 1815 a new Corn Law was passed, abandoning the 'sliding scale', so that import was free at or above 80s per quarter and prohibited below this.

The state, by authorising a flood of Enclosure Acts from the early eighteenth century (these being placed under a standardising code from 1801), enforced a land reform of great importance. It made possible larger and improved farms, but dispossessed many smaller holders or deteriorated their condition. It also brought a new commercial spirit into farming that was inimical to the cottars, those with no claims in law or custom to access to the land. All this was done not as a concerted policy, but by the ad hoc approval by a landed parliament of a series of particular enclosure schemes put to it by the men concerned. The state by helping to create the conditions for improved agricultural output saved lives: the population increase begun earlier in the century was sustained. A lower proportion of the labour force was now necessary to generate the food supply, a necessary condition for the growth of the industrial sector. Enclosure also meant the effective dispossession of many humble rural families, together with a great reduction of tolerance in the countryside of the less productive or indigent labourers. But the English village, though changed by the new age of innovation and efficiency, could still survive as a community. The state by sanctioning enclosure confirmed the classic English pattern of landowner, tenant farmer and farm labourer. Insofar as protection and enclosure were responsible for improving the efficiency of agriculture they provided a condition necessary for the rise of an urban industrial society, though this was not, of course, its intention.

For a short period a Board of Agriculture (1793–1822) struggled to promote better farming practice and to act as a focus for the collection and dissemination of information, but this fruit of the Enlightenment did not long survive; it was before its time.

9. *The freeing of the internal market*

Since 1707 England and Scotland had been a unified economy, with no interior barriers deriving from the state or from regional magnates as on the continent. Similarly the consumer protection that had come through from the middle ages had been abandoned. The laws against forestalling, regrating and engrossing in regional grain markets had fallen into abeyance as such markets expanded to become pretty well a national system. There were still some controls on quality of production as with Yorkshire cloth, worsted and Scottish and Irish linens, but they were fast becoming obsolete. The last great price and quality control over basic needs, already moribund, went with the ending of the Assize of Bread in 1815. The state had formally withdrawn from private bargains and price and quality control, leaving the consumer to the common law doctrine of *caveat emptor*.

10. *The control of the labour supply*

But controls on the labour supply and its behaviour were not abandoned. They were, on the contrary, strengthened. The emergent class of industrialists by the end of the eighteenth century had learned to fear collective action by their workers. The common law of England was on the side of the employers, for it held that trade unions were in restraint of trade and therefore illegal. Though the same doctrine held for combinations among employers, condemning them also as being against the public interest, the system, though nominally symmetrical, was not so in fact. For it was much easier for the employers to invoke the law against their workers than vice versa. Moreover employers in breach of contract committed merely a civil offence, while employees who did so were criminals. This imbalance was confirmed by the Combination Laws of 1799/1800, passed in wartime in order to prevent sudden withdrawals of labour in a condition of labour shortage: they introduced summary prosecutions against striking workers. The penalties were, however, relatively mild (three months in prison), and there were not many prosecutions under the Act.

The state, at the same time that it was refusing to workers the right to combine, was withdrawing its own traditional supervision of wages. The Elizabethan Statute of Labourers (1563) had been the basis of an effort to regulate wages for a wide range of occupations over many generations. The Justices of the Peace had been charged by the statute, in effect, to apply to wages the doctrine of the 'just price'; they were to set either minima or maxima such as to 'yield unto the hired person, both in the time of scarcity and in the time of plenty, a convenient proportion of wages'. The difficulty always was that when goods, especially food, were scarce, a rise in money wages simply aggravated the rise in prices. The practice of wage regulation was falling into disuse by the mid-eighteenth century. Parliament did not, however, wholly desist from regulation: an Act in 1768

27

covered the journeymen tailors, and the Spitalfields Act of 1773 provided for the London silk workers. Indeed in 1795 Samuel Whitbread, with the support of the Whig leaders Fox and Sheridan, proposed that the state should prescribe minimum wages based on the cost of living, to ease the conditions of the working classes under wartime inflation. But Pitt, invoking the name of Adam Smith, rejected the idea, preferring an easing of the poor law.[1] In 1813 the system of state regulation of wages was finally ended. The price of labour was thus rendered wholly free of official intervention, except in the sense that the state forbade actions in restraint of trade from either side of the market.

So too with the conditions of entry into the labour market. The Statute of Labourers, by imposing a seven-year period of training for journeymen, had asserted the control of entry into many crafts in the interests of those already in possession, thus giving state recognition to the right of masters to control recruitment and impose conditions of training. In 1803 certain masters and journeymen petitioned for a more effective enforcement of this law. But there was counter-petitioning by other masters who wanted to increase their labour force and their output by using less skilled men, that is, by dilution. The latter won the day; the apprenticeship laws were repealed in 1814: in future no conditions of entry to a trade by service or skill were to be enforced by the state.

In addition to the refusal to give unions the sanction of the law, there was another sense in which the state and the parishes continued to operate on the labour supply. The Settlement Laws of 1662 had legally tied men and women to the parishes of their birth, or to that parish where a 'settlement' had been acquired. Under the law workers could not move freely and as of right from one parish to another in search of work (unless they had what was in effect a labour pass from their parish authorities); they could be thrust back to the place of birth or settlement if they seemed likely to become a public charge. The more prosperous parishes, likely to attract the indigent poor, favoured this restraint on labour mobility. Though the enforcement of the Settlement Laws was gradually relaxed in the course of the eighteenth century they remained on the statute book.

1. See chapter 3, section 3 below.

11. The ameliorists' programme

Just as interventionist mercantilism operated without benefit of an integrated system of thought capable of producing an analytical explanation of the economy, the proposals of the humanitarian ameliorators suffered from the same lack of system. Of such men the most notable was Samuel Whitbread (1758–1815). He and those who shared his views took the 'something must be done' position. The attempts made during the French wars by Whitbread and others of like mind to ease conditions for the labouring classes by public policy involved many of the proposals that were to have a more or less continuous advocacy throughout the nineteenth century through one group of reformers or another. But Whitbread could not overcome even his own misgivings about the consequences of state regulation of wages. He sought also, under certain conditions, to make relief available to the able-bodied unemployed, independent of a means test. He thus touched upon another classic problem, namely how to distinguish those in need from those who were not, without at the same time penalising the provident. Education was seen by such men as Whitbread as a means of helping the labourers and their families to help themselves. But though a good many reformers were ready to rally to the educational banner, there was disagreement about the proper content of instruction, especially its religious component. For in a diffuse and intuitive way men were aware that publicly sponsored education was an extension of state action that involved the formation of mind and personality, together with the promotion of value systems. The Whitbread group noted the housing difficulties of labourers, and urged public subsidy for the provision of cottages, together with ground for a garden and a cow. But again their arguments failed because of the criticism that this would be yet another unjustifiable interference with the market mechanism. Finally, there were proposals for public works to generate employment, but here also the government was unwilling to embark on such an undertaking for fear of distortion of the market economy, not to speak of enormously extending the field for patronage and corruption.

12. The state and the economy

What trends are detectable in state policy as affecting the economy between 1776 and 1815?

Internal markets were being freed by the abandonment of consumer protection and the state's withdrawal from wage bargains. This might well be construed as a victory for the new groups of businessmen, seeking to be free of hindrances to commercial initiatives. Externally there was no such simple progression: the 1780s and early 1790s saw Pitt's attempts to lower tariff barriers by international agreement with France, but the war reversed this trend, placing the emphasis once more on protectionism. The British economy was thus made capable of more flexible responses domestically, but in its external relations once more withdrew into a mercantilist view of foreign trade.

The state insisted that wages be determined by market forces and not by collective bargaining (taking no account of the fact that labourers and employers were not equal bargainers). It rejected any role for itself in this matter. It continued to control geographical movement of labour by the Settlement Acts, lest people should move about excessively, causing areas of prosperity to attract the poor on too great a scale.

The landed parliament confirmed its own dominance by its continuance of the corn laws. Yet the expanding classes of commercial and industrial entrepreneurs were becoming ever more important in the economy. Debates on the income tax from 1799 brought out the clash of interest between the landed and the business classes. The international capitalists who controlled the Bank of England and the great chartered companies benefited from the mercantilist manipulation of British trade. They were increasingly subject to attack by the outsiders, 'free-traders', in London and in the outports, who resented their monopoly position and who watched and worked for opportunities to weaken it. The growth of the public debt provided a new range of opportunities for monied men, both old and new, for great gains could be made by speculating in it.

It was within this curious, complex and historically formed picture that successive British governments, themselves the outcome of historical processes, proceeded by marginal adjustments, each a response to shifts in effective economic and political power taking place within and between the various components of the national life. In the background there was a growing general predilection among intellectuals for a freeing of trade. There is much debate on the extent to which theories of the society and economy can be abstract philosophical constructs, independent of practical limitations or the influence of vested interests; in the Britain of the industrial revolution this question is as difficult as at any time in British history. Politics then was, as is always the case, a mixture of the pragmatic, the vested and the theoretical, with the latter able to operate only to the degree that the former two permitted it to do so.

2

Core and periphery: England, Wales, Scotland and Ireland

1. The multiple perspective

Britain was not a homogeneous entity, with a single unified society, but embraced peoples of widely different traditions. To understand the course of English public policy towards its three neighbours, Wales, Scotland and Ireland, and the feedback of these upon itself, a complex and painful perspective is necessary.

Wales, though never to lose her national consciousness, had by the later eighteenth century come close to England, with no distinction of institutions, with common access to markets and personal status, and with representation in the English parliament.

To the north, Scotland had maintained her autonomy through bitter wars until, in 1707, under the Act of Union, it was agreed by the two parliaments to merge as one economy, one polity and in some senses one society. Scotsmen and Englishmen gained equal rights in each others' countries, and both were to be ruled by a common parliament at Westminster. The Jacobite Rebellions of 1715 and 1745 had been put down, and a policy of pacification of the Highlands was actively pursued, involving the ending of the clan system. But Scotland continued to have her own distinctive institutions and practices: these included her established church (in the Presbyterian form), her judiciary and legal system (though with final appeal to the House of Lords), her educational structure, the Gaelic language over at least half of the country, her poor law system, and, deriving from these and other elements in her past, her own ethos and sense of nationhood.

Ireland, accessible by sea from England, with few natural defences, fertile over much of its area, had been since the twelfth century a great temptation to the English. It was also a threat, being a potential base for an enemy, especially France. It had failed to achieve a sufficient consolidation to repel the English, but was stubborn enough to make foreign suzerainty a difficult and uneasy affair. Each recurrent revolt against English occupation had led to further expropriations and the extension of an alien Anglo-Irish landlord class. Similarly the retributive spirit that followed each rising had led to further disabilities being heaped upon the Catholic population. By the later eighteenth century these were repressive in the extreme. There had been an Irish parliament for centuries, but it was under the control of the Anglo-Irish; moreover from the end of the fifteenth century Poyning's Law had given the English parliament the right to override the Irish one, and indeed to legislate directly for Ireland. The Penal Laws as enforced since 1690 denied the Catholics the right to hold office, to bear arms, to sit in the Irish parliament, to buy land or to own a horse worth more than £5; members of the Protestant 'ascendency' of course enjoyed all these rights.

Thus by 1776, the year of the revolt of the American colonies, a kind of symbiosis of dominance linked the English parliament to its three neighbouring societies, ranging from the near-assimilation of Wales, through the somewhat one-sided partnership with Scotland, to the continuous coercion of Ireland. British politics and public policy had to function under the conditions set by these deeply rooted complexities.

2. Two views of the state and society: Scotland and England

The terms upon which England and Scotland had emerged from their respective reformations in the sixteenth century were reflected in the differences in attitude taken by the two states toward social matters generally. The Scottish state after 1560 was modelled, under the influence of John Knox (*c.* 1513–72), on Calvin's Geneva. It was frankly authoritarian with a strong theocratic element, intended to regulate the life of the people, largely through the parish mechanism of the Kirk Session. Education was seen as central, an essential social function to be provided under the authority of the law of the land. The state fixed a duty on the landowners (the heritors) to provide parish schools, through a levy or tax upon themselves. It is true that no effective appeal against default was provided, and there were in consequence a good many delinquent parishes. Also, in the rapidly growing towns such as Glasgow a system based on the rural parish, in spite of an attempt to modernise it, simply broke down. It is clear that the Scottish educational system, under the impact of urbanisation, was by 1815 losing generality and direction. But over a good deal of Scotland, especially in the Lowland parts, much of the intent and practice of the educational principles of John Knox were still present in 1815. Where there were prosperous villages and caring heritors, or towns with baillies (magistrates) who honoured the Presbyterian tradition of schooling, the level of literacy in Scotland was as high as anywhere in Europe. To this achievement England provided no parallel: there was no question of general literacy as sponsored by state and church; England did not have even a skeletal educational system. At the same time English life was not subjected to the kind of moral surveillance that was practised by the Scottish Kirk.

The poor law provided a second great difference. Whereas in England since 1597, in Elizabeth's time, there had been parish provision for the able-bodied poor (under certain circumstances) as well as for the aged, infirm and infant,[1] the Scottish system denied the legal right to such aid to the able-bodied. The difference between the two countries from the 1780s became even greater. The Scots philosophy of the poor was that they should be self-reliant, that families should support their own indigent, and that the heritors should assist voluntarily in the relief of the impotent in need. The able-bodied should rely upon themselves and their families, and upon the social bond that linked the classes.

It was thus possible for England and Scotland, because of differences in outlook, to be the obverse of one another with respect to both the poor law and education. The Scottish state required no legal provision in the parishes for the able-bodied poor, whereas the English did; the Scottish state made legal provision for a parish school system for all, whereas the English did not. In Scotland there was a link between the two social needs – education was seen as a strengthener of character and an improver of employment opportunities and thus as contributing to the solution of the problem of poverty; in England on the other hand this connection was not made, for English social policy was never brought under the kind of review prompted by the reformation in Scotland.

1. See chapter 3, sections 2 and 3 below.

34

3. Regional policy in Scotland

Under the aegis of the English-dominated parliament at Westminster there was a form of regional policy for Scotland, most of it concerned with the Highlands. It arose from the need after the final Jacobite rising of 1745 to make the Highlands governable, and to create conditions appropriate to modernisation, in short, to release the region from the iron circle of insecurity in which it had been bound, and on which the clan system depended. The first necessity was the establishment of law and order. This involved the ending of the 'heritable jurisdictions' whereby the clan chiefs ran their own justice, together with the setting up of a system of legally enforceable property rights. A programme of road building, initially for military purposes in the main, was undertaken; indeed this had been begun following the rising of 1715. In 1803 two parallel Commissions were set up with a remit to build roads and bridges, together with the Caledonian Canal through the Great Glen, and the Crinan Canal. By 1825 the Commissioners had created a second Highland road system, planned for civilian use. Much earlier, in 1727, there had been established the Board of Trustees for the Improvement of the Fisheries and Manufactures; the Board had its special Linen Committee to encourage that manufacture by the establishment of spinning schools and by other means; bounties on linen production were provided by the state. Bounties were also made available for the support of the fishery (Adam Smith complained of those who fitted out boats not for the primary purpose of catching fish but to catch this subsidy); the Fisheries Act of 1808 created an official organisation for the Scottish industry. The Scotch Distillery Act of 1786 provided more favoured fiscal treatment to Scottish than to English producers of whisky. The Commissioners of the Forfeited Estates tried to rationalise and develop lands taken from rebels after the '45 and to demonstrate better farming methods. Employment was provided also by the recruitment of Highlanders to the armies of the empire.

In these ways, by a development programme consisting of various governmental and quasi-governmental agencies and financial provisions, the British state tried to assist market forces to hasten the liquidation of tribal pastoralism in the northern half of Scotland. But the prospects of economic development in the Highlands on the scale necessary to retain the population had faded by 1815.

4. *Ireland: the colony within the kingdom*

Ireland was a regional economy within Britain, but with certain very distinct features. It was also a society that was partially merged with that of England through its landlord class, and by 1815 through the movement of Irish labourers to and fro across the Irish Sea.

British rulers for generations were to vacillate between two attitudes toward Ireland: should it be treated as a true component of Britain, or should it be regarded as a colonial dependency, with its economic initiatives restrained wherever there was a danger of damaging the interests of England? It was the second attitude that, by and large, was still operative as the industrial revolution in England and Scotland accelerated in the early 1780s. The result of the suppression of Irish industrial initiatives was to confine activity very closely to agriculture. All attempts to provide alternative forms of investment or employment had met with the restraining hand of England, and with the indifference of an alien landlord class. Ireland was treated as a colony under the Navigation Acts, its role to be confined to that of a primary producer. The largest Irish industry, the manufacture of woollen cloth, had been destroyed after 1699 by a prohibition on exports. Irish cattle could not be shipped to England. The exception was the linen manufacture. It was a branch of industry in which England had no great interest. But nature too had been unkind to Ireland. She was seriously deficient in the natural resources upon which the new industry was being built – coal and iron. The result was a country that was overwhelmingly agricultural.

This single basic industry was itself in a most unhealthy state. Ireland was owned by landlords, most of them of the Protestant ascendancy, and many of them absentees, who were confirmed in their position by the occupying forces of Britain. Most of the tenants were not men of some substance, as was to a considerable extent the case in England, but very small occupiers, often little more than labourers. In an economy with such a restricted economic base, the only direction in which a man could bring his energies to bear was the soil; access to a piece of ground was essential. The result was a very far-reaching sub-division of the land, with petty tenants bidding up the rents of their scraps of land until only a tiny margin of crop return was left for themselves. There were many cottiers, working the land under the 'conacre' system, a tenure for eleven months only, with no rights in any improvements they might make in the land, and hence no incentive to adopt better methods. The cottier could be evicted at will. These men often took to the road in the summer, either in Ireland or in Britain.

The introduction of the potato from the mid-eighteenth century had given some temporary relief by raising the food output per acre. But population increases had pushed relentlessly on until this once-and-for-all benefit was lost. For England, it was Ireland that seemed most dramatically to exemplify the Malthusian devil of over-population. In general, such cash as the tenant received for his crop went to the landlord in rent, leaving the labourer very near subsistence. Yet he could survive (at least when nature was not too harsh), and over many generations had often come to accept his lot, for it meant, at least, that he was subject to no discipline in his daily and seasonal work. But when the potato crop was poor he was in a sorry plight indeed, for there was no compulsory provision for the poor such as had been available in England since the time of Elizabeth I. It is hardly surprising that the peasant often responded to his condition by violence against the landlords, and could be appealed to in the name of his nation and her lost liberty. Between landlord and labourer–tenant in Ireland there was virtually no middle class, certainly nothing approaching the English gentry or the smaller Scottish lairds.

The mass of the population lived in conditions that never failed to shock the visitor. Even among the landlords the system was showing serious strain. Many of them, through their own profligacy and rent default by their tenants, were heavily in debt. A kind of closed circle had come into being. The landlord, even when inclined, could or would do little to alter the situation. Attempts on his part to create larger units of cultivation, the necessary prelude to improved husbandry, meant evicting the petty occupants. The more deteriorated the situation, the more difficult this was to do. The landlords who tried to improve agriculture in this way earned the hatred and indeed violence of their tenantry.

For the labourer to improve his position by hard work and saving was virtually impossible. To protest violently meant that parliament would pass a coercion act, the army would be brought out and civil peace restored with rigour. Secret societies and violence in the countryside were endemic, centring on the 'Ribbon Societies'. To plead for legal action to lessen the rights of the landlords invariably raised the question of the rights of property in general, a matter with which the parliament at Westminster was very loath to tamper lest the landlord's position in England might be called in question, and with it the entire social structure.

All of this was bitterly compounded by religion. The great mass of Ireland's population, estimated at 5.25 million in the first census of 1801, as against England's 8.9 million, were Roman Catholics, compelled by an alien government to contribute to the 'established' Anglican 'Church of Ireland'. But in the North there was a formidable Protestant minority, the result of the 'plantations' of the seventeenth century. Its members were predominantly of Scottish origin, adherents of the Presbyterian churches. They enjoyed a less exploitive land-owning system known as Ulster tenant right; they also had what there was of an industrial base around Belfast. The Orange Order, founded among them in 1795, helped to put down the rebellion of 1798.

Ireland was thus by 1780 a mass of depressed peasantry, undernourished and illiterate, many of whom were brutalised. Indeed, deterioration had gone so far that a racist attitude toward Irishmen had grown up among many Englishmen, with strong overtones of inherent inferiority. Out of this situation came both local violence and a sense of nationhood. Both of these offered temptation to the enemies of Britain, especially the French. Ireland thus confronted the British state with a dual security problem, threatening it both internally and externally.

5. Ireland: the two programmes, 1782–93 and 1799–1801

Between the 1690s and the 1790s Ireland had the longest period of peace it was ever to enjoy. It was then that the power of the Anglo-Irish reached its peak, with apparently no effective opposing force. But things began to change from the later 1770s. This was partly under the influence of the rebellion of the American colonies in 1776 and the French Revolution from 1789. But at a fundamental level it was due to the aggravation of tensions caused by population growth taking place within a restrictive political, economic and social framework.

What were the choices open to the government at Westminster in dealing with this increasingly threatening situation? There could be no question of root-and-branch reform based upon principles of equity or even of humanity. This would have required the government to impose a reallocation of land, infringing if not destroying the structure of society resting upon landlordism. This would have meant placing in jeopardy not only the Protestant ascendancy in Ireland, but the basis of society in England itself. There was, moreover, the Malthusian fear that the Catholic peasant, if endowed with a parcel of land, would simply increase the size of his family, until he was as badly off as before. Moreover, the English parliament held a patrician view of the best structure for society: it was that coherence and initiative could only flow from land-based hierarchy.

Broadly speaking the government could operate on two fronts. it could seek to redress wrongs and remove disabilities from Irishmen, and it could sponsor some kind of development programme that would ease the economic pressures. Parliament at Westminster responded in two phases, the first centring on the years 1782–93, and the second coming to its consummation between 1799 and 1801.

The highlight of the first phase was the award of autonomy to the Irish parliament in 1782. Henry Grattan (1746–1820), the architect of this achievement, announced it with the phrase 'Ireland is now a nation'. This was a considerable step, even though the viceroy in 'the Castle' in Dublin was still responsible to the British cabinet, retaining far-reaching executive powers that could be brought into play if necessary. The Anglo-Irish landlords were enthusiastic for the Irish parliament, for they regarded themselves as 'the lords and commons of Ireland'.

But it was becoming necessary to do something for the great mass of Catholic Irish. This was only possible to the extent to which it was consistent with acceptance by the Anglo-Irish. The French Revolution, with its implied threat to Ireland, pushed the ideas both of many of the Anglo-Irish and the British cabinet in the direction of conciliation. The crux of the matter was Catholic Emancipation. In 1791 a large part of the Penal Laws was repealed in the interest of national unity. In the following year mixed marriages were freed from legal disabilities and Roman Catholics were admitted to the practice of the law and freed of restrictions on their education. In 1793 the Catholics were admitted to both the Irish parliamentary and municipal franchises on the same terms as Protestants. But the

39

property qualification was such (at 40s) to exclude all but the most prosperous Catholics. Yet they could now bear arms, their right to own land was unrestricted and almost all posts in the bureaucracy and the military were to be open to them. Their only real disability was their exclusion from membership of parliament: the Irish legislature continued to be a monopoly of the Protestant ascendancy. The Catholic Irish were not satisfied, and the Anglo-Irish were divided in their attitudes to these concessions.

On the economic front Pitt, the principal author of the political reform of the 1790s, sought to combine reconciliation with economic growth. In 1783 the British colonial market was opened to Ireland and many Irish goods were allowed to enter Britain. But Pitt's main effort took the form of his ten 'commercial propositions' of 1784–5. In effect he proposed to go a long way toward free trade between Ireland and Britain, with Ireland paying a share of imperial expenses. The manufacturers of Britain and their political allies, together with hostile Irish politicians, killed Pitt's programme; the hoped-for economic assimilation did not take place.

The rebellion of 1798, associated with the name of Wolfe Tone (1763–98), was put down with 12,000 rebels killed. It was a demonstration that the Irish problem, in spite of all that had been done, was more pressing than ever. Pitt was ready for his second attempt to pacify Ireland. It had three components: a union of parliaments, the economic assimilation of the two countries and Catholic Emancipation. By an enormous political effort among the factions of Britain and Ireland, aided in Ireland by fear, agitating agents and bribery, the constitutional crisis over Ireland was resolved: the Act of Union of 1800 merged the Irish parliament with the English on 1 January 1801. There were to be 100 Irish seats in the British House of Commons. By the sixth article of the Act free trade between the countries was introduced. Ireland, in the constitutional and economic senses, was placed in the same relation to England as was Scotland, symbolised in the Union Jack. It was hoped that Ireland would assimilate as Scotland had done. But Catholic Emancipation could not be carried: Pitt and his ministers could not remove this last great disability. Not surprisingly there was a feeling of betrayal among the Catholic Irish.

The intentions behind the legislative union were to break down both the sense of Irish separateness and the barriers between the components of Irish society, as well as to reduce the direct power of the Anglo-Irish ascendancy. The immediate incentive for Pitt was to pacify Ireland in order to be able to wage more effective war on the French. The resultant direct rule of Ireland from Westminster was carried out by the traditional executive arm at Dublin Castle with its Lord Lieutenant and Irish secretary, with whom the Anglo-Irish outlook had powerful influence. But with the disappearance of the Irish parliament an instrument of the ascendancy was removed. The creation of a free-trade area was intended to foster Irish commerce and agriculture. But its implications for Irish industry were more dubious. Indeed it has been argued that the Union was economically ruinous, through its damage to Irish manufacturers, especially after 1820 when their interim protection was removed. The refusal of Catholic Emancipation helped to vitiate the whole scheme. The agitation for Emancipation continued, now centred not upon Ireland, but on Westminster. Ireland was never to pass from the British political agenda.

At the basis of Irish life the land tenure system and the ownership of the soil were left untouched. Landlord and labourer each saw himself as justified, and the other as perverse and even evil. There were, indeed, Anglo-Irish landlords who were concerned about the welfare of their tenants and who sought to bring about improvements, but in the main complacency or defeatism had overtaken most of them; it was often accompanied by moral indignation against the Irish peasants. The latter for their part continued to resent and resist, sporadically turning to violence against the landlords, especially at times of bad harvest.

3

Social values and social policy

1. The evangelical injunction, natural law and Benthamism

Throughout the eighteenth century and well into the nineteenth it was the farm worker who dominated the minds of those who thought about the labour force and its behaviour. A view, as expressed by Arthur Young (1714–1820) and others, had gained a strong hold on upper- and middle-class minds, namely that men would only work if they had to, that if the goad of hunger was removed or eased by higher wages, the result would be less work for more money, rather than an increase in output. But against this there grew up an alternative moral perception of the workers. The religious revivals of John Wesley (1703–91) and George Whitefield (1714–70), working upon susceptibilities in the national life that ran back into the seventeenth century and earlier, generated the evangelical movement, widely disseminated among all levels of society. The evangelicals took deeply to heart the injunction of Christ to feed the hungry. Under the impetus of their beliefs, and to a significant degree independent of their class interests, the evangelicals became profoundly concerned for those in poverty, in distress and without defences. A powerful force for the promotion of morality and human sympathy thus came into being. It lay behind the final victory over the slave trade with its abolition in 1806–7, as well as the promotion of penal and legal reform, together with the movements to improve factory conditions and to provide education for the working classes. But the greatest challenge it encountered was the mass poverty of the rural poor and the law and conditions governing its relief. The case of the children was particularly moving – the foundlings, the underfed, the parish orphans put out to work for masters under the parish apprenticeship system, or used as chimney sweeps or in other dreadful occupations. A notable succession of

42

evangelical philanthropists built up a tradition of ameliorative thought, action and pressure: Jonas Hanway (1712–86), Thomas Gilbert (1720–98), George Rose (1744–1818), Elizabeth Fry (1780–1845), John Howard (1726–90), William Wilberforce (1759–1833) and many others. Their influence grew so that by the time William Pitt became Prime Minister in 1783 they were a highly potent force in terms of the poor law and other ameliorative proposals.

The evangelicals themselves thought their movement was a force sent from God, a redemptive intervention in the affairs of men intended, among other objectives, to call the state to its duty. It may be that as part of an inherent tendency of a society to preserve itself, significant minorities will be generated who will assert the principles necessary for such reforms as are required for social coherence. Or perhaps evangelicalism was simply a class affair, a response by the dominant group, intended to maintain its position against a proletarian threat? Such a view would have to be reconciled with the fact that evangelicalism would develop a strong working-class base through Methodism, the Baptists and other nonconformist sects: indeed, with its middle-class and popular elements evangelicalism may by the 1830s have approached the status of a 'moral majority'. Certainly in the 1790s it was renewed and strengthened by fears of the French Revolution and of British radicalism, both seen as a punishment sent from God upon a venal aristocracy and a business class who had gone over to Mammon.

But the view that the labouring classes must accept the discipline of necessity received a restatement: it came largely from the political economists. There were elements of it in the writings of Adam Smith. It gained great impetus from the ideas of the Reverend Thomas Robert Malthus (1766–1834) who, with his theory of population, reasserted the need for self-control among the labouring classes. If the procreative potential of man was governed by a geometric progression, and his capacity to produce food could, at best, increase in an arithmetical progression, then the entire system of society must either accept a combination of personally imposed population control and hard work, or the excess of numbers would be purged by the calamities of famine, disease, vice or war. Such a view meant that easing the conditions of relief for the poor carried with it grave risks. This was especially so with respect to able-bodied men: their incentive to work would be impaired, together with their willingness to limit the numbers of their children. There were further implications. Sir Frederick Morton Eden (1766–1810), he who had negotiated the trade treaty with France, voiced a widely held opinion when he urged that poor law payments weakened the capacity of employers to pay wages and so to make employment available (he was no less against money raised by taxation being spent on popular education, for this too was a diversion and a waste). Instead, like many others of his kind, he urged self-help (by saving through Friendly Societies), together with voluntary charity. This belief that the economy of society was governed by universal laws which man should discover and to which he should conform was related to the enormous prestige of the physical sciences, resting largely on the astro-physics of Newton. It has been called the 'natural law' view of society.

Many well-meaning men and women of the upper and middle classes were thus placed in profound difficulty. The evangelicals from their religion derived a responsibility for the less fortunate (on the response to which the health of their own souls depended), but from the new rational, scientific approach to society they learned that to be too assiduous in removing the pains and penalties to which the mass of the labourers was subject would be to disturb the natural order of things. Revealed religion and a science of society thus provided the horns of a painful dilemma. It was the more acute because of the size of the problem of the poor. A high proportion of the labouring classes was at a near subsistence level, consisting of men and women with little means of support except their daily labour. To ease their plight significantly by transfer payments from the better-off would be to operate on the economy and society on a frightening scale, with perhaps pernicious results.

It is in terms of this conflict of ideas, and the sense of precariousness that surrounded it, that the social policy of the state in the eighteenth and early nineteenth centuries must be viewed. Indeed the choice between sympathy and science, and between relief and rigour, continued to be basic, in one form or another, to 1939 and beyond.

There was however a third strand of thought that could in some cases go some way to reconciling the other two. This was the attitude to society developed by Jeremy Bentham (1748–1832) and his followers. They applied the pragmatic test of utility to policy

44

choices: the correct course was that which promoted the greatest happiness of the greatest number. Utilitarianism could thus take the side of the natural law school on some matters, but not on others. The market system could be modified or even superseded in a good many areas of policy, especially where the market had failed to promote the public interest, or where it was inefficient.

2. The poor law and the philanthropists

In terms of social provision in both England and Scotland the poor law was the sole source of social policy as it directly affected the mass of the population. But the central government at Westminster, though it presided over the provision for the poor by altering its operation by statute, had no direct role: the British state had no social organs of its own whatever.

Each English parish was a tiny fiscal entity, taxing the better-off parishioners by levying a poor rate.[1] It was also a petty welfare administration, paying out the funds it levied. Each parish had its vestry which assessed the poor law rate; it chose the overseer of the poor and made him accountable for expenditure. The vestries were answerable to the Justices of the Peace, who were county office holders; appeals could be made to the Justices against the overseers. Localism and regionalism were thus the great characteristics of poor law provision. The system in consequence had generated an enormous diversity.

But there was also a national aspect. The state had to adjudicate the system by statute, regulating from time to time the general relations intended between the poor and the parish. Though since Tudor times the English poor law had established the right of Englishmen to maintenance, it was minimal and was confined to the parish of birth or settlement. Just how minimal depended on how bad were the times, how heavy were the burdens on the ratepayers of the parish and how strong was the sense of obligation prevailing in each parish.

In rural regions the state, through its poor law statutes, mediated a traditional society of landlords, farmers and labourers, setting in very general terms the relationships that should subsist between

---

1. For the Scottish system see chapter 2, section 2 above.

them. These were matters which in turn rested upon population trends, harvest yields and market conditions.

But though the parish poor law was the sole source of relief prescribed by statute and enforceable by legal sanctions, it was by no means the only provision. Alongside it there operated another system, that of private charity, often providing more relief than did the poor law. It was wholly outside the legal framework, except insofar as the latter enforced general standards of responsibility and morality on administrators of charitable funds. Indeed the hope had been strong since the sixteenth century that the responsibility of the state and the parishes might be kept to a minimum, and the voluntarist principle maximised. Such a hope, of course, rested upon a view which saw society in patriarchal terms, with a bond linking the social classes, powerful enough to withstand corrosive influences, with the better-off sustaining the poor.

Such philanthropy took two general forms. There were the efforts of individuals, giving privately and often secretly to those in need. But there was also a corporate or institutional aspect. Groups of men and women (especially in the towns from the later eighteenth century) came together to form charities. Among the most important of these were the hospitals or infirmaries. Indeed such institutions became quasi-official, combining the civic with the philanthropic role.

The parish poor law officers and the local philanthropists, in a complementary relationship to one another, struggled over the generations with the problems of the indigent. The old, the infant and the impotent (that is, those who could not support themselves) constituted the least divisive aspect of the problem. Because they were not part of the labour force, such help as was afforded to them would have no effect on the willingness of labourers to labour, or upon the level of wages. To assist them was, therefore, morally necessary and economically neutral. The level of poor law aid required by law to be given to the able-bodied was nowhere prescribed by statute – it was a matter of local decision by the poor law guardians and overseers. There were quarrels between parishes as to which one was responsible for particular persons seeking relief: this argument was regulated by the Settlement Laws. Moreover, so far as the philanthropists were concerned, there were often conditions attached to their giving, for example such that only infants without

46

families were taken in; charitable regulations concerning the old usually stated that they should be of good character to deserve relief.

In levying the poor rate the guardians and overseers in England and the Kirk Sessions in Scotland acted in the light of a number of considerations. Their own value judgments were relevant, though not made explicit, as they assessed the parish (including themselves). They took account of the weight of the burden they might be imposing and its effect upon costs of production (especially those of farming), and placed these considerations against their general estimate of social need. At the personal level of the individuals to be relieved, a further range of judgments would be made both as to need and deserts. Finally, if in an English parish the Justices of the Peace (usually the local landlords) were appealed to over the guardians (often tenant farmers), a different, and usually more generous, set of standards might be imposed.

In aggregate terms the scale of social transfer was small; no really significant redistribution of incomes between classes took place through the poor law. But in bad times the burden on farmers could be considerable. Moreover, they tended to regard it as a marginal addition to costs, and thus critical to their position when crops were poor or grain prices low.

Crucial to the English system was an emotive general question. What sanctions, if any, should be applied to the able-bodied pauper? The traditional view had always been that relief given without conditions would debauch the recipient and have a demoralising effect upon the labouring population generally. The most obvious solution was to put the paupers under discipline – to take them into a poorhouse or workhouse. There the level of comfort would be minimal and work could be required, some of which might help to pay for their keep.

3. The easing of the poor law

But the trend under Pitt's first government from 1783 to 1799 was the other way. Pitt himself was considerably affected by the rise of evangelical and humanitarian sentiment as it affected the poor. Gilbert's Act of 1782 made it legal for money to be paid to the able-bodied outside the poor house, though not in the towns; it also permitted the combining of parishes into 'unions' in order to create

47

larger and more efficient poor law units. The Act of 1795 allowed the Justices to prescribe outdoor relief for anyone, in times of sickness or 'temporary distress', for short periods. From the same year, under what was to become known as the Speenhamland System, relief was in effect indexed to the cost of living, rising with the price of bread; moreover it made provision for all of a man's dependents, whether his children were legitimate or not. Inevitably the cost of English poor relief rose, provoking expressions of concern both over the burden and over the effects on the willingness to work.

In 1796 Pitt produced his Poor Law Reform Bill, providing for greater expenditure. Though the opposition was too strong for it to succeed, Pitt was able to introduce changes piecemeal over time, further easing the conditions of poor law provision. By the turn of the century the ameliorists had gained much momentum. At the same time the demand for social data had grown: national poor law returns were available from 1785 and the first population census was conducted in 1801.

But the government tried to do more than relieve: under the influence of men like George Rose it sought also to encourage independence based upon thrift. Rose's Friendly Societies Act of 1793 placed such Societies under the guardianship of the Justices of the Peace and gave them legal identity to sue and be sued. Moreover, for members of Friendly Societies the Law of Settlement was eased: such members were not removable to their parishes of birth or settlement until they had actually become a charge on the poor law. By 1815 membership of the Friendly Societies was almost a million, though many Societies were ephemeral; so was launched the most important of all voluntarist organisations, to play a considerable part in British life for more than a century. An unintended consequence of Rose's Act was to provide a framework for workers' organisation within which, in spite of the prohibition of trade unions, it was possible to form combinations to raise wages.

But though the humanitarian, evangelical momentum could significantly ease the poor law, it could not tempt parliament into the ultimate interference in the economy, namely the regulation of wages and hence of costs, involving a general redistribution of the national product.[1]

1. See chapter 1, section 10 above.

4. The first state protection of workers

The emerging industrial pattern, resting largely upon coal mining and factory production of textiles, was entirely without state surveillance of any kind until the beginning of the nineteenth century. Men, women and children were wholly in the hands of their employers so far as conditions of work were concerned. The Health and Morals of Apprentices Act of 1802 was the first parliamentary assertion that the state had not only the right but a duty to interfere with market-oriented business by imposing minimum humane standards. But it required the energy and application of an individual, the evangelical mill owner Sir Robert Peel (1750–1830), to bring this about. The Act stopped infant labour; it limited the working hours of parish children apprenticed to the cotton mill owners to twelve and required school attendance of such children. Though there was provision for 'visitors' to inspect factories, they were ineffectual, having no real powers. There was, too, the difficulty of establishing the age of young persons, the registration of births by the parish ministers being by now notoriously incomplete.

Pitt's administration stood aloof, taking no part in drafting or implementation. But a precedent of some importance had been set, namely that state regulation was acceptable in principle, beginning with the most vulnerable, namely the parish children. The matter was seen by a significant element in parliament not as one of industrial efficiency, but of human decency. The state thus entered upon this vast commitment through the new factory children, though tentatively and ineffectually.

5. The self-confirming educational system

The state in England had nothing to do with the forming of the minds of the young by a general educational programme.[1] Education was an affair largely financed by voluntary contributions, often through the churches, and by fees paid by parents; it thus rested on a mixture of the philanthropic and the market principles. By the later eighteenth century the endowed grammar schools, set up to help the children of those who could not pay for the education of their sons,

1. See chapter 2, section 2 above.

were in serious financial difficulties. The result was the development of a system of fee-paying; this caused such schools to become a facility for middle-class parents, with a consequent abandonment of the children of poor parents. There were also grammar schools in the founding of which the local town had taken part. The outcome was a complex of private venture schools, some of them run by dames, old charitable foundations now fee-charging and town schools. Needless to say, the use made of schools diminished sharply at the lower end of the income scale.

The most important educational innovation was the Sunday School Movement began by Robert Raikes (1735–1811) in 1780. It represented both an achievement in providing far and away the most extensive educational facility for the mass of the population, and an aspiration in pointing towards the ideal of universal popular education. It sprang from the evangelical religious impulse as felt by the lower middle class, working on voluntary lines, but soon embodied a large element of self- and mutual help deriving from the working classes themselves.

It hardly occurred to the traditional country squire or the emergent industrialist that the masses could be educated, much less that they had a right to be so treated. Squires and business men failed to respond to Adam Smith's urging that 'For a very small expence the publick can facilitate, can encourage, and can even impose upon almost the whole body of the people, the necessity of acquiring those most essential parts of education.' These were 'to read, write and account'; they could be learned early in life so that the torpor generated in a man 'whose whole life is spent in performing a few simple operations' can be overcome, so that he may, among other achievements, be able to proceed to some understanding of 'the great and extensive interests of his country'.

But those with political power and responsibility in England did not share this view. Indeed when they thought of the matter at all two questions arose in their minds, namely what need did labourers' children have for schooling, and would it not be dangerous artificially to widen the horizons of children who, when they became adults, might be prompted to question the structure of society and the state and their own place in these? Moreover under the prevailing conditions the labourers themselves made no claim upon the state for education. Samuel Whitbread's Parochial Schools Bill of 1807 was rejected by the House of Lords on the ground that a literate poor would become discontented.

The educational structure was nevertheless highly relevant both socially and politically. The upper classes, through the development of the public schools and the two English universities, provided the training appropriate to elitist rule. Barbarous as the treatment of privileged boys in the public schools often was, and delinquent though the English universities and their constituent colleges often were in the promotion of learning among their charges, the system provided the conditioning for Britain's future rulers in the House of Commons and the House of Lords. It was largely based upon the study of the classics, intended to give the boys and young men the strict training of grammarians, the felicity of expression of rhetoricians and a view of their country as a successor of Greece and Rome. Such education continuously confirmed the pattern of rule: the commonalty were excluded and landed privilege dominated, but there was a certain open-endedness permitting upward mobility from the commercial and industrial middle classes.

In Scotland the commonalty were in a sense a good deal better off, benefiting from their parish schools. Class distinction was thus to some extent reduced. The four Scottish universities were more open to the lad of parts, and had played a striking role in the European Enlightenment. But Scotland too was ruled by a tight oligarchy, largely composed of landlords, many of whom had succumbed to the English educational system.

6. State surveillance of belief and conduct

No set of governors can avoid involvement with the beliefs held by the governed. The state itself indeed both depends upon beliefs and is capable of operating upon them. It may do so in the interests of general stability, or in the interests of those who constitute the ruling element in society, or in the belief that the two are identical. But this is a matter of great complexity.

The Anglican or Episcopalian religion had become dominant in England, able to identify itself with the state with the restoration of the monarchy in 1660. In 1680 parliament eased but did not remove the disabilities imposed upon the nonconformists. The basic theory of church and state continued to be that England was a society unified by religion and civil obligation: men and women were free to choose their own religion and were not persecuted by the state for so doing; on the other hand anyone refusing to subscribe to the state religion had to forgo full civil citizenship. By 1815 this meant that the nonconformists, together with the Roman Catholics[1] and the Jews, were still subject to serious discrimination enforced by the state. Under the Corporation Act (1661) they could not hold municipal office; under the Test Act (1673) anyone who refused the Anglican sacraments was excluded from public office. Moreover no marriage performed in a dissenting chapel was legal; their ministers could not conduct burial services in parish cemeteries. Dissenters had to pay rates to the Church of England. The latter hung on to education so far as it could through the parish schools and the grammar schools, and excluded nonconformists from the universities. In these ways the state was used in an attempt to coerce nonconformist Englishmen into the Anglican Church. These disabilities were deeply resented; the nonconformist mind was profoundly and lastingly affected by them, creating a deep division in English society. The Church of England became complacent and self-righteous and the nonconformists burned with resentment.

Attitudes to social conduct, and to the use of the state to regulate it, produced a division within the nation that had the same historical roots as that between Anglicans and nonconformists. At the time of the Commonwealth the puritan view of conduct had prevailed, with its belief that life should be governed by self-discipline and not self-indulgence. Physical and material pleasures were deeply distrusted, the notions of purge and renewal were strong. The law was used with vigour to regulate behaviour. The restoration of 1660 had brought a lax morality, almost at the opposite pole from the puritan. Though most people did not stand at the extremes, they did incline in one direction or the other. The two points of view were in continuous contention, the more puritan/nonconformist element seeking to use the state to regulate conduct, both of the wealthy and of the masses.

The principal areas of community and state impact upon behaviour were prostitution, obscenity and profanity, blood sports, gambling

---

1. For Roman Catholicism in Ireland see chapter 2, section 4 above.

and drink. Though there was general disapproval of prostition on both moral and health grounds, Britain attempted no statutory control before the 1860s. Prostitutes were dealt with under the Vagrancy Act of 1744, together with disorderly persons, rogues and vagabonds. Profane swearing (treating frivolously the name and attributes of God) was prohibited by an Act of 1745. Obscenity and profanity of course involved the problem of freedom of speech and publication. Both were, in effect, left to the discretion of the courts. Stage performances had been subject to censorships by an examiner of the stage since the Licensing Act of 1737.

But of all the areas of state regulation of conduct, drink was far and away the most important. As well as being a temporary reliever of personal tensions it was the great releaser of anti-social behaviour in terms of public violence and of private abuse of others, especially within the family. But the ale house was also the centre of much working-class life, rivalled only by the chapel. The devices available to the state in this regard were the rationing of facilities (controlling the number of public houses) and the rationing of drinking time (the limitation of opening hours). These things could be done by blanket rules for the country as a whole, by making the decision one for the constituent regions or towns on the basis of local option or by handing the matter over to the discretion of the Justices of the Peace who would issue licences according to their discretion. The latter had been the English practice since the seventeenth century.

7. Crime and punishment

Like all states, that of Britain was confronted with the problem of how the ultimate sanctions of imprisonment, physical suffering and death were to be used against offenders against the law. There were three great sets of crimes or misdemeanours, namely those against the person, those against property and those against the code of decency. The latter had to do with blasphemy, obscenity and sexual behaviour. The rules governing all three rested upon a code of morality. The question was, whose morality?

On this matter two general perspectives are possible. It can be argued that all human societies must have a structure of discipline of some kind, and that there are universally necessary requirements under these three heads for the functioning of any peaceful, ordered and, indeed, just society. The state, in the face of recalcitrants or deviants who threaten its basis, must choose between coercion or capitulation. But what forms and extent of coercion are justifiable?

Alternatively, it can be asserted that there is no such universal code upon which justice can be based, nor can there be. The only possible exception to this, it is urged by some, is the case of a propertyless and hence classless society. On this view, the moral code and the law enforcing it derive from property, and are merely the means of promoting and preserving the interests of the dominant class. In the British case the mechanism for making and enforcing the law are parliament and the judiciary. This line of thought leads to the conclusion that in British history no objective justice has ever existed, and that the rule of law has been a class-imposed fraud.

In historical terms it is probably reasonable to say that some justification of both views can be argued. There can be no doubt that, as Adam Smith pointed out, a major intention of the legal system was to protect property, and hence the fabric of society that rested upon it. The degree to which the system is acceptable thus depends upon the justification for so doing. In terms of the later eighteenth century the old coherence of agrarian society was breaking down, making it necessary to find a new basis for social discipline.

Much will depend upon the extent to which there is a clear social configuration so that a single 'dominant' class can be distinguished. In Britain in these years the class pattern was a complex and changing one. Moreover countervailing factors operated. There can be no doubt that there were men who strove after an objective justice, and who sought to promote it, and perhaps even more men who sought to modify unfair or unhuman rules either through statute or by judgments in the courts. This concern with justice may well have been reinforced in the minds of such men and others by the sense of the power of the lower orders of society to protest where their sense of fitness was outraged.

There can be no doubt that by modern western standards the code was harsh. But it always had been, back to the re-emergence of cohesive society in the dark ages. The 'rules' were generally agreed by all classes, even by those whose share in property was minimal. Even the prison reformers like John Howard did not question the general need for rules protecting the person, property and propriety, or indeed the particular rules then in operation. There was certainly no suggestion of an inverse morality that argued that just as the lunatic in the asylum was the truly sane, so the convict under sentence in prison was the truly innocent. But there was sometimes a feeling that the poacher, for example, might be less guilty than the grasping landlord who sentenced him, and, more generally, that some criminals were people who had some justification in refusing to accept the place allocated to them in the new industrialising society, or who understandably tried to ease by means of theft the deprived conditions under which they and their families lived.

The trend of the law was clear: from the Black Act of 1723 parliament greatly increased the number of offences for which death could be the penalty. In 1815, 225 offences were punishable by death, including poaching, sheep and cattle stealing and maiming, housebreaking, machine breaking, forgery or rioting. So, too, was sodomy: in 1806 six men in England were executed for this offence as against five for murder. On the other hand, only a small and indeed declining proportion of those convicted of capital offences were hanged, though the number of transportations to the colonies rose. It is thus difficult to establish any simple relationship between the treatment of crime and the protection of property by a dominant class. Moreover, at this period when the law seemed so severe, the poor law, the other great means of social control, was going through a phase of easement.

As for the prisons, there was no national provision or surveillance. They were an affair for the counties and boroughs: indeed any suggestion that the state should take central powers were resisted by the magistrates. Before 1775 there was relatively little need for prisons, except in a very large city like London. But those that existed were fearful places. The growth of a more humanitarian outlook in the later eighteenth century meant that such conditions were brought under criticism, beginning with Howard's *State of the Prisons* of 1777.

The American War of Independence closed one great means of disposal, namely transportation across the Atlantic. The hulks (ships' hulls moored in the Thames) were introduced as a replacement. Demobilisation of the army and navy in 1783 and after, together with trade depression, brought the system to crisis, with overcrowding and gaol fever. The Penitentiary Act of 1779 represented the first British attempt to arrive at principles of prison construction and operation, based upon a philosophy of criminality. The penitentiary was to be quite literally a place for penitence, where men and women would learn the error of their ways through contrition and a sense of guilt, with solitary confinement at night (to isolate them from criminal contagion and to provide a setting for remorse) and drudgery during the day. The old physical brutalities were to be greatly lessened: as Howard put it 'punishment directed at the body' should be replaced by 'punishment directed at the mind'. But though the Act embodied a societal view of criminal punishment, the two major penitentiaries planned under it were not built. The opening of transportation to Australia from 1788 eased overcrowding as well as providing the basis for new colonies on the other side of the world. Thus the reforming influence had passed by the mid-1790s. The prisons were still bad, and in no condition to deal with the increased crime generated by a rising town-based population.

8. *The areas of social passivity*

Apart from the poor law, the state and local authorities before 1815 were largely passive with respect to the conditions of living. Public health intervention in the localities was confined to the general law of nuisance as enforced by the courts, together with local bye-laws in the towns; indeed public health was, and always had been, a local affair, a matter of restraining and removing nuisances. One of its principal concerns was the disposal of human wastes in the towns by surface drainage. Promoting the national interest in terms of health did not go beyond the quarantine laws as affecting incoming ships; they made some contribution to the containment of plague and smallpox. With education the state had no involvement, except its requirement of instruction for factory children in the Act of 1802. In housing too, the state had no part, rejecting Whitbread's plea of subsidies for cottages.

Towns and cities grew spontaneously, without state regulation. Some had obtained incorporation from the state, thus gaining identity, legal powers and the right to perform certain functions. Men of substance in some parishes or groups of parishes, in the attempt to improve the local environment, or to undertake limited programmes of partial urban renewal, had obtained from parliament

Acts authorising the appointment of Improvement Commissioners with defined powers. There were some 300 such bodies in England, all local, with varying functions including paving, drainage and street widening and straightening, operating separately from the local civic corporations and councils. But in general the framework of local government was largely archaic by 1815, ill-suited to the strains being imposed upon it.

9. *The machinery of government*

The organisation available to governments by 1815 for the discharge of their accepted tasks, though in many parts out of date and in most cumbersome, was simple in outline. There was the Treasury, the financial focus of government and source of advice to the Chancellor. It operated on a simple year-to-year basis. It accepted no responsibility whatever for the stability of the economy or the level of employment. Its principal concern, in a somewhat inefficient and ill-defined way, was with the demands of the spending departments and the management of the national debt. In time of war and active preparation for war the Treasury was especially involved with the needs of the Admiralty and the War Office. But there was a distinct lack of scientific principles in its working. The personal expenditure of the Crown and the expenses of government were not distinguished. So rudimentary were the financial procedures that the House of Commons (so jealous of its constitutional control of finance since the Restoration), having voted money, had no effective control over the manner of its expenditure. But at least Pitt in 1786 had created the Consolidated Fund, which brought the government's accounts together. In addition Pitt had done something to bring government contracts and sinecures under control. But nepotism, corruption and patronage were strong, and accountability was weak, confirming the contemporary distrust of the state.

For the rest, there was the Foreign Office, together with the two internal departments, the Home Office (responsible for the civil peace), and the Board of Trade, founded in 1786 (responsible for matters of commerce, including trade treaties), both with a limited range of functions. The revenues on consumer goods were gathered by the Department of Customs and Excise, and the income tax by the Department of Inland Revenue. The implementation of the poor law involved no central organ, relying wholly on parish organisation under the Elizabethan and subsequent statutes.

This was the rudimentary structure, deriving from the eighteenth century and earlier, with which the British government, having assisted in disposing of Napoleon, embarked after 1815 upon the transfer from war to peace of the unique proto-industrial economy of Britain.

PART II

Assimilating the industrial revolution, 1815–51

4

The trend to economic laissez-faire

1. The course of prosperity, power and policy

The thirty-six years from Waterloo to the Great Exhibition of 1851 saw the industrialisation and urbanisation of Britain accelerate and extend. But the trend was neither simple nor consistent. It took something not far short of a decade for the effects of war against France to be assimilated. In a crowd skirmish at Peterloo near Manchester in August 1819 eleven people were killed, largely by the undisciplined action of the amateur soldiers of the yeomanry. Government was obliged in November to contain unrest by a partial suspension of civil liberties by the Six Acts under the authority of parliament and the Home Office, using the police and the yeomanry. There followed in the later 1820s and 1830s a time of impressive progress in output and of gains in real wages for the more skilled. But there was little betterment for the labouring classes generally, and retrogression for some. The economy and society showed renewed stress in the later thirties and early forties, producing a new range of protests and challenges for the state. Thereafter there was improvement, so that the Great Exhibition could be something of an assertion of new confidence.

The political dominance of the landed classes, confirmed by the Corn Law of 1815,[1] received its first great challenge in the Reform Act of 1832. By the Act the new business world gained its first effective footing in the House of Commons, though men of commerce and industry were to remain a minority there for a generation more. Systematic registration of voters was introduced in 1832 for the first time: the electoral roll was henceforth to be the ultimate basis of the state.

1. See section 9 below.

61

The state was confronted with two sets of challenges coming from working classes. These were pressures for the right to organise and operate trade unions, and a demand to participate directly in politics.[1] The former involved the relations between classes, as affected by state power but without challenging it; the latter raised the question of participation in state power itself. As to political aspirations there was to be no labour vote at the parliamentary level until after 1867. This meant that the resentments and aspirations of the masses could only be expressed in large-scale, loosely co-ordinated movements. There is some analogy with peasant times. But Chartism, the major focus of discontent in the first half of the nineteenth century, coming to its climax in 1848, was a fusion of working-class and middle-class interests. Just as one element of the middle classes had a stake in Chartism, another assisted in its defeat. This was the urban bourgeoisie who ran local government in the principal cities. They, in collaboration with a still largely aristocratic central government, acted to contain radicalism. Indeed in terms of the general geographical distribution of power, this phase of Britain's history was characterised by bourgeois control of the cities and towns, while the landed men ruled in the shires and in parliament.

Meanwhile ideas and attitudes relating to public policy were changing. In terms of the economy they began to move in the 1820s in the direction favoured by Adam Smith and his successors, involving the dismantlement of a good deal of obsolescent control, and so found confirmation and support among the economic philosophers. In social terms there were the beginnings of new codes governing conditions of living and working. Though parliament, in spite of the admission of the middle classes, was still largely landed based, the Whigs, when they came to power on a wave of reformism in 1832, found themselves committed to a wide range of new policies reflecting Benthamite demands for more effective government. The call for efficiency was accompanied by a continued growth in humanitarianism that concerned itself both with human debasement at home and plantation slavery overseas.

By 1851 the British state had responded to the challenge of major post-war economic adjustment, had presided over a period of

1. See section 11 below.

fundamental change in its own constitution, established the principal outlines of its relationship to the functioning of the economy, begun its move in the direction of welfarism, taken its first great step in legitimising the formation of trade unions, reduced the affront to Catholic Ireland and made its first attempt to improve Irish agriculture.

It does not follow, of course, from this impressive catalogue of policy responses, culminating in the beginning of a period of high prosperity and world leadership, that the story was one of continuous and disinterested progress toward an ideal society. There were divisions and conflicts over every item, with vested interests and diverse ideologies producing at least two sides to every matter that forced itself onto the state's agenda. Moreover the lowest orders of society suffered greatly and were kept under discipline by those above them in the income and opportunity scale. But there was a minimum of coercion by the state as compared with most other countries. Somehow or other British society, for all its tensions, remained coherent.

2. The legacy of war: deflation and the debt

With the coming of peace the rulers of Britain were confronted with three sets of problems – those arising directly from the re-conversion from a war to a peace economy, those that represented the heritage of the war extending over a generation or so and, more remote but more fundamental, the long-term challenges posed for an agrarian society by industrialisation.

Painfully, and at the peril of civil peace, monetary deflation was imposed; Britain returned in 1819 after twenty-two years of suspension of the gold standard to sound money at the eighteenth-century parity. The contraction of state demand and of the money supply lowered prices and generated large-scale unemployment. Some 300,000 returning ex-servicemen added to the tensions thus created. Workers' resistance at the industrial level was ineffectual, because of the illegality of trade union organisation, still prohibited by the common law and by the Combination Laws. In spite of a good deal of unrest, the economy adjusted itself, so that the worst unemployment and distress were over by the early 1820s.

But the war left behind a debt of unprecedented size. With the fall in the price level the real burden of the debt, and the gains to creditors, were increased at a time of great suffering for a large part of the population. David Ricardo (1772–1823), the leading economist of the day, proposed that it be amputated from the body politic by the drastic remedy of a levy on capital. So concerned was this advocate of the market system with the long-term implications of a swollen national debt that he was prepared to urge this difficult and perhaps dangerous operation. Under it a large-scale transfer would take place within the wealthier classes, and the economy would be relieved of a burden that would otherwise have to be borne by all (largely through a regressive tax system based upon charges on consumer goods). But the government would have nothing to do with such a remedy. William Cobbett (1762–1835) urged that there be an 'equitable adjustment', namely that the debt should simply be written down in proportion to the rise in prices. This proposal was no more acceptable to the government, fearful as it was of disturbing the money market in this way, and of damaging its own standing as a borrower and so limiting its future capacity for action.

The income tax, evolved during the war into a system that combined ingenuity, efficiency and a fair degree of equity among those liable, was summarily ended in 1816. Though Lord Liverpool's government pleaded for even a short-term continuation of this important tax engine, the landed and the monied classes combined in parliament to reject it. It was distrusted and resented by those liable to it as too powerful a weapon to leave in the hands of the controllers of the state. It was bitterly condemned as inquisitorial.

The growth of the London money market had been much accelerated, accompanied by an extension of the monied interest with its political potential. Industry too had been greatly stimulated, accompanied by a rapid increase in the business classes in general. The towns had grown on a scale that could amaze and frighten contemporaries. In the countryside enclosure had proceeded at a rapid rate, causing an irreversible change in land use and in village life. The poor law system had been greatly relaxed, increasing the levels of local taxation and inspiring fears of a debauched peasantry.

3. The post-Waterloo economic strategy, 1815–30

In the fifteen years following the defeat of Napoleon, political economy, or the classical economics (as later labelled), based on

Adam Smith and developed by Ricardo and others, was refined, consolidated and injected into the mainstream of British thinking. Its message, in spite of qualifications and shadings, was clear, namely that a market system uninhibited by state intervention was the best formula for all concerned. Though this belief was making progress with some politicians, the policy choices made between 1815 and 1830 were a mixture of the classical economics, the older mercantilism and improvisation.

The return to gold and an automatic monetary system (1819) was a crucial step in the direction of the prescriptions of political economy, carried out at the cost of painful deflation. There was also the ending of the income tax (1816) and the beginning of an attack on the old restrictions on trade.[1] But mercantilism survived in the usury laws, and was reaffirmed in the Corn Law of 1815.[2] The old absolute barriers intended to preserve an atomistic labour market, in which simple contract ruled, could no longer be maintained, but the new permissiveness toward trade unions embodied in the Act of 1824 was much reduced by the Act of the following year.[3] The national debt too was a puzzle for politicians: to continue it was a great burden on the state, aggravated by deflation, and involved the state in the operation of the money market and the economy generally; to remove it or any large part of it, however, would require a gross state interference with capital. No action was taken.

In arriving at this mix of policies the governments of Lord Liverpool, Canning and Wellington were certainly not simply prisoners of the natural law thinking of political economy. Either they were seeking an economic balance that reflected the changing pattern of class, or they were following a pragmatic and disinterested perception of the nation's needs, or both elements were present.

4. The shift of power: the Reform Act of 1832, the GNCTU and the Chartists

Inevitably there were challenges for the electoral control of the state. They came from the middle classes and the working classes, centring upon the parliamentary reform agitation of the early 1830s

1. See section 8 below.
2. See chapter 1, section 8 above.
3. See section 11 below.

and the Chartist movement of the later thirties and forties. The reform movement had its great dynamic among the middle classes, but considerable support came from those lower down the income and status scale. The landed men were unable to fight off the assault, though they resisted as long as they could, yielding in 1832 only to the threat on the part of King William IV, on the advice of his ministers, to create sufficient new Whig peers to swamp the Tory dominance of the House of Lords. This capitulation of 1832 was, however, very partial. It conceded the franchise on a household (in effect an income) basis, so that only men of some substance could vote. The result was to increase the electorate of Great Britain from some 440,000 adult males to some 717,000; this meant that one in five Englishmen and one in eight Scotsmen could vote. The Irish figures were very much lower, reflecting a different electoral law.

The Reform Act of 1832 was the outcome of a highly complex pattern of interests and attitudes. But it is clear that the nub of the matter lay with the expanding middle classes. Macaulay spoke for the Whig position when he expressed the hope for such a reform as would produce a House of Commons the votes of which would 'express the image of the opinion of the middle orders of Britain'. But among the more politically conscious members of the working classes there was a feeling that they had been betrayed by the middle classes. The effective definition of the middle classes lay in the property qualification for the franchise, namely that a man must occupy a house of a rental value of at least £10 per year.

But the middle classes, though taking their place in a reformed Commons on these terms, by no means superseded land-rooted power there. Moreover the House of Lords continued on its traditional landed basis. Yet the constitution of the state had been profoundly changed. The House of Commons had now moved to the principle of representation on the basis of a defined franchise, so that ministers were answerable to a truly elected body of a new kind. This provoked much discussion on the principles involved in the concept of representation of the people.

All this fell far short of the ambitions of activists among the working classes, and indeed of the more radical component of the middle classes. The attempt to coerce government by a mass movement, namely that of the Grand National Consolidated Trades Union, following Owenite–syndicalist ideas, failed in 1833–4. The

Chartist movement arose out of the disappointments with the Reform Act and the failure of the GNCTU. The many supporters of Chartism, with their widely divergent substantive programmes, were agreed only on the need for a new kind of parliament, less class-bound, more able to conceive of the welfare of the nation as a whole, especially that of its largest element, the labouring population. The Six Points of the People's Charter of 1838, if implemented, might indeed have produced a different kind of Commons, for they included full adult male suffrage, vote by secret ballot and the abolition of the property qualification for Members of Parliament. Something approaching a general strike took place in 1842, seeking universal male suffrage. But the Commons as reformed in 1832 had no sympathy with these further steps, representing as they did a frighteningly unpredictable future. The Chartist movement, though reaching peaks of support, could not sustain itself; its final grand demonstration and petition to parliament came in 1848. The continental revolutions of that year found no real parallel in Britain; 1832 had brought a new equilibrium in the structure of the state that neither the GNCTU nor Chartism could disturb. The revolutionary impulse in Britain, though frightening to some members of the ruling classes, was never a real challenge to the state.

5. *The monetary and fiscal system*

After the resumption of cash payments in 1819 the money supply became again a politically neutral issue. It is true that in times of commercial crisis the government could be subjected to strong pressures to suspend cash payments as indeed it did in 1847. But the monetary system was in general seen as a commercial and technical matter, and not a political one. The tax system, on the other hand, could never be detached from politics, for it was concerned with the imposition of overall burdens on a scale to be set by government, and according to such a pattern of individual and group liability as the state might determine.

Though the government clung to the idea of a market-determined money and credit supply, from 1826 it was obliged to enter upon a course of legislation intended to restructure the banking system in such a way as to assert the centrality of the Bank of England, especially in terms of the note issue, and, through it, of the credit supply. The devices adopted in order to do so are given separate consideration in section 6 below. The income tax was resumed by Peel at a modest level in 1842. This was presented as a temporary expedient, needed to finance a reduction in tariffs until the anticipated growth in trade redeemed the shortfall. But it meant that the state once more took power to investigate and levy upon private incomes, putting all incomes ultimately at its own disposal.

There was a third respect in which the government could not avoid interference in the economy, and indeed involving itself in conflict with certain interests. This had to do with the government's borrowing, heavily encumbered as it now was with debt. The money market of the City of London was the only source to which it could turn. In theory the City was a competitive market, capable of generating an objective price for money for the government, as for any other borrower. But the government's needs were now so large that it was possible for the great money dealers to combine to resist attempts by the state to borrow as cheaply as it thought proper. The Chancellor of the Exchequer could thus find himself confronted by the City of London resisting reductions in interest rates. But the government had a weapon in the form of the Sinking Fund: the Chancellor in 1816–17 was able to keep the market favourable for a short time for its own borrowing by instructing the Commissioners of the Fund to buy the government's own stock, in this way keeping its price up, and interest rates down. Both the City and the state thus had devices for manipulating the money market, at least in the short term. But this did not impair the general view that the money supply was governed by autonomous and self-equilibrating forces.

These attitudes toward the money supply, the fiscal system and state borrowing were adopted by politicians in order to suppress in their own consciousness the fact that a major industrialising economy, subject to the stresses of cyclical instability, had to move, however cautiously, in the direction of a degree of monetary control, fiscal command and, from time to time, large-scale recourse to the money market. But it could only assume these roles in the forms, at the speed and to the degree which prevailing conditions permitted.

6. The concentration and regulation of the money supply

With respect to the money supply, successive British governments devoted their ingenuity to the construction of a regulative system within which the market ruled. But even this approach could not remove the necessity for judgment and action. This the government in effect delegated to the Bank of England, still a private corporation dependent for its continued existence on the periodic renewal of its charter by the state, and enjoying considerable gains from handling the government's affairs. But the Bank too was reluctant to accept a central supervisory function. Nor was the task an easy one; somehow by reading various indicators like the course of the exchanges and the relationship between its own gold holdings and its demand obligations, together with opinion in the City of London, the Bank had to expand or contract the money supply, acting correctly both as to amount and timing. Moreover it had to bear in mind the interests of its own shareholders in terms of profitability and security.

Government policy with respect to banking and the monetary supply was embodied in three principal statutes. The 1826 Bank Act, following the crisis of 1825, suppressed the £1 notes in England (though not in Scotland). More importantly, it marked the beginning of joint-stock banking in England by removing the six partner rule, allowing banking concerns to be formed in England with any number of participants provided they stayed beyond a radius of sixty-five miles from London. In addition the Bank of England itself was made more competitive by the award to it of powers to open branches in any part of England. The 1833 Bank Act made the Bank of England's notes legal tender throughout England except at the Bank or its branches, where gold continued to be payable. This had the effect of focussing internal gold drains on the Bank itself, making them a more readable indicator; it also promoted a centralising and economising of the gold reserve. The sixty-five mile limit was removed, but all banks entering London had to abandon their note issues; the 1833 Act thus prepared the way for the ultimate concentration of the English note issue in the Bank of England.

But the most important legislation was that of 1844, the Bank Charter Act, which provided the fundamental basis of British banking until 1931, and indeed in some senses beyond. Under it the Bank of England was given the final power necessary for it, over time, to concentrate the issue of notes in England upon itself. No new banks of issue were to be permitted, and provision was made for the Bank to replace lapsed issues. The Bank's issue was, however, to be made subject to a code of rules, such that it would act as nearly as possible like the metallic money it had replaced. This was done by allowing the Bank to place with the public a 'fiduciary' issue of notes up to £14,000,000 backed by securities; any further notes had to be backed pound for pound by gold, thus requiring gold to be held in strict proportion to the issue in excess of the fiduciary; this part was to become by far the more important component of the money supply. This rule obliged the Bank in effect to constrain the money supply within the limits of its gold holdings. The Act of 1844 was a kind of permanent paradox: the theory upon which it was based was inadequate if not wrong, and yet it did the job. Consistent with the principle of an automatic money market the government repealed the usury laws as affecting bills of exchange in 1833; the price of short-term money was made independent of the law.

Thus was a simultaneous trend toward centralisation of the note issue and its regulation by 'automatic' rules initiated by parliament. But the very facts of centralisation and of regulation meant that the state, though it preferred to stay out of banking, could, should it so decide, take control of the monetary system. The note issues of Scotland and Ireland were regulated by separate Acts in 1845.

By 1844 it was also necessary to set rules for the conduct of the joint-stock banks, so rapidly proliferating in England after 1826. Under the Joint-Stock Bank Act of that year such banks were required to incorporate themselves, to make public the names of shareholders, to publish the size of shares and their distribution between shareholders; a minimal paid-up capital of £50,000 was prescribed.

7. The rejection of employment policy

The advocates of monetary management as a tool for generating employment were not the only group to urge upon governments the need for an active employment policy. There was also considerable advocacy of public works to be undertaken to this end. Malthus and other theorists argued that unemployment could be generated by failure of aggregate demand due to excess savings. But most protagonists of public works simply urged that it was better that men should not be idle and become a charge on the poor law. The Poor Employment Act of 1817 was a temporary aberration by the government in this direction; it had only a minor effect and the principle it embodied of public works to generate employment was dropped.

8. The general freeing of trade

In foreign trade the trend was consistent: it was in the direction of dismantlement of state-created regulations. There was a considerable clean-up by William Huskisson (1770–1830) of obsolete restrictions in 1822. Huskisson, with his Reciprocity Duties Act of 1823, made possible a wider range of treaties with most of Europe, together with the USA and Latin America. The most-favoured-nation principle was adopted in relation to Prussia and was extended to other countries. Skilled artisans were permitted to emigrate from 1824, though the control on the export of machinery did not go until 1842. In 1833 the East India Company's monopoly of British trade to China was ended; this was the signal for the western impact on that mighty country to assume new proportions. Various duties sheltering various trades were reduced or ended – on timber, silk and cotton. Peel carried Huskisson's efforts further in the budget of 1842, reducing or removing the duty on 750 items, and freeing the export of machinery. He ended the Corn Laws in 1846. The Navigation Laws as they affected foreign trade were repealed in 1849.

The two moving spirits in the culmination of free trade, Peel and Gladstone, starting from conservative positions, were pushed by observation and practical judgment in the direction of Adam Smith. The young Gladstone told the young Queen that unemployment was the main cause of Chartism; the freeing of trade would bring Chartism to an end by generating work and incomes. It would also obviate the destructive activities of the middle-class zealots of the Anti-Corn Law League, stopping them from advocating courses of action that could only set precedents of pressure and even violence that threatened the stability of society.

The alternative to free trade and state withdrawal from the economy was to move equally strongly in the opposite direction, adopting a policy of generalised economic management, aimed at preserving stability through the restraint of the forces of change. Such a policy had a considerable range of advocates. One of the most vocal of the opponents of industrialisation was William Cobbett, though, like others, he was unclear as to what governments should do to resist it. To regulate industrialisation was impossible, and for two reasons. The components of such a policy of controls and the pattern of their interaction raised far too complex a set of problems, both in terms of the necessary conceptual model and in terms of the requisite data. No less daunting was the political impossibility of such a reversal, given the generalised pressures exerted by the enormous increase in population and by the strength of the new economic interests that had arisen step by step with industrialisation. Peel and Gladstone were driven to a policy of giving these forces and interests their head, slipping the lead on the economy and society.

9. *The end of agricultural protection*

In the post-war years the agricultural interest had been obliged to accept a two-part package. The Corn Law of 1815 had confirmed their protected position against foreign wheat, allowing none in below the very high price of 80s per quarter. This was in part in consideration of the fact that farmers had entered into long leases at wartime rents, were encumbered with debts contracted in the optimism of high prices and were saddled with heavy poor law rates: all these obligations had to be met in the face of a collapse of corn prices. But the landed interest consisting of landowners and farmers had to accept a *quid pro quo*, namely the deflationary policy necessary to bring about a return to gold at the old parity in 1819; this of course lowered prices generally in Britain as well as increasing the burden of agricultural debt.

But the post-1815/19 balance of advantage between economic groups could not, of course, last. The corn law was brought under continuous attack both by those who wanted it made more flexible and by those who wanted it abolished altogether. It was modified in 1827 and 1842 by the revival of the sliding scale, whereby the import duty moved inversely with the home price, so that the higher price of wheat in Britain the lower was the duty on imported supplies. By 1846 this compromise had run out. The potato famine was the final detonator: the failure of this high-yield but disease-prone crop meant that the ports had to be opened to corn. Peel, as Prime Minister in a House of Commons based on the powerful Tory majority of 1841, and as leader of the Tory Party, carried the Commons with him in 1846 as he rose above party, and indeed defied it. He used the sovereignty of parliament to subvert the most powerful interest in the land, depriving it of its most sanctified support.

Inevitably Peel's action in exposing cereal agriculture to foreign competition split his Conservative Party. The landed men, unable to exclude the middle classes from the Commons in 1832, were unable in 1846 to maintain protection for the cereal agriculture upon which their incomes, status and power had for so long rested. Peel had finally opted to allow Britain to draw freely on world grain supplies, and in so doing had opened the possibility of reducing to some degree the cost of industrial production and of living in an urban–industrialised society. But the landed class, though potentially impaired in 1832 and 1846, continued largely in command of the nation. This was partly because British cereal agriculture responded to exposure to competition by greatly raising its own efficiency, and so maintained its size and income.

There has always been some danger of placing too much stress on the importance of the corn law and its repeal, just as Engels exaggerated the role of the cotton factories. It may well be that both aspects of the Britain of the 1840s were inflated in the contemporary mind and have continued so since. The corn law was certainly a highly emotive subject; it had become a symbol of the basic food of the populace, of the prevailing social and political pattern of landed dominance and of the increasing challenge of the industrialists that the economy should function on their terms. All this has been dramatised by the glosses of historians and others. Moreover the price of corn, because of the classic inelasticity of both its supply and demand, was highly volatile. In an industrialising country the corn law was now capable of drawing to itself for a time pretty well all aspects of economic, social and political debate. Thus it could explode the Conservative Party, creating a political fluidity, not to say confusion, that was to last for more than a decade.

The repeal of the corn laws was followed by the establishment by the government of a fund of £2 million to subsidise the improvement of English agriculture (with an additional £1 million for Ireland). It was a kind of compensation for the loss of protection to cereal agriculture, but aimed at improving its efficiency in order to meet the threat of foreign corn.

10. *The control of business: company formation and the railways*

By 1825 business needed to be set free of legislative constraints. In that year the Bubble Act of 1720 was repealed, so that joint-stock companies could be freely formed. Moreover, the market in shares was now largely uninhibited, Barnard's Act of 1733 having fallen into abeyance. Under the Companies Act of 1844 the law gave its first general recognition to companies that were not incorporated (e.g. did not have a charter or letters patent), but limited liability was still withheld.

Scarcely, however, had the new atmosphere of freedom of company formation been established when the state became aware of the need for surveillance of business enterprise in another sense. Monopoly had always been inherent in transport, in canals and the turnpike-trusts. The railways presented this problem in a new and pressing light. Should the state stand aside, allowing the railways to charge what they wished and to make as much profit as their monopoly or quasi-monopoly position permitted? By the early 1840s, with company promotions, amalgamations, manipulations and specu-lations rife, the answer was no. Gladstone's first Railway Act of 1842 set up a Railway Department at the Board of Trade to collect information from the companies, to promote public safety and where necessary to send inspectors and initiate prosecutions. This was an action in a sense analogous to that of the Factory Acts, aimed at promoting safety, though of consumers rather than producers. Gladstone's second Railway Act of 1844 went much further. In the case of new lines, railway profits were not to exceed 10% on capital, otherwise the Board of Trade could either force the rates for carriage down, or compulsorily nationalise such offending lines by purchase, subject to a specific Act of Parliament in each case. In 1846 a Railway Board was set up to control directly the rates charged, but it was suppressed in 1851. In addition all companies were obliged to run a daily passenger service each way, stopping at all stations with a maximum charge of a penny per mile – the 'Parliamentary Train'. This was the first attempt at state surveillance of the functioning of a sector of the economy, doing so by the control of profits through pricing policy and enforcing by statute a basic service. But in spite of these controls imposed on the railway companies building costs were outrageously inflated, and there was enormous speculation in shares contributing greatly to the commercial boom and collapse between 1844 and 1847.

The state was the creator in law of all railway companies: each received its birth certificate in the form of an Act of Parliament.

Indeed it was parliament which not only brought the companies into being, but also made their activities possible by empowering them to supersede the property rights of others, by taking from owners of rural and urban land, under compulsory purchase, such property as they sought. The state, responding to claims made by the railway companies claiming to act in the name of the common good, thus carried much further the impairment of the inviolability of private property (already challenged by the Enclosure Acts and the Canal Acts), as well as making itself, in a sense, both the creator and controller of a revolutionary agency, namely the railways.

State control of business down to 1851 was thus limited to general company law (especially as affecting company formation), the regulation of railway services and charging and the setting of the framework for a restructuring of banking.[1]

11. The challenge of labour

Parliament had no wish to sponsor new sources of power in the form of trade unions. But by the 1820s it was impossible to maintain the classic doctrine that they were unlawful because they were in restraint of trade. In simple, pragmatic terms the realisation was growing that the great mass of men could not and should not be denied indefinitely the right to combine for collective action. But neither could parliament concede to workmen the lawful right to combine entirely as they might choose, making it possible for them to bring pressure to bear on wages and costs free of legal constraint.

There was, first, a major concession in the Act of 1824 repealing the Combination Laws made by the House of Commons scarcely aware of what it was doing. This in effect made combination as such a free right. Unions were no longer to be criminal associations. But there should be no 'threats, intimidation or acts of violence'. The hope was that once the right to form unions had been conceded it would be exercised with voluntary restraint. So far as a good many political economists were concerned unions could not affect the course of wages against the pressure of market forces, so that workers would soon learn their futility and abandon them. The response among workers was quite otherwise: the Act of 1824 was

---

1. See section 6 above.

followed by an alarming proliferation of unions and demands made by them, inspired by the workers' urge to gain a larger share of the product under conditions of expanding trade and rising prices.

Parliament, alarmed at what it had done, and under strong pressure from employers, partially reimposed constraint. The Act of 1825, though it continued the basic legality of unions, made more stringent rules governing the ways in which the majority element in a union could enforce its will on the minority. There was to be no coercion to enforce workers to join a union; all members of a union were to have free choice whether to strike or not. Unions were thus made legal, but on restrictive conditions that greatly constrained their ability to present a united front to their employers. The climate of the times among legislators was that though workmen should be conceded a right to join unions, and within them were free to choose whether to strike, and to seek to persuade others, they were forbidden any form of coercion. A union was seen in effect as a means of making it possible for workmen voluntarily to confer and to concert their actions, and not as a means of consolidating all workers against their employers. The provisions against violence and intimidation were strengthened by the 1825 Act, and the purposes of unions strictly confined to seeking improvements in wages and hours. But the great gain of 1824 stood, namely voluntary combination remained a legal right for the workers.

In this way the British state in 1824–5 for the first time conceded to organised workers the right to exert pressure at the industrial level. But the practical terms on which this could be done continued to be obscure, leaving the way open to restrictive interpretations by the courts. The most dramatic of these occurred in 1834 when six Dorsetshire labourers, the 'Tolpuddle Martyrs', were convicted under an Act of 1797 forbidding the taking of illegal oaths: their attempt to create solidarity by pledge earned them transportation to Australia. Though five of them were permitted to return within four years, they were the first true martyrs of trade unions.

A new state function was embodied in the 1825 Act. It sought to promote conciliation and arbitration between workers and employers: the contending parties might appeal to the Justices of the Peace who might appoint mixed panels of masters and men; if no settlement was reached the Justices could make the final award. But this machinery of conciliation was scarcely used, for both parties declined to be bound in advance.

A somewhat forlorn attempt was made by John Fielden (1784–1849) and others in 1835 to revive the principle of state regulation of wages. He moved a Bill in the House of Commons to protect the now obsolescent handloom weavers: local boards would construct wage averages and enforce these as minima. But the Bill was defeated, largely by those who asked how was the product, already unsaleable, and now made to carry these additional wages costs, to be marketed?

12. Ireland, the tragic component

The policy agenda for Ireland continued to contain three great items: how to remove the grievances of Irishmen by the granting of rights, dignity and participation in government, how to promote a programme for economic improvement and how to relieve the desperate condition of so much of the peasantry. These three challenges were interlocked not merely with one another, but in terms of the pattern of politics, property and religion in Ireland. A great though grudging concession to the status of Irishmen came with Catholic Emancipation in 1829, removing civil disabilities for all Catholics. But nothing was achieved by policy in terms of the productivity of the Irish economy through its principal element, agriculture. Instead nature, in the form of the potato blight, brought famine in the years 1845–9, amputating the population, and thus altering the fundamental ratio of men to land. There was a rising in 1848 but it was pathetically ineffectual.

Catholic Emancipation was brought about under the pressure of great popular meetings addressed by Daniel O'Connell (1775–1847), and the fear of disturbance they inspired in government. Irish Catholics could now have direct representation at Westminster. The franchise was, however, narrowed by raising the property requirement from 40s to £10, making it the same as in England. The Anglo-Irish landlords, who had for so long enjoyed the sympathy of the administration at Dublin Castle, now felt themselves betrayed by it, while the Roman Catholics and the liberals regarded it as an ally.

The wretchedness of the majority of the Irish peasantry had by the 1830s become a matter both of political danger and evangelical–philanthropic shame. A Commission under Archbishop Whately (1787–1863) recommended a system of relief appropriate to Irish conditions. But the government insisted that Ireland have the same poor law system as had been embodied in the English Act of 1834.[1] Ireland thus in 1838 acquired the workhouse system, with poor law districts, guardians, poor law rates and the principle of less-eligibility. The hope was that this provision would help to arrest the flow of Irish destitute to England. There was, too, the idea that it would ease the problem of eviction, necessary in order to create larger and more efficient farms. The system was confirmed by the Poor Law Extension Act of 1847.

The new Irish poor law was not intended to deal with the endemic famines that haunted the country. Much less could it relieve the appalling conditions of starvation and disease between 1845 and 1849 when the potato failed. Ireland at this time was one of the most densely populated countries in Europe; in August 1847 some 3,000,000 people were being fed daily at the expense of the British Treasury. Whereas in 1841 the population of Ireland had been 8,175,000 people, by 1851 it was 6,552,000. Taking account of the loss of natural increase this meant that numbers had been reduced by almost 2,000,000 by death and by emigration. From then on Irish nationalism assumed a much more bitter character both at home and in the United States. Indeed, the Irish problem was now compounded by the rapid growth of a support base in America.

On the other hand the pressure on the soil was relieved: the number of holdings fell from 690,000 in 1841 to 570,000 in 1851. It was now somewhat easier to consolidate the land into larger and more efficient units. The Encumbered Estates Act of 1849 set up a special Court that could cut through the many legal impediments to the sale of land by exercising its power to put estates on the market on application either from the owner or encumbrancers (chiefly those who held mortgages). The hope was that by thus freeing the sale of land, tenants could more readily buy, and English cultivators and capital would flow in.

The programme for the regeneration of Ireland urged by the English political economists was for the state to create conditions under which agricultural productivity could be raised by replacing petty cultivation with the English system of large farms with a three-part relationship between landlords, substantial farmers and wage labour. It was believed that this formula would promote investment

1. See chapter 5, section 7 below.

and modernisation. It would also replace improvident Anglo-Irish landlords with improving Whig gentry. But the principal effect of the Act of 1849 was to open the door to speculators in land who were often more oppressive than the traditional landlords. Moreover there had always been a rival programme more closely related to Irish conditions and more attractive to Irishmen: it was that there should be small-scale peasant proprietorships, with the peasant owning his modest parcel of land. The advocates of capitalist farming took as their objective the maximisation of output; those who favoured peasant proprietorships sought to promote the security and independent status of the labourer. The advocates of the landlord–tenant–labourer relationship argued that it was more likely to act as a constraint on population growth than would peasant owner-occupancy. The reduction in the population by the famine made possible attempts in both directions, but both were subject to serious difficulty.

13. *Economic policy from the 1820s to 1851*

In the generation down to 1851 the general trend of economic policy in Britain is clear. These were the years of commitment to the market system, and to increasing economic abdication by the state. By 1851, though some further steps were required, this development was irreversible. But on closer scrutiny the idea of a simple self-reinforcing trend requires qualification. In each aspect of action there was a strong air of pragmatism, of politicians in parliament seeking to deal on an ad hoc basis with a range of evolving problems, by a balancing, in a series of specific situations, the common good against the configuration and relative strengths of power groups. The body of generalised sanctioning theory derived from Adam Smith, Ricardo and others was certainly not strong enough in its hold on the minds of politicians to determine the result. Nor was class interest, simply viewed, the governing circumstance. William Huskisson, Robert Peel and William Gladstone progressively freed Britain's markets because each protective device, when brought under inspection, was seen as pointlessly inhibitive, reflecting past realities, if any at all, and so lacking in the strength of backing necessary for such devices to hold their ground. The tariff had proliferated for more than a century, generating paper and engrossing manpower, often with the most meagre net return, indeed in some cases hardly this. Inevitably there was criticism of so irrational a system. Even the great centre-piece of protection, the corn law, succumbed to this kind of scrutiny. Though it had been powerfully reasserted in 1815, when in 1846 the realities were differently perceived it went down, amid the wreckage of the Conservative Party, and against the economic interest of the dominant class, the landowners. To produce a new, rationalised tariff system to replace the old was out of the question. Partly this was because the protagonists of the growth industries had no interest in such archaism, and were indeed hostile to it, and partly it was because no theoretical system upon which a revamping of mercantilism might have been based was available.

In the monetary field, however, the state could not follow the path of total abdication. Though British governments declined to accept direct responsibility for the money supply, they knew perfectly well that the institutional form of the banking system had to be brought under regulation. Without a centralisation of the English note issue in the Bank of England there could be no means whereby any conscious control of the system could be operated by anybody; such monetary impotence was unacceptable. After 1844 the Bank could move more effectively toward a central banking function through the device of central control of note issue through variations in the Bank's own lending. Though it was now possible that the Bank itself could be outdone in size by joint-stock rivals, its central position within the system, that of a private concern with public powers and responsibilities, could never henceforth be challenged.

In fiscal terms the state had by 1851, in large measure, come to terms with the tax system and the debt. The income tax had been resumed in 1842, never to be abandoned. The debt was brought under control in two senses – as to size (it diminished from a peak of £844 million in 1819 to £790 million in 1851, while national income rose from £291 million to £523 million) and as to management (the state, through the Treasury and the Bank, was learning how to relate its borrowing to the money market and hence to the general supply of liquidity).

But the most difficult and dangerous problem had to do with labour supply. The working classes had been successfully excluded from the franchise in 1832 and again during the Chartist campaigns.

The state, through parliament, was thus able to continue to preside over the masses with no concessions to their participation. The demands of workers for a place in parliament could be resisted largely because of the tactical configuration. Those wanting the franchise to include the working classes had to be able to induce a sufficient level of fear in the upper and middle classes such as would bring the necessary concession; this required a higher degree of sustained organisation than was then possible. For middle-class radicals in alliance with the working class to generate the necessary level of fear would have meant accepting the risk of bringing the country close to open conflict, a prospect which an insufficient number of workers or workers' sympathisers were prepared to accept, especially when the disturbances over the 1832 Reform Act were so recent.

In spite, however, of exclusion from the state, the working classes gained something at the industrial level through the trade union legislation of 1824–5. Once the legitimacy of the union principle was conceded, there could be no returning to the notion of simple contract between individual workers and their employers, and no denial of the workers' right to combine. The problem was: how were the proper limits of action by workers' combinations to be determined and enforced?

5

The social action equation and the *zeitgeist*

1. The social agenda

The industrial–urban society coming into being between 1815 and 1851 was confronted with four principal social areas in which it would be obliged to act. First there was the care of an increasing number of social casualties, to be provided by means of the poor law. Secondly there was an altogether new problem, namely the need for state surveillance of the conditions of work, chiefly in the factories and mines. Thirdly, because of the new concentration of people and industries in the cities, the state could not avoid an involvement in the conditions of living, chiefly through measures to promote public health. Finally, there was the question of education: what should government do about the needs of society and the rights of individuals in this respect? These were the four basic social functions into which the state was to be drawn between 1815 and 1851 in order to ease and contain the pressures of industrialisation and to fit the working population for their tasks. On the question of the supply of housing for the working classes, a matter in which the market was in a chronic default, the state did nothing.

There were five further elements of the national life, of a more implicit kind, upon which the state acted. Firstly, the family was the basic cell form of society; the state could not avoid a relationship with it through divorce law and the rights of married women to property.[1] Moreover the general structure of society was involved in the state's attitude to the family. At one extreme the laws of property could concentrate wealth in the hands of dominant families, and at the other the poor law could break up working-class families. Secondly there was the question of belief, especially as expressed in religious terms, in which the state was considerably

1. See section 12 below.

involved. Thirdly, and also related to belief, the state could not avoid becoming a custodian to some degree of morality and conduct, especially with regard to profanity, drunkenness, prostitution and obscenity. In so doing it accepted a responsibility for the control of considerable ranges of behaviour, delimiting the liberty of the subject in the interests of a set of concepts concerned with the common good. Finally, where the state was confronted with deviants, the criminal law operated, together with the penal system; ultimately the state could not avoid the coercion of those who were recalcitrant towards its rules.

2. *The socially innocent state*

In much of Europe under absolutist cameralist regimes, as in Prussia, the state had for generations had a wide range of positive welfare functions; this was not so in Britain. Governments, lacking a paternalistic tradition, were confronted by the social dislocations of industrialisation. These challenges appeared over little more than a generation of thirty years. Even by 1830 there were less than 100,000 factory workers, far fewer than those making boots and shoes; there were more tailors than coal miners. Moreover England had always depended on child labour: most children in pre-industrial times had worked in one way or another before the age of ten.

Not only did the state have no experience of industrial and urban surveillance; it could not know what and how to regulate until some sort of pattern had emerged. By the time this had happened very bad conditions had been generated over many industries and in many cities. Also, deterioration in industry was to a significant degree specific to each principal line of output. Just as the modes of production were different as between cotton spinning mills, potteries, iron works or coal mines, so too were the relations in these industries between owners, managers and the workers, consisting of men, women and children. There could be no question of blanket statutes which could, from a moment in time, regulate them all according to a single formula. As to living conditions in the cities, government had never been seen as responsible for these. At both the centre and at the local level, governmental organs had to be created appropriate to new needs.

Yet the conditions of work and of urban living were the two areas in which, in addition to an attempt at radical revision of the poor law, the state first responded: there was significant provision concerning these by 1851. On education there was a beginning, but it was tentative; on housing nothing was done until very much later. Thus the agenda of social amelioration produced a distinctive timing.

3. *The conditions of social action*

Social policy in industrialising Britain did not really begin until the Reform Parliament, elected in 1832. The poor law continued to embody all statutory social provision of any real significance prescribed by parliament right down until the years in which the first industrial revolution is commonly thought to have been consummated in the 1830s, and, indeed, far beyond. The first industrial revolution, as commonly conceived, had taken place before the state became a significant agent for social improvement.

There could, of course, be no generalised social policy arising from a systematic view of society. Rather, it was necessary to begin at the other end – with particular needs, abuses and defaults. The grossest and most dangerous of these first forced themselves into view. Specific social challenges had to mature to the point at which pressure for action was able to overcome the prevailing obstacles. There was thus in operation what might be called the law of necessary deterioration. A second law, related to the first, was also involved, namely that of precluded alternative. It states that politicians who anticipate a problem, and act in advance so as to prevent it, make themselves vulnerable to criticism, for the evil has, by assumption, now disappeared, but the costs and enmities generated in precluding it remain. For these reasons, and because the changes in a traditional society as it moved into industrialisation were so all-pervading and so immense in aggregate impact, only patching was possible. The first industrial nation found itself alone in this regard as in so many others.

This challenge involved three sub-circumstances. First, each specific situation had to reach such a level of deterioration as to be an outrage upon public opinion. Secondly, the indifference and hostility that stood in the way of remedy had to be in some manner and to some degree weakened. Thirdly, the forces pressing for improvement had to attain such strength as to be effective. We thus arrive at what might be called the social action equation: thus *Statutory Action* in a given area of social concern will occur when *Deterioration + Reformism* are greater than the *Inertias + Resistances*. This expression, of course, is a tautology, like the quantity theory of money, but it may help us to recall the components of each of the social challenges and the relationships that linked them. Deterioration and reformism also had to have a publicity dimension, for only if public attention was attracted could they impinge on policy.

Social reformism was the product of the interplay between general ideology (the presence of evangelicalism, humanitarianism, philanthropy and Benthamite utilitarianism) and the apparently semi-fortuitous appearance of dedicated individuals. As to inertias, the element of ideology operated (in the form of a predilection for laissez-faire), together with the prevailing class configuration and the attitudes and responses it engendered. Downright resistances and hostilities could range from particular vested interests likely to be threatened by a particular social reform (such as factory owners), to a generalised complacency or conservatism. Moreover resistance could come even from those intended to be benefited, especially where the working classes took a short-term view of their own interests (for example resisting attempts to control the age and working hours of their children), or where they or their spokesmen detected an attempt at social control.

Both reformism plus philanthropy, and inertias plus resistances, mustered their respective tactical power over each issue. Something of a standard sequence developed, acted out in each area of social need. The reformers would make their bid in the form of a parliamentary bill. Their opponents would then bring into play the complete range of blocking or emasculating tactics. Even if the bill became law, there would follow a continuation of the struggle in the form of a contest over more effective implementation through an inspectorate or by other means.

By and large these contests went on without significant direct intervention from the working classes. Certainly there were occasional proletarian voices, and the emerging trade unions were heard from time to time. There were short-time committees, and Chartist and other protests against cyclical unemployment, all reflected in a considerable working-class press. But no sustained and pointed initiative came from these quarters, such as materially to affect the parliamentary outcome. The working classes were in a state of confusion, suspicious of state control of conditions of work. In their social movements and political protests the demand for social reform was not directly prominent; an extension of the franchise in their own direction was what the activists among them really wanted, in the belief that from this a whole range of benefits would flow. The struggle over conditions of work lay largely within the middle and upper classes. To this generalisation there is one partial exception: working-class pressure certainly availed in frustrating the principles of the Poor Law Act of 1834. But this was largely unorganised and instinctive resistance, the spontaneous resentment shown in one parish or union of parishes after another, with occasional demonstrations. On this view of the matter then, social policy perhaps to the 1870s was settled by processes operating chiefly within the middle classes; the social action equation was largely a bourgeois affair.

4. The humanitarian urge; the professionals; the opponents

In a sense the urge for reform was the paramount requirement. It was the dynamic, the source of the drive to change the situation. It was expressed in the evangelical–humanitarian movement dating from the eighteenth century, that extraordinary heightening of the sense of what the minimal conditions for human existence should be.[1] Somehow there had been generated in a sufficient element of the middle classes a social conscience that found the abuse of fellow humans, beyond a certain point, intolerable. In the nineteenth century humanitarianism became an expression not merely of concern over particular categories of social suffering, but a desire on the part of those moved by it to work toward some new moral order appropriate to an industrial society, necessary to replace the moral bond of agrarian society. Lord Ashley (1801–85, Lord Shaftesbury from 1851), for example, never tired of urging the manufacturers to remember their 'great sea of duty to the poor', in order that the labouring classes would respond by embracing 'piety and peace'.

The result was a dual one. There was a growing reservoir of general and diffused feeling which, under propitious conditions, could be tapped. There was also generated a set of philanthropists who,

1. See chapter 3, section 1 above.

though small in number, were potent, pressing in and out of season for their favourite lines of state action. These were not earnest, powerless intellectuals, writing books that had no impact: they were men of some position, using, especially, the provincial power base of the industrial cities, hard-headed and skilful in their tactics, and persistent in their strategy. They are a fascinating lot, both in terms of their own personality formation and of the vulnerability of the liberal system to their single-minded tactics. They were men and women of determination often amounting to obsession, but whose zeal did not run to ineffectualness through zealotry. Lord Shaftesbury was perhaps their great exemplar – something of a manic depressive, pursuing his cause with passion, but with strong tactical sense, performing the work of God, but unwilling that his efforts should be known to God alone.

There is a further problem. What supplied the driving force that made success cumulative, pushing the system into ever further state intervention on behalf of the vulnerable? The philanthropic urge did not diminish, and there was no failure in the supply of ameliorative activists. But the professional was also moving onto the scene in increasing numbers, to provide institutional form and to generate an *esprit* of practitioners. The professional came first with men like Chadwick, Simon and Trevelyan as legislative and administrative inventors. Then, in factories and mines, health and education, came the inspectorates. More and more windows were opened upon industrial and mining conditions, on health and homes. Data was gathered, reports published, techniques of control developed. Not least, the inspectors formed their corps, becoming prime movers in new legislation. They had been given their role: they seized upon it and amplified it, infusing it with their own integrity and urge to achieve. At the same time they were successful in gaining control of their own role and of exercising influence in a manner not envisaged by the legislators who created them.

There was of course, a counter-attack by the anti-collectivists. But social policy, because of its disparate elements, produced no great synthetic prophet offering a coherent philosophy. Therefore it could not be identified as a target. Its opponents, in spite of the fact that their own ideology was unified under laissez-faire, could not bring this dispersed, pragmatic, guerilla enemy of philanthropists, inspectorates and administrators to formal battle.

Such interest groups must not be underestimated, with their potency, ingenuity and plausibility. They included mill and mine owners who could emasculate and delay legislation, civic oligarchs who saw municipalities as their fiefs and landowners who resented the poor law. But they were slowly and eventually brought under a degree of control or replaced, largely by the pressures generated by other parts of the middle-class community.

5. The reforming parliament after 1832 and social questions

Though it is necessary to think in terms of the operation of the social action equation in each of the leading areas of action, there was, nevertheless, a sense in which things held together as a single national whole. Down to the 1830s there was a collective indifference or minimising of the deterioration of social life and working conditions, together with a mutually reinforcing set of inertias and resistances among the land-owning and business classes, so that the reformers were struggling against the *zeitgeist*. There was a need for a major discontinuity in the nation's political life, a new beginning, so that men, though still steeped in preconception, became more conscious of the new social needs.

Such a new atmosphere was made possible by the parliament elected after the passing of the Reform Act. The long and bitter fight for an extended franchise had generated a new set of expectations in both the middle and the working classes.[1] Like every such renovating parliament, that of 1832 was still governed by great underlying continuities even in its most reformist period, and it tired of improvement after a time. But it had its phase of active scrutiny and vigorous response to an impressive range of social challenges, and the trends it set going were not to be reversed. The legislative floodgates were opened: 1833 saw the first effective Factory Act, the first government grants for education and the ending of slavery throughout the empire; in 1834 came the new Poor Law; in 1835 the Municipal Reform Act was passed and a prisons commission set up; in 1836 the University of London was chartered; in 1840 a Royal Commission investigated child labour, the progenitor of the Mines Act of 1842.

1. See chapter 4, section 4 above.

6. Social versus economic policy

The social action equation in each of its aspects, and in aggregate impact, had of course its financial implications; any policy of amelioration involves costs for someone. Yet the national budget was not affected, except to a very minor degree. Nothing done on the social side seriously involved the Exchequer – the charges were borne either by local property owners, as in the poor law unions, or by the businesses affected by the factory and mines acts. By the same token, because the Exchequer incurred no significant burden, social policy and general economic policy could be kept distinct.

Moreover, with social costs dispersed in this way, and with the expenditure involved relatively modest, social policy intruded only to an insignificant degree into the market economy. In spite of loud protestations by business men and others, the scale and direction of official social expenditure, kept at a modest level, left wages and prices largely unaffected.

7. The new poor law of 1834

The poor law in 1815 was not a system, but an accretion, governed by antique statutes, but without any central organisation, left to the discretions and vagaries of the parish guardians.[1] It was also the most complicated social concern, in that it embraced all categories of social casualties and was the only public provision for them.

By the 1830s the challenge of the poor law was seen by dominant opinion not as one of lack of provision, but as one of excess. The question posed was: how could the system be purged of its corrupting and expensive leniency and brought back to rigour? The natural law view of society as exemplified by the political economists was in the ascendancy over the evangelical–humanitarian view. The new poor law of 1834 embodied this outlook: it asserted that pauperism, even when relieved, should be painful. But in its new form the poor law could be presented by its enemies as an abuse of the poor and an occasion to organise and protest on their behalf. Thus whereas poor law agitation before 1834 was aimed against amelioration, after 1834 the rigour of the new poor law generated a counter-pressure in

---

1. See chapter 3, sections 2 and 3 above.

favour of easement. The Act revived the spirit of humanitarianism among sections of the middle classes; they could join in protest with a new force, namely working-class resistance.

So far as the legislating classes were concerned, there was a conflict between, on the one hand, the demands of humane feeling and, on the other, the need for social discipline involved in the link between poor law provision and the willingness to work; the balance between these two views altered with the 1834 Act. There was also the question of which formula, easement or rigour would yield the greater degree of political and social stability.

The Poor Law Act of 1834 was unique in three aspects. It was, in a sense, archaic and irrelevant as soon as it was passed. Unlike factory and mine reform, or health and sanitation, the thinking that drove it was rural rather than urban based. It was this which helped to make possible the adoption of a programme entirely unsuited to and unworkable in the industrial urban setting of the northern cities. Thus accident and timing could determine the shape of legislation. Once embodied in a major statute, as in 1834, the elements of the situation were fused in the heat of the hour, like a chemical combination that could not be undone.

Secondly, 1834 was the outcome of a generalised view taken of an entire range of problems. The Royal Commission of 1832–4, however biassed and inadequate its inquiries were, represented an attempt to embrace in terms of investigation and policy prescription the entire challenge to society of those who had failed within the market system or who had been failed by it. Certainly the Report and the Act both stressed the former, taking a moral rather than an environmental view of the poor. Within this important bias the Report and Act aimed at comprehensiveness and internal consistency.

The third element of uniqueness in the poor law lay in the fact that the 1834 Act created the first effective element of centralised British bureaucracy, intended to preside over a general social policy, to be carried out by prescribed and centrally supervised local machinery. The three members of the Poor Law Commission set up by the Act, with Chadwick as their secretary, could try to make the system 'national' in a sense in which it had never formerly been, enforcing and inspecting the application of the principles of the Act.

The most important of these was that the able-bodied male unemployed should no longer receive relief outside the poorhouse;

within 'the house' there should be applied the principle of less-eligibility, under which the condition of the best-off inmates would be significantly inferior to that of the worst paid employed workers. There was also to be segregation of the sexes in the workhouse and the breaking up of families. The merging of parishes into unions was to be facilitated. In these ways the canons of deterrence and of centrally supervised efficiency were to be enforced.

In part the intentions of the legislators of 1834 were fulfilled. A direct responsibility for the poor, having been assumed by the state in a supervisory way with a view to inducing uniformity of treatment, was never to be abandoned: the inescapable trend toward centralisation had begun. The reports of the Poor Law Commissioners, based on the work of its travelling inspectors, exposed the matter to public and parliamentary scrutiny. This aspect of local government, too, assumed a new form, for the new poor law system brought the dawn of a local civil service on any significant scale, though on a parish or 'union' basis. It is doubtful, however, whether the poor law achieved one of its principal objects, namely that of restraining the fecundity of the poor.

A simple reversal from relaxation to rigour was not possible. It could succeed to a considerable degree in the agriculture shires, as in the south of England, but matters were different in the industrial north. There the new poor law guardians represented the introduction into poor law affairs of the electoral principle; they soon became potent elements in local politics through the patronage associated with the poor law and by other means.

The standardising intentions of national legislators came almost at once into conflict with the responses of local people who had to deal with the realities of immediate situations. The humanitarian feelings of many boards of guardians were placed under stress; there was also a lively awareness on the part of such local men of the social tensions with the realities of immediate situations. The humanitarian feelings too much rigour. They could and did ignore the instructions of the Commissioners, evading and stonewalling, temporising until the Commissioners were frustrated. Even rural guardians soon learned that outdoor relief could not be withheld in a seasonal employment like agriculture. Eventually such feelings could permeate even to the centre, where in the minds of the Commissioners they generated a kind of schizophrenia when placed alongside the concepts embodied in the governing Act of 1834. But they could nevertheless produce concessions to common sense and common humanity. And yet the Commissioners did have a case; they were well aware, among other things, that the implementation of the new poor law, like the old, in town and country alike, was riddled with nepotism, malpractice and corruption, as well as being an important source of local political power and patronage, and so should be brought under rule and inspection.

The implementation of the new poor law of 1834 demonstrated for the first time two great aspects of social legislation in a complex industrial society. First, it provided the first real case of conflict between the demands of centralisation (where theory and even dogma are likely to entrench themselves) and the responses of local government (where improvisations and inertias are so important). Secondly the new poor law was the first great example in modern times of the immense difference that could arise in the social field between what is prescribed by statute and what is done in practice in the localities.

Though the guardians so often declined to enforce the full spirit of 1834, there is no doubt that terrible things were done under the Act, especially perhaps in its early years before resistance could build up. Even in the north (as in Manchester) there were unions where the guardians sought to enforce the full rigour required of them. There are harrowing accounts of appalling diets, penal workhouses, families torn apart and old people stripped of dignity. The poor could be desperately abused because of a combination of indifference to their plight bred of ignorance, and of dogma as enshrined in the Act, leading to a kind of social zealotry.

Significant administrative changes were made by the Poor Law Amendment Act of 1847. A new Poor Law Board was set up in that year, with a president who was a government minister, together with two secretaries, one of whom might be a Member of Parliament. Chadwick was deposed and the administration of the poor law brought directly under parliamentary control. The new Board could make a new start, free of the demoralisation of the Commissioners. A tentative beginning could be made in terms of social realism and sympathy at the centre. The first schools for pauper pupils were established in 1848.

The traditional twin of the poor law, namely private philanthropy, did not cease; in this sense the care of social casualties still relied heavily upon the voluntary principle. This was especially so in the provision of schools for the children of the poor, alongside the workhouse schools.

The poor law after 1834 has been taken by some scholars as exemplifying in a classic manner the basic class relations in England, and the way in which they affected public policy. Were the middle classes and the Commission of 1834 and the Select Committee of 1838 using a system of ideas deriving from their own interests, but projected as neutral social science ('political economy'), in order to bamboozle the working classes into acceptance of a repressive poor law regime? Was there a working-class response that can be properly regarded as being based upon some kind of integrated consciousness?

The links in middle-class minds between the corpus of political economy and poor law policy were complex. The 1834 Act was intended to be an attack on a structural problem, namely the conditions and behaviour of the labouring poor, chiefly on the land; it was intended to combat indigence and careless procreation, and to stop confusion between wages and relief. But the classical economists like Ricardo were uncertain about the effects of 'machinery', that is, technical advance causing a replacement of men by capital. A good many members of the middle classes were aware of the inadequacies of political economy (for example in explaining and prescribing for the trade cycle), and were properly sceptical of attempts to construct a social science on which national economic and social policy must be based; this was demonstrated by their refusal to implement the Act of 1834 in its full rigour.

On the working-class side, that there was a popular attack on the principles of 1834 is clear. But obscurity surrounds the extent to which the proletariat was becoming an integrated force or had an organised consciousness. On the whole it would seem to be straining the evidence to maintain that a polarity of view, based upon differences in observation and reasoning, existed between the classes. But the Act did indeed have a class aspect, namely that labourers as a group, when they could not support themselves and their families, were to be subsidised only to the minimal degree consistent with survival, thus placing them under a discipline imposed by a state in which they had no part.

8. *New labour codes for factories and mines*

As technology gained in strength it became at last, in the 1830s, necessary to invoke the state on a serious and sustained basis to regulate its application. Society began the long search for a new set of values appropriate to the new productive powers now being released, such that public policy could contain their impact within some concept of the common social good. But the economic power already generated by the new technology was not easily to be tamed.

Moreover both employers and labour became the prisoners of attitudes determined and often made compulsive by their respective roles. Employers could, in one industry after another, forge lengthening chains of misery, passing on insensitivity and repression to those below them. They regarded their position as defined by circumstances beyond their control, namely those of the competitive market. They were not constrained by the shame that might follow exposure, or by the law, or (in the early stages at least) by the threat of workers' violence. Most men in such a position will inevitably lose contact with human sympathy. Even religious piety could be subverted in such men, so that they could adopt the external usages of church or chapel going, with little or no effect on the greed and indifference to which a good many of them had conditioned themselves. Even workmen, where the gang system (as in the potteries) or the butty system (as in some of the mines) made them 'contractors', often passed the pressures on to those below them. Finally, drunkenness among the workforce, as an escape from pressures, could become endemic, thus seeming to confirm the belief in many employers that the workforce would not respond to better treatment. Nor could trade union organisation have much effect upon working conditions in the years down to the 1830s and 1840s, for unions had to come into being and, like the state, had to learn to play a role in industrial amelioration.

Masters and men were related to one another by simple contract; so far as the masters were concerned both the labour of men and the use of machines had to be bought in the market. Thus it was that industrialisation created a new set of relationship patterns, baffling to those who wished to use the state to ameliorate them.

The Health and Morals of Apprentices Act of 1802[1] was in 1819

---

1. See chapter 3, section 4 above.

extended from the parish apprentices to cover all textile factory children. But the Factory Act of 1833 was the first really effective statute for the control of workers' conditions. For though it was confined to children, and applied only to the textile mills, it brought into being an inspectorate. Though there were initially only four such men for the entire country, and though their brief deriving from the Act was carefully restricted, they represented an irreversible advance. Inspection was the prime condition of effectiveness, for it not only made enforcement possible, it also provided a continuous source of information in the form of reports that were in effect annual surveys of the conditions of workers in a range of factories, mainly cotton, wool, linen and silk. The compulsory regulation of births under the Registrar General came in England and Wales in 1837 (Scotland in 1855), making possible the ascertainment of a child's true age; invaluable demographic data was thus a direct by-product of the determination to regulate the hours of work of the young in relation to their age. From the Act of 1833 children under thirteen might not work in the regulated trades more than forty-eight hours per week (i.e. an eight-hour day), and those from thirteen to eighteen were limited to sixty-five. Two hours of schooling per day was required for children. This made the factory owners responsible for the provision of what was potentially the largest element in the school system. Regular meal-times were stipulated. The inspectors were given powers to make rules about ventilation, temperatures, the speed of machines and the quality of materials.

The provisions of 1833 were extended by the Factory Act of 1844. It increased the child protection afforded by the 1833 Act, and brought the hours of work of women under control. Children were to work no more than six and a half hours per day, on a 'half-day' basis, the other half to be reserved for schooling or recreation. Employers were required to fence the more dangerous machinery. The inspectorate was significantly strengthened; the chief factory inspector from 1833 to 1856 was Leonard Horner (1785–1864), a man of great force of character. In particular the inspectorate was given some powers over educational provision so that the 'coal hole schools' could be replaced by something better; three hours of schooling per day instead of two were prescribed. State control of working life was further extended by the Ten Hour Act of 1847, and by the legislation of 1851 and 1853; women and young persons (to the age of thirteen) were henceforth to work a maximum ten and a half hours per day, from 6 a.m. to 6 p.m. with one and a half hours for meals. This rule obliged the mill owners to adjust their total working, prohibited a range of ingenious abuses that had grown up around the shift system and indirectly provided a degree of protection for the men of the labour force.

Over all this there was, of course, a long and bitter political battle; a series of major national debates took place with intense publicity. The factory owners (with some notable exceptions) were largely hostile to state control, but it was imposed upon them. It may be that the landed interest gave backing to the Ten Hour Act of 1847 as a retribution on the manufacturers for their campaign against the corn laws of the previous year. The scale of abuse as revealed by protestors (including an important element among the factory owners themselves) and the propagandist and lobbying skill and persistence of men like Lord Ashley – both groups acting in an atmosphere of increasing humanitarianism as projected by evangelicals and others, and supported by landowners – bore down the opposition of the factory men and the arguments of certain economists. Moreover the reports of the factory inspectors from 1833 had generated knowledge of what was going on.

One effect of the legislation was a significant improvement in human terms within the textile industries. With the Factory Acts came an insistence by the state that a range of costs, formerly imposed upon society and especially the workers, should be borne by industry. Moreover cost conditions were thus equalised as between producers, to the prejudice of the smaller and often marginal mills. Such costs could be passed on to the consumer, could be absorbed out of profits or could be compensated for by higher productivity due to the consequent improvement of working conditions. Or they could provoke the response, especially after 1847, as Marx argued, of a rapid increase in labour-saving mechanisation, together with an improvement in the efficiency of machines. In this way the limitation of labour supply through the curtailment of hours may have had profound effects on employment and technology. It would seem that the masters in their resistance to the Factory Acts failed to foresee that mechanisation could be a means of meeting labour pressures, but subsequently learned this. Certainly Peel and other politicians feared reduction of output, increased costs and loss of markets. It is to be remembered, however, that factory legislation

96

was, until the 1860s, confined to textile factories, the places upon which Engels in 1844 had concentrated his critique; most of the labour force was still left unprotected.

The Bill of 1833 as originally proposed by Chadwick and others had represented a much more comprehensive programme than that finally adopted, but it was cropped of its more radical features. Under factory-owner pressure the educational provisions for factory children proposed in the Bill were much reduced, the inspectorate was made weaker than it might have been, both in numbers and in powers, and the proposal that employers should be made financially liable for accidents was dropped. In the case of the 1844 Bill rearguard attenuation meant that far-reaching educational proposals were killed, namely for state provision and supervision, special schools, proper finance and expert control. In this way the road to a general system of elementary education was blocked.

There were also the coal mines – places where the abuse of working conditions was even greater. *The Report of the Commission on the Employment of Women and Children in Mines and Collieries* of 1842 is perhaps the most often referred to horror document of the late industrial revolution. It revealed appalling conditions of degradation in many mines, especially in the smaller and more inefficient ones working thin and difficult seams. Lord Ashley was the father of the Mines and Collieries Act of 1842. Women and children were at one stroke excluded from underground working. But inspection in the coal mines was still lacking. The Coal Mines Inspection Act of 1850 provided it, together with powers to enforce standards of safety, lighting and ventilation.

By 1850 the conditions of work in textile factories and in coal mines were, by this sequence of legislation, brought under a degree of control, reinforced by inspection. It is difficult to say when serious deterioration had first manifested itself in these two rapidly growing sectors: perhaps the years after 1815 might be taken as a benchmark. If so, the first elements of a code of control, inadequate though they were, had appeared within some twenty years in the factories and some twenty-seven years in the mines.

9. The beginning of the health code

The General Report on the Sanitary Condition of the Labouring Population in Great Britain of 1842 heralded the third great item on the ameliorative agenda, namely the health of the cities. European cities as they had grown larger had always produced wastes, mainly human, which defeated disposal, so that a self-generated toxicity hung over them, controlling urban numbers by generating periodic epidemics. Out of the *Report* came the Public Health Act of 1848. It applied only in England and Wales; Scotland had to wait until 1867 for a similar Act. Following the analogy of the Poor Law Board, a General Board of Health was established in London, with Chadwick as one of its three members. It was to act in a general supervisory capacity in the provision of minimum standards of domestic drainage and of water supplies. The corporate boroughs created in 1835, and those subsequently to be established, were empowered by the Act to set up Local Boards of Health, and so were placed in a position to begin sustained action against bad sanitation and the sickness it generated. But the Act was permissive rather than obligatory. Indeed the intentions of Lord Morpeth (1773–1848), its father, were in many respects frustrated by the emasculation of his proposals. Nor were the municipalities at all eager to accept the new responsibility, so that by 1853 only some two million people lived under Boards of Health. The General Board in the first instance worked locally through the guardians of the poor, but in boroughs where the death rate was abnormally high it had the power to enforce the setting up of a Local Board of Health.

The tone of the Public Health Act of 1848 was not mandatory as was that of the Poor Law Act of 1834; in spite of cholera and typhus, government was unwilling to adopt too strong a policy of enforcement from the centre. It hoped that local initiative would produce actions appropriate to local conditions. The situation was greatly complicated by debate concerning the nature of disease and the best methods (both technically and in terms of cost) of dealing with it. But in spite of the weakness of the obligatory powers of the Act of 1848 it was an important beginning.

Chadwick and his colleagues pressed forward on many other fronts, sponsoring Bills on drainage and waterworks, burials and common lodging houses, challenging a wide range of vested interests in the form of water companies, engineers, vestries, cemetery trustees and undertakers.

10. Education becomes a state concern

The lack of general public provision for education in England was modified to some degree before 1851. There were signs of a growing acceptance of the need for public involvement. There had long been a vague responsibility attaching to the poor law authorities for the children in their care, reaffirmed in the Act of 1834. The Health and Morals of Apprentices Act of 1802 had placed an educational responsibility on factory owners. The Factory Acts of 1833 and 1844 imposed upon the textile industrialists the duty of supplying a further element of schooling.

But the main battle was fought elsewhere. The Church of England and the nonconformist denominations had each developed their separate elementary school systems. The Anglicans sponsored the 'National Society for Promoting the Education of the Poor in the Principles of the Established Church' (1811), and the nonconformists founded the 'British and Foreign School Society' (1812).[1] Both were largely based on the monitorial principle advocated by the educationalists Joseph Lancaster (1778–1838) and Andrew Bell (1753–1832), under which the older pupils taught the younger, thus economising on teachers. The two sets of schools shared a modest grant from the government. It began in 1833 at £20,000 for England and £10,000 for Scotland, but increased with the years. It was intended to augment 'Private Subscriptions for the Erection of School Houses for the Education of the Poorer Classes in Great Britain'. This was the beginning of British governmental finance for education. It was passed in a half-empty House of Commons.

But by 1839 the pressure from both sides of the Protestant religious division had become such that the government knew it had to do more for popular education. It dared not attempt a statute, but instead, against a House of Lords protest, the Royal Prerogative was used to set up the Education Committee of the Privy Council. It was to administer the funds provided by the government. To assist in this the Committee established an inspectorate in the same year. It lacked effective power and was harassed by the two religious factions. From 1846 the Committee, disillusioned with the monitorial system, accepted the need to sponsor a teaching profession: it began

1. For the state and religion see section 13 below.

99

to subsidise the salaries of teachers, set up training colleges and made provision for retiral pensions. It introduced the pupil–teacher system, and it sponsored the compilation of the necessary text books. All this was presided over by Sir James Kay Shuttleworth (1804–77), the first great figure among British educational theorists and administrators, operating a concordat with the Anglican authorities. In addition to the state-aided Church of England and nonconformist schools there continued the miscellaneous range of establishments run as benefactions or private ventures, the latter often with a single 'dame' or untrained master.

Two sets of ideas and aspirations were at work in invoking the state to act as an educative agency, namely those of the middle classes and those of the working classes. Of the former, Henry Brougham (1778–1868) in 1820 introduced a Bill into parliament to create a national system of education based upon the Church of England; it failed in the face of a nonconformist onslaught. Men like J.A. Roebuck and Thomas Wyse called in parliament in the 1830s for a national system of education; in the 1840s the Cobdenite radicals took up the same cry. But such men believed that the system should emanate from the middle classes: they had no doubt about the rightness, indeed necessity, of middle-class control. But there was also to some extent a growth of working-class radicalism which was beginning to recognise the strategic importance of the educational system in the setting of social values; it of course resisted middle-class dominance. There were thus two conflicts over education, the first within the middle classes, in terms of the Church of England versus the nonconformists, and the other between middle-class educational advocates and working-class radicals. It seems probable that, so far as most members of the upper and middle classes were concerned, it was still the case that no great benefits were thought to attach to education for the children of the masses.[1]

How, in the face of traditional unwillingness on the part of governments to become involved in education, was education pushed onto the state's agenda? One set of pressures came from the philanthropists. Some of these were concerned with the pauper children in the workhouses; it was under their influence that the Poor Law Act of 1834 made educational stipulations. Philanthropists

---

1. See chapter 3, section 5 above.

also took up the question of the condition of the factory children; they were largely responsible for getting the educational requirements written into the Factory Acts. Others were disturbed by the non-factory children who roamed the streets as vandals and juvenile criminals, being led into bad ways for life; the object of philanthropists concerned with such children was to use schools partly as a means of getting them off the streets. But there was no hope of this without a general elementary educational provision.

Much more potent in its educational consequences was the contest between the two religious groups, the Anglicans and the nonconformists. They were in competition for the loyalties and souls of the young, a contest that had a strong obsessive element. In a sense education became a projection of the religious conflict begun at the Reformation. The Church of England believed itself to be under attack from the state, with the nonconformists admitted to civil rights in 1828, the Catholics emancipated in 1829 and ten Anglican bishoprics suppressed in Ireland in 1833; in the latter year began the Oxford Movement splitting and yet revivifying the Church of England. It was inevitable that there should be a reassertion on the part of the established church of its claim to control national education. The nonconformists for their part still smarted from the traditional exclusiveness of the Church of England and sought to press their advantage. State backing for education was the newest battleground. As a consequence the educational lethargy of the eighteenth century was dispelled; each party derived new energies from the contemplation of the pernicious ambitions of the other.

This meant that the content of courses and the principles of pedagogy attracted little attention, except perhaps with the Educational Committee as it became more deeply involved in the task. Even with the Committee the essence of elementary education lay in the three Rs (reading, writing and arithmetic or 'reckoning'). These could be viewed, in themselves, as being politically neutral and without social content.

But there were further implications which could not be so simply regarded. For the masses to be made able to read had implications on three fronts. First, and primary in the minds of many middle-class advocates of popular education, was the opening of the Bible to the working classes. Many, perhaps most, members of the middle classes (the great supporters of the Bible Societies) seemed to think that the Bible would have a quieting influence, providing spiritual solace that would diminish the inclination for industrial or political unrest. But the Bible could also be read in a radical vein, especially the New Testament with its anti-clerical overtones and its condemnations of wealth, privilege and power expressed by Jesus himself. Secondly, there was the question of educating workers on the nature of economic and social processes: here political economy was the core. Authors like Maria Edgeworth (1767–1849) published books of 'tales', intended to illustrate the workings of the irrefragable laws of economy. This was clearly a quietist endeavour, aimed at inducing in the working classes a sense of inherent limitations of programmes of intervention or amelioration by the state; instead the way to improvement was through self-help in the form of hard work and thrift, and in a productive economy free of confrontation. Thirdly there were the writings of radicals and revolutionaries, like those of William Godwin (1756–1836) and Thomas Paine (1737–1809) and the numerous popular simplifications of these, clearly likely to disturb working-class acceptance of prevailing society and their place in it.

In this curious way religion provided the first two great dynamics for educational progress – through the Sunday School Movement,[1] and through the rivalry between the Church of England and the nonconformists. It can be said that it was religion (quietist in both its Anglican and nonconformist forms) that gave the worker his first access to learning and the means of pondering and arguing about his own material condition. But religion also had an inhibiting and distorting effect, for it delayed any national system for a further generation.

11. Housing

The state made no move whatever in the direction of housing before 1851. There was no way in which the social action equation could operate to repair this failure of the market mechanism. There were by 1851 (and indeed a generation earlier) large and dense slums in the cities. But there was in a sense an acceptance of this. Moreover it never entered upper- and middle-class heads that they, as a section of

1. See chapter 3, section 5 above.

society, should be taxed to provide or subsidise houses for the lowest section of the population. For these reasons even advanced social reformers had no housing programme. Nevertheless Ashley, that great alleviator, did begin the participation of British government in housing. He did so through his Lodging Houses Acts of 1851. They were concerned with the wandering homeless, often looking for work; the Acts made the licensing and inspection by local authorities of all common lodging houses compulsory. Local authorities were also empowered to raise a rate to build common lodging houses, but this was a dead letter.

12. The family

The family was, of course, a spontaneous social unit, coming into being and functioning according to circumstances with which the state had little to do. But there were two respects in which public policy did bear upon the family, the one affecting the middle and upper classes and the other the labourers.

So far as the wealthier classes were concerned, the law of property meant that the state, through the legal system, was used not merely to protect property in a general way, but also to affect its distribution both as between families and within them. English law sanctioned primogeniture, which made the eldest son sole heir, thus avoiding fragmentation of the estate; it also made possible entail, whereby the heir enjoyed only a life interest and so could not dissipate the capital of the estate, and it enforced marriage settlements aimed at consolidating inter-family alliances and allocations of wealth. Within the family the male was the owner of all property, including that of his wife (unless specially provided for in the marriage settlement). Wealthy families were thus structured in terms of property and human relations, using the law and marriages to implement and confirm these arrangements. A second factor seems, however, to have operated alongside the opportunities presented by the law, namely a reduction in the number of children among landed families, with the consequence that the eldest son was not saddled to the same extent with portions, endowments and other payments to sisters and brothers and other relatives. The result of these legal and demographic factors was an increasing concentration of landed wealth in relatively few families.

At the other end of society the poor law reformers, in their consideration of the provision to be made for the indigent, of course encountered the family. But the general notion of the sanctity of the family could not stand up to the three middle-class ideas that were destructive of it, namely less-eligibility, the refusal of outdoor relief and making the workhouse a place to be feared, not least by the breaking up of families within it.[1] When a family came upon the poor law it was regarded as having ceased to be a family, having failed as an economic unit.

So it was that at one extreme of society the state reinforced the family as a unit of wealth and power, whereas at the other it attacked the family as a source of mutual support when it was most needed.

13. The state, belief and conduct

Out of a complex political struggle in the 1820s and 1830s came a weakening on the part of the state in its attempts to control belief. This was related to a fading of the idea that there could be a kind of unity between the state and an established church. This linkage was attacked from two angles: the nonconformists wanted the removal of their 'disabilities', and the Roman Catholics wanted 'emancipation'.[2]

In 1828 the Corporation and Test Acts were repealed, giving nonconformists full political rights. In 1836 marriages in dissenting chapels were made legal. But the other discrimination remained. The nonconformists resented two aspects in particular, namely the Anglican claim to dominate education, and the obligation to pay church rates to a church based upon false doctrines. Indeed by the 1830s the dissenters had begun to develop the idea that the proper religious principles should not be those of the hierarchical Church of England, but their own views of religious democracy as embodied in their own theology and church order. As a natural development they began to seek the disestablishment of the Church of England. They became particularly potent in municipal affairs.

All forms of religion, however, backed the state in its controls on conduct, though the evangelical nonconformists took the lead in this. In 1824 prostitutes were put explicitly under the Vagrancy Laws. The Metropolitan Police Act of 1839 was to be for 120 years

---

1. See section 7 above.
2. See chapter 4, section 12 above.

the basic legal weapon against prostitutes; their punishable offence was still not against morality, but against public order, namely annoying passers-by and behaving in an unseemly manner, that is propositioning men in the street in indecent language. The Theatres Act of 1843 strengthened surveillance of the stage, placing the Lord Chamberlain in charge of its morality. Such controls upon speech, publication and acting imposed a tight constraint, reflecting the outlook of the day, severely restricting what might be said or written on matters fundamental to human conduct and happiness. But in the case both of obscenity and of profanity the accepted conventions of the day were such that it was they and not the law that were the real constraints.

The suppression of the cruder blood sports was perhaps the simplest of the problems of state control of mores. Bear-baiting was prohibited by parliament in 1835. Cock fighting, having thrived in England for six centuries, was made illegal in 1849. Bare-knuckle prize fighting was killed off by the establishment of police forces in England after 1835; though revived in the form of glove fighting, the legality of boxing contests remained doubtful until 1901. Field sports, or the various forms of hunting, which were a recreation largely of the wealthier classes, escaped control.

But the gambling habits of the upper classes were brought under quite severe regulation by the Gambling Act of 1845. It made gaming houses illegal and all gaming or wagering agreements unenforceable in any court. Openly organised gambling at cards or dice disappeared from the social life of Britain, though it could proceed in homes and clubs. Lotteries had already been suppressed in 1826. Thus the state gave some recognition to the puritan view that gain should be commensurate with work done for the glorification of God.

The idea of freedom of entry to the drink trade had gained ground. In 1830 a disastrous step was taken. The state virtually abdicated from drink control: the tax was taken off beer in England, and the Beerhouse Act made it possible for any householder paying the poor rate to open a beershop. No less than 31,000 new beer-sellers came into existence, servicing an appalling outbreak of drunkenness. It was from this abysmal level that the nonconformists began to exert themselves for stringent governmental control of the drink trade.

The state was thus available as an ultimate regulator of social behaviour. It had inherited this role from the church, perhaps unwillingly. Some state prohibitions were above discussion, like those against obscenity, profanity and homosexuality: these taboos reflected a compelling set of values on sex and religion. The cruder blood sports attended by baying crowds were also by the 1830s an affront. But drink, gambling and prostitution were not susceptible to simple treatment. They reflected deep urges in various parts of society, not easily regulated. The puritan/evangelical/humanitarian interest had thus had some success in causing the state to embody their view of society, but on the most important issue, drink, they had lost.

Anglicanism versus nonconformity can perhaps to some degree be projected as the correlatives respectively of the landed aristocratic view and that of the rising business bourgeoisie. But the two elements were agreed on the most important aspect, namely that society should undergo no radical change. Whereas the Church of England promoted deference, with the landed magistrates controlling the behaviour of the workers in the shires, the nonconformists no less reinforced the civil power by stressing law and order. But the rival zeal of these two 'classes' in promoting literacy among the working classes, deriving in large measure from their religious differences, was bound, in the longer run, to weaken working-class deference and promote assertiveness. There were strong elements among the Anglicans who shared the nonconformist desire to use the state to promote a more worthy pattern of behaviour, moving away from the brutalism that was so pervasive in pre-industrial times and which in some senses was aggravated by the new industry and urbanisation. There was, indeed, a fair measure of agreement that it was necessary to operate upon the behaviour pattern of the working classes by statutes governing a range of conduct.

14. Criminals and society

The opening of Millbank Penitentiary in 1816 (on the present site of the Tate Gallery) marked a new beginning in the treatment of prisoners. It was the first national prison in Britain, and the largest place of incarceration in Europe. But the crime rate was still rising steeply. In the same year Elizabeth Fry began her work among the women in Newgate Prison, giving them occupation and dignity and indeed a kind of communalism by putting the rules proposed to the vote. Her success raised the hopes of those who saw the role of prisons as redemptive rather than punitive.

The Gaols Act of 1823 produced the first effective prison code for England. It recognised the desirability of the separate system that would isolate the prisoners from one another, but not from staff or chaplains. But it authorised departures from this principle where overcrowding was too great, which was, indeed, the general condition. Dietary standards, hours of work, exercise and rest were prescribed. Staffs were to be salaried, in the hope of putting an end to prison bribery. But no inspectorate was established, partly because of the hostility of the magistrates to control by the central government. Instead the magistrates were to submit annual reports which appeared in the parliamentary papers.

An inspectorate did come with the Prisons Act of 1835. The inspectors, like those in factories and schools, quickly developed a philosophy of their function. They embraced separate confinement as the right governing principle, especially for the protection of children, unconvicted prisoners and those new to crime. They followed Howard in his preference for 'punishment directed at the mind', in order to bring about reformation. They shared with him the view that the criminal had lost the capacity to judge his own actions by moral criteria, and that therefore the role of the prisons was to provide a setting in which a moral perspective by which to make such self-assessment could be re-established. A sense of guilt, thus self-induced, could be a means both of individual salvation and social coherence. The separate system was adopted at Millbank at this time. Pentonville was opened in 1842. It was a model prison, adopting the separate system as its basic principle, built on the cellular system to make this possible. The Pentonville Plan as it became known was copied by prisons throughout the country.

By the standards of the day the new prisons were advanced constructions, based upon a theory of penal treatment that was intended to be humane. The advocates of the separate system did not mean by it solitary confinement: in theory the prisoners were to be in contact with the prison officers (themselves to be trained and sympathetic) and with the prison chaplains. Hard labour and physical punishment virtually disappeared. Thus physical harshness in the prisons was abandoned in principle at about the same time

107

that the rules governing the poor law were tightened up. But punishment directed at the mind involved profound suffering for those subjected to it. They were isolated from their fellow prisoners (wearing peaked caps that were pulled down to form masks when they were unavoidably brought together, as in the exercise yard). The intended supportive contacts with their gaolers never really developed. The prisoners, spending long hours enclosed and alone, often suffered hysteria and hallucinations. They became timid and suggestible, exposed to the frightening sermonising of the prison chaplain. In this way Howard's humanitarianism produced a manipulation of minds, aimed at inducing a sense of sin in those who had transgressed the laws of society.

And yet, because hard labour had been abandoned together with most physical punishment, and there was less of the old practice of administering a 'lowering diet', it could be said by the advocates of the retributive school that the prisoners were being pampered. The prisoners, it was insisted, should be under such conditions of rigour and denial as to keep them below even the meagre standard of the poor law. Thomas Carlyle, for example, in 1850 denounced the model prisons, demanding a return to the punishment principle.

Meanwhile the severity of the law had been, in a sense, reduced. By 1849 only eight crimes still carried the death penalty, only four of which were within the effective scope of the working classes, namely murder, burglary, robbery accompanied by violence and arson of dwelling houses with persons therein. In 1825 Sir Robert Peel had consolidated the law relating to juries and greatly reduced judicial abuse by removing the perquisites and fees of judges and raising their salaries.

The responsibility of the central government for public order continued to be discharged through the Home Office, concerning itself with major riots, enemy aliens and sedition. In the towns and shires law and order were the responsibility of the magistrates and their part-time constables. In 1829 Sir Robert Peel replaced the old Bow Street Runners with the first modern police force for London: with their top hats of a carefully non-military design the 'bobbies' were a force intermediate between a feeble implementation of law and order and calling out the military.

15. Municipal reform and local government

The Municipal Reform Act of 1835 can be seen not as a direct attack on substantive problems, but as a first step in making the towns and cities capable of responding to the new and frightening range of challenges that now confronted them. By removing the archaic and oligarchic corporations and replacing them with elected bodies, parliament made it possible for a new spirit eventually to enter city government. The immediate results of the Act were not striking. Whereas at the parliamentary level reform had been the prelude to action, at the municipal level the new elected rulers of the town showed no eager activist response. For they were middle-class liberal political reformers, Whigs who had helped to carry the Reform Bill of 1832, anxious to depose the Tory town oligarchs whose power had rested on business success in earlier generations, and to cut away the expenditure and patronage their predecessors had sponsored. They were largely without active plans for civic improvement, especially where these would involve increased local taxation. It was not until the later 1860s that the first real stirrings of modern civic activism were to be seen in the cities.

Three kinds of municipal action can be distinguished after 1835. There were those functions imposed upon the corporations by parliament (of which the only case in the 1835 Act itself was the requirement to provide a municipal police force and gaol facilities). Secondly there were those functions that were made permissible by the 1835 Act and subsequent statutes; these included sewerage, street lighting and libraries. The hope was that the municipalities would make their own choice of constructive actions within the powers thus granted. Thirdly, where corporations wished to undertake functions not imposed or authorised, they had to seek specific powers through private Acts of Parliament. In particular this applied to borrowing powers where a city proposed to undertake a long-term capital-intensive project. So began a new relationship between central and local government within a unitary state. For though parliament was prepared by 1835 to concede the representative principle in local government, it was not prepared to leave the ratepayers at the mercy of the local council in terms either of taxation or borrowing. The Act authorised the Improvement Commissioners to pass their functions to the new municipal corporations, but did not compel this, so that each set of Commissioners faded away as they voluntarily surrendered their powers.

The wealthier members of the middle classes led the physical withdrawal from the cores of the cities – this may well have meant a loss of impetus for civic improvement; it certainly meant that over time in many cases the higher reaches of the urban patriciate abandoned the Council Chamber, making room for small traders including the shopkeepers. The Act of 1835, like the Reform Act of 1832, through the property qualification, embodied the principle that men of property were the proper custodians of the public purse and the taxation demands it might make upon them. Scotland had obtained its Municipal Reform Act in 1833.

The cities, like the central government, developed their own civil services headed by senior officials. There was a good deal of admiration for German urban efficiency in this regard. The senior civic bureaucrats could begin to constitute themselves a power in the land. With the growth in complexity of civic affairs the nominal masters, the civic politicians, became increasingly dependent for information and advice upon their ostensible servants, as at Westminster.

16. The growth and efficiency of central government

The central administrative system by 1851 reflected the imposition upon the civil service of new duties. In 1834 a great step in the direction of effective control of expenditure was taken by the dismissal of sinecure holders and the appointment of a Comptroller of the Exchequer. The Inland Revenue Department had been revived in 1842 to administer the five schedules of the income tax. The Poor Law Board was an independent entity with its ministerial President. There were by 1851 inspectorates of factories, mines, sanitation and prisons, all under the Home Office. The Board of Trade had extended its activities, especially in Mr Gladstone's time in the early 1840s, in the preparation of commercial policy and legislation. Attached to the Privy Council was the Education Committee, with its inspectors. The office of Registrar General in England was set up in 1836; to it fell the duty of registering births, marriages and deaths under the Act of that year, and of conducting the decennial census. Similar action was taken in Scotland in 1854.

The English Act was mutilated in the Lords so that medical certification of cause of death was not made compulsory.

These extensions of functions meant a growth in the civil service from about 25,000 in 1815 to some 39,000 in 1851. But greater size did not bring improvement in quality. It was used as a means of placing sons or other relatives, friends and clients. There was thus at work a principle of inverse selection: parts of the civil service came to consist largely of men who had failed to find a place elsewhere, though others drew on the cream of the university output. The general result was a mass of extravagance and incompetence as described by Sir Charles Trevelyan's inquiry in 1849. By the mid-century the state was confronted with the challenge of remaking its own organs of administration.

17. Amelioration and social control

It seems reasonable to see British society in the first half of the nineteenth century as one in which group antagonisms were of a scale and kind that they could be controlled by a generalised sense of minimal equity, and eased by the effective intervention, on specific issues, of the philanthropists and the public servants. On this basis a significant degree of social amelioration could take place.

But such a situation had no universality. It was the outcome of a specific historical configuration. There is no inherent historical necessity that such a degree of control and acceptance should emerge, merely that under certain circumstances it could, and in Britain, between 1830 and 1850, to an important extent it did. It can be argued that the state should have been used to do more for those placed under pressure by industrialisation, and that the humanitarian response was feeble relative to the challenge. But to reason thus is perhaps to colonise the past with the values and mechanisms of the present.

PART III

The Victorian apogee, 1851–74

6

The market triumphant

1. *The expanding economy; the extending franchise; the harmonious society*

In the quarter century following 1851 Britain reached its world peak economically and politically, achieving leadership in both aspects. Because of the increase in her productivity and her consequent dominance of world trade, real incomes rose for almost all classes. This was the high Victorian age, beginning with the Great Exhibition of 1851 and ending with the first signs of economic faltering in the 1870s.

Half way through the period the second Reform Act of 1867 brought a radical change in the structure of political power. The working classes, hitherto excluded from voting and from membership of the House of Commons, now made their first entry into the constitution. Though there was only a partial opening of the door, it was such as to increase the electorate of Britain from about 717,000 adult males in 1832 to 2,226,000 after 1867. In qualitative terms this tripling of voters (while the population had increased by two-thirds) meant that the political parties had now to adjust their presentation of themselves to an electorate with a major new component. In the shorter run many of the new voters shared the values of the upper and middle classes; few would have any hope of entering a parliament which still demanded a property qualification. But in the longer run they would inevitably develop an outlook deriving more directly from their own view of their own interests. This would bring new pressures for yet further extensions of the franchise. In 1872 the secret ballot was adopted: so ended the open voting of the hustings with its uproar, drunkenness, bribery and intimidation. The property-based franchise and geographical con-

115

stituencies were the two principles underlying British parliamentary democracy.

Meanwhile the political parties had begun to learn a new style of party organisation and political appeal. It originated in Birmingham under Joseph Chamberlain (1836–1914) in the later 1860s. The party programme, the caucus and the professional organiser were coming into being. The function of the party was to merge a sense of what was required in the interests of the nation with what was acceptable to its political system, as seen from the perspective of the interests represented by the party. Politics began to become a specialist career field for both politicans and organisers. The railways were revolutionising the relations between politicians and voters; cheaper and more rapid movement, a condition of political democracy in a nation state, was now becoming available.

2. *Learning central banking on the basis of gold*

It was in this phase of the emergence of popular politics and party machines that British governments succeeded in reducing the role of the state in the economy to the smallest compass it was ever to have. At the same time, and as part of the same trend, both domestic and foreign trade were to achieve a brief span of freedom that was to be unique in British, or indeed any other, history. In the years 1851–74 the monetary system was committed to market forces within the principles of the 1844 Bank Act; the abandonment of the tariff and with it imperial preference was completed thus opening Britain and the empire to the trading world; the income tax was reduced almost to vanishing point.

The 'automatic' working of the monetary system was punctuated from time to time when, in commercial crises (as in 1847, 1857 and 1866), the government suspended the restriction placed upon the fiduciary note issue as it had been laid down in 1844. The effect of suspension of the Bank Act by the state was to restore confidence very quickly, so that cash payments could be resumed after a short interval. The concentration of the English note issue in the hands of the Bank of England continued, so that by 1874 the Bank's notes were by far the greatest element in the paper currency, though the smallest was of £5. In Scotland the £1 notes of the Scottish banks had pretty well driven gold from circulation; in England gold sovereigns and half-sovereigns were the basic coinage. A classic statement of the working of the system appeared in Bagehot's *Lombard Street* of 1873.

And yet the Bank of England was by no means clear and confident as to its role. The suspensions of the Bank Act, especially those of 1857 and 1866, seem to have frightened the Bank and caused it to draw back from general responsibility for the money market. This it did by reducing much of its current business. It could partially abdicate in this way because of three fundamental circumstances – the strength of British exports and hence of sterling, the injection of new gold into the world's monetary system (largely from California and Australia from the 1850s) and the modesty of the government's borrowing requirement. These were the conditions that continued to exempt the British government from the need for a monetary policy. Even the crash in 1866 of Overend Gurney & Co., one of the great discounting houses of the City, though it came close to breaking the financial structure (and caused a suspension of the Bank Act), was successfully weathered. Fate thus allowed British governments to deny themselves effective machinery for control of the money supply.

But the Bank was not so passive an agent as was the government. With the ending of the usury laws in 1854, it could begin to develop a policy of operating upon interest rates in the money market; such manipulation of the cost of borrowing could often be more effective in controlling the economy in the shorter term than variations in the money supply. This tactic was accompanied by 'open market operations'; they were established practice after 1873: under them the Bank would buy or sell government securities. By purchasing such securities the Bank created credits on itself held by the sellers; these individuals or companies then placed these credits with the commercial banks, thus enlarging the balances of such banks with the Bank of England. In this way the liquidity of the banks was increased, making it possible for them to lend more. Conversely, by selling securities the Bank could reduce the banks' balances with itself, making them reduce credit. If necessary the Bank could create a stringency sufficient to force the market 'into the Bank', thus making it necessary for borrowers to go to it, thus making the Bank Rate effective as ruling the market.

Even though the state was a modest borrower in the money

market, it was anxious to fund as much of its debt as possible at long term and at the lowest rates of interest. It was largely in order to provide the government with an independent source of borrowing that Gladstone began the Post Office Savings Bank in 1861. Such an action also fitted well with the Liberal government's policy of increasing the range of possibilities open to small savers.

3. *The zenith of international free trade*

In the fiscal field the high point of free trade was reached when, in conjunction with Gladstone's final ending of the tariff system in his budgets of 1853, 1860 and 1861, Britain and France joined in the Cobden–Chevalier Treaty of 1860. Under it virtual free trade was agreed between the two great commercial nations of Europe. The abandonment of the tariff made it possible for the British government to avoid the traditional invidious task of adjudicating between its home producers in terms of the protection each might be awarded against foreign competitors. Britain was thus a free and open market both internally and externally. Agriculture, like all other lines of output, had to hold its own against all comers; this feat it triumphantly achieved. The traditional position of landed wealth and political power (both based upon rents) was sustained by the performance of British farming. To contemporaries in Britain it could well seem that something like Adam Smith's views of the ideal economy had been realised.

The rest of the world, however, was not for long to be weaned from traditional protectionism. With the fall of Louis Napoleon in 1870, consequent on the defeat of his armies by Germany, France reverted to protectionism. The United States, though hostile to state intervention generally, reaffirmed its belief in the tariff; Germany was wholeheartedly protectionist.

4. *The economics of empire*

British free trade meant the end of empire preference. The British West Indies were the greatest imperial casualty of this policy, for sugar, its basic crop, now had to compete in the British market with that of all-comers, including Cuba, on equal terms: colonial and foreign sugars paid the same duty from 1854, and in 1874 the entry

118

of all sugars was freed. The decline of the West Indies was greatly accelerated by the loss of protection, but the British urban–industrial consumer got sugar much more cheaply. Canada, having confederated in 1867, went its own way, adopting a 'national' policy of tariffs similar to that of the United States. So arose the curious phenomenon of a great empire, the components of which made little or no special economic concessions to one another. Britain, indeed, having opted for free trade, had no concessions to give.

But Britain did have the power to deny fiscal autonomy, not to the new and under-populated Anglo-Saxon dominated Dominion of Canada, but to the sub-continent of India. It was thus impossible to provide infant-industry protection for Indian manufacturers by means of a tariff; Indian markets were kept by the British parliament fully exposed to low-cost British manufactures, especially cotton goods.

5. The income tax nearing extinction

Gladstone had shared Peel's view that the resumption of the income tax in 1842 was a temporary and extraordinary expedient. Twice he tried to abolish it. In 1853 as Chancellor of the Exchequer he presented his first budget, establishing his rank as one of the foremost ministers of his day; in it he planned the abandonment of the income tax over a seven-year period, stressing its threat to liberty because of its inquisitorial character. Moreover there were its inevitable anomalies, its damage to morality through evasion, and the foreign policy temptations it offered to interfering or imperialistic British governments by providing them with an almost unlimited resource. But Mr Gladstone's proposal was overtaken by the demands of the Crimean War beginning in 1854. In 1874 as Prime Minister he again announced a scheme to end the income tax. Such a programme seems more realistic when it is remembered that in that year the tax stood at its lowest ever rate, namely 2d in the pound (0.8%). Gladstone proposed to serve redistributive justice and to readjust the burden between landed property and industry in favour of the latter by replacing the income tax with a reconstruction and enlargement of the legacy duties; indeed he fought the general election of 1874 partly on this programme. He was defeated. Thus did Mr Gladstone make his last effort to get rid of the income tax, just as the age of mass politics was beginning. Never again was it seriously to be proposed that the British state could abdicate the taxing of incomes as it had abandoned the taxing of imports; the door remained open to the state to levy at will on the incomes of its subjects.

6. *The regulation of business*

The rules for business set by the state were extended in two directions. Additional Factory and Mines Acts and the Alkali Acts further defined the conditions of work and production, and hence the levels of cost.[1] Secondly, the principle of limited liability was introduced by the Companies Acts of 1855 and 1862. Whereas formerly partners and shareholders were held liable for the debts of their businesses to the full extent of their assets, it now became possible for firms not only to incorporate, but to become impersonal entities, and for the shareholders to be liable only to the extent of their subscriptions to shares. Company promoters wanted limited liability in order to make the formation of companies easier and to facilitate the mobilisation of capital; those with investible funds were also in favour of the new principle. A good deal of misgiving was expressed that the state should exempt men from the traditional responsibility for their actions (*The Times* called the 1855 Act the 'Rogues Charter'); but the arguments for the need for accumulations of capital on a new scale, and the need for a new form of company organisation, bore down the opposition. With limited liability came the potential for an enormous increase in the size of firms and for the manipulation of assets.

In the longer run an impersonalisation of relations between employers and workers followed. The older paternalistic links often existing between the owner–manager and his men could be replaced by a hierarchy of officials, with the directors often cut off from the labour force and insensitive to their outlook and responses. Moreover the increase in the size of business could make employers more powerful than ever as bargainers, provoking an urge on the side of labour for stronger unions. But the extent to which business made immediate use of limited liability must not be exaggerated: it took time for business to adjust to its new opportunities.

1. See chapter 8, sections 2 and 3 below.

Other aspects of company law had to advance with the needs of the times: a major codification of bankruptcy law was carried through in 1869, setting out the rules under which creditors could take action against defaulting firms, forcing them into liquidation.

The common law of England continued to evolve, reflecting the lawyers' view of the state and its role in regulating conduct, including that of business. Before about 1770 the English lawyers had thought in terms of the requirements of justice, seen in terms of the social and economic context in which bargains were made, rather than enforcing contract in the strict terms of the bargains entered into; the law had exercised a kind of paternalism over bargains, a reflection of the paternalism of a landed society. Then, for about a century, culminating perhaps in the 1870s, the idea of individualism replaced the notion of social justice; men were seen by the judges more as atomistic bargainers, required on the one hand to stand strictly by their agreements, and entitled on the other to enforce them to the letter. The great age of economic expansion thus correlated with an individualist view of rights and liabilities: law and political economy went together.

7. *The miniscule public sector*

The public sector continued to be tiny, being largely confined to the defence establishments and the Post Office. The latter had been obliged by the Act of 1839 to make its services cheaply available to all by the adoption of the penny post, under which a letter would be delivered in any part of Britain for a penny. Communications had been much improved by the construction of a system of electric telegraphs (by 1858 much of Europe was provided with the new miracle of communication). Here, as with the railways, the problem of monopoly rates had arisen, but in an even sharper form. The government's solution in 1869 was to nationalise the telegraphs, the first real addition to the public sector since the founding of the Post Office in the seventeenth century.

The state continued to refuse to involve itself either in the structure of industry or in its efficiency. In the one area in which it might have affected production methods, pushing them closer to those of America, it did not do so. The nationally owned Enfield Armoury, set up in 1854, did not distinguish itself in standardised production of interchangeable parts.

By 1874 the politicians had arrived at a set of mind which made it very difficult for them to think in positive terms of an enlarged state role. But some of those whose thinking began from the physical sciences did not suffer from this inhibition. William Siemens (1823–83), one of the foremost scientists and inventors of the day, urged in 1873 that the government should take into its purview the production and consumption of what was virtually the nation's sole source of heat and energy. Parliament, he urged, should have a fuel policy: it should 'insist upon knowing whether a proper balance between the supply and demand of coal cannot be re-established, also what can be done to prevent the wholesale conversion of fuel into useless and positively hurtful results'. But no nineteenth-century government could for a moment contemplate accepting such a responsibility.

8. Ireland, the land laws and nationalism

There was one exception to the triumph of the market and private property. It lay in Ireland and was embodied in the Land Act of 1870. There the question of property in the land was basic to the fabric of society.[1] The 550,000 Irish peasant–tenants wanted to be made secure against the demands of their alien landlords. This was the Irish problem at its most basic. But to meet this aspiration the British parliament would have to cut into the rights of landlords. There was hope in England that with a new ratio between population and the land after the famine the tension would go out of Ireland. But the governing relationship had not changed, namely, the claim made on the peasantry by the landlords through rents. By the later 1850s the grievances of tenants were once more being expressed. Moreover the form of Irish agriculture was changing. Tillage was yielding to the raising of livestock, largely because of the demands of the English market. Cattle and sheep meant larger farms, with the small men forced out and increased displacement of labour. Industry was growing round Belfast, providing employment, but the rest of Ireland needed protection for its infant industries, a facility denied by British free trade.

Meanwhile a new element had appeared in Ireland and America, namely the Fenian Brotherhood, founded in the early 1850s. There

---

1. See chapter 2, sections 4 and 5 above.

had been violence and secret societies for generations, but the Fenians were different. They were a close-knit organisation, begun by those who had taken part in the Young Ireland insurrection of 1848, and with strong support in America. They were dedicated men, holding the sacredness of nationality as an absolute. Constitutional means against Britain were rejected as futile; immediate violence and tension was the policy, centred upon a programme of assassination. The Roman Catholic Church condemned the Fenians for this. A rising in 1867 was abortive, but the Brotherhood continued with its campaign, confirmed in its rightness by its growing accumulation of martyrs.

When Mr Gladstone became Prime Minister for the first time in 1868 he declared 'My mission is to pacify Ireland.' He began in 1869 with the Irish Church Act, disestablishing the Anglican Church in Ireland. It was left still well endowed, though it lost half of its wealth, a good deal of which was used over the next ten years to pay off rent arrears and for education and the relief of the poor.

Gladstone then turned to the land question. There was still much bitter resistance to using the law to strengthen the tenant: Lord Palmerston called such action 'communistic . . . a subversion of the rights of property'. On the other hand even exponents of the classical economics like John Stuart Mill (1806–73) and J. E. Cairnes (1823–75) had come to realise that highly capitalised large-scale farming on the English model was inappropriate in Ireland, and that in so basic a matter as access to the land each society must be seen in terms of its own evolution and needs. The problem accordingly became how to make small-scale agriculture in Ireland work. Mill believed that the challenge was not the maximisation of Irish agricultural efficiency, but the happiness of the people, so intimately bound up with their relationship with the land.

The only real solution was to end landlordism, giving the land to those who worked it. This could be done either by confiscation or compensation. The former was unthinkable. The latter would mean a state loan to finance mortgages to the peasantry to buy their land, but the finance required was too vast and the administrative difficulties too great. There remained the less radical solution of an operation on landlord–tenant relations.

This was embodied in Mr Gladstone's Irish Land Act of 1870. It rested on the assumption that the occupier had a right in the land just as did the landlord; it was a reversion to status and custom, resting on the principle that men who had worked the land had acquired customary rights that could legitimately be enforced against the rights of property. Thus a tenant who had improved his land was entitled to compensation when he left his tenancy. Those who were evicted for any cause other than non-payment of rent were to be compensated for improvements, on scales based upon rent. In short the principles of Ulster tenant right prevalent in the north were extended to the whole of Ireland. This was the best Mr Gladstone could do in the prevailing political situation in Britain. But though important in the sense of encroaching upon the doctrine of absolute property in land, and asserting the ancient principle of the rights deriving from custom, the Act had little effect. It failed to provide direct security of tenure (which would have involved a much larger breach of landlord right) which was the real desire of the Irish peasantry. Even in its own terms the Act carried so many qualifications (imposed by the landlords in their counter-attack) that few peasants availed themselves of its provisions.

In the same year as the Act the Home Government Association was formed. Its members had no policy as such except to work, by constitutional means, for an Irish parliament. In 1873 it became the Home Rule League; in the general election of the following year it won fifty-nine seats in the House of Commons. An Irish party pledged to Home Rule had arrived at Westminster. It could operate as a group on British politics, especially when either of the two great parties lacked an overall majority. The Irish question was now an active force in the British House of Commons, with Irish Members of Parliament seeking points of leverage within the British political agenda.

9. The public economics of the Gladstonian age

In 1874 Mr Gladstone's first and greatest ministry came to an end. Simultaneously the Victorian economy entered upon the period of arrestation and misgiving, often referred to as the Great Depression. It was the culmination of an era in another sense, namely that of public policy.

Governmental involvement with the macro-economic aspect had been reduced to minimal dimensions. The money supply was market-determined within the rules of the gold standard game. The state was left with no monetary role except perhaps the ultimate one of presiding over major liquidity crises. Free trade had become a reality: Britain provided free entry and exit of goods, money, technology and people. The empire had ceased to be a closed trading system; there was no imperial preference to integrate it economically. In sum, the state had abandoned all control of and responsibility for the direction of economic development, or for its structural form. By the same token there was no scope for the manipulation by the government of economic matters.

There was certainly no thought of using direct taxation as a means of redistributing incomes from the rich to the poor. Indeed, with the reduction of the income tax to levels of insignificance, the tax structure (dominated by its indirect taxes) had become more regressive, bearing proportionally more heavily on lower incomes. The public sector too was minimal in size and scope, concerned principally with internal and external security, its only commercial activities being those of the Post Office and the electric telegraph. Moreover welfare expenditure was largely a charge on the local authorities. This, then, was the system of economic laissez-faire in its most advanced form.

For the Gladstonian the economy was self-adjusting in terms of stability, growth, structure and equity. Or, more precisely, where it was not, the state could do nothing about these matters that would generate a net benefit. Just as the state should not disturb the world by international aggression, so too it should not disturb the economy and society. The Gladstonian thought all this in pretty well the first and last phase of British experience in which it could be thought. Mr Gladstone has been criticised for his seeming indifference to welfare questions, but his unwillingness to embark on any general attempt at using the state to promote welfare was simply part of the general pattern of his outlook, based upon the minimising of the state.

But in one direction the state had interfered in the system of private property and market relations in a fundamental way, namely Ireland. There the idea that property was sacrosanct was given its first great blow, in an attempt to establish civil peace in Ireland based on consensus.

10. The Treasury consolidates its financial control

An essential part of the philosophy of economic withdrawal was an insistence upon the strictest accountability in the discharge of what governmental functions remained. This meant placing one government organ, namely the Treasury, firmly at the centre, with a strict surveillance over all other departments of state through their finances.

From 1862 the Public Accounts Committee was a permanent part of the financial machinery of the House of Commons. In 1865 the Exchequer and Audit Departments Act had at long last made it possible for the Treasury to exert effective control over all government expenditure. The primacy of the Treasury was explicitly recognised in 1867, when its Permanent Secretary was placed above the heads of all other departments. By the later 1860s, then, parliament, through the Treasury, had consolidated its financial control.

The Chancellor of the Exchequer was the head of the Treasury; his principal job was to prepare and present the budget on a strictly annual basis, mutually adjusting the expenditure and income to arrive at a balance. Parliament could thus view the entire finances of the nation at the same time each year, treating them on an almost penny-cash-book basis of ingoings and outgoings, jealously guarding against a deficit. The Chancellor had also to assign the tax burden that resulted. These tasks he discharged as the national housekeeper, not as controller of aggregate demand, nor, to any significant degree, as the imposer of national equity.

7

The state and the claims of labour

1. Labour as a problem for the state

The period 1851–74, which saw economic liberalism at its peak, was subject to two great counter-tendencies, namely an extension of the public provision of welfare in its various forms,[1] and the making of concessions to the labour force in terms of its right to organise against its employers. In both cases the liberal creed was in principle minimalist, anxious to keep both kinds of concessions as small as possible. In neither, however, could governments wholly resist the trend toward extended involvement.

But there was an important difference between the two. Welfare proceeded on many diverse fronts, each with its peculiar circumstances, whereas the concessions made to labour had to be governed by general rules, applicable to all. It is true that the judiciary also played its part by the interpretation of trade union statutes through case law, handing down verdicts in the particular cases presented to the courts. But these verdicts then became of general application; they gave meaning to the law where statute was ambiguous or silent. In this way the state presided over the contest over wages by setting its rules.

In a sense this was the most difficult of all problems for governments. For it raised the great issue of what posture the state should adopt, at one remove, toward the distribution of the national product, in particular the wages' share against profits and rents. The contest had to be fought out over a great many fronts, consisting first of particular firms, then regional groups of firms (as, for example, in coal mining), then all the firms in a given industry, and ultimately between great alliances of workmen against employers in general, and, indeed, the state itself.

1. See chapter 8 below.

127

There were a number of responses available to governments. They could revive the practice of setting minimum or maximum wages in particular trades, in the seventeenth- and eighteenth-century manner, acting through the magistrates or some other body. But the tenor of the times was now strongly against the direct interference in market forces which this kind of action involved. Or the state could set up a system whereby it arbitrated between employers and workmen, hearing the respective submissions and deciding what compromise to impose upon them. But this mode of action was too close to the first, and was subject to the same great criticism of involving the state in the labour market. In any case neither employers nor workmen wanted such intervention. There remained the third choice, and the one adopted, namely to confine the role of the state in the main to regulating the terms upon which bargaining and the trial of strength took place, doing so through a body of trade union law.

Having assumed this role the state found itself confronted with a series of challenges, succeeding one another over the decades and the generations. Union rights and immunities were conceded step by step, each extension being made within the conditions and assumptions prevailing at a given time. Each new relationship thus created, once it became the norm, was placed under strain as organised labour, using it as a base, sought from the state a further alteration of the rules in its favour. At each stage there would be a legislative struggle followed by what looked to the unions like a rear-guard action by employers and the courts, and a new concession to the unions would finally emerge. The employers, on their side, were not of course defenceless; they evolved means by which to counter union pressures. But the trend was against them: the enormous advantages enjoyed by them over their workers in Adam Smith's time, as duly noted by him, were subject to a long-term erosion, especially as the political franchise was extended, bringing the strength of the contestants closer to one another, and consolidating each more and more as a compact, self-conscious and self-justifying entity, thus making the general contest over the division of the national product more and more explicit. The story is thus of a fight – a long and real one.

In the skilled trades the craftsmen often gained the power to control entry to their part of the labour market through the apprenticeship system, and to demarcate jobs between craftsmen, thus regulating the labour supply in terms both of quantity and quality. It was this aspect which chiefly led to the charge that they were a conspiracy in restraint of trade. The state was confronted with the challenge of whether those in possession of a given range of skills should be entitled to exclude others, thus limiting the growth and adaptive capacity of the economy.

The question was made the more difficult in the light of the fact that the professions, especially the law and medicine, relied heavily on this kind of exclusiveness. Moreover industrial employers, on their side of the market, often had means of combining of a more or less informal kind, very difficult for the law to perceive.

Within this long-term trend of concession to the unions a pattern can be discerned. The first questions to be raised by the unions had to do with the basic requirement of recognition, together with the need to escape from the taint of criminality as being conspiracies in restraint of trade. This had been conceded in general in 1824 and was never to be revoked. But the right of unions to exist had little value without further sets of concessions.

Secondly, then, the legal identity and status of unions had to be defined. This was a question which involved giving them both rights and protection, but which could also make them vulnerable to attack. Thus the unions desired such legal identity as would make it possible for them to protect their assets against embezzlement by their own servants, but they did not want to be defined in such terms that they could be proceeded against in the courts for damages caused by their withdrawals of labour. In principle the choice for the state lay between recognising the unions as corporations or as combinations. Business concerns and charitable organisations were often corporations, with full legal identity in a form well known to the law, so that they could enter into contracts and sue and be sued in connection with these. This kind of identity had its attractions for the unions, for it meant that having bargained a wage settlement, the employers would be bound to honour it during its currency. But by the same token an undertaking by the unions to supply labour at a given price over an agreed period would also be enforceable against them in the courts; a withdrawal of such labour would expose the union to damages. Strikes, under these conditions, could only be called safely when a labour contract expired. Moreover there were difficulties concerning the power of the unions over its members; the unions in their turn had no legal recourse against their members who took unofficial action.

A combination, as opposed to a corporation, was not visible to the law, and so was neither capable of entering into a contract nor of being sued. But it was necessary that it be given some sort of identity so that it could, for example, hold assets and take action against its own officials should this be necessary. The employers, down to the 1880s, were as hostile as were the unions to the principle of incorporated unions, because they on their side did not wish to be obliged to enter into binding wage contracts, but like the unions wanted to preserve their flexibility of action. The idea of incorporation and enforceable contract was thus rejected by both sides. The unions, in the eyes of the law, continued to be combinations.

Thirdly, and closely related, there was the question of union liability for damage caused by industrial action. Striking meant using damage as a weapon to extract better pay and conditions from employers. From the union point of view it was essential that the damage be borne by others, preferably by the employers, but, if the effects could not be confined to them, by third parties or even by the community as a whole.

The fourth kind of status sought by the unions concerned their ability to persuade or coerce workers, both within the membership and outside it. Within a union, should the majority have the right to subject the minority to its will? This was the power denied by the Act of 1825, which reasserted the right of a worker, even though a unionist, to agree his own wage bargain with his employer. With respect to those outside the union, should the law concede the right of unions to coerce all workers confronting a given employer or set of employers to join the union? That is, should the law be used to promote the closed shop?

Fifth and finally there was the question of the weapons permissible in strike action: should picketing be allowed, and if so, how should its limits be determined in terms of harassment, intimidation and violence? The issue of picketing was given additional emphasis by the use by employers of blacklegs (the introduction of labour from other places to break a strike), an action which the law did nothing to inhibit. Picketing under such conditions could hardly be confined to simple peaceful persuasion. How far should the liberty of the subject be abrogated in order that the unions might be strengthened? Beyond the liberty of the subject lay yet another disturbing question, namely that of conspiracy against the community and the state.

The judges regarded themselves as having two functions in connection with unions. The first was to interpret the law where this was necessary, doing so within the specific contexts of particular cases. The second was to act as custodians of the common good of the nation as a whole. This meant protecting the consumer from price rises, caused by employers passing on the effects of granting higher wages to the unions, and from inconvenience, loss or damage caused by industrial stoppage.

From the unions' point of view the matter was seen as a fight against repressive employers and the state. Their thinking did not run in terms of the state having a responsibility to create a balance of power between themselves and the employers; to them the concern of liberal-minded legislators and the judges with civil liberties and the common good appeared simply as an alliance with the employers, aimed at keeping wages down. And yet the unions did not want to see the state subverted. They, in their own way, wanted the state as they knew it to survive as the arbiter between themselves and their employers.

The five challenges posed by labour for the state were thus legality, legal identity, immunity from liability, the closed shop and the limits of persuasion or coercion. In terms of these, governments and the courts sought to balance the rights of organised labour against those of their employers and the community.

2. Unions versus employers

From the 1850s the workers among the more skilled trades, like the political parties, were learning to organise in a highly effective way. They formed what were later to be called 'New Model' unions, with a select membership of craftsmen, together with professional paid organisers. Such unions pursued carefully chosen objectives and conserved their strength and their funds for these non-revolutionary ends. The extension of the political franchise in 1867 made it possible for an important range of working men to participate in politics as electors. Such men could hardly fail to gain in confidence, developing their own views of the proper role of the state, both as affecting the labour market and more generally. It was no accident that the first Trade Union Congress took place in 1868.

The state, in addition to its attitude to the unions, had also to take carefully into account the responses of employers. Some of these rested on a straightforward determination to resist any encroachment on the authority of ownership and management. All employers, however, were involved in two intrinsically difficult problems. Union pressures on the wage level could affect competitive production costs, especially in foreign markets. Secondly, and closely related, there was the question, what general limits should the employers demand be imposed by the state upon the collective actions of workers? This dual concern by employers with costs and coercion runs through the long and complex story of labour legislation.

3. The definition of union identity

The narrative of developments in statute and legal judgments is a complicated one. It was widely believed that the Friendly Societies Act of 1855 provided both identity and protection of assets to the unions, subject to their conforming to the requirements of the Act by registering as Friendly Societies. In 1867, however, in the case of *Hornby* v. *Close* the Court of Queen's Bench ruled that trade unions were not protected by the Act against embezzlement by their own servants. Vigorous protest followed, to which parliament responded with the Trade Union (Protection of Funds) Act of 1869; this temporarily secured the unions' position. This recognition of the right of a union to act against its own servants was the first fruits of the franchise extension of 1867.

At the same time an inequity in the law was removed. Since Tudor times an employer who broke a contract of employment had been subject merely to a civil action; an employee was liable to criminal prosecution and penalties. The Master and Servant Act of 1867 prescribed that either party could proceed against the other, on equal terms, in a civil action. But criminal actions against workmen for breach of contract in withdrawal of their labour were still possible in what were called 'aggravated cases'.

There were indictments of unions before the courts for conspiracy in 1842, 1847, 1852–5 and 1865–8, arising out of their efforts to impose a closed shop. The Molestation of Workmen Act of 1859 was an effort to clarify aspects of the 1825 Act. It permitted picketing, but left it to the courts to decide, case by case, what picketing actions were justified in terms of the continued prohibition of intimidation. The government thus passed the problem of picketing to the ad hoc common sense of the judges. Acts of violence against those who refused to join unions were, of course, illegal. The 'Sheffield outrages' of 1866 (in which violence was used against workers in the cutlery trades who refused to join unions), together with other aspects of union behaviour, caused the government to appoint a Royal Commission on Trade Unions: it sat from 1867 to 1869. Its *Report* is one of the great nineteenth-century documents on a subject fundamental to the state and to the economy. Though the Commission had its origin in the outrages, its report went a long way toward convincing the public of the justification of unions.

The outcome of the national inquiry into the unions was the passing by the Gladstone government of the Trade Union Act and the Criminal Law Amendment Act, both of 1871. The former finally removed all remaining danger of prosecution of unions on the ground of their being in restraint of trade. It also confirmed their right, granted in 1867, to register as Friendly Societies, thus consolidating an aspect of their legal identity and securing their protection against embezzlement by their own servants. The trade unions were thus recognised in 1871 as legitimate and fully legal bodies: their legality and legal status were secure.

4. The limit of persuasion or coercion

Critical to the debate was the mode of persuasion, centring largely on picketing. The Gladstone government elected in 1868 was strongly opposed to any form or suggestion of intimidation by trade unionists. It believed that only such persuasion of other workers as was wholly peaceful and without threat, real or implied, was permissible. Accordingly the Criminal Law Amendment Act effectively prohibited picketing by making strikers liable for prosecution for intimidation, molestation and obstruction. The unions were thus deprived of their most effective means of mass persuasion and of direct action at the scene of conflict. This was especially serious for the unskilled unions, with their limited funds and vulnerable membership. The concept of intimidation was then stretched by the courts to include a threat of refusal to work. Thus, though in principle there was a right to strike, a threat to do so could be interpreted by the courts as contrary to the Criminal Law Amendment Act. A cloud of ambiguity still hung over the whole matter.

5. The Gladstonian stance on labour

The defeat of the Gladstone administration in 1874 owed a good deal to the rejection by working men enfranchised in 1867 of the 1871 legislation. They repudiated the Liberal insistence upon the dangers inherent in trade union coercive action against employers, against non-unionists and against the general public. But the liberal creed, in requiring that coercion in any form be prohibited, almost as an absolute principle, in effect ignored the fact that employers, though relatively weakened, were in general still in a more powerful position than their employees. Unions had the right to exist, and to persuade, but not to coerce.

8

The advance of social collectivism

1. The politics and finance of amelioration

British politicians of the third quarter of the nineteenth century, like their predecessors, did not enter upon social problems until they became serious, even critical. Most politicians were still part-time amateurs with an inclination toward a minimum of state action in the field of social welfare, as elsewhere. There was little belief in the idea that the state should or could solve the residual problems of society. Moreover, in order to operate an extended social policy, it was necessary to tax and regulate on an increasing scale; this met with powerful resistance. The process of social amelioration therefore continued to be one largely of patching-on. Each such action was promoted by those of the middle classes who were affronted by bad conditions of living and working, and who were now often in alliance with the growing strength of organised labour. Each was contested by those whose interests or opinions were threatened, using the weapons of attrition and minimalisation.

Other circumstances confirmed this situation. Though a good deal of the nepotism and corruption of earlier times disappeared as British politicians and civil servants moved toward the unprecedentedly high standards of honesty of later Victorian times, there was still enough patronage and corruption about to make those concerned with the standards of national life cautious about generating new ministries and new bureaucracies. Generalised distrust of the state was reinforced by the problem of the relationship between central and local governments. To use parliament to coerce local authorities could lead to trouble, but to leave local authorities to themselves might mean serious dereliction of their social duty. Not only was this a question of authority; it was also one of finance. Parliament was not anxious to increase the burden of national taxation, and local governments were not anxious to provoke hostility among their ratepayers.

The Conservative Party, under the unlikely leadership of Benjamin Disraeli (1804–81) proposed to reinstate the philosophy of the social bond by the promotion of a new paternalism. Disraeli spoke of two nations within Britain; the second of these was composed of the working classes, a large part of which laboured under severe deprivation. There was thus a continuing Tory tradition of concern for the moral rights of the less fortunate. But between this almost mystical ideal and real measures there was a gulf that was difficult if not impossible to bridge without bringing about a radical change in society and the principle of property on which it rested.

Gladstonian Liberalism, on the other hand, did not propose to use the state to unite the social classes: it explicitly stood for minimal state action and minimal taxation and expenditure – money should be left 'to fructify in the pockets of the people'. This should be accompanied by maximum efficiency throughout the civil service. Gladstone was not indifferent to social suffering. But he was fearful that mistaken meddling in the economy and society would make things worse. Nor did he passively accept the existing pattern of property-owning – he was, on the contrary, hostile to the new 'plutocracy', the men who had made money by the manipulation of money. But his political philosophy provided no remedy.

2. Factories, mines and other employment; humanitarianism as social control

The continued caution of government in accepting responsibility for the surveillance of the conditions in factories and mines was reflected in the step-by-step nature of control. A standing tension grew up between the more demanding inspectors and the more recalcitrant and cost-conscious of the employers. This was a reflection of the fact that few absolute criteria were available amid the immense variety of factories, workshops and mines.

But one thing was clear. The government could not indefinitely confine its factory regulation to the textile manufacturers. In 1860 bleaching, dyeing and lace making were brought under surveillance. Under further pressure from reformers a Children's Employment Commission was set up; its *Reports* of 1863, 1864, 1866 and 1867 revealed cases of deplorable abuse. The practice of forcing boys to clean chimneys by climbing up into the filth and darkness was stopped by Acts of 1864 and 1867; an Act of 1864 brought six noxious trades under control, including the making of lethal lucifer matches. In 1867 came a complex statute, bringing the workers in a long list of named trades within protection in places where more than fifty persons were employed (the quantitative definition of a factory). Accompanying this extensive Factory Act was a Workshops Act covering all children, young persons and women in small production units. But the Workshops Act was merely permissive, so that local authorities which thought that there was no serious reason for concern with conditions of work in their area could ignore their responsibilities in this direction. In consequence, in 1871 the inspection of workshops was transferred from the local authorities to the Home Office.

In the mines there went on a parallel struggle for and against control. The Coal Mines Inspection Act of 1850 imposed regular inspection of the mines, affecting safety, lighting and ventilation. Safety provision was further improved in 1855, when the first code of General Rules was brought in. The Coal Mines Regulation Act of 1860 strengthened the Rules and excluded from mining operations all boys under twelve years of age. The right of the miners to appoint checkweighmen was conceded, but at the same time it was enfeebled because the colliery owners were given the right to dismiss them; the Coal Mines Regulation Act of 1872 made the checkweighmen secure. Also colliery managers were obliged to have state certificates of their qualifications.

In farming, the Gangs Act of 1867 gave a degree of protection to seasonal itinerant women and children. The Agricultural Children's Act of 1873 forbade employment of children under the age of eight and required that educational provision be made for those in employment above it.

So far as many of the employing classes, both at the works and in the home, were concerned, there was a general lack of knowledge of, and *a fortiori* of empathy with, those whose labour they bought. There continued to be, in many instances, abuse of worker by worker – where one worker organised his group or gang, the wages of its members being at his discretion.

The middle classes were able to continue to generate a degree of interior social control of themselves.[1] To this the rise of social science made a contribution, for working conditions and the industrial relations associated with them were subjects well suited to the inquiries of the Social Science Association, founded in 1857. On its Council were civil servants greatly concerned with social welfare like Chadwick, Simon and Kay Shuttleworth, together with lawyers like Lord Brougham, all men who believed in the need to produce scientific evidence as the basis for social action by the state.

Children, because they were impotent (to use poor law terminology), could be brought under factory legislation without conflict with the principle of adult responsibility. Adult males, on the other hand, ought not, according to the individualist philosophy, have their rights to bargain with their employers intruded upon by Factory Acts. In between stood the women. Some reformers, like the economist Henry Fawcett (1833–84), anxious to bring equality between the sexes, flatly opposed treatment for women different from that of men. But other reformers, and parliament over time, chose to include the women with the children, thus ensuring protection for the women, and through them the men with whom they worked.

3. Urban sanitation, health and the environment

It became apparent in the third quarter century down to 1874 that public health had three aspects: improved sanitation and water supply, the adoption and enforcement of health regulations and the provision of medical facilities in the form of doctors and hospitals. The state acted with some vigour in terms of the first two, but medical facilities were left to the poor law guardians, and to the doctors and the philanthropists. The poor law, in spite of the intended rigour of the Act of 1834, provided an ever-increasing medical service.

There was a growing awareness that sickness was a *cause* of pauperisation, and might, indeed, be a principal cause. Moreover it was increasingly realised that sickness could not be dealt with on principles derived from less-eligibility or the workhouse test. There had to be a degree of comfort, so that sick paupers often received better treatment than those in employment.

1. See chapter 5, section 17 above.

The doctors sponsored hospitals partly because of their scientific and educative value in making possible the observation and treatment of a wide range of patients: the knowledge thus gained and the teaching provided benefited society as a whole. The philanthropists collaborated with the doctors, raising funds and organising, so that the hospital sector (apart from the poor law element), grew up entirely in private philanthropic hands. There was no serious suggestion that the state or local authorities should move into this field.

One aspect of health provision was indeed made obligatory on the general population: compulsory vaccination for children was introduced by Act of Parliament in 1853, and strengthened in 1867. This intrusion into civil liberties was bitterly fought by the Anti-Compulsory Vaccination League. It sought, at the least, relaxations in the compulsion, but these were not made until 1898. The state thus passed the child population into the hands of the doctors, the price imposed by parliament on the nation for the conquest of smallpox by the end of the century.

Sanitation and water supply involved heavy public investment, on a local basis. But whereas the enforcement of minimal conditions of work was largely paid for by industry, becoming a charge on production, the purging of the cities under the Health Acts was a charge on the local rates. There was another great difference, for, whereas the Factory and Mines Acts involved relatively small adjustments, not too difficult to be assimilated by the firm, sanitation and water supply on the scale now necessary demanded investment in sewage and water systems for large areas, involving local authorities in engineering and financial problems on a new scale. The most difficult of sanitation areas lay in the hearts of the great cities, densely built over, with a complex of property rights. To construct the sewage systems of the cities required men of vision and drive – the greatest of these was Joseph Bazalgette (1819–91) who provided London with its modern system. He did so after 1858, 'the year of the great stink', when the Thames was like an open cesspit. Some cities were very slow to meet their responsibilities. As late as 1870 Leeds was pouring its sewage, entirely raw and untreated, into the River Aire; both Leeds and Birmingham had to be forced by court injunction to take action.

In the drafting and enforcement of health regulations there was some apparent retrogression. In 1854 the Board of Health was greatly weakened and in 1858 it ceased. This was partly as a reaction by local authorities against centralisation, and partly in resentment of Chadwick and his insensitive activism. With it ended Chadwick's official career. But the trend toward surveillance and control was too strong for effective resistance. In 1858 a Medical Department of the Privy Council was set up.

At its head was placed the remarkable John Simon (1816–1904), one of the great civil servants of the nineteenth century. He had already served as medical officer to the Board of Health. His personality and tactics were very different from those of Chadwick; he was an excellent publicist, with his annual reports eagerly read, as well as being a conciliator and facilitator. In consequence Simon's Medical Department gradually took over responsibility for a medley of health functions. Like Chadwick he sponsored an impressive number of Acts creating powers to deal with various aspects of sanitation, epidemics, burials, food defilement and adulteration and venereal diseases.

The Act of 1871 created the Local Government Board which took over central government health functions; the Public Health Act of 1872 defined and consolidated powers at the local government level; the Public Health Act of 1875 codified the legislation of the previous forty years. The Births and Deaths Registration Act of 1874 made registration of these matters in England virtually complete for the first time, making the certification of cause of death compulsory. This reflected pressure from the local medical officers of health who needed to have the figures improved in order to use statistics to locate and define health problems in their districts.

In addition to human pollution there was the question of industrial wastes, now being generated on an enormous scale. Nothing was done by statute to regulate solid wastes, so that ugly tips and slag heaps became part of the industrial landscape. But gaseous wastes were a more obvious threat to health. With the extension of the heavy chemicals industry, based as it was on the use of sulphur, action had to be taken. The first Alkali Act was passed in 1863 to control by means of an inspectorate the diffusion of industrial gas into the air. One of its consequences was that industrialists sought ways of recovering noxious gases, thus providing valuable by-products. But not all the costs of cleanliness could be recovered in this way: the inspectors were in continuous contest with the manufacturers, operating a compromise. In the absence of absolute standards, just as in factory law, it was a question at any given time of setting what was socially tolerable against production costs and the consequent impeding of economic development. Subsequent Alkali Acts of 1868 and 1874 extended these controls.

The state began its surveillance of the quality of the food supplied to the public with a series of Adulteration of Food Acts in 1860, 1872 and 1875. Public analysts were appointed with powers to prosecute. They could be effective because scientific analysis, using chemical discoveries and the microscope, had now reached the point at which standards could be set, inspections carried out and prosecutions successfully conducted. The state had begun its role as watchdog over the quality of the nation's food.

4. Literacy for the masses and education for the elite

Elementary education for the English masses first became the subject of serious national inquiry in 1858. This was undertaken by the Newcastle Commission, reporting in 1861. By this time the annual parliamentary grant for school building begun in 1833 had reached £813,441. But elementary education was still basically regarded as a charity. The grant was administered by the Department of Education which superseded the Education Committee of the Privy Council in 1856; the Department was thereafter represented in Parliament by a Vice-President, who was a kind of proto-minister of education. Its most active and successful civil servant was its Permanent Secretary Kay Shuttleworth (1804–77). The Department's system of school inspectors, of whom Matthew Arnold (1822–88) was one, revealed the sad deficiency of the system.

The real public attack on general illiteracy in England was a response to the Newcastle *Report*; it began with the Revised Education Code of 1862, adopted by the Department of Education. In it was overcome the general resistance to state action in assisting in the provision of elementary schooling. The state, through the Department, now assumed a central role. But two conditions had to be met. One had to do with religion: the mutual hostility between the supporters of the Church of England and the nonconformists continued to mean that a unified secular system was impossible, so that the principle of general compulsory education under a national system could not be adopted.[1] Secondly the new scale of expenditure required that there be cost-effectiveness. Government grants were made subject to a periodic monitoring of the efficiency of the schools; they were tied to satisfactory examination performance by the children, under the eye of the inspectors, on the basis of the three Rs. The inspectors, unlike their colleagues in the factories and mines, were obliged by the Code of 1862 to judge the quality of the output, cutting the grant if insufficient pupils performed to standard. This led to a good deal of drilling of pupils by teachers, a serious displacement of the goal of education. The provision of schools was still to rest on a voluntary basis, under the rival National and British Societies. But the system continued to be full of gaps and to be inadequate in other ways. This inspired the formation by Joseph Chamberlain in 1869 of the Birmingham Education League, a largely nonconformist body demanding a general system of elementary education that was to be compulsory, free and non-sectarian. The supporters of Anglican education in response formed the National Education Union. In this way the old conflict between Societies was broadened, and education was made explicitly political.

The condition of elementary education in England by 1870 is a matter of debate. It has been argued that the weaknesses of the system of private provision of schooling have been greatly exaggerated, that on average working-class children had some sort of schooling to the age of ten, and that illiteracy, at least in its crudest forms, had been largely eliminated and that the voluntary system was continuously improving. On the other hand there is the more traditional view that voluntarism as a provider of general elementary education had failed seriously and that only state action could redeem a deplorable situation.

There can be no doubt, however, that whatever the state of things by 1870, the Elementary Education Act of that year marked a new beginning. It was brought in by W. E. Forster (1818–86), providing for the establishment in England and Wales of elected School Boards wherever the provision of elementary schools on the voluntarist principle was inadequate. The Boards were empowered to raise local education rates; the franchise for election to the Boards was such as

1. See chapter 5, section 10 above.

to admit women, their first break into a political role. It also provided a means of entry into an important aspect of political life to members of the working classes. In this way a form of the democratic principle was brought into operation in elementary education. The politics of education became highly complex. The dissenters through their National Education League rallied to the Board Schools, in which a neutral Protestantism was taught. The supporters of the Church of England clung to the 'voluntary' principle, making vigorous efforts to improve and extend their schools in order to preclude the demand for Board Schools. The Boards were to decide religious education policy in their schools, on the 'undenominational' principle: there was to be Bible reading and Christian explanation of the basis of morality and religion.

But the old divisiveness remained so compelling, not to say obsessive, and so contentious did the religious issue in education continue to be, that it largely pre-empted the public debate: there was still little real argument about the nature of secular education, it being assumed that reading and writing and arithmetic pretty well exhausted the matter. Because of the structure of English society neither the established church nor the nonconformists could deal a fatal blow to the other; the contest was complicated by the claims of the Catholics. Forster's Act did not, therefore, provide a new system of elementary education in England, but supplemented the old by filling the gaps. The disruption it caused in the Liberal Party contributed to its defeat in 1874.

There was an increasing professionalism among teachers, encouraged by the Department, though the system of payment by results put them under stress. The inspectors continued their work, including their reports. Buildings of good quality were provided, standing out impressively in the poorer parts of the towns.

All this reflected a growing sense of national need. The economy required clerks and counter hands on an ever-growing scale as the service sector developed: these functions could not be performed without at least an elementary literacy and numeracy. In skilled work among the artisans there was also a need for these accomplishments. Indeed, though religion dominated the educational debate in one sense, the real business was how to meet the nation's requirements for the new kind of labour force.

Education for the English masses was to lead, inevitably, to public provision on a very large scale, of buildings, teachers' salaries, training colleges and of local and central administration; the 1870 Act was a big step in this direction. But there remained an unwillingness to abandon the voluntary principle, partly because it, accompanied by locally elected Boards, provided a means of contact with the diverse wishes of the community.

As with the regulation of the factories and mines, the arguments over popular elementary education went on to a large degree over the heads of the intended beneficiaries. To it was brought upper- and middle-class preconceptions as well as improving zeal.

The Scottish Education Act came two years later in 1872. It differed from its English counterpart in three respects. It at once imposed compulsory education on all children (with fees removed in stages). This was an action in the tradition of John Knox.[1] If there was poverty in the home the parents could apply to the poor law guardians for such help as was needed to keep their children at school. The desire for a comprehensive system made possible the third difference from England, namely the taking of elementary education out of the hands of the Protestant churches: their schools were placed under the united jurisdiction of the School Boards, making a full rationalisation possible on the basis of an unde-nominational Protestant Christianity. A Scottish Education Department was set up under the act to supervise and integrate the system. The Catholics retained their schools in both countries.

Local authorities were also given power to provide other means of popular self-improvement. The Public Libraries Act of 1850 in England, and its counterpart of 1853 in Scotland, empowered local authorities to spend up to the equivalent of one half-penny on the rates to make a supply of books publicly available, though there continued to be a heavy reliance on charitable provision. Local authorities also began to follow the lead set by philanthropists in establishing art galleries, public parks and recreation grounds.

The gap between the provision of education for the masses and that for the wealthier classes in England was almost absolute: the two systems were seen as wholly separate. There was almost no thought of working-class education proceeding beyond the elementary stage. Social division was thus built deep into the educational

---

1. See chapter 2, section 2 above.

system. The wealthy parts of society, as in the past, of course had no need for state aid in the education of their children. The system of preparatory schools followed by 'public' schools extended rapidly: it contained a hierarchy of schools which reflected the wealth and social standing of the families who paid the fees. Even so, however, the Public Schools Act of 1868 was necessary in order to bring about modernisation of endowments: new schemes for governing bodies were brought forward for approval by the courts. The sharpness of class distinction, undiminished though refined, was thus confirmed in English social life.

The endowed grammar schools continued to be largely the preserve of the middle classes. They, like the public schools, were badly in need of overhaul. The Taunton Commission reported on them in 1868. In 1869 the Endowed Schools Act set up Commissioners who were to supervise a revision of the use of endowments and to extend their benefits to girls. A good many grammar schools were revitalised under the Commissioners, with a greatly improved use of resources and with new curricula. Similar Commissioners, with a similar role, were appointed for Scotland in 1874.

Elitism continued to be strong at the university level. The colleges of Oxford and Cambridge regarded themselves as autonomous entitites not answerable to the state. But there were the stirrings of reform, including the examination system. The Universities Test Act of 1871 was an important step in reducing Church of England influence by ending religious tests for holders of university and college teaching posts. But the public schools and the universities continued to express and confirm the class structure.

5. Housing seen as sanitation

In the housing of the working classes there was an even stronger adherence to voluntarism than in education, though for quite different reasons. The provision of housing was an activity in which participation by the state was even more dubious, for it was a major area of property-owning and economic activity. House building was a highly complex affair involving financial provision, business organisation, land availability, labour supply and wages and many other factors. But it was also a great and growing area of default. During the age of Victorian expansion the supply of houses for the unskilled lower-paid workers, not to speak of those who could not work effectively at all, was becoming more and more inadequate. The slums grew as the cities did, accumulating concentrated masses of decayed and congested houses. This was so in spite of the devoted, though sometimes autocratic, activities of philanthropists like Octavia Hill (1838–1912).

There were four lines of action open to the state in seeking to meet the housing shortfall: it could build and own houses, thus involving itself in the role of landlord, it could subsidise private building, it could regulate the standards of house construction or it could acquire property, clear the sites and offer them for sale to redevelopers. The first two possibilities were utterly remote from contemporary thinking. Of the second two, only the raising of standards was as yet possible, and this to only a minor degree.

In 1866 came the Torrens Act which put local authorities in a position to compel the owners of insanitary houses (e.g. the most deplorable of the stock) to make improvements. This was the first step in state imposition of minimal standards upon landlords. Some slight improvement in quality was thus brought about at the worst end of the scale, but it raised costs, with consequent effects on supply. The state took no further housing action down to 1875.

6. *The continued ambivalence of the poor law*

Throughout all this the poor law continued as a kind of varying constant. The general governing rules as set out in the 1834 Act remained largely unchanged. But within them Boards of Guardians over the country continued to act in a largely discretionary way. The humanitarian and working-class attack on bad conditions in the workhouses, together with the unwillingness of guardians to provoke local hostility, had caused much diversity and easing of poor work management. By the 1860s outdoor relief was being given on a large scale, especially in London, attracting the inevitable criticism. The three issues that raised legislative concern were those of chargeability, the relations between the parish guardians and those of the poor law unions, and the problem of high regional unemployment.

In 1861 came the Irremovable Poor Act, under which a pauper with three years' residence in a parish could not be removed to the parish of birth or settlement. The Act also required that parishes make payment to the common fund of their unions, not, as formerly, in proportion to their relief expenditure, but as related to their rateable value. Here was a belated but now essential recognition of the problem of the adequacy of the parish tax base in relation to the demands made upon it. In 1862, chiefly under the influence of the cotton famine in Lancashire arising from the American Civil War, it was laid down that within a union the less burdened parishes must assist the less fortunate. As between unions, the more heavily burdened were given powers, in an emergency, to borrow. The Public Works Act of 1863 authorised the Treasury and the Public Works Loans Board to make loans to unions and to local authorities on the security of the rates in order to finance employment by drainage and other works. The Union Chargeability Act of 1865 finally superseded the parish entirely as a unit of rating and settlement, placing these matters in the hands of the union and its Board of Guardians.

The basic problem remained much as before – namely how should the able-bodied unemployed worker be treated? By this time a belief in the inhumanity and degradation of the workhouse had been securely established in working-class minds. The bad cases seem to have occurred less in the new purpose-built workhouses put up by the active unions, than in the older obsolete institutions. It was this decaying tail of the system that made it so feared, together with the fact that entering 'the house' was widely regarded among the working classes as the final debasement of loss of identity.

As always with a subject of such diversity the truth is hard to come by, both on a regional and on a temporal basis. The Goschen Minute of 1869 expressed grave concern about the growth of abuse of outdoor relief, so that in the early 1870s the Local Government Board (to which responsibility for Poor Law Administration passed in 1871) embarked on something of a campaign from the centre to rehabilitate the spirit of the 1834 Act. Moreover though it was beginning to become apparent that the only escape from the anomalies and inequities of the poor law was a national provision based upon national taxation and centralised administration, history and tradition, as well as local patronage and politics, required the continuance of the principle of locality.

7. *The control of belief, morality and conduct*

In the matter of rules and sanctions for the control of personal belief and behaviour, as with welfare generally, the state appeared to act ad hoc, responding to a series of apparently separate challenges.

But behind these seemingly disparate responses of the British state there still lay two sets of concepts. The first was that of a God-fearing society, accepting the morality of the Old and New Testaments, based upon the family, the latter being strongly patriarchal. The second was that of political stability, based on the security of private property. The church, with its theology of reward or retribution in an after life, confirmed these moral values and indeed to some degree the political ones as well, but it now fell to the state to enforce them. Thus between church (and chapel) and the state there had grown up a concept of what constituted respectable behaviour and its reverse, namely various forms of deviance. To this the great bulk of the middle and working classes subscribed.

But there was bitter division between the Anglicans and the nonconformists. There was the chronic question of how the established church, with its public duties, should be paid for. Church rates, to maintain Anglican church buildings, churchyards and burial grounds, could be imposed by the vestry on all inhabitants of a parish. After more than a generation of bitter controversy, and a good deal of nonconformist passive resistance, Gladstone ended compulsory church rates in 1868.

In a sense Britain by the 1860s was one of the freest countries in the world. The 'taxes on knowledge' in the form of the newspaper tax and the tax on paper had indeed been serious constraints on freedom of expression. The newspaper tax by 1815 had been raised to 4d, making the cost of newspapers prohibitive to all but the better-off, but in 1836 the tax was reduced to 1d and in 1854 abolished. The advertising tax disappeared in the following year and the tax on paper in 1861. *Habeas Corpus*, and the right of free speech and assembly, were honoured by parliament and the courts. The state, though it stood ready to preserve its governing authority and the social order, did not feel the need to restrict expression of opinion. This relaxed attitude reflected a kind of general consensus among the British public, or at least the feeling among legislators and the courts, that there was no group of dissentients anxious and able to attempt the overthrow of the state. The struggle between the individual and the state, present in all societies, had in Britain been reduced below the threshold of danger by the peculiar nature of British historical experience. This permitted certain freedoms to become regarded as the inherent rights of British subjects, a matter of pride to those who enjoyed them.

On the morality side, concern over behaviour centred on two general aspects, namely the suspension of responsibility in the individual through drink, and the dangers of depravity through anti-social sexual behaviour in various forms. Both were seen as threats to the family.

The drink question was the classic ground of conflict between those who upheld the doctrine of the natural right of the individual to sell and to consume, and those who argued the responsibility of the state to exercise control over both activities where there was risk of social damage. The advocates of the former view insisted that in this matter the state had no right to compel morality, forcing virtue upon the individual as consumer. Nor had it any right to restrict the liberty of the subject as supplier by licensing, for this would be to create monopolies for those who were so favoured. Against these arguments the temperance movement stressed the terrible damage and degradation caused by drink among the working classes. The great source of temperance advocacy was the evangelical non-conformist element, with its demands for restrictions on the drink trade. Its members were largely on the Liberal side: indeed it was something of a paradox that supporters of the minimal state should seek to push the state into far-reaching control of so important an aspect of personal life.

The Liberal Party down to the 1870s included a high proportion of the brewers and distillers, together with their populist spokesmen, the publicans. But the temperance element won: Mr Gladstone's government passed the Licensing Act of 1872 (Bruce's Act), which placed important restrictions on the trade. The result was a movement of brewers, distillers and publicans into the Tory Party, leaving the temperance element dominant among the Liberals. In this way Mr Gladstone's attempt to regulate the drink trade significantly altered the political configuration of England.

The sexual preoccupations of the state centred upon three aspects, namely homosexuality and 'unnatural' sex acts, obscenity and pornography, and prostitution. The first category had always been illegal: this was confirmed by the Offences against the Person Act of 1861, though in somewhat more lenient terms. It was still a serious affront to publicly acceptable behaviour, so that social ostracism and a broken career were perhaps more fearful sanctions than the law, exposing public men to blackmail and disgrace.

Obscenity and pornography involved state surveillance of publications and the stage. In 1857 the Obscene Publications Act was passed, promoted by Lord Chief Justice Campbell. It was provoked by the growth of hard-core pornography in London, centred upon Holywell Street, and was supported by a powerful social purity lobby. The Act provided the judges with a definition: an obscene work was one written with the sole purpose of corrupting the morals of youth, and 'of a nature calculated to shock the common feelings of decency in any well-regulated mind'. Lord Cockburn's judgment of 1868 set up the further criterion of likelihood 'to deprave and corrupt'. This search for a definition of course reflected the intrinsic difficulty for the state in regulation of this aspect of conduct. Too rigorous an application could have a seriously damaging effect upon the creative self-expression of authors and artists. The stage continued to be governed by the Theatres Act of 1843, intended 'for the preservation of good manners, decorum or the public peace'.

In these various ways the state underpinned Victorian morality. The advocates of freedom of action and of expression were opposed by those who believed that certain kinds of behaviour were wrong in an absolute sense. A larger group of people, perhaps the majority of the nation, though they thought that certain actions were noxious to the social good, wished to restrain them in relative terms only. But these relativities were very difficult to define in law, without damaging the right to self-expression and to the exploration of the human condition. The police had a hard time of it in trying to respond to the often ambiguous dicta of the law. The system of regulation arose mainly from pressure from the middle classes, especially perhaps its lower reaches. But it appears to have been accepted by all classes. The exception to this was perhaps the rise of the music-hall from the 1850s in which a fairly uninhibited kind of expression developed for the entertainment of the working classes.

The prostitution question raised a related but distinct set of problems for the state. It involved the demand for and supply of a special service, and one which was profoundly offensive to prevailing views of womanhood and the family. Yet so powerful was the demand side, involving not only soldiers and sailors, but a significant proportion of males of all classes seeking sex outside of marriage, and so powerful were the incentives on the supply side, including difficulties among women of obtaining employment, that the state could not make prostitution illegal. Instead English law continued to take no cognisance of prostitution as an offence in itself, but was directed against the action of soliciting (treating 'common prostitutes' as vagrants and street nuisances) and against the procurer, living off the earnings of prostitutes. In 1864 the state tried to go a step further, largely because of the fearful problem of venereal disease in the armed forces. The Contagious Diseases Act of that year, and subsequent Acts in 1866 and 1869, authorised a system of registration of prostitutes in eleven garrison and naval towns. Women suspected of prostitution in these places could be obliged to undergo an examination for venereal disease. This effort at containment of disease soon aroused strong public protest, for it exposed respectable women to the risk of being apprehended and inspected.

8. The family, the role of women, divorce

There were two further issues that precipitated debate on the family as the basic unit of society and the responsibility of the state for it. The first of these was the right of a married woman to hold property, and the second was divorce.

The law of England had long proceeded on the principle that the family was a single unit, that the husband was its head, and that, in consequence, all its income and assets were his, including those brought to the marriage by the wife or earned or acquired by her during it.[1] This arrangement had, of course, its class significance. The middle- and upper-class woman was certainly seriously affected by it, but there were devices available to her father before marriage whereby certain assets could be secured to her. The working-class wife had no such protection, and so was economically wholly dependent upon her husband. If he refused her a part in the financial management of the family, taking her earnings as well as his own, and squandered them, the result could be disastrous for all.

1. See chapter 5, section 12 above.

In the 1850s elements of the middle classes began to concern themselves with this question. The Law Amendment Society and the National Association for the Promotion of Social Science (earlier called the Social Science Association) were the two most important bodies to do so. The initiators and sustainers of debate were a few dedicated middle-class women. They drew upon the writings of John Stuart Mill, especially his *Subjection of Women* of 1869. A first parliamentary Bill failed in 1857; a second was brought forward in 1867.

The proceedings of the Select Committee and the Commons debates reveal a good deal about middle-class attitudes toward themselves and toward the working classes. The assumption of the propriety of male supremacy in this matter largely continued to be held so far as the middle-class family was concerned, for the *pater familias* was a fundamental Victorian figure. Complementary to him was the notion of the wife as the angel in the house, diligent and self-denying, deferentially serving her protective husband. The legislature should not be invited to lay rough hands on this arrangement. But where roughness was already present, as was thought to be the case with working-class husbands, the matter could be different. There was the possibility of the brute husband terrorising his wife, making it difficult if not impossible for her to exercise her moral influence, sustaining the family and making the most of its resources. There was in the minds of some the consideration that as working-class wives lost their pay to their husbands they had little incentive to work, thus limiting the labour supply, but there was also genuine concern for the working women, as in the case of Lord Shaftesbury.

The Bill of 1867 was greatly diluted in the Lords. It emerged as the Married Women's Property Act of 1870. It laid down a plain rule with respect to earnings: women were to retain what they had worked for. But with respect to property the Act was much less generous. Married women could retain inherited property and monies up to the value of 200 guineas, together with their own savings bank accounts and shares or other investments up to the same amount. Though partial and ungenerous, these concessions were an important modification of the respective status of husband and wife. They were the outcome of debate largely within the middle classes, for this was not a subject on which the working classes could yet be articulate.

Divorce, down to 1857, could only be brought about by private Act of Parliament, though the ecclesiastical courts could grant separations. Divorce was, thus, of course, a very expensive business, available only to the most wealthy. Marriages were in essence church and chapel affairs (the latter were licensed by the Marriage Act of 1836). Marriages were thus regarded as bonds forged by religion, pledges given before God, and indeed in some churches were sacraments. But by 1850 there was a considerable demand for the reform and cheapening of divorce law: a Royal Commission on Marriage was set up that year under Lord Campbell. Its fruit was the Matrimonial Causes Act of 1857. It set up a Court for Divorce and Matrimonial Causes. All jurisdiction on such matters passed to the new secular Court, and away from the ecclesiastical courts. The grounds for divorce were prescribed as adultery, cruelty and desertion without cause for two years or more. A double standard was adopted with respect to adultery: in a husband's petition for divorce simple adultery sufficed, but where a wife petitioned additional aggravation had to be proved. This provision was intended as a protection against imposing upon the husband an heir not of his blood.

But the expense of a hearing in London was still prohibitive for most people. Marriage continued, in effect, to be indissoluble for life, for all but the rich. Within marriage the husband, in spite of the Married Women's Property Act, was still paramount. The state was thus, by its unwillingness to intervene in marriage except to the minimal degree demanded by men of large property, a bulwark of the patriarchal family. The great mass of the people, in spite of a good deal of desertion and unmarried cohabitation, accepted marriage as a properly irreversible act for themselves, and looked askance at their betters who were showing the first signs of casualisation.

9. Criminals and prisons

In the treatment of criminals the philosophic basis was changing. There was growing disillusionment with the separate system upon which so many of the gaols were based.[1] The stresses imposed upon the prisoners were being made obvious by the growing extent of mental disorder, softening of the brain as contemporaries put it, and

---

1. See chapter 5, section 14 above.

suicide. This was a heavy blow to those who placed their confidence in self-redemption. Moreover the system became incoherent as more prison governors brought back physical punishments to accompany the separate system and not as a straightforward alternative to it.

A third possibility was revived at this time, namely that of industry in the prisons, so that the inmates might work for 'marks' which they could spend in acquiring comforts, and which could also act as credits towards an earlier release. The protagonists of this principle urged that the prisoners should be offered objectives and the chance, to some degree at least, to affect their own lives. But there was no great enthusiasm for an incentive-based programme of this kind, partly because of the difficulties of organising work on the scale necessary.

When the transportation of criminals to Australia was suspended in 1853 Britain had to face the problem of incarcerating all her convicted malefactors. It was necessary to provide a national system of prisons. Some relief was, however, found by the adoption from 1853 of a parole system under which 'ticket-of-leave' men were released under surveillance.

By 1860, in spite of new prisons and the use of paroles, the system was in considerable disarray. At this point a new direction was imposed by events. There was in 1862 in London an outbreak of garrotting (robbery with violence, usually strangulation). Something of a public panic was created. Legislators went through a crisis of nerve, as shown in the recommendations of a House of Lords Committee and a Royal Commission in 1863. The result was the Penal Servitude Act of 1864 together with the Prisons Act of 1865, which made deterrence paramount, bringing in hard labour, hard fare and hard beds. The system had returned to the physically punitive principle making men pay for their crimes not by the torture of solitary self-assessment, but by discomfort, futile labour and humiliation.

Meanwhile the police system was being further elaborated. The County and Borough Police Act of 1856 made grants available to local authorities, and made provision for a national inspectorate. Provincial police forces were made more efficient; there were no less than 231 of them by 1888. In general the middle classes regarded the police as their friends; so did a considerable part of the working classes. But at the nether end of society, not surprisingly, they were often regarded with suspicion and active hostility.

10. The state involvement in welfare by 1874

In spite of all the difficulties, there had been progress on the welfare front since 1851: by 1874 the aggregate effect of social intervention was considerable. The worst abuses in factories and mines were greatly lessened, and the expanding parts of the cities were provided with drainage of a new standard. Indeed, conditions of working and of living had at last, and within limits, gained general acceptance as a right and proper responsibility for governments. Certainly much further legislation was to be required, and the notion of what was reasonable in terms of working conditions was to rise continuously, but the involvement of the state was now a settled obligation.

Education for the masses was doubly bedevilled (by continued religious controversy, and by the debate on how to achieve cost-effectiveness), but even here there was a degree of advance even before the legislation of the early 1870s. Thereafter the scene was set for further expansion, in the effort to render the whole population literate in a minimal basic sense.

Housing for the lower-income workers, and the related problems of the quality of urban life, though still not effectively tackled, were moving forward on the agenda of discussion. Housing was perhaps both the most pressing and the most baffling welfare issue, for any attack on the shortfall of houses on the scale required would involve a fundamental abandonment of market principles, together with a challenge to cost-effectiveness even more formidable than that posed by education.

But there were countervailing tendencies. In spite of the increases of wealth and income in Britain, the slum parts of the cities were by the 1870s generating poverty and pauperism of a scale and intensity never before known, with London providing the most atrocious case. At the same time the cyclical instability of the economy, in spite of the general trend of expansion, caused such unemployment, especially among the unskilled labourers, as to generate in the worst times widespread feelings of civil insecurity. Yet the poor law, as evolved by the 1850s, continued through the 1870s to be all the provision there was. The diversity of regional responses by the guardians continued and indeed increased, but there was no significant change in the system. The dislike and distrust of centralised control was still strong in the areas of both poor law and health. There was an insistence by those immediately dealing with these problems on the need for local knowledge and autonomy; this conflicted with the unifying and standardising thinking and instructions emanating from the centre.

Localism had another dimension. It bore the chief costs of welfare provision, with the finances of the central state down to the 1870s little affected. As these costs rose, and as units of local government increased in size and powers, the question of who paid for urban welfare partly depended upon the arrangement of city boundaries. The wealthier people, already moving out of the cities in consequence of urban deterioration, now accelerated their exodus in order to avoid its social costs as imposed by local taxation. Having moved out, they then fought against the extension of city boundaries to avoid being re-embraced by the more heavily taxing authorities.

The belief in the voluntarist principle continued to be powerful; it rested on the idea that the middle classes would assist the working classes, and the latter would practise self-help and mutual aid. In matters of morality and of the family, the state was in general loath to act, and could only be made to do so under sustained and powerful pressure.

11. The bureaucracy

The general structure of government departments was subject to no great elaboration in the quarter century down to 1874. The greatest change in this sense was the setting up of the Local Government Board in 1871. It took over four elements, namely the Local Government Act Office, the Registrar General's Office, the Medical Department of the Privy Council and the Poor Law Board. The President became, in effect, the minister for local government. But the effectiveness of the LGB was to be seriously impaired by feeble ministers and strong Treasury control. The Home Office continued to be responsible for conditions of work in factories, mines and agriculture. The Department of Education was responsible for the school system.

The Factory and Mines Acts and the Education Acts had generated inspectorates; the prison system was under similar surveillance. There were also the inquiries and reports of the School Boards, especially those of the Attendance Officers. In these ways windows were opened upon work places, schools, homes and prisons. The new information and insight thus gained could be used as weapons against complacency and as the basis of new campaigns.

The civil service had grown from 39,000 members in 1851 to 54,000 in 1871. In the qualitative sense, too, it was changing. For though from about 1800 there had been some degree of training, with salaries graduated by responsibility and regular promotion, entry had always been by patronage. From 1855 under Mr Gladstone's influence (following the Northcote–Trevelyan Report of 1853) the principle of competitive examination was introduced in the home civil service, under the newly established Civil Service Commission (this indeed was the origin of the term 'civil service'). In the face of strong opposition Gladstone and his colleagues sought to promote efficiency and economy and to demote the long-established political families by depriving them of the patronage of the civil service, replacing it by the notions of equality of appointment for gifted men. This reform was carried further in 1870, opening all departments to competitive entry, except the Foreign Office, that final bastion of patronage. The state could now draw to its service from the whole range of talent of the middle classes; the age of bureaucratic meritocracy could begin.

Local government continued to consist of a number of fragments, including civic corporations, School Boards and Poor Law Unions. On the other hand the various bodies of Improvement Commissioners progressively passed their duties to the corporations after 1835, so that streets, sanitation and local building bye-laws became municipal matters. But the day of the civic gospel had not yet dawned.

12. *The philosophy of the state*

The extensions of the functions of the state down to 1874 necessarily gives rise to the question: had the philosophy of the state in Britain altered in any important way? Group antagonisms had been capable of a considerable degree of reconciliation before 1851. This trend continued and was indeed further strengthened over the next quarter century. The conflict model of society, though always implicit, had faded in the general consciousness. Welfare provision in its various forms had made some contribution to this. Constructive policies on many matters continued to be carried through by a process of balancing of interests and pressures (though such policies could be much attenuated in the course of the manoeuvres involved).

But this way of proceeding was, in essence, ad hoc. Indeed in parts its success depended on the keeping apart of the various issues, so that the overall tally and trend might not be too plain. This, of course, had its price – it meant that the elements of policy could be unco-ordinated or even inconsistent. But as policy actions accumulated it was becoming plainer that at least a degree of co-ordination was necessary, for example, as between poor law, health, sanitation, housing and education. This meant that the old posture of parliament – waiting for private members to lay proposals before it in the form of private Bills – was too patchy and too difficult to control. There was a need for the political parties to become programmatic, offering a more or less coherent set of proposals. At the same time a system of ministries had to be elaborated to execute policy.

Behind the ministries lay the problem of ethos and instruction of senior civil servants. It was necessary for a concept of the public good to seize hold of them, generating in them a combination of dedication and disinterestedness rather like that of Platonic guardians. This condition was indeed largely met as the new generation of civil servants came forward. It could be said that ultimately they were the creatures of the ruling classes, but to substantiate such a view it would be necessary to deprive them of any significant autonomy or inter-class sympathy. This would be a difficult case to argue, given the complexities of the British class structure, especially among the 'rulers'. Three conditions must be borne in mind, namely the moralism that impregnated so much of British life, the ever-present aberrants from middle-class complacency who could always be relied upon to exercise reformist and philanthropic pressures, and the perceived need even among the unidealistic to make concessions to the working classes.

13. The four levels of state action by 1874

It is possible to view the role of the British state by 1874 at four principal levels. With respect to the macro-controls – monetary, fiscal and expenditure policy – the state had effectively abdicated; it had withered away so far as it was ever to do so. Secondly in relation to labour and its claims, the state had accepted a responsibility to set the rules for the contest between labour and employers; concessions consistent with a liberal conscience had been made, but a careful line had been drawn limiting union action. These concessions were related to the extension of the franchise in 1867. Thirdly, there was an improvement in the treatment of workers by the courts, reflecting a growing recognition of their rights as full citizens, so that justice was more even by the 1870s than it had been in the 1830s. Fourthly, on social questions – caring for the poor, improving working conditions, promoting public health and providing elementary education – a general obligation had been adopted: it had been irreversibly conceded that the state had a role and responsibility in these four matters.

The extension of working-class voting power since 1867 and the revelations of deprivation which social welfare action itself generated meant that the commitment to social amelioration contained the seeds of its own extension. The age of laissez-faire was losing reality in terms of social policy. But the extension of social action did not involve the state in significantly higher expenditure, for most of it fell on industry or on the local authorities. This allowed the central state, still largely controlled by an interplay of the landed aristocracy and the middle classes, to continue to minimise its intervention in the economy through the tax system. The ability of the unions to generate monopoly conditions on their side of the labour market was still under formidable constraint. Thus could economic laissez-faire, a partial state tolerance of trade unions, a growing recognition of the legal rights of workers and a considerable degree of social collectivism co-exist.

PART IV

Industrial maturity and the ending of pre-eminence, 1874–1914

9

The continued freedom of the market mechanism; the state-induced changes in its operating conditions

1. The late Victorian and Edwardian challenges

From the 1870s Britain's world economic dominance waned; indeed some scholars detect deceleration of economic growth as beginning as early as the 1860s. Britain's high Victorian lead over trade rivals, especially Germany and the USA, shrank; by 1900 it had gone. The country was entering upon the phase of industrial maturity, in some ways presenting its governments with problems more intransigent than those of the first industrial revolution. Cereal agriculture was in serious difficulty, causing landed incomes based on rents to fall. France was replaced in the 1890s as the great disturber of continental stability by Germany, a nation whose aggressiveness, inspired by a newly found political unity, had at its disposal the means of making war on a scientific and industrial basis.

Mr Gladstone's first Home Rule Bill of 1886 made Ireland the dominant and most divisive issue in British politics.[1] Large additions were made to the empire, especially in Africa. The Boer War (1899–1902) shocked the British people, for it was no easy task to subdue guerrilla fighters on their home ground. Out of it came a new imperial philosophy, closely related to concern with national health and efficiency at home. The challenge to modernise India prompted the Morley–Minto reforms of 1909, intended to carry the sub-continent toward self-government.

The women made their bid for the vote, some of them employing violence.[2] Perhaps most frightening of all was the end of social harmony within Britain itself, marked by a revival from the 1880s of

1. See chapter 10, section 5 below.
2. See chapter 13, section 10 below.

working-class unrest reminiscent of the 1830s and 40s, reaching a peak in 1911–1912.[1]

Toward each of these threatening circumstances, unprecedented in their complexity and staggering in their scale, the British state had to assume a posture.

2. *The extending franchise; the new politics*

At the same time the distribution of political power in Britain was undergoing further dramatic change. The Representation of the People Act of 1884 and the Redistribution of Seats Act of 1885 are often referred to jointly as the Third Reform Act 1884–5. The 1884 Act brought a third general widening of the franchise, including its extension to rural and mining areas: the electorate increased from some 2.2 million in 1867 to just under 5 million. In consequence of the new franchise two in three of the adult male population had the vote. The working classes thus numerically dominated the electorate from 1884. From 1907 Members of Parliament received a salary from the public purse (£400 per year); in this way was provided an important degree of financial independence for members, an essential condition for widening British politics to include direct working-class participation. The landed interest, though gradually diminishing in political potency, and economically threatened by the fall in cereal prices and farm rents, still retained a powerful influence. But the founding of county councils by Lord Salisbury's government in 1888 replaced landed power in the countryside with elected bodies. The industrialists increased in number, generating new sectors and adopting monopolistic or semi-monopolistic tactics where markets made this advantageous and possible. But an element of the business world was showing an increasing concern with welfare, and with industrial peace through arbitration and conciliation.

With the extension of the franchise, politics was increasingly carried by the politicians and their parties to the people. It was the ageing Gladstone, seventy in 1879, who showed what could be done in this new direction: his famous Midlothian campaign of that year, moving by train from place to place, greeting the electors and addressing unprecedented mass meetings and attracting wide re-

---

1. See chapter 12, sections 5 and 14 below.

portage, meant that a new age of appeal to the populace had begun. But Mr Gladstone saw the direct participation of the masses in very limited terms, laying it down in 1878 that 'It is written in legible characters, and with a pen of iron, on the rock of human destiny, that within the domain of practical politics the people must in the main be passive.'

The Conservatives too were obliged to respond to the new conditions. Under Lord Salisbury (1830–1903; Prime Minister 1885, 1886–92, 1895–1902) the old Tory reliance upon patronage and loyalty was to be replaced by a vigorous and efficient party organisation to bring the voters to the polls. Salisbury, the last great political exemplar of landed aristocracy, ruling Britain and the empire from the House of Lords, detested the new plutocracy of industrial and financial wealth (just as Mr Gladstone did). Moreover he deeply distrusted democracy. But as a realist he turned to the working man as enfranchised in 1867 and 1884. He thus revived the Conservative Party, left in disarray by Disraeli, and found for it a renewed element of support, namely the Conservative working man. The greatest political good in the mind of Salisbury was the empire and its honour; the greatest evils were collectivism and socialism.

With the rise of political parties in the modern sense from the 1870s, they came to be regarded as the basic unit of government, rather than the traditional loose groupings of more or less like-minded men. The two-party system, composed of Conservatives and Liberals, confirmed itself. Party programmes were increasingly conceived in terms of mass appeal, launching British politics on the dangerous course of competitive bidding for votes.

Yet even such a system was not inconsistent with the existence of party philosophies. The Conservatives under Salisbury continued in the role of custodians of the theory of the organic–hierarchic society as it had been elaborated in the eighteenth and early nineteenth centuries by Burke, Coleridge and Southey, and held by Disraeli; a view which saw the relationships between classes as governed by a natural harmony, and sealed by a sense of moral responsibility on the part of property owners. In this way of thinking the conflict between classes, with its basis in gross inequality of wealth, could be muted. This approach was not without its appeal to a significant section of the working classes. The Tories, because of their organic–hierarchic view of society, had never suffered from inhibitions about state ameliorative action. Their difficulty was to decide what actions to take.

The Liberals too inherited a tradition, namely that of radicalism. They, like the Tories, were in a quandary how to fulfil their role. In the 1880s, with Mr Gladstone exclusively preoccupied with Ireland, and with the strength of the evangelical nonconformists reaching its apogee, the Liberals found it hard to establish their direction. They were exposed to much ad hoc pressure, sometimes referred to as faddism, especially in the form of attempts to impose temperance programmes. The senior members of the Party had a profound distrust of socialism, in which they included most forms of collectivism: Lord Rosebery as late as 1909 described socialism as 'the end of all, the negation of faith, of family, of property, of the monarchy, of the Empire'. There was, however, especially among the younger Liberals, a perceptible development of new attitudes toward social amelioration and trade union claims, as these might be affected by state action.

But the new politics of both Tory and Liberal Parties were not to take pronounced shape until, in the aftermath of the Boer War, Joseph Chamberlain polarised debate by offering a programme of economic management starting from tariff reform. Its rejection in 1905–6 split the Conservatives and brought the Liberals to over-whelming power in the House of Commons. What was to be done with a mandate that was at once overwhelming and vague?

3. *The monetary automasticities continue*

In economic terms the debate between 1874 and 1914 was successively dominated by three issues: the inconclusive and unfocussed discussion of bimetallism from the 1870s to the 1890s, the national debate on the protective tariff as a means of national renewal and imperial coherence between 1903 and 1906, and the conflict over the taxing powers of the Commons centred on the budget of 1909 culminating in the constitutional crisis of 1911.

The monetary and banking system continued in the forty years between 1874 and 1914 largely on the self-adjusting basis established in 1844.[1] This was the great age of what Professor Sayers has called 'the traditional automasticities'. Changes in Bank Rate were seen as

1. See chapter 4, section 6 above.

a technical affair of bankers, with no serious implications for the level of trade, and were free of politics in the sense that the Bank of England was independent of the Treasury. Bank rate was also regarded as remote from industry, having nothing directly to do with the liquidity needs of firms, much less the structural problems of the economy. All this was based on a simplified form of the quantity theory of money.

Britain's export performance relative to imports, in spite of everything, continued to be reasonably strong, being reinforced by her invisible earnings. In the 1870s other countries (Germany, France and the USA) were committing themselves to gold, and ostensibly to the system of free movement of funds which it represented. It is not surprising that the gold standard system had become a state of mind, almost unquestioned, within the Bank, throughout the City and in the outlook of governments. It provided a set of monetary principles appropriate to a country that stood at the centre of the world's economic system.

It is true that there were certain aspects of this monetary system which worried the more far-seeing of the generation before 1914. Chief of these was the concern about the Bank's liquidity base in terms of gold, for the City of London was exposed to large international movements of funds. London was becoming increasingly vulnerable to external gold drains of an arbitrary nature, some of them arising from the needs and policies of foreign states and foreign nationals holding reserves in the City. There was also a growing volume of securities in London that could not readily be realised on the markets of the continent should London liquidity be threatened – Indian, colonial and American. Further, though London was the only effectively free general source of gold, the Bank of England in the 1890s held on average only 24 million, against 95 in gold and silver at the Bank of France, 50 at the Bank of Germany, and 142 in the United States Treasury. It was becoming apparent that variations of Bank Rate were often impotent to staunch outflows of gold when politics or panic provoked them. The arbitrage of money dealers could have a stabilising effect in 'normal' conditions, but when there was the possibility of mass movements of assets between countries the guesses and actions of dealers and speculators could greatly amplify the uncertainty.

The most sustained and general controversy in the City in the last

167

quarter century centred around the intricate question of bimetallism, namely the proposal that both gold and silver, at an agreed parity between them, should serve as the basis of the British monetary system. Huskisson had proposed such a scheme in 1828, but Wellington as Prime Minister had vetoed it. The 1870s brought a vigorous revival of the idea, based on concern for the adequacy of the money supply on a world basis. Here was an issue at once intractable, yet touching all the fundamentals of the money system and much else besides. If the monetary base of Britain and the world was unsound, the City must be disrupted, the trade to India and the East confounded, international capital movements distorted, rivals possibly favoured and general monetary disturbance threatened, with consequent effects on wage pressures. In a sense bimetallism was a challenge to answer all questions at once. The debate resumed in strength in the depression beginning in 1873, reached its peak in Britain with the Royal Commission at 1888, and was still going strong in some circles at the end of the century.

British governments, though they sent representatives to inter-national conferences in 1878, 1881 and 1892, had no enthusiasm for any form of bimetallism which required an internationally agreed parity between gold and silver. Experience had shown that it was exceedingly difficult to get agreements between nations on anything, let alone on monetary matters, at once so delicate and so fundamental to national interests. Britain, together with Germany, at Brussels in 1892 destroyed the attempt, led by the United States, to establish an international silver standard. The flow of South African gold into the world's monetary system from the 1890s greatly lessened the constricting effect of gold.

Britain, because of her industrial and commercial pre-eminence, had a strongly active balance of payments. By continuously re-lending her surpluses abroad she spread the gains and losses of industrialisation over the world at large. The state did not interfere with this vast emission of funds, but left the export of capital entirely to its owners. The charge has been made that this search for higher returns for capital outside Britain had a harmful effect on the economy at home by starving it of capital, and that, by implication, the state should have controlled this export of funds. But in order to judge this issue two enormous ranges of assumptions have to be made. One concerns the effect such 'forced' investment would have had on the home economy, and the other involves the implications for Britain herself of a curtailment of world economic growth that would be the result of a refusal by her to re-lend her foreign earnings.

As it was, successive British governments left the economy entirely open, with British industry committing itself more and more eagerly to world markets, and thus making itself, quite unwittingly, more and more vulnerable should they be disrupted. A tariff had to be granted to the white dominions, together with their general domestic autonomy. But where such a right could be withheld, as in the case of India, it was refused.

In the matter of periodic commercial crises the government relied upon the City. But the City was perilously weak in analytical power. There would be earnest discussion on the direction of the late over-extension, and accounts of the course of the crisis would appear. The City would then place a label upon the recent breakdown: excessive foreign loans, railway investment, post-war restocking, speculation in the Eastern trades, gold discoveries. This would go out to the country as the City view. There, so far as the City in general was concerned, the matter would rest. As recovery came there was usually a tendency to look for the symptoms associated with the previous collapse (and possibly one collapse removed), and, if these were weak or absent to conclude that the expansion was sound. Little attempt was made to see the new phase in its own terms, to be comprehended not by looking for the reappearance of earlier circumstances, but as a set of relationships only to be understood by systematic thought that embraced both general laws and the specific conditions of the moment.

The City view of banking was dominated by one prime consideration – how to deal with illiquidity. So long as the banking system could contract without serious losses, then all was well. But to control investment, or equalise prices, said Grenfell, sometime Governor of the Bank, was no business of the banker, drawing him into a labyrinth of problems. In 1890 the City demonstrated that in a time of major financial danger it could act together and so preclude the need for governmental intervention: the banking crisis of that year, caused by the suspension of one of the greatest of financial houses, that of Barings, was met by the Bank of England's initiative in organising a guarantee fund subscribed to by all the major banks. The money market, under the Bank, thus learned that it could act co-operatively and voluntarily to forestall unnecessary liquidity crises. But it could not generalise this experience. Yet, perhaps because of their naivety, the Bank and the City could quickly recover from their frights, and revert to a fundamental confidence in a monetary system governed by market considerations and independent of government. The erosion of the basic assumptions upon which the system rested was largely ignored.

The fundamental but almost imperceptible changes affecting the British monetary system had to do with three factors: the actions of foreign governments, the spending demands of the home government and the attitudes of trade unions. Even in strictly monetary terms foreign governments could distort the system by sterilising gold inflows so that they did not raise their price levels; they could also compete for gold holdings in such a way as to produce a serious international maldistribution of this basic element of liquidity. There was too the increasing vulnerability of the British economy to governmental demands for resources, for the age of modern welfare and warfare had begun, especially from 1900 to 1914. But in spite of increased spending on a scale to worry contemporaries, tax revenue was sustained, so that the size of the government's borrowing requirement did not significantly affect the money supply; moreover most of the public debt could be funded at long term without great difficulty. Perhaps most threatening of all, industrial unrest, especially in 1911–12, ought to have made it plain that governments could no longer assume that wages were flexible downward to the degree required by the assumption of self-adjusting price levels on which gold standard theory rested. The Bank and the City in closing their eyes to the implications of these developments set the general tone. Politicians and governments for their part were not going to press gratuitously for a new view of such complicated and dangerous matters. The classic gold exchange standard system, in spite of its inadequacies, could thus survive to 1914 as part of the basic psychology both of business and of parliament. In this curious and limited sense, therefore, the monetary system continued to be apolitical.

4. *The threat to free trade is defeated*

The struggle between 1903 and 1906 to bring back the tariff as a regulatory mechanism for the economy failed, but it did so in a resounding fashion. A great national campaign was mounted to restore to the state this great macro-policy weapon. It rivalled in verve and divisiveness that of Gladstone on Ireland. In consequence of it the Conservative Party, from certain members of which the campaign emanated, was split, going down to devastating defeat in the general election of 1905–6. But in the process the protectionists had hammered the divided Liberals (split in the 1880s over Home Rule for Ireland) into a new unity based upon a reaffirmation of free trade. The Liberals, having won office by the nation's negation of state interference in the economy in the form of the tariff, then embarked on a far-reaching programme of state-sponsored social intervention.

The dominant figure in all this was Joseph Chamberlain. He had begun as a nonconformist, business man, radical Liberal. But in 1886 over Ireland he had abandoned Mr Gladstone and the Liberals, choosing to fight alongside the Conservatives for the maintenance of the Union. In so doing he had torn the Liberal Party asunder, creating the Liberal Unionist Party, later simply Unionists. He then turned to the second of the Victorian Britain's great divisive issues, namely free trade. The Cobden–Chevalier Treaty had lapsed in 1872; France had reverted to her traditional protectionism. The Great Depression beginning in the 1870s shook confidence in free trade even in Britain. In the 1880s the National Fair Trade League fought for a 'balancing' tariff to compensate for the discrimination against Britain practised by other nations. The League had failed, but by the 1890s the ideas it embodied attracted Chamberlain.

He was already at the centre of the policy debates of his time. His early reputation was based upon his programme of civic action in Birmingham in the 1870s. His Unauthorised Programme of 1885 had combined Benthamite ideas of efficiency with collectivist/socialist devices. For Chamberlain taxation was not on principle to be minimised, but was to be used positively as an instrument of income redistribution and of welfare provision. Chamberlain was a man of programmes rather than isolated causes, a man who sought a series of measures appropriate to Britain's performance and position as her high Victorian prosperity began to fade. But Mr Gladstone hung on to the leadership of the Liberal Party so long that Chamberlain was denied the opportunity of wielding that party as his weapon of reform.

As Colonial Secretary Chamberlain attended the Colonial Conference in 1902. There the premiers assembled from the empire set off in his mind an explosive sequence. Could there be a new British economic policy based on tariffs, within which a general imperial preference could operate? Chamberlain resigned from the cabinet to launch his national appeal for tariff reform from his power base of Birmingham on 1 May 1903.

The trade of Britain's leading rivals was subject to mercantilist manipulation; Chamberlain and his supporters played upon Britain's vulnerability in such a world. The fear of German rivalry was particularly potent. In Chamberlain's scheme both agriculture and industry had their places, but as his proposals developed through the campaign rhetoric, industry became the dominant element. At the same time there was much stress on the benefits to be enjoyed by the working man through sustained incomes and employment. Chamberlain came out for a 10% duty on foreign manufactures.

It was no longer possible, in the face of so much foreign tariff-building, for Liberals to argue for the universal application of the principle of comparative advantage on a world scale, under which each nation would specialise in the production of that range of goods and services for which it was best suited (e.g. had the lowest relative costs), thus increasing the wealth of all. Instead the argument had now to be a much more limited one, in British terms only, resting upon the British need for tax-free imports of foodstuffs and raw materials, and stressing the dangers of adding further to the international movement of building protective walls. It also emphasised the need to keep British industry exposed to competition in the interests of efficiency, and the perils of exposing trade continuously to politics through the tariff-seeking activities of interested groups. Behind all this, of course, there was the fear that Britain was so heavily committed in her industrial and commercial structure to world trade that it would be madness for her to try to recede within herself. The Liberals could also accuse Chamberlain of a fundamental inconsistency, namely that if protection did keep out foreign goods, then the tariff would yield no revenue for welfare.

Arthur Balfour (1848–1930) as Conservative Prime Minister, together with a good deal of his party, was susceptible to the idea of a moderate tariff. But Balfour could neither find a compromise that would stabilise his party, nor arrive at a view of his own so that he could lead it. From this time onward there was a Tory predilection for some form of protection, albeit a cautious one.

5. Growth, stability, structure and location are left to the market

After three years of massive assault, free trade and the unmanaged economy prevailed with the electorate in 1906. The British state took upon itself no responsibility for stability and growth, leaving them to the market.

It is true that by the award of naval contracts the state could have some effect on aggregate demand and on regional activity, but this was a relatively minor aspect. The powers given to local authorities under the Unemployed Workmen's Act of 1905[1] did authorise regional public works, financed by local government, but the response was minor. There were voices raised on behalf of public spending as an anti-cyclical device, as in the case of the Minority Report on the Poor Law (1908–9), but as yet such pleas commanded little attention among legislators. The first Census of Production of 1907, under Lloyd George at the Board of Trade, was a harbinger of official interest in questions of output and efficiency as seen in quantitative terms, but it was not completed. Contemporaries did not have available the kind of calculations later made of the performance of the economy, both in itself and in comparison with rivals; even if these had existed they would have provided no obvious and unanimously acceptable clue to the correct direction of state action.

Moreover the industrial structure of the country was a matter for businessmen and not for governments. So too with the pattern of location of industry and of the population. For, in spite of the increasing concentration of activity and people in London and the South-East, it hardly occurred to politicians that governments had a role in such matters. The only device adopted by the state to promote one sector of activity over another was the Agricultural Rating Act of 1896, which cut the property rates levied on farmers in half. The public sector owned and controlled at the centre continued to be minimal; even at the local government level, where there was indeed a notable extension of enterprise, it was conducted on market principles.[2]

In sum, the operation of the economy in its many aspects was the concern of the market and those who traded in it, and not of the central state. Britain had suffered no great shock as in the case of

1. See chapter 12, section 10 below.
2. See chapter 11 below.

France, so heavily defeated by Germany in 1870, or, as with Spain, losing the last of her colonies in 1898. Nor was Britain subject to a great exhilaration, as with Germany after her unification. So it was that the triple tenets of the liberal market economy continued to be the basis of economic policy, namely the gold exchange standard, the balanced and minimal budget and free trade. These were the three pillars of the anti-collectivist temple.

6. But the outflanking of laissez-faire proceeds

Yet the market by 1914 was not what it had been in the high Victorian age. Governments had taken actions that over the longer run were to affect profoundly its workings. Though the monetary system was left to the 'automatic' operations of the gold standard, the fiscal system was altered by the taxation of inheritance on a new scale, and by the introduction of the progressive principle into the income tax: these measures meant that the way was opened to continuous redistribution of wealth and income, with the state thus operating upon the fundamental shape of society. Secondly, the development of a public sector, mostly by the actions of local authorities with central government approval, placed the state in its local form in the position of owner–manager of large monopolistic enterprises providing water, gas, electricity and trams.[1] The state in these ways became a massive entrepreneur, replacing private enterprises and itself providing a wide range of services essential to the growing cities. Thirdly, the state made great concessions to labour in the form of trade union legislation which placed the unions in the position of consolidated wage bargainers, with powerful persuasive and even coercive powers.[2] Thus a large part of the labour market ceased to be governed by simple contract between individuals, but operated by negotiation between organised employers and organised workers, armed with the sanctions of the lock-out and the strike. Finally, the state in its greatly increased commitment to welfare provision, especially in terms of pensions and unemployment insurance, undertook to underwrite to a certain extent the individual and the family.[3] All these actions were to alter the context within

1. See chapter 11, below.
2. See chapter 12 below.
3. See chapter 13 below.

which the market functioned. But the market system remained the mainspring of the economy, strong enough to sustain these impediments to its working.

7. *Active redistribution of wealth and income enter the tax system*

The British tax system was under no very serious strain until late in the nineteenth century. It is true that the income tax had risen from 2d in the pound (0.8%) in 1874 to 8d (3.3%) in 1886, to comprise one fifth of the total tax revenue. Disturbing though this was to contemporaries, it was far from crippling. Moreover debate on the tax system could proceed on terms that Adam Smith would have approved, emphasising the taxpayer, his rights and liberties against the state, together with a concern for simplicity and economy in collection.

But preoccupation with civil liberties and efficiency was increasingly encountering another theme, that of fairness as between people with incomes of different sizes. Chamberlain's Unauthorised Programme of 1885 proposed to treat the income tax not as an undesirable inquisition and an imposition, but as an instrument of social reform: it should be progressive, a means of systematically redistributing incomes. From the 1880s the principle of graduation gained adherents. But there were still misgivings: Mr Gladstone, always an enemy of the income tax as an illiberal and inquisitorial device, argued that once the progressive principle was adopted, it could become confiscatory.

Changes in economic theory had, of course, their bearing on the matter of taxation. The classical economics of Ricardo, with its emphasis on the aggregative distributive shares of the national product (rent, wages and profits), had carried a strong class connotation (landowners, capitalists and wage-earners). In the 1870s and 1880s came the development of the subjective utility theory of value; it stressed that on the demand side the utility of any good, including income, was subjective. To this was added the marginal principle, namely that the utility of a good to an individual will diminish depending on how much of it he possessed. The notion of marginal utility thus seemed to confirm the case for greater equality by implying that a marginal transfer of income from a rich to a poor man would add to the national aggregate of happiness. The implications of the debate were important. The belief that higher rates of taxation of the rich would increase societal welfare placed those economists who accepted the theory of diminishing marginal utility of income outside the philosophy of laissez-faire, at least in this regard, bringing them alongside socialist thinkers.

Meanwhile the tax system was being amplified in another direction. Just as principles of utility and equity were applied to discussions about income, so too with wealth. John Stuart Mill and others had pointed out how grossly unequal was the wealth pattern in Britain. From the 1880s proposals on general grounds for the state to operate upon it were becoming difficult to resist. But there was another theme present. The most resented category of hereditary wealth-holders were the landed aristocracy and gentry. At least this was the case so far as the new business-based, radically minded class were concerned, for whom such families were perceived as representing a continuing feudalism. Landed wealth could thus become a target, especially for the Liberal Party.[1] It could also become a source of government finance.

It was the Liberal Chancellor William Harcourt (1827–1904) who was the real architect of the estate or death duty. His budget of 1894 marked a new age of fiscal policy. He extended the taxation of inherited wealth, using the progressive principle. The scale ranged from 1% on petty estates between £100 and £500 to 8% on the great estates of £1 million capital value or more. Modest though these rates may seem, especially in the upper range, they were a radical new beginning, in practice, in theory and in social philosophy.

In addition they had profound implications for landowners as a class. Landed aristocratic power as late as the 1880s was still great, and in some senses still dominant. But now the axe was to be taken to the tree of landed inheritance.

Harcourt was a financial Gladstonian in the three principal senses. He was against the waste that so easily proliferated if Treasury control was relaxed, he was against heavy spending by the war departments (too easily to be employed in continental or colonial aggression) and he was against class fiscal privilege on the scale prevailing. But there was serious concern over the warlike intentions of the French, so that the Admiralty was able to promote a

1. See chapter 10, section 2 below.

substantial expansionist programme. Harcourt as Chancellor was faced with a deficit of £5 million, a prospect which he could not accept. His death duties taxed land like any other asset, and at its true capital value. In so doing Harcourt acquired a new source of revenue, without affecting British industrial costs or working-class incomes.

Rosebery, Harcourt's Prime Minister, pleaded that such a tax, once seized upon by Chancellors, would mean the end of the great landed estates. The Queen and many great lords, including Devonshire and Salisbury, agreed. To this Harcourt replied that well-run estates – those of the Fitzwilliams, the Bedfords, the Portmans, the Devonshires, the Northumberlands – could easily make the necessary provision, by life insurance or other means, while the ill-run ones deserved to be broken up. So it was that Harcourt, this scion of landed privilege, could take the first step in a course which was to end in taxing the great landed families out of existence.

From 1894 all property passing at death was to be seen by the state not as embodying a natural hereditary right, but as a windfall rightfully to be taxed. All estates on the deaths of their owners were to be treated as being the result of 'unearned' incomes, and no cognisance was to be taken of the spacing of testators' deaths, so that an estate could be repeatedly levied at short intervals. Landed estates, already suffering diminutions in rents, were thus further threatened, and with them an important traditional element in British society. Not surprisingly, and with justification, the landed interest saw the Liberal imposition of death duties in the same light as Home Rule for Ireland – as an attack upon themselves.[1]

In the background there was the question of the national debt. Concern over its size had revived after the Crimean War, when it stood at just over £800 million. The government's obligations thus became a major element in the money market, a development inconsistent with the liberal view of the economy. Moreover there was a growing feeling that it was improper to saddle posterity with this burden. This view had been about for some time; it was focussed by W.S. Jevons' book *The Coal Question* of 1866. Jevons (1835–82) argued that Britain's prosperity rested upon a wasting asset, the fundamental one of energy, of which posterity was being deprived at

---

1. See chapter 10 below.

a frightening rate. But there were other considerations. A large national debt meant correspondingly high levels of taxation to service it, involving transfers from the more creative elements of society to rentiers. It also meant that the government itself was at the mercy of changes in the level of interest rates. This in turn raised the old question of the relationship between the Treasury and the City: could the City hold the government to ransom by keeping the rate higher than was justified?

Considerations such as these lay behind the Sinking Fund set up in 1875 by Sir Stafford Northcote (1818–87) with a view to redeeming the national debt. Annual contributions were made to it from budgetary surpluses, out of which debt redemption took place. As a result the debt was steadily reduced, to £724 million in 1886 (less the value of earning assets acquired, chiefly the telegraph system, taken over in 1869, and the Suez Canal shares bought by Disraeli in 1875), to £635 million in 1899. In spite, therefore, of increasing expenditure, the principles of sound finance had been more than honoured, causing the debt to be brought down by one-seventh. It was not altogether unrealistic to begin to think in terms of a debt-free state. Moreover as the floating component of the debt was so small the Treasury had no need to keep going to the money market.

The Boer War brought a new situation. It affected the attitude of politicians to taxation in two ways. The appalling expense as it then seemed was a blow to social reform. By 1903 the debt had risen to £798 million. But on the other hand the war was a revelation of the taxable capacity of the state, once nineteenth-century inhibitions had been swamped by war demands. The income tax had reached 1/3d (6.2%) in the pound by 1903, though it fell thereafter. This first hint of the potential of taxation of incomes was by far the stronger element at work, preparing the ground for a new generation of big spenders, beginning with Lloyd George. He responded to the challenges of arming against the Germans and of meeting a new dimension of expenditure on the social services. In so doing he raised taxation so effectively that by 1914, in spite of greatly increased expenditure, the national debt had been reduced to some £706 million, an astonishing outcome.

The victorious Liberals found in 1906 that promises and power had brought a daunting fiscal problem. Having denied themselves a tariff revenue, they had to turn to domestic sources. Their long-standing obligation to the progressive principle, already embodied in the death duties, was now revived. After bringing the debate to a head with a Select Committee on the Income Tax in 1906, H.H. Asquith (1858–1928) as Chancellor in the following year took the first, and irreversible, step in introducing the progressive principle into the income tax. Earned incomes under £2,000 per year paid 9d (3.75%) in the pound, those above paid 1s (5%), while those below £160 paid nothing at all.

8. Taxation provokes a constitutional crisis

But it was the Liberal budget of 1909 which heralded the new fiscal age. Out of argument concerned with the distribution of national burdens came a constitutional crisis to rank with that of 1832. British politics was polarised in 1909 and the two years that followed in a manner that had not occurred throughout the sixty-four years of Victoria's reign.

Lloyd George (1863–1945) was the great precipitator. As a rank outsider, a protagonist of the little man/working man, raised by his cobbler uncle in a remote Welsh village in an atmosphere of resentment against the local landed squire, he was free of the continuities and inhibitions that had impregnated so many intellectuals, civil servants and politicians.

The voting power gained by the Liberals in 1905/6 placed the Commons as a weapon in his hands. The government's mounting commitment to social provision and warfare preparation (chiefly old age pensions and dreadnought battleship building) had generated such a demand for revenue that the tax base simply had to be extended. In this way the necessary psychology of action and the imperative needs of the state converged. The trends which culminated in 1909 were fundamental; but the timing and the immediate configuration, including the personalities involved, were powerful short- and medium-term conditioning elements. It is for this reason that Lloyd George takes his place alongside Joseph Chamberlain as a prime mover in British politics, insofar as an individual can be such.

Lloyd George's budget extended two existing fiscal devices. Earned incomes between £2,000 and £3,000 were levied at 1s in the pound, and those above £3,000 paid 1/2d. The death duties too were raised to new levels so that, for example, estates over £1 million paid

15%. There were three new departures: the super-tax, the land tax and the tax on undeveloped lands and minerals. The super-tax was an additional levy of 6d in the pound on incomes over £5,000 per year (but levied on the amount by which they exceeded £3,000). Such incomes thus represented a sharp discontinuity; on them a new level of direct taxation was to be charged, making, in all, 1/8d (8.3%) in the pound. The land tax was entirely novel: it took the form of a 20% levy on the rise in site values. This was a further impost on landowners, both in terms of their country acres and their urban properties. Finally there was a tax of ½d in the pound on the value of lands or mineral resources left undeveloped; this was an attempt to curtail the gains of those who held such assets idle in the hope of a rise in value. Of the radical nature of the budget there can be no doubt: 'This', said Lloyd George, 'is a War Budget. It is for raising money to wage implacable war against poverty and squalidness.'

The Lords, dominated by the Conservatives, had been consistently blocking Liberal measures since the new parliament of 1906. The budget of 1909 became their sticking point. They determined to use their power as the second chamber to reject it outright. They were, of course, defending their own wealth and privileges. Lloyd George made great play of this in his baiting of the dukes. But they were also (though inadvertently) defending the settlement of 1688 which seemed to have made property and income, apart from taxation levels of an accepted and modest kind, inviolate against the state.

A whole set of questions affecting state and class power in Britain suddenly became explicit. There was the constitutional one, namely how far could parliament go in taxation, and, in particular, what powers of restraint did the hereditary chamber have? There was the question of classes as wealth-holders and income recipients. Were the Liberals acting as the party of the bourgeoisie, now, at long last, ready to consolidate their victory over the landed class, at the same time protecting themselves from the rising challenge of the working classes by undertaking expensive new social programmes?

The budget was rejected by the Lords. The Liberals were victorious in a new general election in January 1910, though the Tories won back 100 seats. The Liberals, backed by Labour, presented their budget again, only to have it thrown out for a second time by the Lords. Lloyd George at this point tried for a grand coalition of parties to seek agreed solutions to all the great outstanding problems, including Ireland, defence expenditure, the land question and the tariff controversy, but there was insufficient will and trust. Matters reached the point at which the new King, George V, as William IV had done in 1832, agreed to swamp the House of Lords by creating hundreds of new peers, doing so on the nomination of Asquith the Liberal Prime Minister. After a further general election in November 1910, as required by King George, the Lords finally capitulated. Under the Parliament Act of 1911 the Lords, as well as having their delaying powers reduced to two years, were stripped of all control over money matters. This enormous step placed the whole of the wealth and income of the population at the disposal of the elected chamber, leaving the hereditary chamber powerless in this matter. This in turn ultimately meant the full exposure of incomes and wealth to the electorate and to the competing party bids addressed to it.

The budget of 1909 was carried by the new powers of the Commons to become law in May 1911. As an aspect of Lloyd George's radicalism it is to be set beside the adoption of old age pensions in 1908 and unemployment and health insurance in 1911.[1] Taken together they represent his attempt to head off the prospect of conflict with the working classes.

9. *The further regulation of business organisation and conduct; self-regulation*

With respect to the control of capital, employers and managers, the state produced an increasingly elaborate code of company and business law which defined standards of conduct and disclosure. But it also, by the concession of limited liability, progressively increased the power of business to attract capital and to expand its operations. Company law was, indeed, extended more or less in step with the needs of commerce and industry, legitimising their growth and changes in their organisational forms.

By 1914 many of the largest British firms raised equity capital by a public issue of shares on the stock exchange. This was especially so in banking, insurance, transport and in various capital-intensive industries. But down to 1914 most medium and small firms did not

1. See chapter 12, section 13; chapter 13, sections 1 and 7 below.

feel the need to incorporate under limited liability. No obligations toward the workers were, of course, prescribed by company law beyond due discharge of employment contracts, though firms had to accept the step-by-step strengthening of the legal position of the unions.

Driven by the economies of scale, and at the same time seeking to minimise the risks that scale involved, firms in various sectors of industry were beginning to generate greater control of their situation by moving in the direction of monopolistic market regulation. This involved agreements through trade associations, together with amalgamations; there were powerful incentives to seek to control sources of materials or markets for products by means of vertical or horizontal integration. These tendencies were strong in iron and steel, in building materials, in salt, in chemicals and other industries. While Germany officially blessed cartels (essentially market-regulating agreements), and the United States attacked the 'Trusts', governments in Great Britain, in spite of a good deal of discussion, took no action either way. But there was public apprehension as to the implications of the trend toward size and market control. Large firms might well seek to destroy competitors, thus behaving in a way so long resisted by the common law of England, acting in restraint of trade. Their defence would be that they were acting in the interests of efficiency, made possible by the creation of orderly markets, and were serving the general good by so doing. Left-wing critics became increasingly vocal against monopoly, especially the Fabians.

There can be no doubt that much German cartel building had as a major objective the consolidation of business power over the economy. British industrial combines were fewer and weaker, with more limited aims: they were concerned with countering innovative rivals as in the alkali manufacture, fighting off restrictive legislation as with the brewers, or coming to terms with large-scale foreign rivals as in tobacco.

But there were stirrings of a British business consciousness and the first moves toward collective identity. In 1898 the Employers' (or British) Parliamentary Council was formed to take action with respect to any Bills introduced into parliament affecting the interests of trade, of freedom of contract and of the employers' relations with labour. But the effort to organise British business in this way was premature: a large part of it stood aloof from the Council. A

Manufacturers' Association of Great Britain was formed in 1905. At a different level, however, employers' organisation thrived: by 1914 there were some 1,200 employers' associations in Great Britain, the Association of Chambers of Commerce of the United Kingdom (f.1860) had a membership of 109 Chambers by that year, and the Chamber of Shipping (f.1887) had pretty general coverage. But such bodies as these had achieved only very imperfect market control and their access to the ear of government was very limited.

There was a healthy and perhaps inevitable aspect also to the amalgamation movement, as larger and more efficient enterprises were formed from smaller ones. There was a striking series of mergers among the English banks, ostensibly producing a stronger financial system. Indeed the complexity of the problem of state intervention in business, as the Americans had discovered, was very great. The fear of doing the wrong thing, together with the belief that it was not the business of government, precluded any attempt in Britain to use the state to stop the market system generating monopoly positions. Successive governments lacked a theory of the firm that would guide them in legislation; no less important, public opinion on the matter was not strong enough to force them to seek one. The competitive market system could thus accelerate its own impairment.

At the same time it could be argued with much plausibility that there was a range of factors limiting monopoly. The principle of substitution under which consumers could choose products not subject to monopoly manipulation would act as a control on price rises of many goods, and the inherent difficulties of maintaining agreement as to selling quotas would make much control transitory. Moreover in Britain, with its early industrial start, there were a great many family firms with little interest in amalgamation; indeed this may have acted as a disincentive to the development of the higher management skills, thus prejudicing Britain in her competition with the USA and Germany. Finally, Britain had no tariff, that prolific mother of monopoly.

As to the railways, the state, unable either to leave the prices of carriage of goods to the market, or to set general principles to govern such prices, handed the matter to a body of reasonable men, namely the Railway and Canal Commission set up in 1894.

At the fringes of the Edwardian money market there was much

dubious activity. This was partly the result of the fact that London, as the centre of the world's money transactions, attracted an enormous supply of funds whose owners were eager to make money beyond modest, safe returns. But it was inconceivable that the state should seek to regulate the complex and delicate mechanisms involved in the placing of private funds. The socialist critics of capitalism were not slow to suggest that at the heart of the nation's economy was not a rational system for the allocation of the nation's resources, but a casino.

10. The state and the economy by 1914

By 1914 the British economy was somewhat curiously composed. The three great sanctities of Gladstone's time still stood, namely a 'free' monetary system based upon the gold standard with a minimum of state intervention, an open trading system free of tariffs and a fiscal system under which the budget was kept more or less balanced taking one year with another. In consequence of these three forms of non-intervention the state continued to be Gladstonian in a fourth and fifth sense. It accepted no responsibility for the growth of the economy or its stability, and had nothing to do with the structure and location of industry.

But action had been taken that threatened this passive view of the state. Spending at the national level had increased significantly, in response to the demands for more and more costly defence and welfare provisions. New principles of taxation, of great potential potency, had been adopted, involving a commitment to operate upon the pattern of wealth and incomes in a redistributive way. Governments were on the one hand asserting that the state should remain passive in relation to the economy, and yet were being pushed into economic intervention as a by-product of their own need for income for the purposes of war and welfare. At the local level advanced urbanisation had brought into being a new range of functions for government, a response to pressing social needs that could no longer be treated minimally.

10

Land and rule in England, Wales, Scotland and Ireland

1. The divisive issues: the land, class interests and nationalism

The question of national identity scarcely arose in England; the Englishman, secure in his own country's dominance, tended to see the nationalism of others in the British Isles as a manifestation of irrationality, likely to bring barriers and conflict. In Wales nationalism began to revive in the 1860s; in Scotland it accelerated in the 1880s. In Ireland it was to become the most difficult of all issues, confounding the entire British system of politics.

2. The land question in England

There had for generations been a tradition in England of radical attack on the landed interest, that embodiment of the principle of private property; indeed it went back to the Levellers of the seventeenth century if not earlier. By the later 1870s the question of 'landed monopoly' was moving forward again on the political scene. There was a demand for 'free trade in land', namely that the legal constraints on the land market should be removed. By a range of devices[1] the landed families had secured and indeed strengthened their position. The 'New Domesday Book' of 1876 suggested that some 4,200 men owned half the land of England. The reformers believed that a change at this level would bring about a better political and social structure. England was virtually without peasant proprietors. There were enough landed estates badly run to justify the charge of inefficiency and idleness.

The landed men, on the other hand, justified their position by their notion of themselves as a paternalistic land-owning class

---

1. See chapter 5, section 12 above.

presiding not only over the countryside but also over the nation. Moreover they were not a closed caste; men who had become wealthy in trade or industry had always been able to acquire land (in spite of the legal system), and to join over the generations the older families. Many benefits flowed to the owners of land. Not least of these was patronage: the landed class were accused, with some justice, of placing their sons in public posts, doing so in spite of the introduction of the examination system into the civil service in 1855. The aristocratic principle was indeed being spread over the empire through the Foreign Office and the colonial service just when it was being challenged in the metropolitan country.

The landed interest sustained a series of heavy blows: there was the Reform Act of 1884 enfranchising the farm labourer, the setting up of the county councils in 1888, Harcourt's inheritance tax of 1894 and Lloyd George's proposed land tax of 1909 (the aspect of the budget most responsible for the intransigence of the landlord-dominated House of Lords). There was also the progressive encroachment into the position of landlords in Ireland ending in their virtual disappearance,[1] and the agricultural depression bringing a collapse of cereal rents (though the landed families enjoyed a cushion of urban rents and miscellaneous investments).

A section of the middle class urged that the state should be used for a direct attack on landed property, based upon moral principle rather than ad hoc adjustment, insisting that the landowners' claims rested on nothing but 'force and fraud'. So too did parts of the labour movement, especially after the four visits to Britain in the 1880s made by Henry George (1839–97) the celebrated American land reformer, author of *Progress and Poverty* (1879). The middle-class advocates of an attack on landed property saw it as a means of spreading individual ownership of property; for the labour side of politics it had the potential for a form of socialism. But for many other members of the middle classes a generalised attack on landed property based upon an absence of moral right held frightening implications for property in general.

A series of particular interventions into land-holding was made. There were Agricultural Holdings Acts in 1875 and 1883, passed under pressure from the Farmers' Alliance, in order to implement

---

1. See section 5 below.

the tenants' rights to the improvements they made. The Ground Game Act of 1880 made the landlords share with their tenants the right to take hares and rabbits. The Settled Land Act of 1882 gave the tenant-for-life the full management of the land he worked, as if it were his freehold. The Allotments Act of 1887 and the Smallholdings Acts of 1892, 1907 and 1908 gave state aid in the form of loans, under county council administration, to those wishing to acquire small plots, though the number of smallholders thus established was small. These enactments were the sum total of land reform in England; land law remained largely as it had always been, in spite of the setbacks received by landowners on other fronts. Their fate lay in the fields of the franchise and taxation rather than in a direct attack on their tenure. The budget of 1909, with its increased death duties, land tax and tax on undeveloped land, made this clear.[1]

3. Wales: nationalism frustrated

In Wales from the 1860s there was the beginning of an assertion of national consciousness. It was based on the concept of *Gwerin*, namely that the Welsh people had a real and abiding identity, sharing the same language, way of life and system of values from time immemorial. With this went the belief that the true Wales was a community of equals, owing allegiance only to God. As in Ireland, there was in Wales an imposed and alien Anglican Church, allied with an English-based landed class. This was the setting in which Lloyd George grew up and upon which he based his early career.

In 1896 a Royal Commission on the Occupation of Land in Wales reported: it split on the question as to whether there should be a land court on the Irish (1881) and Scottish (1886) models, with the result that nothing was done. But in that year there was a concession in the direction of education: the Welsh Intermediate Education Act provided for a new range of secondary schools, to be supervised by a Central Welsh Board. In 1907 a Welsh Department was set up at the Board of Education in London. The long fight for the disestablishment of the Church of England in Wales ended with the Welsh Church Act of 1914, becoming effective in 1919, with a good deal of the revenues of the church going to secular purposes, especially education.

1. See chapter 9, section 8 above.

These victories reflected the rise of Liberal power in Wales: in the election of 1885, following the Reform Act of the previous year, Wales returned thirty Liberals and four Conservatives. Wales as a national unit thus joined Scotland as a Liberal bastion, a supporter of the Liberal reforms of 1906–14. But it is necessary to distinguish between a loose and general Welsh national sentiment as a force favouring the Liberals, as opposed to Welsh nationalism, just as in the case of Scotland. In the 1880s Cymru Fydd was formed; a movement aspiring to Welsh autonomy. It lapsed when Lloyd George and others of its leaders entered the higher reaches of British politics. The achievements of Welsh nationalism before 1914 were slight, with no real recognition by Westminster of Welsh identity.

4. Scotland: the dilemma of the Highlands, national identity

The land question led in Scotland to a similar, though perhaps more muted, attack on the great estates. But there was a special dimension to the question in Scotland, not very different to that of Ireland. In the Western Isles and the glens of the Highlands lived the crofters, small tenants with no security of tenure, no control of their rents and no title to such improvements as they made. They had a strong sense of identity, sustained by the Gaelic language and the bitter folk memory of the Clearances. They lived amidst great scenic beauty but few natural resources. Even sheep farming, so attractive to the landlords who had carried out the clearances in earlier generations, now provided no great return. The crofters' homes were often 'black' houses, without sanitation, ventilation or water supply, where disease, especially typhus, could easily take hold.

The state had attempted regeneration by a regional development programme in the late eighteenth century;[1] this had long since been abandoned. There was still some support for road building, and the links by sea between the Isles and the West Highlands and the Clyde were subsidised through the postal service, but the official view was still that emigration was the correct solution.

The long arguments over the Irish Land Acts helped to awaken the Scottish crofters to their condition. A Scottish Land and Labour League was formed, similar to the Irish Land League, but stopped

---

1. See chapter 2, section 3 above.

short of Irish violence. Moreover attitudes to the Highlands were changing. They had been rediscovered by Queen Victoria and Prince Albert, and romanticised by the paintings of Landseer. The Highland potato crop failed in 1882, causing some rioting and attacks on rent collectors.

The government's response to the Scottish crofters' plight was the Napier Commission, reporting in 1884. From its consideration of the problem of the Highlands and Islands two lines of action suggested themselves. The one derived from the crofter's relationship with the landlord, leading to the idea of granting security to the tenant by encroachment upon the landlord's position, thus meeting the crofter's sense of justice and confirming him in the continuance of his traditional way of life on his tiny holding. The other possibility was to seek means whereby the old ways of life could be changed so as to make the land more productive and the regional economy self-supporting at some reasonable level of population and standard of living. There was thus a clash between the security of the smallholder and the efficiency of the system he worked, similar to the Irish dilemma.

The Commission tried to combine the two approaches. The Crofters' Holding (Scotland) Act of 1886 scheduled the crofting areas (mainly Argyll, Inverness, Ross and Cromarty, Sutherland and Shetland), awarding the crofters the unique status of tenants in perpetuity (with rights of bequest to members of the family), and rents were to be controlled by a Land Court. On the Irish model, rents were reduced by a quarter to a third and there was much writing-off of arrears. The landlord thus lost his right of eviction or sale, of replacement of a tenant at death and of determining the level of rents. A Crofters' Commission was set up to encourage the enlargement of holdings by consolidation. But it could do little in the face of the almost complete security of occupancy now awarded to the crofter and his family.

A second Royal Commission reported in 1892. It stressed the failure to modernise Highland agriculture. The Congested Districts (Scotland) Act of 1897 was intended to promote efficiency through rationalisation. A Congested District Board was established to sponsor the enlargement of holdings and the creation of new ones, and to encourage crofting-related industries such as weaving and fishing as cash earners. But the crofters' new-found security on the land stood in the way of this development programme. A further effort was made with the Small Landholders' Act of 1911: a Board of Agriculture was set up to sponsor improvement. It also took over the land settlement role of the Crofters' Commission and the Congested Districts Board. The Act inadvertently made it possible for crofters to be absentees, subletting or leaving the land idle.

In 1914 the dilemma of the Highlands still confronted governments. How should the state act in relation to a marginal peasant economy which, though it had long since lost its clan leadership and such coherence as had derived from it, was traditional to a high degree, with its own language and its own Kirk (the Free Church of Scotland), anxious above all to gain security of individual occupancy of the small pieces of land it worked (thus achieving recognition of a long-standing moral claim), but which failed to generate a form of life and a level of incomes that was acceptable? The Highlander was unwilling to abandon his traditional claims of right in favour of any plan aimed at making the township and the region viable by the consolidation of holdings.

Meanwhile Scottish nationalism was showing its first signs of re-emergence as a cultural and political force. From the 1880s there were those who wished to assert a Scottish identity, both in its own terms and as against the English. A realisation was dawning in some quarters of the extent to which Scotland had been assimilated to English ways and to the empire. There was, also, a sharing in the feeling developing in parts of Europe that advanced industrialisation was promoting cultural destruction and perversion; in Scotland, as in Wales, this had the effect of causing some people to look back in the hope of recovering old values. There were fears that the Gaelic culture of the Highlands, with its distinctive language, might disappear. As to Scots law, it was becoming apparent to the percipient that any body of law which relies upon an external court as its final arbiter (as Scots law related to the House of Lords) is bound to be weakened over time as decisions were taken without cognisance of or sympathy with a very different legal tradition. In education, under the senior civil servants responsible for Scottish schooling, Craik Sellars and Sir Henry Craig, the men who implemented the Scottish Education Act of 1872,[1] did a good deal to anglicise Scottish education.

1. See chapter 8, section 4 above.

The main element of the Scottish economy, namely the industrial west, had become both heavily dependent upon world trade and economically integrated with the rest of the United Kingdom. The industrial labour force was not susceptible to appeals to nationalism. Governments at Westminster had always known that it was an unprofitable business to offend the Scots, with the result that much legislation, especially in the social field, was embodied in separate Scottish statutes. The Liberals, dominant in Scotland since 1832, had considerable power to promote legislation when they were so moved. In 1884–5 Scotland secured parliamentary representation in proportion to her population.

The accumulation of separate Scottish legislation was so great by 1885 that an Act of that year provided for a Scottish Secretary; by this and the amending Act of 1887 there was transferred to the Scottish Secretary a wide range of responsibilities, including those for law and order, education, poor relief, public health, local government and fisheries. The responsibility for many of these functions continued to be entrusted to a set of Boards, as in the past, but with the Scottish Secretary now appointing their members and supervising their work instead of the Home Secretary. This separate 'civil service for Scotland' continued to be located in the Scottish Office in Dover House, Whitehall. The Scottish Grand Committee (the Standing Committee on Scottish Bills) was begun in 1897.

These steps did not satisfy those concerned with Scotland's identity: a Scottish Home Rule Association was founded in 1886. Meanwhile the General Assembly of the Church of Scotland was moving clear of its old preoccupation with doctrinal conformity and was beginning to constitute itself a kind of surrogate parliament. It had long been concerned with social questions, especially the poor law and education; this kind of involvement extended with a Committee on Social Work of the General Assembly from 1904.

5. Ireland: the liquidation of landlordism and the Home Rule contest

Ireland combined the land question and nationalism in its own peculiarly intensive way. The civil disabilities of Catholics had been removed, and the Land Act of 1870 was an attempt to improve the position of the Irish peasant–tenantry.[1] But the concessions always

---

1. See chapter 6, section 8 above.

lagged far behind Irish aspirations. Moreover with a home rule group in the House of Commons from 1880, obstructionism could operate at the heart of British policy making. Even more serious in a sense was the increase in direct action in Ireland. The Fenians and a range of secret societies were increasingly active; from 1879 they were joined by the Land League. It adopted the tactic of boycotting, that is ostracising any landlord guilty of evicting his tenants or otherwise abusing them: in this way a formidable campaign was mounted against the landlords. This was more effective than the older violent methods, causing a striking fall in evictions.

In 1880 Mr Gladstone became Prime Minister for the second time. Ireland at once engaged his attention. Two Acts were passed in 1881 – a Coercion Act, giving the civil authorities greater powers, and a Land Act. The latter embodied the 'three F's', namely fair rents, fixity of tenure and freedom for a tenant to sell his occupancy. Land Courts were set up to implement the Act. The landlord was now reduced to being a mere receiver of rents, on terms regulated by the state in favour of the tenant. To those who wished to buy the land they worked the state would lend three-quarters of the price (as set by the Court), repayable over thirty-five years. This provision was, however, little operated, largely because of the inability of tenants to find the necessary one quarter capital. The government extended its efforts to find a settlement of the Irish problem in general. But it was frustrated by the murder in Phoenix Park in Dublin in 1881 of the Irish Secretary and the Under Secretary by a group calling themselves 'The Invincibles'. A new Coercion Act followed.

The Tories, resuming power in June 1885 under the great English landowner Lord Salisbury, passed the Ashbourne Act, giving much more generous terms to the Irish peasants in acquiring their land, advancing the whole sum and making it repayable over forty-nine years. The peasant could now acquire his land by paying the equivalent of some 70% of his former rent. But both the Tories and the Liberals were now badly split over the Irish question.

Gladstone became Prime Minister for the third time in December. He declared for Home Rule, bringing in his 1886 Bill. It provided for an Irish parliament, with its own executive in Dublin. But certain powers were reserved to Westminster, namely those necessary to preserve a federal unity within the United Kingdom: these were matters affecting the crown, defence and foreign relations, together with a delimitation of fiscal powers. There remained the question of continued Irish representation at Westminster, the classic dilemma of British devolution. The Bill was accompanied by a scheme of land purchase that would have bought out pretty well the whole landlord interest in Ireland, passing the soil to those who worked it. Night after night the aged Gladstone (he was seventy-seven) fought for his Bill in the Commons, defending it clause by clause, struggling to cut through the problem of Ireland by handing over its domestic affairs to an Irish parliament. But the Tories, the Ulster MPs and elements of his own party combined to throw the Bill out by 343 votes to 313. The Tories returned to power, to rule for twenty years except for a brief interval. This came in 1892–5; in 1893 the aged Gladstone succeeded in forcing his second Home Rule Bill through the Commons, only to have it defeated in the Lords. It marked the end of his career.

The Tories, rejecting any devolution within the United Kingdom, made land purchase the centre of their Irish policy. There were Land Acts in 1891 and 1896. It was Wyndham's Act of 1903 that in effect brought an end to landlordism in Ireland, doing so on terms that both landlords and tenants found acceptable. But such a step, important though it was, did not solve the problems of Irish agriculture. As in England and Scotland, Irish farmers were hit by agricultural depression in the 1880s and 1890s as the cheap cereals of the new world reached Europe. The trend to cattle-raising was accelerated, but even this could not save much of the rural population from poverty.

A major operation was needed on agricultural efficiency: this was now the real 'land problem'. The government made a limited attempt in this direction from 1891 with a Congested Districts Board, financed mainly from the funds confiscated from the disestablished church. The Board sought to improve the infrastructure by building harbours; it assisted the fisheries, sponsored cottage industries and sought to improve agricultural methods. The Board represented, indeed, the return to regional development policy, last practised in the eighteenth century in Scotland.[1] In both cases regionalism was provoked by the need for pacification.

But the terms for peace and tranquillity in Ireland had now changed. Though one of the fundamental historical grievances had been removed, namely Anglo-Irish landlordism, a consuming desire

1. See chapter 2, section 3 above.

to assert an Irish identity had been generated in the course of the long struggle. The self-esteem of Catholic Ireland had been long and deeply affronted; the terrible memory of the wrongs done in the countryside over so many generations would not pass away. But to compound the tragedy the irresistible urge in Catholic Ireland to be separate, to assert an intrinsic identity, was matched by a no less equal determination in the Protestant north to be part of Britain, to be loyal to the memory of the victory of King William over the Pope in the seventeenth century and to reject a Catholic ascendancy enshrined in a Dublin parliament. Each side set about providing the other with martyrs, the betrayal of whose blood would be unthinkable. On both sides the young stepped forward to fight the battle inherited from the old.

From 1911 the Liberals in the House of Commons were in thrall to the Irish Nationalist Party, needing its votes in order to be able to govern. In a highly troubled time Ireland became the most pressing issue in Britain, for it called in question the basis of the state itself, just as the struggle over the House of Lords had done. Indeed the votes of the Irish nationalists had been necessary to carry the Parliament Act of 1911. Moreover that Act deprived the Lords of its power to veto Irish Home Rule, placing the matter of Ireland at the disposal of the Commons. The Conservative Unionists had lost three general elections in a row; they exploited Ulster's hostility to assimilation to an independent Ireland as a political weapon against the Liberals.

Asquith, the Liberal Prime Minister, could not avoid taking up the challenge that had twice defeated Gladstone. He introduced the third Home Rule Bill in 1912, its operation to be delayed for six years. It envisaged Home Rule not only for Ireland, but for Scotland, Wales and even England. The government, backed by the Irish nationalists, could not be defeated in parliament. One response remained for those who were hostile, namely to support Ulster resistance, to the point of arming that part of Ireland. Sir Edward Carson (1854–1935) organised the Ulster Volunteers, and Bonar Law (1858–1923), leader of His Majesty's Conservative Opposition, supported this para-military force. The British army itself was divided, having a good many Ulster officers unwilling to coerce the north. The south formed the 'Irish Volunteers'. Civil war seemed dangerously close. The Bill was passed by the Commons in 1914. But with the outbreak of war the government put the matter into suspense. The United Kingdom entered the fight against Germany with a deep internal division between Ireland and England.

11

The emergence of a public sector, chiefly at the local government level

1. The state and the public sector

The central government continued to own and manage the Post Office and the telegraphs, together with the naval dockyards and the arsenals;[1] from 1912 the Post Office acquired an effective monopoly of the telephone system. There were two additions to the business role of government, both of them involved in foreign policy. One was the acquisition by Disraeli in 1875 of shares in the Suez Canal Company sufficient to control it, giving Britain mastery of this great link to India and the Far East. Secondly, the British government was from 1911 in search of an oil policy, involving it deeply in the politics of Turkey and the Middle East.

Oil had become a vital concern for Britain's Admiralty because of the need to have a secure supply for the navy. Winston Churchill (1874–1965) became First Lord of the Admiralty in 1911; he committed the navy to conversion to the new kind of oil-burning marine engines. Mesopotamia and Persia offered the best prospects for an oil supply. In 1914 the British government, after much complex negotiation by the Foreign Office, acquired a majority shareholding in the Anglo-Persian Oil Company.

Oil indeed in a sense epitomised the new struggle for world resources that was to characterise the new century, drawing British governments into extensions of their diplomacy and informal empire and bringing the state and business into a new close (though often covert) collaboration. The resources of South Africa in the form of diamonds and gold and the business interests involved had already drawn British governments into heavy involvement with

---

1. See chapter 1, section 3 above.

southern Africa. To keep the state and business apart in the final imperial efflorescence was impossible.

At home voices were beginning to be raised urging the nationalisation of certain industries: they came from the Fabians, members of the Labour Party and some unions. But no substantial and sustained body of opinion embraced such ideas. The central state had by 1914 taken very little under its direct ownership and control.

But it had taken very real powers over the local authority sector. These the government exercised in three ways – by prodding local authorities into action, by restraining them and by giving them optional powers. Where heavy capital investment was involved the central government was in control through its powers over local government borrowing.

Central government and local authorities thus constituted a dual system. At the centre the problem was to determine the national interest in terms of necessary provision. This was divisible under four principal heads, namely communal welfare facilities (of which water supply and sanitation were the most important), employment measures, public utilities (chiefly gas, electricity and tramways) and urban redevelopment.

There was, especially with the utilities and urban redevelopment, a third party to the relationship, namely private enterprise. It had been the pioneer in many directions, exploring the potential and experimenting with techniques; it would not willingly be displaced. The problem for the state was, therefore, to arrive at an optimal combination of three principles – central surveillance, local initiative and free enterprise.

2. Local government: its politics, functions and finance

The extension of the functions of local government was in the main the outcome of specific local initiatives, with all their vigour and variety. There were, of course, attempts to impose compulsion and conformity from the centre, as with the poor law, health and education, but these the local authorities could resist or modify in execution without too much difficulty. But from the 1890s, with a further great extension of the local government role, the power of the centre over the periphery grew. Yet the periphery did not capitulate. By the 1890s local governments had formed associations so as to co-ordinate their actions and to strengthen them in their dealings with central government. As government grew, officials at both local and central levels built their empires and constructed their spheres of influence.

Local government became increasingly organised on the committee principle, with the business being pre-arranged before being passed through the full council. Preliminary discussion of this sort, with a view to arriving at consensus and containing the more outrageous dissidents, became, as the activities of local authorities increased in complexity, a necessary condition for reconciling representative government with effective action. But it meant, on the other hand, the growth of caucus power and the danger of corruption. The Municipal Corporations Act of 1882 prescribed that a business contract with a municipal corporation disqualified the maker of it from sitting on the council. But no mention was made of directors of limited liability companies, so that the rule became more and more irrelevant.

London posed a unique problem. It was far and away the largest conurbation in Britain. But it consisted of a great number of separate jurisdictions for different purposes, including boroughs, poor law authorities and the Metropolitan Board of Works (f. 1854 to tackle the problems of sanitation and street improvement). The historic Corporation of the City of London, with its obstructionist attitude, bore a great deal of responsibility for this continued confusion and inefficiency. In consequence the London boroughs had fallen behind the provincial cities in the provision of public services, even of the most basic kind; a sort of urban impotence prevailed in the world's largest city. The first attempt to provide a unified government came with the formation of the London County Council in 1888. Between 1892 and 1905 Sidney Webb and others used the framework of the LCC to rationalise the plethora of London bodies into a functioning whole, providing its servants with a ladder of preferment and achievement such as would keep the metropolis working effectively, and at the same time bring to its service men of talent. This was perhaps the greatest achievement of Fabian socialism. The national government looked on with some misgiving at this metropolitan giant, within whose jurisdiction stood parliament itself. For it could be made the basis for large-scale collectivist experiments. The Metropolitan Police continued to be under the jurisdiction of the Home Secretary.

With the extension of local functions the problem of finance became pressing. Three formulae were possible: each local authority could rely on its rating revenue (the tax on property values within its boundaries), local authorities in general could be made by the central government the recipient of assigned revenues (e.g. specific taxes raised by the state) or the government could award Exchequer Grants or grants-in-aid.

The basis of the local government system continued to be the rates. This meant that local activities were very much subject to the approval of ratepaying voters. In addition, local authorities could only spend money on new projects when authorised by Act of Parliament. Moreover there were enormous differences between rich and poor localities. From the 1890s advanced Liberals pressed for drastic reform of local government financing so that the poorer might be aided by redistributive devices such as assigned revenues or grants.

Successive governments did indeed vary the formula. For example, when from 1865 the central government required minimum standards in borough and county police forces (enforced by inspection), Exchequer Grants were made available to assist in this. In 1889, a year after the establishment of county councils, ad hoc grants of this kind, broadly speaking, were abolished. Instead the government set up a separate local taxation account to which certain revenues were assigned, including the licence duties for public houses and one-half of the probate duty. In this way Goschen, the Chancellor, provided local authorities with independent and buoyant sources of revenue in augmentation of their rates. He did so in an attempt to release local authorities from dependence upon central government through Exchequer Grants, and thus to invigorate local government. The revenues on wines and spirits were assigned in 1890 by the government to local authorities to assist in financing technical education.[1] But grants-in-aid reappeared in 1896 with monies to assist the cultivation of agricultural land; in 1902 the new Local Education Authorities were similarly supported. Governments, just as they refused to be themselves confined to a single tax formula (for example the income tax), also fought shy of a single formula for the augmentation of local

1. See chapter 13, section 4 below.

authority incomes. They preferred the flexibility and sometimes the obfuscation of pluralism.

On the side of capital works the Public Works Loans Act of 1863 had set up the Public Works Loans Board, responsible for making advances to local authorities. Moreover the cities and counties could, with Treasury permission, go direct to the money market and borrow. Liverpool Corporation led the way in 1880; by 1910 local government in the United Kingdom had a debt of £600 million, much of it serviced by productive enterprises. By such borrowings local authorities could extend their planning from short term to long.

3. Unemployment measures

Unemployment was, in a sense, a local affair, for the men without jobs were, of course, distributed on a regional basis, accumulating especially in the large cities. The able-bodied unemployed had always been the principal worry of the poor law guardians. The central government occasionally turned its mind to giving local authorities powers to finance job creation through the rates; the Public Works Act of 1863 had authorised loans to local authorities on the security of the rates to promote drainage and other labour-absorbing works. The Local Government Act of 1888 gave powers to local authorities to reduce unemployment by subsidising emigration, though not one authority so acted. The Unemployed Workmen's Act of 1905 authorised, but did not compel, local authorities to finance job creation from the rates, but few did so.[1] Local government was clearly unwilling to ease the problems of the poor law guardians at the expense of the rates, and central government did not think it proper to provide the means out of general taxation. As more workmen began to enter local councils after 1888, displacing middle-class members, there was less tenderness about burdening the rates.

4. The new utilities: municipal trading and municipal socialism

But the main battle affecting the public sector at the local level was over the provision of new services, especially gas, electricity and

1. See chapter 12, section 10 below.

tramways. Should the local authorities go into business in these directions, ousting the private companies and conducting monopoly undertakings? The expression 'to municipalise' began in the 1880s; heated debate extended through the 1890s to the 1900s. It was a curious mixture of arguments, including the need for efficiency in the administration of units, the problem of how to control natural monopolies, the case for directing the profits from such enterprises into the municipal coffers in relief of the rates, and the arguments, based on a general philosophy, for socialist ownership and operation. The debate was conducted in the provincial cities and in London, and was adjudicated piecemeal by parliament by its passing, amending or rejecting specific private bills coming from both local authorities and private companies. By 1900 over 300 municipal boroughs had assumed some sort of trading function.

The principle of giving the state the option to acquire enterprises was extended to the local authorities in the Tramways Act of 1870. The Electric Lighting Act of 1882 provided for the setting of maximum prices to be charged by companies, and for the option of purchasing them by local authorities after twenty-one years; the Act of 1888, in order to remove what was argued to be a discouragement to private investment, doubled the period to forty-two years.

Long and bitter battles were fought over the acquisition of private companies, often centring upon the price to be paid. The struggle over gas was largely over by the end of the 1870s, with the local authorities victorious. The gas companies fought hard, but their failure to extend supply to meet social need had become notorious. For in the provision of such a facility the formula for maximum profits was to keep supply well within the areas of denser population, not extending it to provide a wider service. But the fact that many boroughs had acquired or built gas undertakings sometimes made such authorities less anxious to enter upon the new challenge of electricitiy supply confronting them from the late 1890s onward. Bradford was the pioneer of civic electricity in 1895.

Moreover there was the problem of the size of spatial units appropriate to each function: the provision of gas, water and electricity were governed by different technologies. These could change, especially in the explorative stage; electricity supply was passing through this phase when the argument concerning private versus public ownership was at its height.

The approach of the business man, like Joseph Chamberlain, was free of generalised theory. It was to get things done in the most effective way. It became increasingly obvious that this lay through public ownership. In many cities, following the examples of Birmingham and Glasgow, business men developed a strong civic consciousness, energising their practical sense. This mixture of pragmatic attitude and action converged with the programme proposed by the advocates of socialism, who saw the extension of public ownership and operation as good in principle.

Though local government units might be appropriate to water and gas, electricity was another matter. Once it became possible to transmit it over great distances, the need arose to think in terms of larger units. Indeed the private suppliers staged a considerable come-back in the late 1890s and early 1900s with schemes conceived on a regional basis; this was largely a victory over the resistance of the municipalities. By far the most successful electricity undertaking in Britain by 1914 supplied the North-East, namely the private Newcastle-upon-Tyne Electric Supply Co.; it operated the largest integrated power system in Europe. Attempts to extend its principles to London failed because of difficulties as to jurisdictions, party political squabbles within the LCC, and the resistance of the private power companies.

Though the business man and the socialist might find considerable common ground in one city after another, they could not go all the way together. The socialist moved easily from the idea of municipalisation to that of ownership on a national scale; here the business man stopped short. Moreover, even within the municipal context, the business man resisted the idea, favoured by the Fabians, of extending local socialism into a complete system, including fair wages for all local employees, council housing provision, direct works departments, municipal banks, ownership of the docks where present, and so on. The opposition to municipal socialism was most strongly expressed by the Liberty and Property Defence League and *The Times* newspaper. They used the classic arguments against the intrusion of the state into business and property owning, doing so, as the title of the League indicated, by linking, as Adam Smith had done, liberty and property.

Two parliamentary committees considered municipal trading (1900 and 1903), but no statutory principles or practices were laid down. The pragmatic approach of separate private Acts continued.

There was, of course, no question of subsidy for the consumer of the services of gas, electricity and tramways – these were profitable undertakings. The cities did not become the springboard for general public ownership as the Fabians had hoped, but the functioning of local government was profoundly altered by the civic provision of utility services.

5. Shaping and renewing the cities

Yet a further set of problems had arisen to force local government into action and ownership. These had to do with the need to control the form of the cities, to renew already decaying cores, and to act upon the housing supply. These challenges were closely related. But they did not make their impact simultaneously. It was housing and slum clearance that pressed itself first upon the attention of national legislators, beginning with the Torrens Act of 1866 and the Cross Act of 1875.[1] But though local authorities were given powers under Torrens to make owners of insanitary properties improve them, such attempts were largely fruitless. The Cross principle of compulsory purchase and clearance of slums with the intention of resale to private developers had somewhat greater success, but at the cost of making the local authorities owners of property on a considerable scale, much of which was sometimes difficult to sell. In the meantime two municipalities, Glasgow and Birmingham, had embarked upon ambitious schemes for clearing and reshaping important parts of their inner cities. Glasgow ran into considerable difficulties because it took a long time to find developers willing to buy the land it had acquired and cleared; Birmingham's scheme became a much admired model.

The statutory sequence was that health and sanitation needs asserted themselves first; this raised the question of housing; from the problems of slum clearance and housing replacement arose those of town planning. The latter were first entered upon by the Town Planning Act of 1909.[2] Local politicians and administrators came closer to an understanding of the needs of urban life than did central government, but each group of local men thought in the specific terms of their own city.

1. See chapter 8, section 5 above; and chapter 13, section 5 below.
2. See chapter 13, section 5 below.

12

The assertion of the power of labour in industry and politics

1. Conflict or co-operation?

The forty years between 1874 and 1914 saw the emergence of a new relationship between labour, employers and the state. Organised labour sought to extend its control over its role in the mature industrial economy, the business men had to respond to this demand, and the state, itself changing in terms of control and structure, had to find ways of obviating or easing the mounting tensions between two great powers that had developed under its aegis, and which might threaten the basis upon which it rested.[1] What had certainly been important throughout the earlier part of the century, namely the limits to be imposed by the state on labour action, moved to the centre of things, becoming the greatest and most difficult challenge for governments.

Before 1874 stress between labour and capital had been seen largely in terms of the particular firm, or of the industry. By 1914 it could be seen, constantly by a few and occasionally by many, as lying between two great orders of society, capital and labour, being concerned with the general distribution of the product as between profits and wages, and with the power relations this involved. To this set of considerations was related the rate of capital formation and the consequent possibility of raising future productivity by the implementation of new technology; if too much of the current product were to be dispersed in wages, thus impairing the return to capital, would new capital be forthcoming on a sufficient scale? A national question was slowly becoming explicit, namely was the relationship between capital and labour to be seen in terms of co-operation or of conflict, or of some kind of continuous pragmatic compromise presided over by the state?

1. For the general perspective see chapter 7, section 1 above.

At the same time ideological thinking had returned to the trade union movement, largely absent since the first half of the century. Socialist and syndicalist formulae were made available to rationalise the hypothesis of conflict and to sustain a new militancy. By the later 1890s it was customary in a good many parts of the labour movement to make ritual remarks condemnatory of the capitalist system. Even where there was no real revolutionary intention, the convention of denigrating capitalism was firmly established by 1914. But the great bulk of the trade union movement, especially among the more skilled men, was slow to commit itself to radical socialist policies, preferring rather to use improved organisation as a means of exerting pressures on employers for better wages and conditions of work.

2. The judiciary

The judges came increasingly into play both in the interpretive sense and as custodians of the general good. Though governments preferred to leave capital and labour to sort out their differences, the judges could not. For them the law represented the forces of social cohesion; they rejected the view that there should be unrestrained trials of strength in the industrial field, or anywhere else for that matter. For the judges, uncontrolled union power posed a direct challenge to their central concept, namely the rule of law, doing so by placing one category of organisation free of the law, and allowing the power of the organised group of workers to take precedence over the rights of others. At the same time, however, there were cases of interpretation of the law which strongly suggested discrimination against the unions and in favour of the employers.

3. The state and labour: the phasing of interaction

The story of labour and the law between the 1870s and 1914 falls into three phases. There was first the legislation of Disraeli's government in the 1870s, a response to that of Gladstone.[1] Thereafter until the mid-1890s the state was legislatively quiescent. But in this phase the trade union picture, both in organisation and outlook, was largely remade. There followed the third and longest phase, in which first

1. See chapter 7, sections 3, 4 and 5 above.

Tory and then Liberal governments struggled to deal with the new labour assertiveness, backed as it was by the entrance of labour upon the parliamentary scene, together with industrial action unprecedented in form and scale.

4. Disraeli's Acts

The Tories, under Disraeli's leadership, having vanquished the Liberals in the general election of 1874, turned to trade union legislation in fulfilment of one of their implied election promises. They, like their Liberal predecessors, passed two Acts: these were the Conspiracy and Protection of Property Act (1875) and the Trade Union Act (1876). Under the latter the unions were now recognised as voluntary societies with all the rights, freedoms and identity of unincorporated bodies. The Conspiracy Act laid it down that an agreement or combination by two or more persons to do or to procure to be done any act in contemplation or furtherance of a trade dispute between employers and workmen should not be indictable as a conspiracy if such act committed by one person would not be punishable as a crime. The Act rested on the assumption that the immunity against charges of conspiracy that it granted was a limited one, namely that the dispute must be a direct one between given groups of employers and workmen, and in contemplation or furtherance of a specific dispute. Much debate was to develop over the years concerning whether particular trade union actions brought before the courts were or were not objectively in furtherance of the dispute in question or were too remote from that pursuit. But the act also prescribed penalties for conspiracy in another sense, namely where the communal interest was damaged; it tried to distinguish between those actions that were or were not noxious to society as a whole. Thus the notion of conspiracy against the community, in a vague and graduated form, survived. Though threats, intimidation and violence were prohibited, trade unionists had the right to seek to convert non-unionists on the spot to their cause, by giving information concerning their grievances. Conversely, picketing was made equally legal in this sense for those workers seeking to persuade others not to strike. Breaches of employment contracts likely to result in interference with essential public services continued to be illegal.

In sum, by 1876 it seemed that British trade unions had won their fight to exist, to be protected by the law against the effects of their strike actions and to function effectively. The unions assumed that they had been granted immunity from suits for all damages arising from industrial actions undertaken by them. But strike action had to be closely related to immediate industrial ends, there was to be no coercion or putting in fear, and the doctrine of conspiracy survived as a protection for the general public.

5. The new militancy of the 1880s

All this, however, did not bring quiescence. The state of trade union law after 1876 had gone a long way toward meeting the views of the craft unions, with their caution, their careful conserving of funds and their pursuit of defined and limited objectives deriving from their own interests. But the time had come for another element, namely the unskilled workers, to assert themselves. A new unionism was coming to birth in the 1880s, helped by a new, articulate leadership, drawing not upon ideas of respectability but upon ideologies of radicalism. Moreover the law affecting trade unions as amended in 1875 and 1876 had still to encounter testing in the courts. The appearance of a new and more militant unionism and the restraining verdicts of the judges were part of the same atmosphere.

The dock strike of 1889 was a dramatic demonstration of the new phenomenon. The army of unskilled casual labour in the London docks, notoriously abused, was organised for victory, winning its famous 'Dockers' Tanner' (a wage of 6d per hour). A good deal of middle-class support and sympathy was forthcoming. This was a new circumstance, of which legislators and the law now had to take account. For the first time a strike had been organised among low-paid workers in a casual trade, sustained by sympathy from a wide band of society. The dock strike was a portent in another far-reaching and indeed frightening sense. It was the first great demonstration that a strategically placed group of workers, whether skilled or unskilled, could so act as to arrest the activity of a whole community. Reach after reach of London docks stood crammed with idle ships, a new and fearful spectacle, a choking of the city's vital flow. Other strikes confirmed the new militancy. But the employers too had their weapons: they defeated the Amalgamated Society of Engineers by a large-scale lock-out in 1897.

6. The state's search for conciliation

How was the state to act in this new and threatening situation? It could do so by promoting conciliation between the parties, through the interpretation of the law through the courts or by the making of new law.

There was no longer any question of reducing the permissible scope of union action and organisation by statute, for what had been conceded in that direction was irreversible. Statute law was now such that large-scale industrial confrontation between capital and labour could take place within it, without illegality, and there was no prospect of parliament retreating from this position.

The state had now to take a further step: it had to seek means of resolving the differences between the parties. But it could not do so by the implementation of a set of general principles derived from the working of the economy and the society. For these did not exist: the just wage could not be defined in the abstract and then enforced by the state. Instead, after the Report of the Royal Commission on Labour of 1894, the state embarked on the creation of machinery for conciliation and arbitration. Under the Conciliation Act of 1896 the Board of Trade was empowered to investigate the causes of trade disputes and offer mediation; it set up within itself a Labour Department in order to do these things. Previous efforts at legislation along such lines had all been failures – in 1824, 1867 and 1872. For the first time there now existed an arm of government that was to assume a continuous surveillance of labour problems. The Labour Department was to stand ready to be called upon; it was also to provide for voluntary registration of Arbitration and Conciliation Boards. A gifted civil servant, Llewellyn Smith (1864–1945), was placed in charge. Like the Royal Commission of 1894, he emphasised the need for strong organisation on both sides, that would be 'responsible, organised bodies'. He criticised employers (as for example the railway and shipping companies) for their policy of non-recognition. But he was also concerned to stop labour militancy from driving on to a general polarisation of society; he hoped to avoid this by discussion, mutual understanding and reciprocal concession. He and his colleagues were given no powers of compulsion over either side of industry: capital or labour or both could decline their services. The state did not want to take to itself such powers, for fear of involving itself in a direct conflict with labour. Indeed in the great labour disputes of the 1890s the government more than once exerted pressure on employers to enter into negotiation with the appropriate unions.

Inevitably the Labour Department of the Board of Trade, with its mission of conciliation, became a target for the socialist press. The latter argued that the system was dominated by the capitalists and that conciliation was merely a means of perpetuating this situation. Certainly there was no overwhelming enthusiasm on the part of either capital or labour for the Department's services: between 1910 and 1913, of 3,686 disputes 388 were referred, of which 92 were settled by arbitration and 296 by conciliation.

7. The emergence of labour as an organised political force

Meanwhile labour militancy did not abate, but indeed grew. The Trade Union Congress, formed in 1868, became increasingly important as the central forum for organised labour. To industrial action was now added political action. The Labour Representation League had been founded in 1869 to promote the election of working-class MPs. The extension of the franchise in 1884 to rural and mining areas improved the prospects of so doing. In 1893 the Independent Labour Party was formed, with a programme which included an eight-hour day, a legally enforceable minimum wage, full maintenance for the unemployed and the nationalisation of the land and the basic industries.

But there was a good deal of reservation in the TUC about such 'socialist' objectives and the implications they might have in terms of class warfare. This was especially so among the representatives of the craft unions. Nevertheless trade unionists with a socialist outlook won the day, at least in part: in 1899 the TUC resolved in favour of a Labour Representation Committee, though it was left to the individual unions to join the LRC or not. It was formed in 1900, with J. Ramsay MacDonald (1866–1937) as its Secretary. It superseded the League and combined the ILP, the Social Democratic Federation (with its Marxist leadership), the Fabian Society (with its social democratic programme) and a minority of trade unions. The miners and the cotton workers would have nothing to do with the LRC, in which, it was feared, highly articulate middle-class thoughts might well be the dominant element.

Meanwhile difficult questions of party structure and the relationships between it and the TUC had arisen. How was the strength and configuration of the unions, together with their overwhelmingly dominant financial contribution, to be reflected in party affairs? The answer was the trade union block vote, first adopted in 1894, whereby each union carried votes proportional to its membership (or more precisely, later on, proportional to that number for which each union paid the political levy). Through the block vote the unions asserted their power and authority over the Party, faced as they were at the time with a rising tide of socialist sentiment and activity. Such a voting procedure was, however, difficult to reconcile with democratic principles, for it meant that a minority view within a union, however large, was obliterated in the count. Moreover union leaders, armed with their block votes, could become immensely powerful, almost a new set of barons.

8. Further statutory and legal definition of union powers

While organised labour was thus trying to define itself in political and organisational terms, a whole new set of complications arose with respect to industrial action. As the law came to be applied and tested, certain areas of ambiguity were revealed. It was the duty of the judges to say what in their interpretation the law was. As was so often the case with statute, the weakness lay in those matters which had been overlooked or had been left in an ambiguous state. An important aspect now became central: were the unions immune from damages done to non-involved third parties thus affected? The issue went against the unions in the courts in 1893 and 1896, but a majority decision in the House of Lords, the supreme court of the land, seemed to resolve the matter in 1898: it ruled that not only were employers to have no recourse against union action, neither would the general public.

But this exemption of the unions from the consequences of their industrial actions was not yet wholly secure. In 1901 the ruling in the Taff Vale Railway Case was that it was not. The judges in that case held that 'if the Legislature has created a thing which can own property, which can employ servants and which can inflict injury, it must be taken to have implied the power to make it liable in a court'. This was the concept of 'representative action', which made it possible to proceed against an unincorporated association: it implied that damages could be awarded against a union in certain cases. This decision reopened the fundamental question of the vulnerability of the unions for damages, and the right of recourse against them by those injured by their actions. It was a serious blow to union membership. There was strong union pressure to reverse this decision by a further Act of Parliament. Unions that had stood apart from the LRC hastened to join it. The Conservative government refused this final step of totally acquitting the unions of responsibility; the Tories were replaced by the Liberals in 1906.

Meanwhile a Royal Commission on the Trade Unions had been sitting; it reported in 1906. It recommended that the unions be given statutory recognition as full legal entities, that is to say, become corporations, with a consequent end to their legal immunities, but with their benefit funds kept separate from their strike funds and safe from actions for damages. The new Liberal government was disposed to adopt this solution. But the fifty-four recently elected Labour and Lib–Lab members obliged it to change its mind so that the trade unions remained combinations and did not become corporations.

Moreover under the Trades Dispute Act of 1906 the unions henceforth were under no circumstances to be held responsible for torts, that is for civil wrongs for which damages might be claimed. This was to say, in effect, that for this purpose trade unions had no corporate existence, and therefore could not be proceeded against. An individual, however, who committed acts of violence in pursuit of an industrial objective was not exempted thereby, being still subject to the criminal law. Unions were thus, finally, made inviolate against the consequences of their actions in contemplation or furtherance of an industrial dispute. But the notion of conspiracy against the community still lurked in the background.

Two further matters remained, namely the question of picketing and the use of trade union funds for political purposes. Legal decisions handed down in 1896–8 seemed to place new limitations on the right of picketing. The Trades Disputes Act of 1906 reasserted the legality of picketing and extended its legal scope from the giving of information to include the right to attempt persuasion.

211

But it must be peaceful – the fundamental prohibition of coercion was reasserted. The difficulty of defining and interpreting what was peaceful remained.

The unions had for years been spending their funds for political purposes. In 1909 the Osborne Judgment called this practice into question. The House of Lords ruled that because the functions of unions as defined by the existing law did not include the support of a political party, it was *ultra vires* for a union to spend members' money in this way. The state of the law having been thus explicitly declared, the issue lay with parliament. Here the Liberal government, though it had acted briskly enough with its Trades Disputes Act in 1906, hesitated. The issue in one sense, was: should a political party based on labour be endowed with this potentially very large source of revenue? Moreover the unions themselves were not agreed on the matter. Strong minorities among them were opposed to political affiliation and to socialist policies, believing that the role of unions should be confined to sectional pressure for higher wages and better conditions.

The issue was dealt with by the Trade Union Act of 1913. It gave statutory recognition to the right of a union to devote money to political ends, subject to the agreement of a majority of members by secret ballot, the monies to be kept in a separate fund, subject to the rules of the Registrar of Friendly Societies. But individual union members had the right to 'contract out'. In this way the unions were given the power to finance a political party from trade union dues.

9. *The control of immigration*

While organised labour was thus gaining in strength a new aspect of labour supply had received legislative attention. British governments had not had any control of immigrants and their movements since the Aliens Act passed in 1792 and repealed in 1826, intended to limit the influx into Britain of French fugitives from the Revolution. Because Ireland was part of the United Kingdom from 1800, no restrictions were imposed on the entry into Britain of Irish immigrants, allowing the post-famine refugees to flood in, creating immense social problems, especially in the cities, and greatly augmenting the unskilled labour force.

After the European revolutions of 1848 a considerable number of activists took refuge in Britain. Under pressure from continental powers, and fearing the possibility of war, Palmerston in 1858 presented his Conspiracy to Murder Bill in parliament in order to strengthen the law against the activities of alien refugees against European governments. But parliament rejected the Bill. Britain became the great haven for polyglot revolutionaries with their immense variety of ideologies. The holders of almost every form of continental political belief found shelter in England, including Louis Philippe, Metternich, Louis Blanc, Karl Marx, Victor Hugo, Kossuth, Garibaldi and Lenin. In the popular mind the right of asylum was an aspect of the British view of freedom; in the minds of Britain's rulers it was a kind of compliment to the country's stability, deriving from the granting of moderate liberal institutions.

But from the 1880s a different kind of alien was growing rapidly in numbers. These incomers were not revolutionaries, but an oppressed minority. The Tsars of Russia inflicted fearful pogroms on their Jewish subjects; something like 120,000 Jewish immigrants settled in Britain between 1870 and 1914. They tended to concentrate in the large cities, especially in the East End of London, Leeds and Manchester. They were feared by those whose society they entered, because of their strangeness, and because of their immense tenacity and industry, causing a great extension of the sweated trades. Racial or ethnic hostility thus arose in certain working-class areas. Balfour's Conservative government, concerned about these concentrations of bad feeling, passed the Aliens Act of 1905. It was aimed at controlling the entry of destitute or undesirable aliens. But the latter category was very difficult to define. The Act left much to departmental interpretation. The Liberals, coming to power in 1906, did not press its enforcement, leaving it to lapse as the Jewish influx lessened.

10. The refusal of the right to work; the adoption of mild employment measures

The Labour Representation Committee, having won twenty-nine seats in parliament in 1906, quickly changed its name to the Labour Party; it now felt itself in a position to propose legislation on its own account, free of the Liberals.

The most important of such general issues was unemployment. Though the figures available are inadequate, it is clear that the numbers of jobless was growing, so that by 1908 perhaps some 8.5% of the labour force was unemployed. Labour Members of Parliament and others began to formulate the question: what were the rights of such unemployed as against the state? In July 1907 Ramsay MacDonald introduced into the Commons the measure that became known as the Right to Work Bill. It was inspired by the ILP. It proposed two possibilities with respect to unemployed workmen: either the local authorities under central government aegis would provide work for them, or the local authorities would 'provide maintenance should necessity exist, for that person and for those depending on that person for the necessaries of life'. Here was a clear statement of public responsibility for the unemployed, giving them an explicit claim to work, or alternatively to maintenance, as of right.

The Right to Work Bill was the culmination of a lengthy sequence. As early as 1886 Chamberlain's circular from the Local Government Board had recognised that worthy men could find their services unwanted, that searching for work could be futile and that penalties for being jobless could be unjust. It was, wrote Chamberlain, important that local authorities should provide work schemes so that the working classes might not 'be familiarised with Poor Law Relief'. The circular proposed local job-creation programmes to be financed on the rates. There were Select Committees on Distress from Want of Employment in 1895 and 1896, but nothing came of them. Unemployment was kept largely a bipartisan issue as between Tories and Liberals, for neither party saw any real solution, thus reducing the problem to one of amelioration rather than cure.

But Walter Long, President of the Board of Trade in Balfour's government, revived the Chamberlain line of thought of his Unemployed Workmen's Act of 1905. Local authorities were empowered to finance labour colonies[1] and labour exchanges. Towns with more than 50,000 population were authorised to undertake public works to generate employment, chargeable to the rates. Under the Act there was to be a co-ordination of action between borough councils, poor law guardians and charity organisations; the principal outcome of this provision was the London Central (Unemployed) Body. The Act, though well intentioned, could not solve the problem it was designed to meet; local authorities were not enthusiastic in applying

---

1. See chapter 13, section 8 below.

it. The government, at the same time that it passed the Act of 1905, announced a Royal Commission to investigate the poor law and the problem of poverty.[1]

The Right to Work Bill two years later reflected the failure of the Unemployed Workmen's Act. It could be read either as a plea for the further extension of the job-creation programme on a local basis, or it could be interpreted as imposing obligations on the government such that, in order to ensure jobs or maintenance for all, the state would find itself undertaking more and more interferences in the economy, including public ownership. It would, in effect, be committing itself to socialism; at least this was the view taken of it by Asquith the Liberal Chancellor of the Exchequer. He regarded the Bill as an attempt to bring in a socialist commitment under the guise of an ad hoc measure.

Neither a Conservative nor a Liberal government could face such a prospect. Neither, indeed could the newly founded Labour Party, at least with any unanimity. Philip Snowden observed that of the thirty Labour MPs in 1909, twenty-five were sponsored by the trade unions and so were cautious about supporting socialist measures. The other five represented the radical ILP element with its various proposals for the renovation of society.

The Right to Work campaign as such faded from the scene in 1908, having raised implications which even sympathetic men were not prepared to face. A form of the idea, though not the name, was brought back by the Minority Report of the Poor Law Commission in 1909. Therein was argued the case for a comprehensive provision for the unemployed based on a long-term programme of public works. There was also a proposal that trade union funds used to help the unemployed should receive government subsidies. Neither suggestion was adopted. The problem of unemployment continued unsolved.

11. The first concession to the minimum wage, 1909

The state had withdrawn from the setting of wages in 1813–14 with the repeal of the Elizabethan Labour Statute.[2] About a century later, in 1909, it resumed this role, acting on behalf of the sweated trades.

1. See chapter 13, section 6 below.
2. See chapter 1, section 10 above.

The growth of petty manufacturers in the East End of London, accelerated by the influx of refugees from eastern Europe, had been a concern for some twenty years or more. A House of Lords Committee had reported on the Sweating System in 1889, and although the Factory and Workshop Act of 1891 brought about some improvement, nothing was done in the matter of wages. The Webbs had proposed a national minimum wage to the Royal Commission on Labour of 1894: this had already become part of the programme of the ILP adopted the year before. But for any government to contemplate so far-reaching an interference in the labour market and in income distribution was as yet unthinkable. Moreover there was the fear that the enforcement of minimum wages by law would raise the marginal cost of some categories of labour, making them uneconomic and thus generating unemployment.

The Trades Board Act of 1909 set up statutory bodies in a number of trades with the duty of regulating wages. Though its range was initially fairly narrow, being confined to tailoring, shirt making and confectionery, affecting only some 100,000 work people, the Act was a radical measure, involving the state directly in the setting up and regulating of machinery for wage setting. But the state proposed no guidelines as to amounts: each Trade Board was to formulate its own judgment as to what wage was proper.

12. The improvement of the labour market

The Labour Exchanges Act was passed in 1909, William Beveridge (1879–1963), a protégé of Churchill's and author of *Unemployment, a Problem of Industry* (1909), having prepared political opinion and having done the necessary administrative groundwork. The country was soon covered by such exchanges where seekers of labour and seekers of jobs could be brought together. Some trade union leaders were distrustful of them, fearing they might be used to break strikes by supplying blackleg labour. But 'the boy Beveridge' (as the Webbs referred to him) and Winston Churchill (as President of the Board of Trade) were able to provide reassurance, partly by involving trade union officials in the supervision of the exchanges. But it was only with the introduction in 1912 of insurance benefits that the skilled workers really began to use them. The labour exchanges, in addition to their primary function, were then to become the source of most labour data, especially of unemployment, bringing the first possibilities of manpower planning.

13. *Unemployment: the introduction of the contributory insurance principle*

By 1911 unemployment had become a challenge the state could no longer ignore. Four policy choices were open to British governments in dealing with it. The first was to undertake direct measures to generate jobs. But as had been made clear in the debate over the right to work, neither Liberals nor Tories were prepared to enter upon this path. The return to the tariff having been resoundingly rejected in 1906, the Liberals had precluded the possibility of the state being drawn into the inner workings of the economy by this alternative door. The Labour Party could engage in advocacy of job generation in a general way, but it is by no means clear that had it been responsible for government its protagonists would have been so vigorous of speech.

The second choice was that of non-intervention in the economy, accepting its verdict on unemployment, but making the relief of its victims, at a level to be determined, a full charge on the general tax system. But here too there were immense difficulties. The tax proposals of Lloyd George's budget of 1909, confiscatory as they seemed to those who were to pay them, would have had to have been very greatly increased to sustain the unemployed and their dependants. The fiscal difficulties were thus frightening enough, without taking into account the long-standing fears of the effect such a provision might have on wages, the labour supply, the incentive to work and industrial costs.

Thirdly, there was the possibility of some adaptation and amplification of the prevailing poor law system. Here, though much could be done to improve the system it simply could not meet the need for incomes on the scale required.

This left the final possibility, namely a combination of the contributory and insurance principles. Could a contributory insurance system be devised into which workers, employers and the state each paid, to produce a fund out of which support to the unemployed could be provided, doing so on an actuarial basis? Such an arrangement would relieve the government of the need to intervene seriously in the operation of the economy, it would reduce the strain on the tax system to a tolerable level and it would leave the poor law for separate treatment while at the same time removing one of its biggest and most difficult problems (old age having been provided for in the Act of 1908).[1] Such a scheme, in conjunction with the improvement of the labour market through the exchanges, could reasonably be expected to solve the problem of unemployment.

Part II of the National Insurance Act of 1911 initiated such a system of unemployment insurance. The initial benefit to be paid was 7s (35p) per week for a maximum of fifteen weeks. Clearly the scheme provided much less than 'full maintenance', either in amount or in the period of time covered; it was a tiding-over provision, to serve until the economy recovered. It thus assumed a high degree of employment in the long run. To be eligible for benefit a worker had to have been in employment for twenty-six weeks in the previous five years. Dependants were not provided for. Some two and a quarter million workers were covered (out of some ten million), especially in trades where unemployment appeared regularly, such as building, engineering and shipbuilding. No benefits were payable to men sacked for misconduct. Nor were those put out of work by a trade dispute to receive anything from the fund: this reflected the fear that the state might find itself subsidising strikes. Each worker had to make his choice of an 'approved society' (e.g. one of the Friendly Societies, which by 1904 had 5.6 million members and £41 million of assets), through which he or she would receive benefits. On the contribution side, workers and employers were each to provide 2½d (1p) each per week, with the state adding 25% to the sum thus contributed. Under this formula the able-bodied unemployed in certain industries were no longer to be suppliants, but were to receive insurance benefits by established right.

In spite of the limitations placed upon the benefits in terms of eligibility and period of payment, Part II of the Act of 1911 was the most radical step taken by the reforming Liberals. But it was far from being a state commitment to succour the general labour force; it was tentative and experimental, representing the government's estimate

1. See chapter 13, section 7 below.

of the scope and form of action necessary to pacify the electorate. Because of the unpredictability of its operation and implications it seemed right to limit it. Down to 1914 the sums were correct; the unemployment insurance fund in that year was in credit to the extent of some £3 million.

14. The strike movement of 1911–13; syndicalism; minimum wages in coal, 1912

The new unemployment benefit scheme came into being as the economy was passing through its greatest period of industrial unrest since the hungry forties. The first dispute on a national scale came in 1911: it took place among the railway workers. It was the second massive demonstration of strategic power against the community (the first was the London dockers' strike of 1889). It followed and was accompanied by strikes by seamen at Southampton, by London and Liverpool dockers, and by transport workers in various parts of the country. In February 1912 the miners began a national strike for a minimum wage. The stoppage of the mines meant that the sole source of energy for British industry began to fail; workers in other industries were made unemployed and incomeless. In May came another London dock strike. This time the challenge was not directly to the employers, but to the Port of London Authority, an official agency set up in 1908. The struggle was a bitter one: in August the strike collapsed. The miners' and the London dockers' strikes demonstrated the increasing vulnerability of the economy to industrial action, together with the power of the unions and the counter-power of the employers, both highly destructive.

Anarchic and syndicalist ideas found their greatest scope among the railwaymen, the dockers and especially the coal miners. Their industries provided the most favourable conditions for disruption and the evocation of working-class solidarity. The miners were a crucial case. No industry was more basic than theirs. They were an army of men, amounting to well over a million by 1911. There was an essential need for their product, but its price was unstable, with obvious implications for wages. These were, however, relatively high. But the Coal Mines Act of 1908, enforcing the eight-hour day, became operative in 1910, making it hard for the miners working difficult seams to support their families, giving an impetus to the claim for a minimum wage.[1]

It was in the Rhondda Valley of the South Wales coalfield that industrial unrest on a new scale of intensity was detonated. The miners struck in September 1910. This was an unofficial action, reflecting a new militancy, with syndicalism the most widespread of radical influences. Riots took place at Tonypandy. The government was now confronted with a new problem, namely how to respond when a whole community had reached the point of threatening the civil peace, with attacks on the homes and persons of mine managers and magistrates, the burning of power houses, the looting of shops, the beating-up of blacklegs and bitter fighting with the police. In such a situation revolutionary methods made a powerful appeal. Troops were sent to Tonypandy. Though they were used only once, and though there was only one death (from a stray stone or a truncheon), Tonypandy became the founding legend upon which so much subsequent miners' bitterness was to be based. They regarded the government as acting as the agents of the colliery owners. But the Home Secretary, Winston Churchill, with his aristocratic dislike for the mine owners, and General Macready, with his soldier's distaste for men who had put him in a false position, found themselves confronted with every government's primary duty, namely to re-establish order. The strike continued to the summer of 1911. The miners were defeated. But the Lib–Lab alliance had been irredeemably damaged among the miners and the demand for a minimum wage greatly strengthened.

In 1912 came a four-week national strike by the miners; it was a demand for a minimum wage ('five and two', i.e. 5s per shift for men and 2s for boys). The owners objected to the state setting a minimum wage, especially when productivity per man was falling. The government feared that Tonypandy violence might break out in all the coalfields. But so great was the threat of united action by the miners that it made violence unnecessary. The Coal Mines (Minimum Wage) Act of 1912 was quickly passed through parliament. The Liberal government did not, however, grant all that was demanded. It refused to create national minimum wage machinery, but made provision only on a district basis. Moreover it would not set specific

1. See chapter 13, section 3 below.

rates even for the districts, but committed this to a system of twenty-six District Boards. The new militancy was reflected in the influential pamphlet of 1912 by A.J. Cook (1883–1931) and others, *The Miners' Next Step*, in which he proposed that 'The old policy of identity of interest between employers and ourselves be abolished and a policy of open hostility installed.' Unrest continued in 1913, though on a lesser scale in England and Scotland.

In Ireland there was the harsh conflict between the Irish Transport Workers Union and the employers of Dublin. Its eight-month duration and the bitterness and suffering it caused attracted worried attention throughout Britain. It raised the question of sympathetic action on a new scale and in a new form, to the embarrassment of a good many British trade union officials. It brought to a dramatic and searching focus the difference between the older, more cautious leaders and the militant young.

Were the disturbances of 1911–13 simply an extension and intensification of industrial action, or did they represent a revolutionary challenge to the state? Certainly some participants intended them to be. The syndicalist movement played a considerable part in the industrial actions of these years. Though relatively small, its members formed a determined subversive element, seeking through industrial action (culminating if possible in a general strike) to generate so great a confusion that the existing system would collapse. A new order of society, it was believed, could then emerge. Such an order would be based not upon the existing geographical franchise, with its mixture of classes, but upon a kind of industrial parliament. Each industry would be controlled by the workers within it, organised in a single union. Each would send delegates to a national assembly, which would, presumably, perform the co-ordinating functions previously provided by the market mechanism. In this way, it was believed the state would no longer be coercive, because private property in the means of production would be ended. Elements of this programme had been present in the ideas of Robert Owen and in the Grand National Consolidated Trades Union of the early 1830s.[1] Such ideas flourished in France, stemming partly from P.J. Proudhon (1809–65). But they had also their native British characteristics.

1. See chapter 4, section 4 above.

In June 1914 the 'Triple Alliance' was formed, embracing the Miners' Federation of Great Britain, the National Transport Workers' Federation and the National Union of Railwaymen. This was a move toward one single great union as envisaged by the syndicalists. Though suspended by the war, the idea of such an alliance between massive unions did not die. As a first step toward a syndicalist system it was necessary to rationalise the trade union movement. Indeed in 1909 syndicalists were urging that the 1,168 unions in Britain be reduced to fourteen. This would cut out inter-union conflicts and thus increase union power as against employers and the state.

The notion of locating the sensitive points of the industrial system and working to disrupt them by industrial action was, of course, not consistent with a trade unionism that believed in bargaining within the existing system. Indeed to believe in bargaining was in the eyes of the syndicalists to be 'incorporated' into the system, to be made its victim by assimilation to it. Such a view had no sympathy for the fact that the concessions made on the employers' side and by the government were real, and were cumulative and irreversible.

The programme of disruption leading to breakdown had a powerful cathartic attraction for a minority of men who were more frustrated than the rest, giving them the feeling of power that came with obsessional conviction, conspiracy and even the prospect of violence. This provided the self-appointed and dedicated elite needed to organise and sustain such a movement. Such men rejected all classes but their own. They placed their trust wholly in what they conceived to be working-class experience and potential, both to bring about revolutionary action and to consolidate revolution in a new society free of power or coercion. Their idealisation of the working class (whether they belonged to it or not) as capable of discharging these two roles, caused them to pass over the limitations of labouring men and women, as well as the pains and destruction of a collapsed society, together with the ancient problem of the re-emergence of oligarchy and faction. Such men appealed in their simplistic way to the sense of workers' loyalty to their fellows that had been made compelling by earlier industrial conflicts and was confirmed by every new one.

This kind of uninhibited and unqualified (though not always openly public) attack on the state posed an entirely new challenge to government. Such an approach was insulated by its own convictions

222

from any appeal. Moreover it could work within the framework of legality conceded to the trade unions, and it enjoyed all the civil liberties that constitutional government had provided. Never had revolutionaries found a system so open to attack.

Against this, however, were the reservations of the trade union movement and most of its members, making them unwilling to put all to the hazard in favour of disruptive and eventually revolutionary action. They had learned how fearful a thing it was to have a strike lifted out of their hands by the militant minority, and to be faced with unreasoning uproar at any suggestion of a settlement short of total capitulation by the employers.

15. The extension of conciliation

The principles of conciliation and arbitration were anathema to the syndicalists. They saw them as the most blatant and pernicious attempts to assimilate the working classes into capitalism. George Askwith (1861–1942) at the Board of Trade provided a kind of epitome of syndicalist distrust, advocate as he was of conciliation and enemy of conflict. After the railway strike of 1911 a Royal Commission was appointed to study the working of the Conciliation Boards set up fifteen years earlier. A new scheme was introduced in 1912, intended to improve the working of the system. An Industrial Council was established, to settle those strikes in which both sides agreed that it should arbitrate. But however well designed the machinery, it could do no more than facilitate contact, when such contact was mutually desired.

16. The business men's response

British business men had, of course, to confront the great complex of problems relating to labour, and the actions of the state affecting it. It is possible to make a rather crude, yet useful, distinction between those concerned with the older and the newer industries.

Of the older industries, in which problems had grown in a cumulative way, locking the business men into their set of attitudes and the workers into theirs, the most dramatic example was coal. Colliery owners and mine workers had become total prisoners of their respective cultures. Miners had been forced by their condition to seek protective legislation. A large proportion of mine owners, on the other hand, were members of families that had owned mines for decades. They had conducted a prosperous industry for several generations, and while doing so had adopted the economic philosophy of the market, believing as an article of faith that free competition was best for themselves, miners and consumers alike. They were not, on the whole, indifferent to human suffering, though most were comfortably insulated from it. But they did believe that private enterprise yielded the highest standard of living that was possible, given the nature of the industry and the economy at that moment in Britain's evolution. In this way the cultural attitudes of mine owners and miners were each further 'confirmed' by experience, producing a situation in which a solution, mutually arrived at, became ever more remote.

By contrast, there were the business men who operated in sectors of industry that were able to achieve efficiency leading to profitability. Among them were the chemicals and explosives industries (Ludwig Mond, John Brunner, Charles Tennant), soap (William Lever), artificial fibres (the Courtauld family), glass (the Pilkingtons), retail trade (David Lewis), food and tobacco (Cadburys, Rowntrees, Wills), automobiles (William Morris) and oil (Marcus Samuels). These represented the new element among British business men, innovating and renovating, relying largely on their own efforts and responses, and needing no state adjudication between themselves and their workers.

The business of all of these men was strongly paternalistic. They could look after their workers, paying good wages and maintaining good conditions. So much so that, in spite of the great size of their enterprises and the impersonalisation thus promoted, their workers showed few signs of resentment of the despotism that often went with paternalism. Business men of this breed could adopt the attitude of the landed classes, so that their workers were well treated and content, making no challenge to authority and having no wish to take upon themselves the burdens of management.

By 1914 most British business men in either old or new sectors seldom spoke of the market economy as though it had an innate and universal harmony; the notion of divine wisdom and the idea of social Darwinianism were now both muted, for there were too many discordant elements to be explained. Yet confidence in the market was still fundamental to business men, for it was difficult, if not impossible, for them to conceive of any other principle. They, unlike the worker, had the responsibility of running the system, and so were denied the luxury of posing hypothetical alternatives, unlinked by any safe path to the present. Because the worker still had no say in policy making, the autonomy of the firm was preserved at least thus far; in this sense, the business man was still in control.

But he no longer had a confident rationale of what he was doing, no confirmatory theory of economy and society, and no sustaining set of religious and moral beliefs. As a result business men in parliament were without any solution to offer to governments. They sensed that *force majeure* was building up in certain of the unions. Could it be fought down? More precisely, what were the costs and dangers of attempting this? Or could a policy of conciliation be made to work, reinforced by attempts to educate the unions into seeing the limitations of the employers' position? The latter tactic would, of course, involve conveying to the workers the unattractive idea that the system as a whole was not capable of generating higher levels of wages and full employment for everyone, and was at the same time both subject to cyclical instability and obliged to generate a continuous flow of labour obsolescence as it adopted new technologies. Once the socialist or syndicalist idea had been spread among a significant element of the workers that an alternative to the market economy was available that would be free of all these malfunctions, it would become increasingly difficult to persuade the labour force that there was an identity of interest between employers and workers.

17. The state in relation to labour by 1914

By 1914 there had been conceded almost unlimited freedom for trade union formation and action in pursuit of industrial objectives, together with the use of the unions as the financial foundation for a third political party. The unions could not be sued for civil wrong by anybody. Only two legal constraints remained. In law the unions could not coerce other workers by picketing or other means, and they could not strike against the community. But government had refused any generalised right to state-generated work or to the alternative, namely maintenance by the state. Instead there had been instituted a system of limited unemployment benefits on the contributory insurance principle. In addition the state had set up machinery for the conciliation and arbitration of industrial disputes, and had made a notable improvement in the job market with its labour exchanges.

With the growth of the franchise (itself perhaps irresistible), together with the operation of a party system which rested upon competitive bidding for votes, and with the increased vulnerability to labour action of the industrial structure through its own sophistication, it was inevitable that the state should yield ground to the unions. The fundamental problem for governments presiding over a mature industrial economy was taking shape, namely what were the limits and forms of labour power in terms of which the industrial/ parliamentary system could continue to be viable?

On the union side there was a reciprocal set of questions. What further ground should the movement press the government to concede? With an elaborate system of restrictive practices securely established and used to keep up labour intensity and to secure wage differentials in favour of the skilled men, and with a trade union ethos and interest that defined itself against a familiar set of employer opponents, how far was it worth while to adopt radical formulae with which to challenge the fundamental structure of British society?

13

Welfare and the social democratic urge

1. The politics of welfare

The work of various philanthropists, and of the inspectorates, together with the very scale of deterioration in some parts of society which they revealed, led in the 1880s and 1890s to a kind of rediscovery of poverty and 'the social problem'. It inspired the revealing phrase 'the perishing and dangerous classes'. By the later nineteenth century the evangelical urge had begun to undergo a mutation in the direction of humanism; the redemptive passion, though still powerful, had by 1914 assumed a more or less secular form, as embodied, for example, in the Webbs. It generated a new phase of social data gathering from the mid-1880s, led by Charles Booth (1840–1916) and Seebohm Rowntree (1871–1954).

There was a gradual weakening of the assumption that in a competitive system those who lost out were inherently inferior either genetically or through moral failing in the form of a disposition to idleness; but the old notion never wholly departed, and indeed in some quarters continued an active existence. Its chief protagonist was the Charity Organisation Society, founded in 1863; fundamental to the outlook of the COS was a distinction between the 'deserving' and the 'undeserving' poor. The former were the proper concern of charity, the latter were the responsibility of the poor law. As the old century ended and the new one began, the two great political parties and the emergent new one were being increasingly pressed by a miscellany of proposals toward the adoption of a consistent and to some degree comprehensive view of the welfare responsibilities of the state.

But no radical new step was taken until the introduction of old age pensions in 1908.[1] Until that year there was no generalised national

1. See section 7 below.

provision for any category of social casualty. There was the poor law with its tests and humiliations. There was private philanthropy, and the powerful influence of the Charity Organisation Society. There was the support of family and friends. Finally, there was self-help, largely through the savings banks, the co-operative movement, the Friendly Societies (with 500,000 members by 1886, making them larger than the unions) and the industrial insurance companies (with their army of door-to-door collectors gathering in petty sums). Payments to the Societies and the companies were part of the budgets of careful families. These organisations had constituted themselves a national network of collection and payment built into respectable working-class life, and had attracted to themselves men of humble origins as their administrators. Indeed they had become an institutionalised interest, with their own bureaucracy and their own power of parliamentary lobbying.

Working-class attitudes to welfare provided by the state or the local authorities continued to be equivocal down to 1914. There was the view that what was needed was full employment, higher wages and shorter hours rather than state aid. A good many liberals could share this view because it was consistent with self-help rather than state help and did not threaten the freedoms or moral fibre of the workers by making them dependent upon the state. There were working-class objections to the inquisitorial aspects of welfare, with middle-class officials inquiring into family circumstances; there was often a good deal of hostility to the school attendance officers. For one kind of socialist, state power embodied in bureaucrats was an evil. But from about 1900 there was a growing acceptance among the working classes of the need for welfare support. The fear of the state was alleviated to some degree by growing working-class participation in welfare administration through membership of Boards of Guardians and School Boards, and local government activity generally (the property qualification attaching to local government ended in 1893). The rise of the Labour Party added to this confidence. Moreover the prospect of higher wages through union action was seen as not sufficiently immediate or certain. There was, too, the realisation that large categories of working-class people could not in any case be aided through wages.

From the 1890s the more active-minded Liberals had realised that the Gladstonian age of minimal government was passing; the Tories for their part had never been inhibited in their view of the state. At the same time the Liberals were painfully aware of the damage done to their party by Home Rule, and were fearful of further fissures as nonconformist zealots pressed for temperance legislation, disestablishment of the Church of England or other 'fads'. Not surprisingly, Liberal reformers, anxious for a new party image, had been looking for a major unifying issue. There were two contenders for this role. The House of Lords was a marvellous double target, as a source of unwarranted power, resting on unjustifiable inherited landed wealth. The second great matter was the social question: how far should the Liberal Party go in offering a programme of welfare? As has been seen[1] the two issues converged in dramatic fashion between 1909 and 1911.

Within the Tory Party the creative elite had, as with the Liberals, perceived the need for new postures and policies; the dominant figure among them in this regard was Joseph Chamberlain. Both political parties were thus moving toward social reform, each impelled by its own internal dynamics, and each necessarily responding to the bids made to the electorate by the other.

Meanwhile a second great contender for public money, also with its own imperatives, was making its claims. This, of course, was defence. In the new century such demands, especially from the Admiralty as it reacted to the German programme of warship building, were even more pressing. Parties and governments had somehow to place the claims of welfare and warfare against one another, and within these categories seek to get the highest cost-effectiveness (or, more realistically, the highest political-effectiveness). At the same time they had to propose new tax burdens, doing so in such a way as in the short run not to change the general social and political configuration of Britain in an unwanted way.

To all this there was yet a further set of complications. These took a geographical or regional form. The social problem was much more acute in some parts of Britain than in others, centring as it did on the large cities. London was of course the most pressing case, a mass of contained concentration, especially in its East End. By the 1890s there was something approaching crisis in the inner city of the metropolis, where newly apparent social forces operated to concen-

1. See chapter 9, section 8 above.

229

trate the casual labourers, the sweated trades, the drop-outs and the outcasts. By the later nineteenth century there was among the sensitive element of the middle class a profound uneasiness about the great cities, a compound of compassion, guilt and fear. There was too the challenge to remake the interiors of the cities in the physical sense, especially by improving their layout by cutting new streets: this related closely to the question of slum clearance and to the energy, vision and powers of local government.[1]

The social action equation was still a reality.[2] In each area of proposed amelioration there could be statutory action only where the degree of deterioration plus the strength of reformism, acting in mutual reinforcement, outweighed the inertias and the resistances. A good many philanthropists, though not abandoning the voluntarist principle, were moving toward the advocacy of state action in areas formerly thought inappropriate, as in housing. By an interesting paradox the purging of British politics and administration of the corruption of earlier times, one of the great achievements of the high Victorian age, had lessened the general fear of the state, making it a more acceptable vehicle of social policy. As for the working classes, just as with respect to trade union action, they could find no unanimity in their approach to social welfare. Both the middle and the working classes were thus in confusion.

The only general programme offered before 1914 was that of the Webbs, together with their fellow Fabians and those who thought like them on this matter. It was that there should be guaranteed by the state a national minimum below which no one should fall. But this apparent simplification was itself full of difficulties.

2. Public health and national efficiency

Down to 1874 concern with public health continued to focus upon the four traditional aspects of sanitation, water supply, health regulation and the provision of medical facilities. The last of these was in large measure in the hands of the medical profession and the philanthropists; sanitation and health regulation were the concerns of local authorities acting under general statutes. The Public Health

1. See chapter 11, section 2 above.
2. See chapter 5, section 3; and chapter 8, section 1 above.

Act of 1875 was a great consolidating and innovating measure, passed by Disraeli's government (Disraeli in the election of 1874 had laid it down that 'the first consideration of a minister should be the health of the people'). The Act confirmed the division of the country into sanitary districts (begun in 1872), each with its Medical Officer of Health and Inspector of Nuisances, thus requiring national coverage under the aegis of the Local Government Board in London. Unlimited rating powers were given to local authorities for the purposes of the Act. They were also required to maintain, pave and light the streets, and to ensure that domestic drainage was connected with the sewage system. No new house might be built without being provided with running water and internal drainage. Thus was laid the basis of a hygienic revolution, bringing Britain into the modern era. Local authorities were also given powers under the Act to acquire land for parks. They could also buy up or establish gas and water undertakings. In short they could embark upon whole new areas of municipal activity.[1]

A hospital revolution could also be begun under the 1875 Act, for it empowered local authorities to build their own hospitals, financed from rate revenues. There had been voluntarily supported special hospitals from the mid-century; now the local authorities could begin to provide some further facilities on a 'rate-paid' basis. In 1907 came a further Act to supplement and extend that of 1875. A Royal Commission on the Alkali Acts reported in 1878; a further Alkali Act followed, extending the control of noxious effluvia.

The provision of a water supply to the cities was a splendid Victorian achievement.[2] The improvement of sewage systems also proceeded. But such work was costly, putting a strain on local rates. This in turn had the effect of pushing housing even further out of reach for many workers. Thus housing costs could be raised, through a combination of land costs (mounting steadily in the towns), building costs (also subject to upward pressure, partly due to the imposition of higher standards) and rates (increased by local services such as sewage). At the same time the ability of many workers to pay (as governed by their wages) did not rise proportionately. The housing gap could thus widen, especially among the lowest paid, and this by almost unnoticed degrees.

1. See chapter 11 above.
2. See chapter 8, section 3 above.

The Boer War, however, had the effect of bringing these failures of provision, and a good many others, to the consciousness of many members of the middle classes. Recruitment of large armies for service in South Africa provided data on adult males. It was found that some two out of every five intending recruits were below the standard set for military service. Such data must be treated with some care; it must also be viewed in the light of similar results obtained with recruits from the industrial parts of France and Germany. But it was a shock to contemporary British opinion. There were two disturbing implications. How could Britain compete in foreign markets with a debilitated labour force? How could she defend herself and her possessions if the imperial race was subject to cumulative physical decline? The vogue for social Darwinianism was strong at this time, inspiring a good deal of loose talk about the 'unfit'. A revived romanticism based on the need for contact with nature insisted that deterioration was inevitable when man lost contact with the soil and organic nature. An interdepartmental Committee on Physical Deterioration reporting in 1904 confirmed that there was ground for alarm and need for action. But it rejected any suggestion that deterioration was hereditary: the decline was not irreversible, but could be corrected by improved environment.

As a response to this newly aroused consciousness of human waste and national vulnerability various public figures declared themselves for 'national efficiency'. Lords Rosebery, Haldane and Milner, along with Winston Churchill, the Webbs, Robert Blatchford and the civil servant Robert Morant, together with others, composed a somewhat heterogeneous national efficiency group. Some of them were also Liberal imperialists. Some looked to Prussian initiatives, for German institutions, like the Imperial Insurance Office and the Imperial Statistical Office, were much admired by many British politicians, apparently without realising the implications for their theory of the state. Some were collectivist socialists. The national efficiency school, because of its diversity, failed to capture the leadership of either main political party. But the formation of the London County Council in 1888 under the influence of Rosebery and others did make possible a conversion from chaos to a co-ordinated system of government for the enormous population under its care.[1] Edu-

1. See chapter 11, section 2 above.

cationally, also, the believers in national efficiency had some successes, as with the Webbs in setting up the London School of Economics in 1895, Haldane's initiative in the forming of the Imperial College of Science in 1907, and the reorganisation of London University after 1898. Slowly a response was emerging to the need to train experts for government as well as industry.

Another way of promoting national efficiency was to improve the food and health facilities available to the young. In 1906 the Education (Provision of Meals) Act, following the example set by certain local authorities, encouraged the introduction of school meals by permitting local authorities to make such meals a charge on the rates.[1] In 1907 under the Education (Administrative Provisions) Act a medical department was set up within the Board of Education to supervise the provision of a school medical service. The schools were thus used as part of a nutrition and inspection policy. Neglect or abuse by parents of their child was made an offence under the Children's Act of 1908, known as the 'children's charter'.

3. Working conditions, hours and injury

The Royal Commission on the Working of the Factory and Workshops Act surveyed existing provisions in 1876: its *Report* was followed by the Factories and Workshops Act of 1878, an important consolidating statute. A standard day of ten hours was prescribed, with six and a half hours on Saturday – that is a fifty-six-and-a-half-hour week. But the 1878 Factory Act left men without direct protection, still confining this to women, young persons and children. In the same year the lives of seamen were brought within statute through the persistence of Samuel Plimsoll (1824–98) in pressing his Merchant Shipping Act: under it the condition in which ships put to sea was regulated. In 1886 the first step was taken to limit hours of work in retail trade: the Shops Act of that year limited the hours of children and young persons. The reductions of working hours in 1878 and 1886 for certain groups, though important, did not satisfy everyone: in 1886 Tom Mann (1856–1941) launched his Eight-Hour Movement. In the hard times then prevailing Mann argued that statutory limitation of hours would reduce unemployment by 750,000: the

1. See section 4 below.

state was thus being pressed to control unemployment by statutory work-spreading. Socialists also stressed the need for the state to improve the conditions of leisure as a means of raising the quality of working-class life.

A further extension of control of working conditions came with the Factory and Workshops Amendment Act in 1901, codifying and consolidating. A second Merchant Shipping Act sponsored by Lloyd George was passed in 1906. In the following year, in accordance with the International Conference on Labour Regulation held in 1906 at Berne, Switzerland, there was passed the Employment of Women Act. The Anti-Sweating League was founded in 1905; the Trades Boards Act of 1909 was the government's response.[1]

The question of hours of work came to the fore again in 1908. This time it was the coal mines that provided the focus of attention. The Coal Mines Act of that year embodied the eight-hour principle, limiting the length of shifts below ground to that figure. Many industrialists were greatly alarmed at this provision, fearing an all-round rise in the cost of fuel and power.[2] They urged, as in the past, the notions of the liberty of the subject and freedom of contract. But the Liberal government of the day, as part of its search for accommodation with labour, imposed the limitation of hours. In so doing it breached, for the first time, the principle that adult males should be left to settle their own terms with their employers. It also brought to a head the tensions in the coal mining industry.[3]

Meanwhile two further issues had been moving to the fore, namely pensions[4] and compensation for accidents. As to compensation, a beginning was made with the Employers' Liability Act of 1880. Previously the matter had been governed by Lord Campbell's Act of 1846 which had defined and extended the common law provision concerning workmen injured on the job. The 1880 Act introduced the new principle that compensation for injury must be paid by employers. But it was heavily qualified: it was operative only where the workman could prove his injury to be due to negligence on the part of his employer or of his agents. The onus of proof thus lay on the workman, as did the burden of injury where negligence was

1. See chapter 12, section 11 above.
2. See chapter 6, section 7 above.
3. See chapter 12, section 14 above.
4. See section 7 below.

absent. Chamberlain's Act of 1897 made the employer responsible for injuries whether employer or worker or both or neither were guilty of negligence. Accidents were thus made a general charge upon industry; at the same time workers could not be made responsible for the damaging effects of their own actions or omissions. But the Act was limited in its application to certain dangerous employments. The new principles were applied to agricultural labourers in 1900. The Workmen's Compensation Act of 1906 generalised the coverage, so that all persons working under a contract of service or apprenticeship were protected (except for non-manual workers earning £250 a year or more). The 1906 Act also provided compensation for disablement or death caused by certain industrial diseases. But it contained no requirements that companies carry insurance against their liability, so that when a company failed, benefits ceased.

4. Education: popular, secondary, technical and university

Forster's Education Act of 1870 and its Scottish analogue of 1872 had laid the basis for general elementary literacy in Britain.[1] It is true that there is some danger of minimising what had been achieved by the private school system before the Act. But parliament, by establishing the right of every child to some form of education, began a movement which could only gain momentum.

From the 1870s onward it was inevitable that the nation would move progressively toward a comprehensive state system. The voluntary principle, though it still had its place, was increasingly seen to be inadequate for educating the masses, including the working men newly enfranchised in 1867. In 1880, by Mundella's Education Act, elementary schooling was made compulsory throughout the United Kingdom. But compromise was present here as in so much social legislation: attendance was in general required until the age of thirteen, but children over ten needed only to attend half-time if they had gained a certificate of proficiency. The minimum age for full-time attendance was raised to eleven in 1893 and twelve in 1899, representing victories for the advocates of higher standards, and simultaneously reducing the child labour force. Parents had been

1. See chapter 8, section 4 above.

obliged to pay for the education of their children at a few pennies per week, representing the contributory principle; in 1891 schooling was in effect made free (or more precisely made a charge on the tax system), by the device of giving parents the right to demand exemption from payment. In the 1890s School Boards throughout Britain began to pay increasing attention to secondary education, opening new secondary schools and departments.

Compulsory education involved the School Boards, through their school attendance officers, in a struggle to get working-class children into the schools, especially those of families at the lower end of the scale of skill, employment and incomes. The School Boards eventually won, disciplining the population into general literacy, an achievement that reached its peak in the two or three decades from about 1910. Literacy was a powerful engine of social change, reducing the wage differentials between skilled and unskilled.

What more was brought about is hard to assess. Matthew Arnold (1822–88), in his *Culture and Anarchy* of 1869, hoped that schooling would mean getting to know 'the best which has been thought and said in the world', bringing the young into contact with the highest human achievement. This was an ideal embraced by both elitists and socialists, but their respective choices of the 'best' would perhaps differ.

There was no misgiving about the pedagogic and the didactic: the children were there to be moulded; there was no compunction about using discipline and regimentation where necessary. Indeed the scale of the task was so great that there was little room for Rousseauite self-expression by the children; among educators there was little philosophising about the working of the child mind. The processing of the children of the masses, in spite of many devoted teachers and administrators, could too easily take on characteristics of the factory system.

By 1899 it had become clear that the state's central machinery for educational purposes was inadequate. The Board of Education Act of that year set up the Board of Education to take over the duties of the Education Department, with its responsibility for elementary schooling, and of the Science and Art Department of the Board of Trade which administered grants for technical education. The Board presided over English education until 1944. But though it was responsible for both elementary and secondary education, it was denied the powers necessary for it to promote a fully integrated system.

Yet it provided the opportunity for an outstanding educational administrator, Robert Morant (1863–1920), its Permanent Secretary from 1903 to 1912, to do great things. Morant's achievements centred round the Education Act of 1902, largely prepared by him and Sidney Webb for Balfour's Conservative government. It was intended to make a major contribution to national efficiency. The School Boards of the early 1870s, though they had done useful work, were adjudged to be severely sub-optimal in size. The 2,500 Boards in England were accordingly wound up, to be replaced by Local Education Authorities, 315 in number. The elementary schools were thus assimilated to the local government system and made a charge upon its rates. (The responsibilities of the Scottish School Boards, they having taken over the churches' schools in 1872, did not pass to the local authorities until the Scottish Education Act of 1918.) The LEAs were the county and county borough councils, each of which appointed its education committee. The LEAs took over both the Board Schools and the voluntary (largely Church of England) schools, but the religious instruction in the latter schools was to continue, under Church of England parsons. The principle which Morant was trying to promote was, of course, that of integration at a new level of efficiency, under the local authorities and the central Board.

But religion could still be the enemy of educational advance. Balfour's Act brought a storm of protest from the Liberal non-conformists who argued that their taxes were to be used to propagate pernicious Church of England doctrines, and who resented the suppression of the School Boards. For the first time the state was challenged by passive resistance. A good many nonconformists, led by their ministers, refused to pay the education rate and had their goods distrained in payment. The young Lloyd George rode upon the storm to national fame, on Liberal, nonconformist support. The Tory Church of England Party was no less intransigent in refusing to give up religious education in 'their' schools. But Balfour's government persisted and the Act was passed, a victory for Morant, the national efficiency school and the Church of England. But further Acts were passed in 1906 and 1908 as concessions to the non-conformists, modifying the special position of the Voluntary Schools.

The bitter controversy over the Act of 1902 reveals the power of obsessive beliefs and grievances, so deeply rooted in the past, to continue to obstruct adjustment to the necessities of a new world.

The introduction of school meals (1906), and medical examinations in schools (1907), indicated that the state was ready, subject to local authority implementation, to use the elementary school system as a means of improving the health of the people in infancy and childhood. But the adoption of the power to provide school meals was only gradual and partial: as R.H. Tawney (1880–1962) remarked, such meals were 'confined to children as gravely undernourished as to be unable, in their absence, to profit by instruction'. From 1900 the LEAs were empowered to raise the school-leaving age from thirteen to fourteen.

There was undoubtedly among the middle classes a quietist aspect to education, resting on the belief that if the working classes better understood the necessary workings of society they would be the more likely to accept the limitations of their condition, and indeed of social amelioration generally. As to working-class criticism of the system, some scholars argue that there was a growing antagonism among the working classes to middle-class control of the educational system, beginning well before 1850.[1]

The Balfour–Morant Act of 1902 had a second great concern, namely with secondary education. The Royal Commission of 1895 (the Bryce Commission) advocated the unification of elementary and secondary education. The Board of Education Act of 1899 made this administratively possible; the Act of 1902 took an important step in bringing it about by placing the two elements under the single control of the Board.

Secondary schooling in England had long had two aspects. There were the public schools for the sons of the upper strata of society, and there were the endowed grammar schools, largely a preserve of the middle classes. A third element was now to be added – grammar schools run by the LEAs under the general aegis of the Board of Education, to take both boys and girls. In some areas the LEAs took over existing foundations, but in most they set up entirely new schools. Fees were to be paid at the LEA grammar schools; at this level of education the contributory principle was still insisted upon.

1. See chapter 5, section 10 above.

But from 1907 all such schools were required to reserve a quarter of their places for non-fee-paying pupils from the poorer classes, part of their grant being made dependent on their doing so. Such pupils having passed the free-place examination, made up only some 6% of the LEA total in 1914. This was, however, a component of a rapidly growing number as the first generation of LEA grammar school pupils rapidly expanded. In this way a socially broader band of pupils enjoyed a 'liberal' (i.e. non-vocational) education, and could make themselves eligible for the universities. Yet most boys and girls still left the LEA schools without matriculation, evidence of the fact that there continued to be economic, social and cultural barriers to be overcome before families were fully prepared to back the education of their children. Nevertheless, when Morant left the Board in 1912, the old pre-1902 dichotomy of simple elementary schooling for the masses and secondary education for the privileged had been significantly modified by the growth of LEA grammar schools. These became the most important agency of social mobility for the qualifications gained in them largely determined the subsequent occupation and social status of the pupil.

There was one point, however, on which Morant was vulnerable to his critics. He and the government he advised did not use the opportunity of 1902 to make a corresponding advance in terms of technical, scientific and commercial education that would be both vocational and directly related to the national efficiency he sought to promote in other parts of his programme. English education had long been dominated by two emphases: on the arts side by an addiction to the classics, and on the scientific side by an exclusive emphasis upon mathematics and pure science; indeed the success of the grammar schools contributed to the persistence of this academic tradition. Both outlooks were inimical to education in terms of the implementation of new technologies. The Devonshire Report (of the Royal Commission on Scientific Instruction) appeared in 1872; in 1882 a second Commission reported; in 1884 the Samuelson Commission (the RC on Technical Instruction) laid its views before the public. By the late 1880s the advocates of technical education were at last able to push government into action. In 1889 the Technical Instruction Act of that year authorised local authorities to spend the product of a penny on the rates on technical teaching. This provision was augmented in 1890 by the allocation by the government of the duties levied on wines and spirits to technical education, popularly known as the 'Whisky Money'. Most technical instruction in England continued to be given in evening classes, at a discouragingly elementary level.

Thus the first industrialised nation continued in this extraordinary default, failing to respond to its own fundamental needs. It was deflected from doing so by elements of its own past, rooted in a view of education that derived from the ethos of a hierarchic, landed England. Middle-class parents sought a grammar school education for their sons not merely for the prestige of the formal qualifications they gained, but also that they might acquire the patterns of speech, dress and manners appropriate to the upwardly socially mobile. The result was that before 1914 no British government department, outside of education itself, had the slightest scientific interest: the notion of a national policy on the sciences was not even raised.

The ancient universities of England had always produced the classic syndrome of closed societies – they were prone to loss of initiative, but were vigorous in the defence of their privileges. So great had been their abuse and ineffectualness that the state was obliged in the 1850s, 1870s and 1880s to intervene with inquiries and legislation. The application of the Test Acts to the ancient English universities excluding students who were Dissenters had been finally ended in 1851; fellowships were opened in 1871 to all. With conformity to the Church of England no longer required in undergraduates or dons, a great secularisation could take place. The Royal Commission on Oxford and Cambridge Universities of 1876 resulted in the Act of 1877 which carried their renovation much further, defining their relationships with their colleges, preparing the way for modernisation of the curricula and making better educational use of the endowments. The Scottish Universities, though serving a wider band of society, also needed reform: the Act of 1889 prescribed a new mode of government in which the professors no longer had a monopoly of power, their Senates being placed under the control of Courts on which there was powerful lay representation. In 1893 the three Welsh Colleges joined to form the University of Wales. An Act of Parliament of 1898, together with university statutes of 1900, restructured London University in modern form. From the 1880s a new range of English universities came into being. In 1884 the Victoria University was formed from three constituent colleges: these received independent charters in the new century: Manchester and Liverpool in 1903 and Sheffield in 1905; Birmingham University was constituted in 1900, Leeds in 1904 and Bristol in 1909. To these civic universities the products of the new grammar school system after 1902 could aspire. Traditional English university education based upon Oxford and Cambridge, though largely purged of abuses and lethargy, maintained its position of privilege and esteem. But a second system with a new potential had begun. The products of the Forster and the Scottish Acts, with their elementary reading and writing skills, were present on a significant scale by 1900, those gaining secondary education under the Balfour Act of 1902 became numerous in the twenties, and those who passed through the new red-brick universities were beginning to constitute themselves a new order of graduates by the thirties.

In a way, however, the extension of elementary education was a disappointment, for it was followed by the appearance of a popular press, which often exploited in crude market terms the barely literate, narrowing the new vistas opened to them by their schooling to the simplistic and meretricious, and subjecting them to political manipulation. At the same time, however, literacy did make possible a wider dissemination of information and ideas upon which a better knowledge of public affairs could be based.

5. Housing: the subsidy barrier; town planning

Housing was a matter of mounting concern in the generation before 1914. Four-fifths of the British population could by this time be classified as urban; thereafter the proportion was more or less stable. By 1911 some three-quarters of a million people in London, almost the population of the next biggest British city, were living in overcrowded housing. The scale of the shortfall of working-class provision was made ever more apparent by a succession of debates and inquiries, both local and national. A number of formulae were offered. Philanthropists like Octavia Hill (1838–1912) strove for a combination of economical construction and occupant discipline that would close the gap between costs and the rents that could be paid out of low incomes.

The Artisans' Dwellings Act of 1875 (the Cross Act), the product of Disraeli's government, gave local authorities power to undertake clearance schemes by the compulsory purchase of houses and land. This was the fourth great purpose for which the state had invaded the sanctity of property rights (it was preceded by canal building, the enclosure movement, and the building of the railways). On each of these occasions the state had asserted the principle that the ongoing needs of the community were prior to those of property. In the cases of the canals, enclosure and the railways the state had transferred property rights directly from one group of private individuals to another; with the Cross Act the state was to acquire the land, disallowing the customary compensation for compulsory sale, and was then to resell it for redevelopment. Mild though the Cross Act now looks in retrospect, it was a radical step in its time. The sanitation aspect of policy was confirmed by the Public Health Act of 1875, laying down minimal standards for housing.

Successive governments continued to legislate along these lines. There were some six Torrens and Cross Acts between 1868 and 1890, all aimed at encouraging local authorities to undertake slum demolition programmes. In spite of a few striking examples of the adoption of the Acts the result was disappointing. There was almost no building response, because adequate rents could not be paid. The dishoused simply crowded into the remaining properties, creating ever denser rookeries. The central and east-end parts of the large cities had become self-confirming entities, holding their population by a kind of centripedal logic. This was especially true of London where categories of casuals had to be near their jobs, including dockers and building workers; the families of such men relied on the credit of petty shopkeepers, and could not afford the cost or time of travel.

Select Committees of the House of Commons considered the housing default in 1881 and 1882; a Royal Commission did the same in 1885 and in 1890; their *Reports* reveal a high level of perception of the organic nature of the problem, including the relationship between rents and incomes and the concentrating force of great cities. But their policy recommendations were slight, not to say feeble, perhaps because of the very perception of the scale and intricacy of the problems involved. The Housing Act of 1885 did little more than confirm existing policy. The matter became more pressing than ever, highlighted by a potent plea by G.R. Sims (1847–

1922): *The Bitter Cry of Outcast London*, published in 1883. But in the same year that veteran of so many good causes, Lord Shaftesbury, reiterated a deep misgiving: 'If the state is to be summoned', he wrote, 'not only to provide houses for the labouring classes, but also to supply such dwellings at nominal [i.e. subsidised] rents, it will, while doing something on behalf of their physical condition, utterly destroy their moral energies.'

The Housing of the Working Classes Act of 1885 and the consolidating Act of 1890 strengthened the hands of local authorities in promoting sanitary conditions in the housing stock of their areas. Local authorities, in addition to demolishing insanitary houses, were now empowered to build, but only on an economic basis such that rents met costs. This restriction meant that only slow progress was possible, though the government did try to encourage local authorities to act. The great obstacle was, of course, the unwillingness of ratepayers to be taxed to pay for houses for others. The granting to local authorities of the power to lend money to tenants for the purchase of their homes (the Small Dwellings Acquisition Act of 1899) did a little to improve the situation.

In 1900 the policy of attacking the housing problem by regulating building standards was further extended. The Housing of the Working Classes Act of that year stopped the building of the worst kind of crowded-in houses, the back-to-backs. Medical officers of health were expected to condemn insanitary properties, but how could they do so when no alternative accommodation was available? Like the factory inspectors they had to operate a 'reasonable' compromise.

By now the limitation of the market principle in the supply of working-class houses had become apparent to many observers. All attempts, by philanthropically imposed discipline, by the provision of sites and by the offer of local authority loans, had failed to create conditions of supply to which the market would respond. The stark alternative was subsidy. This was a daunting prospect for governments. It would involve costs that would soon raise housing to the level of a major demand on the public purse. It would also pose the painful question: should local authorities bear the charge on their rates, or should the central government provide funds, or should the two principles be combined?

In 1911 the Unionists (Conservatives) in opposition introduced a

Bill which would have set up a branch of government to deal with the matter (Housing Commissioners under the Local Government Board), to collaborate with local authorities. Much more radical, the Bill proposed to legitimise housing subsidies as a charge on the local rates, supported by a state subsidy. The Liberal government, with the Lib–Lab John Burns (1858–1943) at the Local Government Board, killed the Bill. They were not prepared to open the subsidy door.

Britain thus reached 1914 without embarking upon subsidised housing. Before 1909 only 2% of houses were publicly owned, and these were let at economic rents; between 1909 and 1915 approximately 10,000 houses were built by local authorities on this self-financing basis. This was against some 200,000 built in the same period by private enterprise.

With growth in size of cities and the transport revolution brought by the railways and the tramways, the shape of the cities could no longer be left to contending market forces. The Housing and Town Planning Act of 1909 promoted by John Burns authorised local authorities to prepare town planning schemes. Following the German example, a beginning could be made in the public control of the urban environment. As Burns put it, somewhat optimistically, the Act aimed 'to secure the home healthy, the house beautiful, the town pleasant, the city dignified, and the suburb salubrious'. The Act was somewhat more limited than Burns suggested: its essence lay in the fact that it provided permissive powers for the preparation of schemes for the control of the development of new housing areas. Compensation and betterment provisions were included, though they proved unworkable. The more progressive authorities found the Act a considerable aid. Also, because the Act failed to renew the stipulation that local authorities were obliged to divest themselves within ten years of any houses they had built, it became possible for municipalities to own houses indefinitely. The Road Traffic Act of 1909 gave local authorities powers to buy land adjacent to projected roads in order to provide parkways. Under the Ancient Monuments Act of 1882 the state accepted responsibility for the physical remnants of the nation's past; the 1909 Act also provided for the preservation of objects of historical interest or natural beauty.

6. *The poor law: its extension and fragmentation*

Poor law history between 1874 and 1914 went through a succession of phases. In the first the inspectorate continued its crusade for the workhouse system, deriving from the Goschen minute of 1869, seeking to restore a strong social discipline. But, as so often in poor law history, the atmosphere changed. In the 1890s there was a movement toward greater sympathy. This owed something to the return of more difficult times, and something to a softening of political opinion, no doubt related to the extension of the franchise in 1867 and 1884. Throughout the 1890s a greater humanity entered the Local Government Board's recommendations and the guardians' practice: tobacco, snuff, and personal tea, sugar and milk were often supplied; visiting committees of ladies inspected conditions and recommended their easing; trained nurses were engaged and medical treatment brought additional comforts and improved diet. A Board circular of 1900 recommended outdoor relief for the aged 'of good character'. All this, of course, ran contrary to the principles of less-eligibility. At the same time new kinds of provision were made outside the poor law, especially for children. The Elementary Education (Blind and Deaf Children) Act of 1893 required School Boards to provide special schooling for such children and grants were made available. The children of the poor entered the general elementary schooling system. Until early in the new century then, this second phase of easing continued. Life was still hard, sometimes brutal and always humiliating for those in receipt of poor relief, but it was eased to some degree by continuous local adaptation.

By 1900 there were three sets of people concerned with the operation of the poor law, and each had developed its ethos. The politicians, in general, were more sensitive than the bureaucrats to humanitarian considerations and to votes, and favoured the easing of conditions. Secondly, there were the central civil servants at the Board who, in spite of concessions, clung to the austere principles of 1834, seeking to preserve rigour and promote uniformity. Thirdly, at the implementational level the guardians and overseers, both of whom saw painful hardship arising from the rules, and at the same time had to deal with difficult and idle persons, could not afford to take a simple view based exclusively on either humanity or discipline. The treatment accorded to the poor was the outcome, in any given phase and place, of the interplay of these three levels of participation. The situation had thus produced many anomalies.

Once again, as in 1832–4,[1] it was, by the early twentieth century, time for a new inquiry. The Royal Commission on the Poor Law of 1905–9, set up by the Balfour government, was an attempt to ascertain the real position and to prescribe for it. As with all such inquiries, the outcome was to a significant degree determined by the choice of inquirers. The majority (fourteen members) and the minority (four members) produced separate *Reports*. These reflected, respectively, the older view (subject to modifications) and the newer view, calling for radical change. The majority wished to continue the principles of rigour and less-eligibility of 1834. Their fundamental philosophy was based on the traditional fear that too gentle a handling of the poor would destroy their remaining moral fibre and weaken that of the rest of the working population. But the majority also believed that the poor law could and should be remodelled so as to embrace all that was needful in the care of social casualties; they were therefore hostile to the trend of treating forms of social need by setting up new machinery outside the poor law. But they were prepared to abandon the popularly odious term 'Poor Law', and replace it in word and fact by 'Public Assistance Committees', run by local authorities. In this way the principle of local government followed by the Education Act of 1902 would be applied also to social provision; indeed majority and minority recommended the assimilation of the poor law to the general pattern of local government. Both *Reports* wished to see a greater systemisation of benefits so that the wider discrepancies between areas would be removed. Both approved of labour exchanges, school clinics, old age pensions and a state medical service.

But the *Minority Report* signed by Beatrice Webb and largely drafted by her husband Sidney had its highly distinctive point of view. It proposed that there should no longer be any distinction between paupers and the rest of the population. This would mean the removal of stigma and the treatment of poverty as misfortune rather than as moral failure. Moreover poverty should be seen not as a kind of gross aggregate, but as deriving from distinct sources, each with its appropriate diagnosis and therapy. This led to the advocacy

1. See chapter 5, section 7 above.

of the 'break-up' of the poor law, each aspect of need in each local authority having its own separate committee. Children of school age would become the responsibility, in all aspects, of the Education Committee; the Health Committee would have charge of all the sick (as well as expectant mothers); the Pensions Committee would care for the aged; and the Asylums Committee for the mentally defective. In this way the local authority, through its structure of committees, would provide for each and all categories of need. At the centre appropriate ministries or departments would be created or reformed to co-ordinate and guide.

The *Minority Report* also recommended positive state action to cure or ameliorate unemployment, but its specific suggestions went little beyond the traditional plea for make-work schemes in bad times. It contained proposals also for something approaching a national health service and a ministry of labour.

The two *Reports* provide a source of information and opinion comparable with the *Report* of 1834. But no statute followed. Partly this was because of the obduracy of John Burns as President of the Local Government Board. More fundamentally, it was because the government of the day was confronted by two documents, neither of which it could wholly embrace, and between which no compromise seemed possible. The two *Reports* represented the fundamental difference between the two philosophies of poverty that reached back to 1834 and beyond even to Tudor times. The principle of rigour, retained in the *Majority Report*, was restated in Evidence by the spokesman of the Charity Organisation Society, and by J.S. Davy (1848–1915) of the Local Government Board. For Davy 'the hanger-on should be lower than him on whom he hangs', and a man 'must stand by his accidents: he must suffer for the general good of the body politic'. The moral distinction between the deserving and the undeserving poor must be preserved. The charitable bodies should locate and relieve the deserving so far as their resources permitted; the rest were the responsibility of the state, receiving from it a minimal provision. Davy, indeed, would have made pauperism subject to three penalties of deprivation: loss of personal reputation by stigma, loss of freedom by detention in the workhouse and loss of political rights by disenfranchisement. Though the *Majority Report* would not go so far, it relied by implication on many of the older moral sanctions.

The minority members would have none of this, for to them paupers, being not guilty, were victims; they should be helped at the public cost without scrutiny of their conduct. The Webbs had developed the concept of the national minimum guaranteed by the state, below which no one should be allowed to fall: this was indeed the central element in their social philosophy. It gradually extended its influences at various levels of the national consciousness. But in the shorter run the advocates of the *Minority Report* were too insistent and too uncompromising, attacking the *Majority Report* too harshly and ignoring the common ground, and so achieving nothing.

7. Old age pensions and the contributory insurance principle in health

But already a new phase in welfare had begun. It was that of abstracting altogether from the poor law framework certain forms of care, and making them the responsibility of bodies outside the poor law. The provision of school meals and medical services (1906 and 1907) had given dietary and health functions to the schooling system under the Local Education Authorities.

Much more immediately dramatic was the making available of old age pensions in 1908. This was done on a national basis, as a charge on the budget, paid out through the Post Office branches. All persons over the age of seventy were eligible for 5s per week (7s 6d for a married couple). No contributions were involved. But the 'undeserving' could be excluded, and those with an income over 8s per week had their benefits reduced proportionately. Modest though such payments were, they gave a degree of independence to many aged, removing them from the scope of the poor law, and often inspiring an almost pathetic gratitude.

It must not be thought, however, that the Old Age Pensions Act of 1908 was an impulsive action on the part of the government. From the 1880s there had been much discussion in both political parties of the fearful prospect of poverty, deprivation and dependence in old age for so many members of the working classes. They were a simple case to deal with, in one sense, for such benefits as they received would not affect the general incentive among the able-bodied to work. But the fear was expressed that relief to the aged might weaken the disposition of the active to save and thus provide for their old age. In the traditional agrarian society saving by the peasantry was simply not a significant part of life: in an industrialised society, however, with its money wage payments and its facilities for saving (Friendly Societies, savings banks, industrial insurance companies), thrift, it was argued, might be expected of working men. Indeed a high proportion of them had indeed saved in these various ways. On the other hand social inquiry of the kind carried out by Charles Booth in the later 1880s pointed to the impossibility of saving for those with near-subsistence incomes. Moreover, should the thrifty and the improvident be treated alike in their old age?

By 1895 there was widespread concern about the condition of the aged. A Royal Commission on the Aged Poor (the Aberdeen Commission) reported in that year. Its majority expressed itself as satisfied with 'the general ability of those who are in any regular employment to make direct or indirect provision for old age as well as for sickness and other contingencies beyond the everyday needs of life'. But some easing of the conditions of the aged poor did follow. A Treasury Committee reported in 1898, and a Commons Select Committee (of which Lloyd George was a member) in 1899. A wide range of formulae was produced in an attempt to provide effective relief without damaging working-class budgetary and planning behaviour. One proposal was that nest-egg savings should be state augmented, thus rewarding the deserving. Another was that there should be a means test. But the main argument centred around the contributory principle – should it be adopted as the basis for old-age pensions, and, if so, on what basis? Lloyd George cut through the argument with his Act, coming into operation in 1908, granting the pension, on a non-contributory basis, as of right. But the eligibility conditions were the price necessary to overcome resistance.

In addition to the contingencies of old age and unemployment there were other needs pressing upon working-class families, including sickness, disablement and maternity costs. These eventualities were provided against in Part I of the National Insurance Act of 1911. Such provision was compulsory for most employed persons, and on a contributory basis. Insured workers were to receive sick pay of 10s per week: they were to pay 4d to which their employers added 3d and the state 5d. The need for the contributory principle seemed to be confirmed by the experience with old age pensions: they had cost £8 million in their first year instead of an estimated £6.5 million, thus revealing the potential bill for social relief to the Chancellor Lloyd George. Moreover the feeling was strong that both pride and satisfaction would be promoted if working men bore a share in such provision, thus placing the benefits on the basis of earned right. Thus Lloyd George and W.J. Braithwaite, his civil servant adviser and drafter, preferred the contributory insurance principle to either the *Majority* or the *Minority Reports* on the Poor Law; by adopting it they lifted a large part of the health problem out of the poor law framework, just as had been done in 1908 with the aged. They were also acting within the Liberal credo, and at the same time weakening the case for socialism.

They had also to solve the problems of administrative implementation. The radical course would have been for the state to set up its own machinery, or to adapt the Post Office or the labour exchanges to this additional function. But there were already in the field many trade unions with benefit schemes, the Friendly Societies (Oddfellows, Rechabites and the like) and the industrial insurance companies (the Prudential, the Liver, the Royal Victoria, the Pearl). All were vigorously hostile to the entry of the state into insurance, and all were politically powerful. The industrial insurance companies were pacified by the dropping from the programme of the proposed coverage for funeral benefits and for widows and orphans, much to Lloyd George's disappointment. The scheme was to be administered through 'approved societies', i.e. those societies registered under the Industrial and Provident Societies Act of 1893. Each worker was to choose his society, pay into it and receive his benefits from it. This was a further compromise Lloyd George had to accept.

There remained the medical profession, the direct supplier of health services. This was the first occasion on which the British state had to arrive at an accommodation with a major independent profession; though there had been a state involvement with the poor law doctors, this concerned only about one in six practitioners. The medical profession fought powerfully and persistently to keep itself free of control. It was insistent upon being independent, so far as possible, of both the approved societies and the state. The mechanism for achieving this was provided through local Insurance Commissions set up by the government. Each worker was to select his doctor from a panel organised by the Insurance Commission in his locality. Each doctor thus composed his panel, for each member of which he received a capitation fee. In this way the medical profession was brought into the national scheme with a minimum sacrifice of its own view of itself.

By 1914 the Liberal government, by its provision for old age pensions, unemployment insurance and health insurance, had rejected the idea of working within a renovated poor law. Instead it created separate elements of support quite outside the traditional system. The poor law remained responsible for what the government hoped would be a much smaller army of social casualties, reduced as they had been by the new legislation.

This curious mixture of poor law and other agencies was the outcome of conflicting philosophies (themselves deeply rooted in the divisions long present in the national life). There were also the complexities of the institutional structure, including the political parties, the Friendly Societies, the local ratepayers and all the other groups with vested interests in what might be provided for the social casualties. It was a sense of urgency, begotten both of humanitarian impulse and fear of social unrest, that had prompted new ad hoc beginnings outside the traditional and in some ways deadlocked system. But they were at the cost of yet further incoherence.

8. *Labour colonies: segregation, discipline, retraining and redemption*

There was the belief that it would be in the interests of society if certain groups of persons could be withdrawn for a time from it and kept in labour colonies or camps. This idea had highly diverse origins: they ranged from the punitive to the redemptive, much as did ideas affecting the criminal element in society.

On the punitive side there was the moralistic belief, shared by William Beveridge, that there was nothing to be done with the unsocial, the misfits, the parasitical, the idle who evaded employment, except to take them out of society to a place where they would live under discipline, no longer a threat to their families and to society in general. Reform schools for boys had enjoyed some success: could the principle be extended to adult males? Labour camps would thus be a fourth device for withdrawing undesirables from society, along with the penal system, insane asylums and workhouses. But in spite of a good deal of discussion, no purely segregative or punitary camps were set up. Sir John Gort's Bill of 1904 providing for the detention

251

in labour colonies of 'criminal vagrants' and 'habitual paupers' was defeated. There was perhaps an instinctive realisation that such camps could degenerate into something indefensible.

More positive, resting upon hope rather than despair, were the proposals for camps or colonies for rehabilitation and settlement. There were plans for these to be used as a means of settling men on the land, working collectively in voluntary community settlements; this idea of rural colonies related back to the land movement that had produced the Allotment and Smallholding Acts.[1] Industrial training was also envisaged, with facilities for the learning of new skills more in demand by the labour market. The 1905 Unemployed Workmen's Act empowered local authorities to undertake schemes of this kind. Beatrice Webb included such proposals in her *Minority Report* on the poor law. The idea owed something to her mentor Charles Booth; he sought a social classification that yielded distinct categories, to each of which, including the 'casual residuum', distinct policies could be applied, including the principle of segregation. Booth argued in 1889 that 'the poverty of the poor is mainly the result of the competition of the very poor'. If the latter could be withdrawn from the labour market, earnings of those above such a class would rise – this was, indeed, 'the only solution to the problem'.

Proposals for labour colonies were discussed at length by the Select Committee on Distress from Want of Employment in 1896, partly under Booth's influence, but the Committee was hostile to such efforts to 'employ, retrain or detain the unemployed', criticising both the theory of such schemes and prevailing continental practice. The nearest labour colonies came to public implementation was the Central (Unemployed) Body set up to administer the 1905 Act in London, with its Working Colonies Committee. It established a number of colonies in the London area. But John Burns, President of the Local Government Board, was unsympathetic and would provide no public money: labour colonies petered out.

9. State control of thought and conduct

In the later Victorian and Edwardian age, apart from the laws of obscenity, and of libel and slander, British subjects could say or

---

1. See chapter 10, section 2 above.

publish what they liked. The spread of elementary education after 1870 and 1872 widened the scope of the printed word as it affected the working classes.[1] The new range of popular newspapers, in spite of their power to affect ideas and beliefs, often irresponsibly used, gave rise to no new regulative legislation. The minds of the public were thus opened to whatever the market might supply them.

At the same time, however, the Home Office was confronted with a long-standing dilemma, having to do with free speech and public demonstrations (an expression first used in 1860), and their relation to public order. Though the quarter century down to 1874 was a period of relative quiet, the occasional outbursts of street violence, not to say rioting, against the spokesmen of unpopular causes did pose a problem. Should the state enforce the right of the individual to express sentiments which, though legal, might provoke a breach of the peace? Conversely should the danger of street violence be allowed to impair free speech? The Home Office could find no secure ground in principle, and so extemporised. As to the law, there was no general statutory basis for free speech, only fragments: thus it was provided for by Act of Parliament in Hyde Park from 1872 and Trafalgar Square from 1892.

The power of the church over mind-formation was weakening as the religious component in schooling lost its vitality. It was still possible for one element in the Church of England to attack another, and call the state in aid in so doing; the anti-ritualists obtained the Public Worship Regulation Act of 1874, under which clergy who, seeking to carry the Established Church closer to the practices of Rome, could be prosecuted. This practically ceased after 1888. Thereafter, apart from retaining its jurisdiction over the Prayer Book, parliament did not intervene in church matters.

The market affecting morality, as in the past, had two components: there were the purveyors of prostitutes and there were the purveyors of pornography. The Criminal Law Amendment Act of 1885 raised the age of sexual consent among females to sixteen, where it remained, thus making it easier for the courts to convict procurers and brothel-keepers.

The controls on pornography and obscenity continued largely unchanged under the 1857 Act. The stage remained under the

1. See section 4 above.

censorship of the Lord Chamberlain. But the music-halls had aroused criticism, both in terms of what they presented on the stage and as places of ill resort: Mrs Ormiston Chant (1848–1923), caricatured in *Punch* as Mrs Prowlina Pry, undertook a sustained attack on the London music-halls in 1894, obliging the London County Council to clean up their bawdry, and to stop their promenades from serving as one of London's chief markets for sexual services. The Indecent Advertisement Act was passed in 1889; somewhat perversely it was used as a weapon in the fight against the extension of birth control. Homosexual acts had always been illegal; from the 1870s the British public seems to have developed a renewed detestation of male homosexuality. In 1885 Labouchere's Act made such relationships much more vulnerable to the law and to the blackmailer; it was under its provisions that Oscar Wilde was sent to prison in 1895. A new form of entertainment was covered by the Cinematograph Act of 1909, giving the local authorities the job of licensing cinemas and so overseeing their conduct; in 1912 the British Board of Film Censors was set up by the film industry itself.

The law on prostitution continued to make soliciting the relevant offence. As a result the attack on prostitution was left to local authorities, their police forces, and their watch committees. The Vagrancy Act of 1898 reaffirmed that it was a crime for men to live off immoral earnings of women. The attack on the Contagious Diseases Acts,[1] led by Josephine Butler (1828–1906), was successful: they were repealed in 1886. The attempt at control of venereal disease by registration and inspection had thus failed, largely because of the resentment among women against the attempt to enforce it through the chief carriers, the prostitutes, involving as it did discrimination between men and women. Meanwhile the white slave traffic had become a *cause célèbre*: the Criminal Law Amendment Act of 1885 was aimed at stopping such procuration: because it failed to do so the White Slavery Act was passed in 1912.

Alcohol abuse continued to be a serious problem. The Licensing Act of 1872 (the Bruce Act), pushed through by the temperance interest, had done something to limit the number of public houses through licensing, but drunkenness continued to be a frightening national problem, damaging to happiness and national efficiency. By

1. See chapter 8, section 7 above.

the 1890s many temperance reformers had lost faith in men and women curing themselves in response to educative programmes. To those seeking to promote national efficiency, the reduction of drink consumption, the great vice of the late Victorian and Edwardian working class, was a high priority. But any attempt at increased state control met with the opposition of brewers and publicans (organised in 1888 as the National Trade Defence Association), and their patrons. Against the publicans the nonconformists could use their pulpits and their temperance organisations.

In 1892 and 1895 Sir William Harcourt sponsored Bills to make the control of liquor a matter of 'local option'. This device would have placed the whole matter not on a uniform national basis, but would have made it a question of local discretion. Both Bills were lost, with that of 1895 contributing to the Liberal defeat in the general election of that year. This experience caused many Liberals to regard the temperance question as a liability. But the issue remained strong in the country.

Balfour's Conservative government in 1904 tried a different tack. It sought a means of reducing the number of licences. To do so meant finding a formula that would pacify the brewers. The Licensing Act provided for compensation for the licences withdrawn, not by state payment, but by a levy on the licences remaining. The government justified this by arguing that the Act increased the monopoly value of each of the reduced number of licences. The Liberals in 1908 tried to extend this principle, but their Licensing Bill, proposing a further drastic reduction of licences, was killed in the Lords.

In the cases of drink, prostitution and cinema censorship a good many people were attracted to the idea of authorising local authorities to regulate these matters according to their views of the needs of their immediate communities, rather than trying to regulate by general enactment. In the upshot prostitution and the cinema were in the hands of local authorities, but this principle was not acceptable in terms of the drink trade.

10. The state in relation to women, children and the family

In the years 1874–1914 women began to demand political en-franchisement. Married women property owners were given the local franchise under the Local Government Act of 1894, entitling them to elect and be elected to local authorities and to school boards. But the parliamentary franchise was denied them. In spite of the suffrage movement, with its use of passive resistance and, ultimately, violence, the male legislators would not modify their monopoly until 1918.

A second kind of freedom was now being sought, namely the right to escape from marriage. Under the Matrimonial Causes Act of 1878 abused wives could obtain legal separation and maintenance from husbands. The Royal Commission of 1912 favoured a liberalising of the ground for divorce, but no change was made. The Poor Persons' Rules of 1914 were designed to meet the legal costs of the very poor. But the marriage bond yielded little to the attacks upon it: the peak pre-war year for divorces was 1909 when 694 were granted. Marriage was still very much for life.

But family life was losing something of its standing and sanctity. In 1889 the Prevention of Cruelty to Children Act gave the courts power to intervene where children were being abused by their parents. In 1908 came the Children's Act ('the Children's Charter'), a measure to codify the law on children's rights, to exempt them from the full impact of adult law by instituting juvenile courts and to improve their protection against parental abuse and neglect. This latter meant imposing a new range of duties on local authorities, often involving intrusions by them into the home. The schools were first called to the aid of the family with the provision of school meals and school medical inspection. The state still looked to the family as the fundamental social unit, but at the same time was becoming aware of its inadequacies.

11. The penal code: from retribution to partial easement

In the treatment of prisoners the trend toward physical harshness continued from the 1860s. The Prisons Act of 1877 placed the English prisons under the Home Office, the belief being that the local authorities could not be relied upon to be tough enough. The prisons were thus the first social service to be nationalised. A Prison Commission was given general responsibility. To hard labour and hard beds was added the rule of silence. This programme of retribution and deterrence represented a suspension of thought about the causation of crime, as well as an abandonment of the evangelical sense of social guilt concerning it. Criminals were now simply evil doers who must be punished, providing an example for the rest of society.

But the evangelical inheritance, though in a way secularised, ran very deep. In 1895, in response to criticism outside the prisons and tension and protest within them, a Committee of Investigation recommended a programme of humanisation. There was to be an end of useless toil accompanied by the provision of productive industry; libraries, preachers and instructive visitors were to be introduced; there was to be segregation of first offenders and reformatory training for prisoners under twenty-one. These proposals were implemented under the Acts of 1898 and 1899. A different perspective had asserted itself over that of the sixties and seventies. But there was an oppressive heritage of old buildings, many of them on the cellular plan appropriate to the separate system. The enormous cost of reconstructing the prisons in the physical sense, to meet more liberal standards, was becoming apparent. The prison treatment of the suffragettes produced glimpses of reality that were deeply disturbing.

The system in 1914 thus still rested very largely on deterrence and retribution. It seemed to be successful: the streets were safe places. There is no evidence that the working classes were any more sympathetic to prisoners than were the middle classes; indeed the trade unions sometimes showed resentment over concern with prisoners when their own members were in poverty. The Home Office, with many new duties thrust upon it arising from the Factory Acts and Workmen's Compensation Acts, did its best to draw a veil over the prison system, making investigation by outsiders difficult. The legal profession showed little understanding of poverty as a source of crime.

12. The involvement of the state in welfare by 1914

The pattern of social welfare provision was still by 1914 a collectivity of ad hoc actions, each with its peculiar history and long debate. But though there was no unifying principle or co-ordinated thinking, the trend was clear. It was toward the amelioration of the most obvious forms of social suffering, the improvement of industrial and urban life and the lessening of inequalities of life chances. Yet in spite of this trend, there is much room for argument concerning its adequacy. The forces hostile to welfare concessions in their many forms were still powerful.

British society was thus well begun on the long and continuous testing of a number of related questions. These had to do with the proper size of the welfare share of the national product, the best ways of levying it upon the community through the tax system, how to allocate it between the competing social ends, how to administer it in its many aspects and, finally, how to assess the implications of welfare policy for the productivity of the economy.

13. The bureaucracy

The Treasury continued to dominate the civil service: it was the great centre-piece of the British bureaucracy, drawing to itself the cream of the examination candidates. It practised a detailed scrutiny of the expenditure of all ministries and departments. But it would seem that where there were politically powerful and policy effective ministers they and their departments could sway the Treasury. The Treasury carefully sponsored a public image of neutrality as between contending policies, projecting itself as implementing the remits of the government of the day. But such a posture was inevitably unreal: the men in the Treasury, as elsewhere, had their preferences deriving from their value systems. For example the effectiveness of the Local Government Board, impaired by inadequate ministers, was further reduced by unsympathetic Treasury control.

Nevertheless the idea of Platonic guardians as interpreters of the public good, striving impartially to promote it, continued to be powerful both among senior bureaucrats and among an element of the politicians.

PART V

Total war and troubled peace, 1914–39

14

The policy imperatives of war; the reconstruction debate and the dismantlement of control, 1914–21

1. *Committing the nation to fighting*

Britain and her allies were at war with Germany and the central European powers from 4 August 1914 to 11 November 1918. The conflict cut across the political, economic and social debate of late Victorian and Edwardian times, overwhelming it with an experience of traumatic depth. It brought the greatest state manipulation of society that Britain had ever known, involving all available techniques from persuasion to conscription and civilian coercion.

How far were those who had control of the state justified in the uses they made of it? Part of the answer lies in the nature of these uses, for there is the question of the choice of the most appropriate means in given circumstances in pursuing a chosen end.

But it was with the end itself that the great question of justification lay. Was it right to go to war 'with Germany and her allies, and to persist in such a war for more than four years? Two levels of motivation were at work. There was the moral aspect, having to do with the integrity of small nations and the sanctity of treaties entered into for their defence. When the commitment lengthened, the more fundamental question, that of the security of Britain herself, came to the fore. Since the seventeenth century Britain, by instinct born of geography, had resisted all attempts at continental hegemony. Once more this was the issue. Should Germany and her allies be allowed so radically to alter the balance in Europe as to make herself master, able at leisure to reduce Britain to her will? Or was the whole question misstated? Could the ancient conflicts between European nations be superseded by a new principle, perhaps that of the brotherhood of working men, such that armed combat would become unthinkable? There were those who before the war, believing that war was the result of economic rivalry, had hoped for such a solution, and who, briefly in the confusion of 1917, hoped again that a peace of reconciliation could be negotiated.

The present discussion cannot resolve the difference between those who accepted the justification of the war and those who did not. But this difference is a datum. For those who accepted the war it followed that more and more state intrusion was necessary and justified in order to bring victory. No one at the beginning could know what would be involved before the end; it was a question of ongoing, incremental acceptance of the state's imperatives. Neither set of warring nations dared relax its efforts for fear its opponent would take advantage: even possible peace overtures could be regarded as tactics to weaken the will of the other side.

For those in charge of the state between 1914 and 1918 a necessary and drastic simplification of mind took place. Once embarked on the perilous process of national mobilisation, once manpower and resources had been reassigned on a significant scale from peace to war uses, once the incredibly complex diplomacy necessary to gain allies for the encirclement of Germany had been embarked upon (involving pledges to them of territorial or other gains from *their* traditional enemies), there seemed no course open but to go on. Once men had died in large numbers for the cause, it would be betrayal to weaken. Irreducible conflict, on a world scale, and in an industrial form, had become self-confirming. So it was that the state was used in a sustained and undeviating way in order to turn Britain into a war machine. The liberal, market-based economy and society was set aside, in the hope of ensuring its long-term preservation.

Yet even this dedication to an end had to take account of the new realities that had asserted themselves since Britain's last great war, that against revolutionary and Napoleonic France. The industrial revolution had matured; Britain was now an advanced industrial country. Politicians had to offer and act in propitiation of a largely enfranchised male population. They had also to perform within the limits of acceptability set by a complex and powerful labour force, with its own highly developed organisational structure, together with a capacity for massive and unpredictable action outside that structure. For though it was the middle classes who were dominant in parliament (and not the landed class as in Napoleonic times), they had to beware of the new potency and volatility among the mass of working men and women. The great danger was that at the industrial level critical groups of workers could be appealed to with an immediacy that could override any generalised acceptance of the war. Moreover there was present that small minority of revolutionary activists whose chosen business it was to work upon grievances generated by wage differentials, dilution and falling real wages, in order to bring about general breakdown as a prelude to what they believed would be a better society.

As a counter to this kind of activity, as well as on more general grounds, the government had to concern itself with the shape of the post-war future. It sponsored a reconstruction debate, especially from 1917 onward. In it were discussed the objectives of war that reached beyond victory. An attempt was made to envisage the new Britain, partly as a contribution to morale, and partly in an effort to arrive at an assessment of the longer-term trends and needs of British society.

2. Mobilising the economy

The war was at first thought of as a short-term affair, though indeed a major crisis. The first step for the government was to take hold of the money and credit supply, in order both to reassure the business world and to give the state the powers it needed over this central mechanism. The banks were closed on 4, 5 and 6 August, freezing the system. On 6 August the Currency and Bank Notes Act was rushed through parliament. The gold coinage of England was to be replaced by paper on the Scottish model: the Treasury was to issue £1 and 10s paper notes (previously the smallest Bank of England note was £5). Both kinds of notes were made legal tender. In this way the Bank of England was relieved of its duty to meet its notes in gold on demand; in short, the gold standard was suspended, as it had been in 1797. There was now no control on the money supply except the will of the state: government could proceed to create money and credit to take control of real resources without limit.

As the state freed itself of financial constraint it had to enforce its will upon society at large. The principal means of doing so was the Defence of the Realm Act (DORA), which, with its extensions by Orders in Council, gave the state power to stop almost any action or activity of which it disapproved. *Habeas Corpus* could be set aside, should the government decide this was necessary, along with freedom of speech, press and meeting, and the right of trial by jury could be suspended. The whole structure of civil liberties, so long inviolate against the state, now became subject to state approval. This was acceptable in the first phase of emergency enthusiasm. But it became less so as, early in 1915, there was increasing disillusionment, with reports of mismanagement, errors and delays in the conduct of the war; these brought an urge to express misgiving or to make protests.

In May 1915 the Liberal government was replaced by a coalition which included Liberal, Conservative and Labour members. Lloyd George was made Minister of Munitions of War. From his new Ministry he, to a large extent, took over the economy and society, dealing with output, labour relations, health, housing, morale and even the consumption of alcohol. He introduced the piece-work system of payment. He mobilised Britain with a completeness never before approached; in so doing he imposed immense strains and hastened the evolution of labour attitudes and institutions. But he also sponsored a host of ideas for easing labour relations through industrial welfare, unheard of before the war, including recreational facilities, welfare supervision and canteens and restrooms. New management and production techniques were brought in under the Ministry's encouragement. The Ministry in a matter of months became the core of a state collectivism on a colossal scale, controlling production, raw materials and manpower; in so doing it created a situation in which the trade unions had to be conceded a new power of organisation and of dealing with government.

The government entered upon the production of its own means of warfare, going far beyond the traditional army arsenals and naval dockyards, setting up its own factories. All *punctilio* about intruding into the realm of private enterprise was set aside, virtually without discussion. Bulk imports were undertaken under state agencies – the government thus became the major marketer, as well as the effective controller of imports and exports. The railways, shipping and the mines were all brought under direct control; they were in effect temporarily nationalised. An entire system of economic warfare, based on an all-out blockade of the central powers, was set up.

Inevitably the massive government spending brought pressure at two major points in the economy, namely the balance of payments and the ability of the government to borrow. The first brought a return to protection: under the McKenna Duties 33½% was levied on a range of items thought to be of low priority in wartime. This control on imports was not enough to right the foreign balance: an enormous overseas deficit began to develop. To meet it assets held abroad by British nationals were taken over and sold. Thus the fat which Britain had accumulated in the high Victorian age, and which was so important to her invisible earnings, was rendered down. The government's response to its borrowing problem was a series of massive campaigns to persuade people to buy its bonds. One of the greatest of these was the Victory Loan Campaign, begun in January 1916. The controls on imports and the abstinence from consumption by subscribers to loans eased to some extent the enormous pressure of domestic demand generated by the government itself. But such measures could not stem the rise in prices.

The retail price index (July 1914 = 100) rose from 123 in 1915 to 215 in 1919 (it reached 249 in 1920, falling to 226 in 1921); the wholesale price index (1900 = 100) rose from 117.2 in 1914 to 296.5 in 1919 (it was 368.8 in 1920 and around 200 in 1921). The national debt increased relentlessly, as did the problem of paying interest upon it (it stood at £706 million in 1914; by 1919 it was £7,481 million). In consequence of the government's borrowing policy the banks found their portfolios stuffed with government securities – they had become, in effect, a branch of government, lending most of the money deposited with them to the state.

These problems of economic control were serious enough. But the central and most difficult one had to do with the labour force. It too had to be bent to the government's priorities. Over a large part of labour there was an acceptance of the need to conform to the programme of the government: this disposition was strengthened by the appeal of patriotism and by the unwillingness to deprive the men in the field and at sea of the weapons they needed. But as the war went on some sections of labour were more aggrieved than others; it was here that the problem of conciliation assumed a new urgency.

The systematic mobilisation of the human resources of the nation began with the National Registration Act of July 1915. A complete register of the male population of Britain was compiled, an action formerly unthinkable. At the same time was passed the Munitions of War Act. Under it the government assumed powers of compulsory arbitration, prohibiting strikes in war industries, and allowing job changes in them only by authority of an employer's certificate. The government also took power to regulate wages through Munitions Tribunals. In January 1916 came compulsory military service for single men: conscription was extended to married men two months later. Labour, the trade unions and the miscellaneous socialists wanted conscription of property as well, but there was no sustained insistence, partly because of the inherent difficulty of carrying out such a proposal. The government would not go beyond its general Excess Profits Duty, imposed on all businesses in 1915, and its Rent and Mortgage (War Restriction) Acts of the same year which pegged rents of unfurnished tenancies (about 85% of rented premises) at the 1914 level; eviction was made very difficult.

Meanwhile the war was going badly. The Easter Week Rebellion in Dublin in 1916 meant that the government was confronted with civil as well as foreign war. But more devastating in the short run were the appalling casualties suffered by Kitchener's new army on the Somme in July. The élan went out of the war: there was numbness, lassitude and disillusionment.

It was time for the Prime Ministership of Asquith to end, and for Lloyd George to move to the centre of things. The transfer of power was made in December 1916. In spite of the nation's needs this could only be done by the traditional means of factional manoeuvre. The Liberal Party, at its peak of power only ten years earlier, was fatally split, entering upon its long futility. But Lloyd George, at the head of a government in which his personal supporters were few, rose to the occasion. He saw that the restoration of morale required two things: strong leadership in the prosecution of the war, and the provision of a new incentive in the shape of a vision of a new post-war Britain. He supplied both. His war cabinet was a drastically slimmed-down affair, working at a pitch that had been impossible under Asquith. In February 1917 the cabinet set up a revived and renovated Reconstruction Committee which shortly became the Ministry for Reconstruction. With Christopher Addison (1869–1951) at its head it sponsored seven committees on leading aspects of the national life. A Ministry of Labour was established in January 1917. It took over labour matters from the Board of Trade, providing the labour movement with a facility it had long wanted, namely its 'own' Ministry, able to co-ordinate its interests and to provide a Minister in parliament.

But there now fell new blows, both external and internal. The Irish troubles continued and the French army was in a state of near mutiny. The Russian eastern front collapsed; Germany imposed appalling terms on Russia, depriving her of 34% of her people, 32% of her arable land and 54% of her industry. Germany, in a reciprocal attempt to starve Britain, embarked upon unrestricted submarine warfare. At the same time British labour unrest had entered its most difficult phase with widespread unofficial strikes. Against these calamities, however, was the entry of the United States into the war in April 1917.

The threat to the food supply brought the appointment of a Food Controller (1916), shortly superseded by a Minister of Food (1917). The Corn Production Act of August 1917 gave the Board of Agriculture power to order pasture to be put under crop. It also guaranteed a highly remunerative wheat price, bringing essential help to an industry which had been wholly exposed since the repeal of the Corn Laws in 1846. But in return the farmers had to pay minimum wages, set on an area basis, under a national Agricultural Wages Board.

The sacrifices which the people had sustained were recognised and rewarded in February 1918 by the Representation of the People Act; all males over twenty-one could now vote. So too could women over thirty. In this way the electorate was increased threefold to over 20 million. In a situation in which the British people were more regulated and confined by the state than ever before, provision was made for an enormous extension of political participation.

In March 1918 the great German offensive was stopped: the end of the war was in sight. The British army at the end was sustained by extraordinary confidence and morale, performing high feats of arms as it and its allies advanced.

With victory must come a general election; using the extended franchise, Lloyd George sought to concentrate public attention on reconstruction. But somehow in this last phase of hostilities the urge for retribution gained the upper hand, with cries of 'Germany must pay', and 'Hang the Kaiser'. Perhaps such a response was to be expected to a war which had cost the British empire almost a million lives of men in their prime, together with over 2 million wounded. Moreover, it is possible that in this matter the government fell victim to its own anti-German propaganda. The armistice came on

11 November; the following day the general election was announced. The coalition government awarded its 'coupon' to candidates who supported it, though the Labour Party fought independently. The result was a great victory for Lloyd George's government, but one based more on retribution than reconstruction.

3. Rallying and propitiating the labour force

Just as, before the war, the dominant social phenomenon had been the new assertiveness of organised labour, so too during the war. Though by and large the government obtained labour consent for its actions, this was at the price of a mixture of solicitude, negotiation, manoeuvre, appeal to patriotism and threat.

But there was first something of a phase of common outlook. In August 1915 the TUC, the General Federation of Trade Unions and the Labour Party accepted the war, declaring an 'industrial truce' during hostilities; the Parliamentary Labour Party agreed to join the coalition. The unions decided to postpone large wage claims until the war was over. Out of the Treasury Conference of March 1915 came union acceptance of dilution of skilled labour, together with a surrender, for the duration, of the right to strike. The government on its side accepted that dilution should be under union supervision, and that munitions profits should be controlled. Much of this was embodied in the Munitions of War Act. The setting up of the Ministry of Labour with a Labour MP in charge, in January 1917, seemed to put a kind of seal on the bargain between the state and labour.

The unions were thus left with the challenge of containing the pressures that war was generating among their members. By accepting it, the unions created the conditions for the appearance of a new form of labour representation, that of the shop stewards on the workshop and factory floor. Though many shop stewards were simply non-ideological trade unionists, a small group of them were left-wing socialists or syndicalists. Their dedication gave them more than proportionate power. This was the context in which DORA was most used against civil liberties.

The problem first became serious in March 1916 when there were unofficial strikes among the Clydeside engineers. Certain left-wing leaders were arrested under DORA, removed from the district and kept away. In the May strikes of 1917 industrial disturbances among munitions workers spread rapidly. Under dilution the earnings of skilled men could fall to near, or even below, those of the unskilled, for by means of speeding up the unskilled men on piece-rates could sometimes take home more than did the labour aristocracy. This frustration over lost differentials gave the shop stewards' committees their opportunity. There was a certain irony in the fact that socialist ideologies could find their entrée to industrial power by leading the fight against the egalitarian effects of a reduction in wage differentials.

But the trade unions, in their support of the war effort, and in spite of the challenge from the left, made real gains. Full employment brought them increased power and enlarged membership. Under Part II of the National Insurance (Munitions Workers) Act of 1916, most of the workforce was in effect made eligible for unemployment insurance, though under conditions of full employment the workers tended to resist making insurance payments. The status of the unions in relation to government was greatly enhanced by the consultations to which they were now made party, both as to policy and its implementation. They were moving into the position of autonomous bodies which had to be listened to with great care.

The Labour Party adopted a new constitution in 1918. It declared itself for the creation of a socialist system of society, by the replacement of competitive capitalism by planned co-operation in both production and distribution. To this end, under Clause IV, the Party placed among its objectives the nationalisation of the means of production, 'To secure for the producers by hand and brain the full fruits of their industry, and the most equitable distribution thereof that may be possible, upon the basis of the common ownership of the means of production and the best obtainable system of popular administration and control of each industry or service.'

But between the generalities of the constitution and the conducting of government there stood the question of the Party programme as it might be formulated for each successive general election. Clause V of the new constitution regulated this very important matter for presentation to the public. The annual conference of the Labour Party as a whole would determine what proposals might be included, doing so on the basis of 'not less than two-thirds of the votes recorded on a card vote'. Out of this selection the National Executive Committee and the Parliamentary Labour Party 'shall decide which items from the Party programme shall be included in the Manifesto which shall be issued by the National Executive Committee prior to each General Election'. Joint assent being thus required, it followed that, in effect, both the National Executive and the Parliamentary Labour Party had the power of veto. In particular the Parliamentary Party was free to decline to adopt any policy, even though it had Party Conference approval. In this complex manner it was arranged that the Party as a whole could express itself in Conference (with its powerful trade union card votes), but at the same time its MPs could exercise their independent judgment and consciences in the House of Commons according to their inter-pretation of what was right in prevailing circumstances. Clause V reconciled parliamentary democracy with the extra-parliamentary power of the Party and its trade union basis.

4. The role of business

Business too was made subject to a wide range of state controls. But business men, acting as temporary civil servants, played a large part in operating them. As well as running a good deal of the state apparatus, British business came together successfully for the first time in an organisational sense in 1916 with the formation of the Federation of British Industries. There had been a growing sense of identity and of a need for effective organisation at the national level, in order that business could, like the trade unions, offer a common front to the state. There were models in the United States (the National Association of Manufacturers) and in Europe (the Swedish Federation of Industries). The FBI absorbed the Employers' Parlia-mentary Association, the branches of the latter becoming the District Branches of the FBI. But the FBI did not concern itself directly with labour questions. These were entrusted to a separate body, the National Confederation of Employers' Associations, founded in 1919, later known as the British Employers' Federation. It was to deal with collective bargaining between employers and unions on questions of wages and conditions of employment.

5. The administrative revolution

There had been a continuous growth of governmental functions since the 1830s, with the expert becoming increasingly important in central and local government. But the war brought an explosive extension of the administrative state.

Government was, of course, much gratified that for the purpose of fighting the war it was possible to bring such vast machinery into operation quickly and effectively. But in another sense government had reason to be uneasy at the phenomenon it had so successfully brought into being. It was disconcerting and indeed frightening to discover what immense power a modern state could now take over the life of the nation, making itself the master of the economy and of the people.

6. Discussing and implementing reconstruction

The Reconstruction Committee set up in February 1917 under Addison was charged with forward thinking about the great areas of necessary social action (namely, health, housing, pensions and unemployment insurance, and education). The war had revealed even more dramatically than the Boer War had done the deplorable physical condition of much of Britain's working classes. There were the further challenges of the restructuring of industry, and of fuel policy, together with the two great issues that directly concerned organised labour – the determination of wages and the control of industry. It was a massive set of assignments – in effect all the problems left in abeyance by the coming of the war, and further complicated by it.

After long frustration a Ministry of Health was set up in 1919, with Addison as first Minister and Robert Morant as first Permanent Secretary. To it passed the duties of the old Local Government Board (with its Poor Law Division and its responsibility for health), together with the Insurance Commission. It was to undertake also the main burden of the reconstruction policy of the coalition government elected in 1918.

This involved an entirely new responsibility, that of housing. The government had promised 'homes for heroes'; Addison and Morant were to supply them. The Housing and Town Planning Act (Addison's Act) of July 1919 was a new beginning, breaching the subsidy barrier. War and the claims of ex-servicemen were necessary to bring this about. The Treasury was to provide housing subsidies both to local councils and to private builders.[1] The Ministry of Health was thus

1. See chapter 21, section 4 below.

made central to health, the poor law and housing. Indeed it was charged with a responsibility for the general quality of British social life.

But one important aspect was kept outside its purview, namely pensions. A Ministry of Pensions was set up in 1919, to which the problem of old age was passed. The new Minister appointed a vigorous committee which produced a report which startled the government. It proposed a system of 'complete and adequate public assistance' which would include old age, unemployment, injury and indeed any other incapacity. But the cabinet could not sanction the kind of increase in public expenditure thus envisaged. Instead it passed the Old Age Pensions Act of 1919. This raised the basic pension to 10s; it also removed the pauper disqualification, so that the guardians could, in effect, augment the old age pension. The government would go no further in either money or organisational terms.

This left the question of unemployment benefits. Here too the response was minimal. One of the Ministry of Reconstruction's sub-committees had in February 1918 set out the choice between a scheme of general insurance to cover all workers in all conditions of the economy, and the paying out of extra ad hoc benefits of one kind or another as emergencies arose: it proposed the first of these courses. But its proposal for planned foresight was not acted upon. The government fell back in 1919 on an 'out of work donation', to maintain the unemployed who were without the support of the 1911 scheme. But this did mean that the state, however loosely, had accepted responsibility for providing the unemployed with a minimum income.

The wartime debate on education had begun well before the Reconstruction Committee began its deliberations. H.A.L. Fisher at the Board of Education had introduced a far-reaching Education Bill in August 1917, but was defeated by local authority and industrial resistance. His Education Act of 1918, though embodying much less than he had hoped, was a significant advance. Elementary education was already free; Fisher's Act required local authorities to submit proposals extending the free principle to all branches of education in their charge, especially the important secondary sector. The school-leaving age was to be raised nationally to fourteen. Grants were offered to local authorities for the provision of nursery schools so that the children of busy mothers could be taught good social habits. Moreover education as a continuing experience after leaving school was to be made possible by encouraging local authorities to provide day continuation schools. Educational grants to local authorities were improved. Teachers' salaries were taken from the often parsimonious and certainly unequal hands of local authorities and fixed nationally under a system later to be known as the Burnham Scales: this provided the basis for a much improved teaching profession. Fisher's vision of a state system of educational opportunity from primary school to university was forwarded by his Act, presaging far-reaching changes in British society.

The structure of industry was approached with great caution. A Department of Scientific and Industrial Research had been founded in 1916 in order to facilitate a more innovative approach to technology, a general enough aspiration. But how to use constructive state action to sponsor modernisation of the basic industries in a more general sense was a much more difficult problem. The relevant sub-committees showed no sympathy with the proposal for outright government ownership and operation in peacetime, but pursued the liberal path of seeking means whereby the state could sponsor initiatives from within each of the problem industries themselves. In coal, for example, the emphasis was upon the need to increase productivity through improved mechanisation, and the difficulties involved in doing so. In steel the need for larger-scale units and greater efficiency was stressed; a programme of rationalisation through merger was proposed, together with a single national selling agency to strengthen bargaining power abroad. In shipbuilding there was an appeal for efficiency, with standardisation to play a large part. Suggestions made by some sub-committees, in some sectors of industry, of a pattern of rationalisation that would lead to effective monopoly, clashed with proposals from other quarters that machinery was needed to investigate and control trusts. The reports make interested reading. But their authors must have had the bleak feeling that they were shadow-boxing: that no immediate action was possible, and that such matters would only gain real governmental attention in crisis conditions. The sad paradox was present that the first comprehensive view of the British industrial economy was taken under conditions that could inspire it, but which at the same time made it largely futile.

There were certain subjects that had been high on the pre-war agenda, and indeed had dominated it, which could only be brought into the reconstruction debate with extreme caution. These were industrial relations, wage determination and the control of industry. On this hornets' nest of topics it was all the state could do to obtain agreement to its wartime measures. It dared not open the frightening question of longer-term principles, for the foundations of society itself were involved. Thus the aspects which most determined the shape of the new Britain for which the war was being fought were taboo because they were too divisive.

The Federation of British Industries turned its mind to these questions in 1918 with its Committee for the Organisation of Industry. It stressed the need for a common industrial policy involving close co-operation between firms, namely 'a collective responsibility for efficient and economic production'. This, however, would involve enormous difficulties, for it would require the control of competition, the regulation of prices, the elimination of excess and inefficient firms and the limitation of entry of new ones. The question of how to induce the degree of discipline necessary for collective action inevitably arose. Could order and efficiency be generated without invoking the sanctions available to the state? The Committee, in spite of its insistence on the urgent need for industrial reconstruction, recoiled from the idea of compulsion, frightened by the fear of bureaucratisation of industry and its consequent rigidity, by the possibility of the loss of business initiative and efficiency and by the general prospect of involvement with the state. For the first time British industry, in its corporate form of the FBI, faced the problem of long-term policy. But the conditions of solution, here as on the labour side, were too frightening and divisive to be pursued, beyond the level of general discussion.

Such advance as was achieved was cautious and limited. The *Report* of the Whitley Committee of 1917 suggested that there should be consultations between capital and labour at national, district and works level. In this way a cautious opening of the door of workers' participation was proposed, but no legislative action on these lines followed. The Minister of Labour did, however, approve the suggestion that joint industrial councils (Whitley Councils), consisting of unions' and employers' representatives, should be established, where the parties agreed, in industries where firms were too small for effective union organisation. With the support of the Ministry seventy-three such councils were formed, fifty-eight of which were still meeting in 1923. But they had no place in the great basic industries.

The social reconstruction era may be taken to have run from 1917 to 1921. On the side of failure, the remaking of the poor law and the extension of insurance for old age, unemployment and other eventualities constituted too big a sub-agenda to be dealt with: the result was ameliorative patching-on leading to even greater in-coherence. The exploration of the possibilities of industrial re-structuring had little direct effect, though it provided anticipations of later arguments. With respect to wage determination and workers' participation in the control of industry the issues were too dangerous; apart from the Whitley Councils the situation was left much as it had been in 1914.

On the side of new beginnings the most striking action was the adoption by the state of a positive, subsidy-backed programme of housing provision, though Addison's Act of 1919 was soon to be departed from.[1] Secondly, there was Fisher's Education Act of 1918. For the rest there was little specific governmental commitment. But the setting up of Ministries of Health, Pensions, Labour and Agriculture and Fisheries meant that four sets of problems had been consolidated within their own Ministries, and had been made the responsibility of members of the government, with appropriate civil service support.

As to economic reconstruction, even less was achieved. All the problems of the economy were carried over from 1914, but now were aggravated by the sacrifices of foreign assets and the invisible earnings they had brought, together with the formation of new world patterns of production and trade from which Britain, absorbed in her war, had been excluded.

7. Liquidating the system of control

Both capital and labour regarded themselves as having made 'con-cessions' that were temporary, and which must be ended with the peace. Indeed the hectic and far-reaching adoption of wartime

---

1. See below, chapter 21, section 4.

collectivisation may, in the longer term, have arrested the growth of state control, making both sides yearn for a return to liberty of action. So far as the state was concerned there was neither blueprint nor will – the government simply responded to the immediate demands made upon it, relieved to be able to retreat from the power made available to it by the administrative revolution.

The government's carefully sequential demobilisation plans were made a nonsense: the army largely demobilised itself. The central setter of industrial priorities, the Ministry of Munitions, was wound up as quickly as possible. The unions insisted upon the restoration of the rights they had gained before 1914. The controls on consumption were dropped as soon as the easing of shortage permitted. The McKenna Duties lasted longer, but were discontinued in 1924. The embargo on lending abroad was ended in 1925. The Corn Production Act was extended under the 1920 Agriculture Act, but when agricultural prices fell in 1921–2 guaranteed prices for grain ended, being replaced by small payments per acre of wheat and oats planted; at the same time, as compensation to the farmers, minimum wage regulation was abandoned. The coal mines (in effect nationalised during the war) reverted to their former owners in March 1921, though control over the railways did not really end.[1] By 1921 there had been, over a large part of economic policy, a return to the position of 1914.

Though victory had been the fruit of shared efforts and sacrifices, the gulf between capital and labour was wider than ever. New postures and new consciousness had been generated that would never really be reversed. Labour had achieved a new status and a new access to parliament and the bureaucracy. The business world had shared in the heady delights of centralism and state sanction, and had at last paralleled labour in establishing a degree of unified identity. Government had gained a new sense of what could be done by centralised power, but had no real desire to use it.

1. See chapter 17, section 8 below.

15

The strains of nationalism: Wales, Scotland and Ireland

1. Land, radicalism and nationalism

The land question had long been basic to English radicalism. It had been so also to Irish nationalism, and, to a lesser degree, to that of Wales and Scotland.[1] But in the course of the inter-war years land largely passed from the radical and nationalist agendas in all four countries. In England and Wales it was largely eclipsed by unemployment and the conflicts between labour and industrial capital. The land question lingered in Scotland in the form of crofters' grievances, but did so only remotely. In Ireland both radicalism and nationalism had been largely detached from the land question. By 1929, due to the operation of the successive Land Acts of the British parliament, 97.4% of those working the land in Ireland were owner-occupiers. Indeed the Land Acts had helped to create a deeply conservative peasantry who, though it could be revolutionary in a nationalist sense, was not so in a social or political sense.

But though nationalism in the United Kingdom had been in a sense simplified by the fading of the land question, it was beginning to become complicated anew by the challenge, on what basis should an independent Scotland, Wales or Ireland rest? There were two general possibilities. One was to identify an intrinsic national character as formed in the traditions of the people, and to base a society upon it. This was the path of Ireland with its ancient culture, its Roman Catholic religion and its small peasant proprietors. The other was to seek a social and political structure appropriate to advanced industrialisation. This could lead either to some concept of the mixed economy, or to some form of socialism, the kind of

---

1. See chapter 10 above.

thing that might have been expected in the industrial parts of Wales or Scotland.

But here nationalism conflicted with the theory of the class struggle: industrial working men and their unions were not greatly attracted by nationalism. They turned rather to the notion of class solidarity. Though Lloyd George at Versailles could play a large part in the creation of a set of independent peoples in Europe, fostering the autonomy of smaller peoples in mid-Europe and the Baltic, there was no great demand that he should do so in his native Wales or in Scotland. In Ireland, however, he could not avoid the issue: it forced itself to the fore of public policy during and immediately following the war.

2. The Welsh

In the inter-war years Welsh nationalism was in a state of some confusion. A nationalist party was formed demanding dominion status. But with the Church of England finally disestablished in 1919, and with the rise of the Labour Party among the miners and other industrial workers in South Wales, the sense of shared identity among Welshmen was not powerful enough or did not take the appropriate form to make nationalism a significant political force. And yet Wales had a higher proportion of speakers of its ancient tongue than did Ireland or Scotland, living largely in the mountainous north. The language had not been made the subject of official English attack as in Scotland after the rising of 1745 and in Ireland after 1789, though it had suffered from the effects of the industrialisation of South Wales.

3. The Scots

In contrast with the Welsh the Scots were able to extract further piecemeal concessions from Westminster and Whitehall and to form them into a new system. In 1926 the Secretary for Scotland was made a full Secretary of State, with a place in the Cabinet. In 1928 the main Boards which had carried out most of Scottish administration[1] were made Departments, and in 1939 they were directly vested in the

---

1. See chapter 10, section 4 above.

Secretary of State. The Scottish Office had become an integrated instrument of government, with its Home, Education, Health and Agriculture Departments. These were brought together in a new building, St Andrews House, Edinburgh. Scotland thus achieved a high level of administrative devolution, though no separate legislative identity.

These developments did not, however, satisfy nationalist aspirations. Inspired partly by the setting up of the Ulster Parliament in Ireland in 1921, there were a number of abortive Home Rule Bills for Scotland in the 1920s. The National Party of Scotland was formed in 1928 by the convergence of four small groups. From the outset the conflict between the left wing and the conservative element within Scottish nationalism became apparent: this was compounded by the differences between those who sought total separation and those who wanted Home Rule, or Dominion status. The Local Government Act (Scotland) of 1929 created larger units, destroying the older localism, and in so doing may have strengthened the search for Scottish identity. But the Party could poll very few votes. In 1932 the right-wing nationalists formed the Scottish Party, which merged in 1934 with the National Party. The resulting Scottish National Party, having ingested the two points of view, was badly factionalised. It had a small membership (2,000 in 1939) and could make no electoral progress against the major parties. But the Scottish cultural renaissance of the 1920s had created, at a certain level, a new Scottish self-awareness.

Scotland thus manifested a curious duality. She gained control of much of her own affairs in the administrative sense. But the politicians and bureaucrats of the Scottish Office were not directly responsible to a Scottish assembly but to the vastly preoccupied British parliament.

4. The Irish

While Wales was largely passive and while the Scots were gaining administrative control of their own affairs on a more or less managerial basis, Ireland exploded in civil war, and then divided into two parts – the one an independent republic and the other a home-ruled part of the United Kingdom.

By 1914 rebellion and civil war in Ireland were perilously near, with a uniquely Irish set of preconditions.[1] In 1916 the conflict came, set off by the Easter Rising of 1916. A proclamation of an Irish Republic was read from the steps of the General Post Office in Dublin by a dedicated, far-seeing, but badly disorganised set of men. The rebels were forced by the British army to surrender; fifteen of their leaders were shot. In less than a year the Irish of the south had adopted their cause. Lloyd George's government, engaged in the greatest of wars, was placed on the rack between Republicans and Ulster Unionists. The nationalist movement gained rapidly in electoral power, with the Sinn Fein ('We Ourselves') Party, led by Eamon de Valera, winning seventy-three seats in the British parliament in the end-of-war election of December 1918. These men formed in Dublin in January 1919 the first Dail Eireann, or Chamber of Deputies, and so set up a self-proclaimed government. There followed two years of violence, practised on one another by Republican gunmen on the one hand and the British army and their vicious irregulars, the Black and Tans, on the other. In December 1921 'the Treaty' was signed by the British and Dail Eireann cabinets. It created in the twenty-six counties of the Catholic south and west not a republic, but a dominion, the Irish Free State, with its capital in Dublin. In the Protestant dominated six counties of the north a 'federal' component of the United Kingdom was set up in the form of Ulster, with its parliament at Stormont, Belfast. This arrangement, it was hoped by the British, would stabilise Ireland, recognising the impossibility of reconciling the two views of Irish identity, but giving each what seemed to be the closest approximation to its desires, consistent with the aspirations of the other. In 1937 a constitution was unilaterally enacted by the Dail setting up the Republic of Eire.

Lloyd George's Treaty of 1921 and the constitution of 1937 seemed to many to have solved the Irish problem. There was to be peace in Ireland for forty years, her first experience of such for many generations. British public policy could now function for the first time since 1800 without being haunted by Irish politics. The nightmare of Ireland had been temporarily lifted.

---

1. See chapter 10, section 5 above.

5. The fourth nationalism

England, too, had its nationalism. But belonging to a dominant people, it required no explanation or justification, and gave rise to no faction seeking to promote it. It had been expressed in extending English influence over the non-Anglo-Saxon parts of the British Isles, partly in search of settled frontiers and a secure western flank, and partly in seeking widened markets. Partly, too, it had taken the form of an extension over the globe of imperial and colonial adventure, offering participation to the Welsh, the Scots and the Irish, eagerly accepted. The three lesser nationalisms could neither assume English identity and so obviate distinctions and quarrels, nor establish fully distinct and unified existences. Moreover all four shared certain tensions within themselves, as for example non-conformists versus the state or majority religion, and labour versus capital. The English language was a kind of unifying influence, but the peripheral nationalisms shared with each other the feeling that their own variants of Celtic tongues should be preserved, but worried about them being made mandatory by state action.

In terms of public policy, the peripheral nationalisms were a complicating factor in British politics. They did not bear greatly on foreign policy, for Wales and Scotland thought with England in terms of resisting any continental hegemony, and in the extension of empire overseas. Even in Ireland, though the French were called in aid in 1798 and the Germans before 1914, few Irishmen really wished to see England conquered. In domestic affairs, however, under the general heading of welfare, the three peripheral societies increasingly wished to manage their own provision, giving it the stamp of their own sets of values. With respect to this Britain had no objection, so long as such services could be financed on the local tax base, and not be made a charge on Westminster. As to the macro-controls, they did not develop a nationalist dimension. This was because monetary and fiscal policy, from 1815 to 1931, followed a largely non-manipulative course, and did not change thereafter apart from the reintroduction of the tariff.

16

The advent of peacetime macro-economic management

1. The shift in values and in power

Post-war Britain was a country much changed, bewildering to its rulers, themselves formed in an age which, for all its stresses, had been one in which the appearance at least of a basic continuity had been maintained.

With the old landed families in decline, new men of wealth and power asserted themselves. They were the creators and products of the age of monopoly already apparent before the war, and of the war itself with its immense government contracts and unprecedented finance. A good number of such men had been drawn directly into the war effort as ministers, departmental heads or advisers. They were now almost a new estate of the realm, the custodians of the arcana of big business. There was some inclination among Conservative politicians to think that they should also be in control of public economic affairs. Their outlook was, of course, very different from that of the former mentors of society, the landed class. The minds of the latter had largely been formed by the agricultural estates over which they had presided; their outlook had its roots in the land, its crops and animals and men. The new business men, especially the most powerful among them, the financiers, were often remote from this kind of psyche-building life, being concerned with estimates about the course of markets, or, very often, estimates about the estimates and actions of others.

As the Liberal Party split between the Lloyd George and Asquith factions, and as its prospects faded, a polarisation of political allegiance took place between the Conservative and Labour Parties. Business could no longer choose between two non-socialist parties. Accordingly its representatives consolidated themselves within the Conservative ranks; in the course of the inter-war years the old landed Toryism with its continued ideal of a social bond stressed by Disraeli and Salisbury was increasingly displaced by a business Conservatism.

A third order of men was moving forward in the contest for power. These were the Labour politicians and the trade union leaders. Beatrice Webb from time to time confided to her diary her discouragement about such men, for whom parliament posed a daunting personal challenge, but who could sometimes be captivated by their new positions when their party became the government. A long and arduous learning process had to be undergone so that Labour MPs and union leaders could move beyond the relatively easy posture of protest, to think in terms of the constructive action they would take when responsibility was theirs. All this was made the more difficult by differences within the labour movement, extending all the way from the belief in the inevitability of gradualness, enunciated by Sidney Webb and held by Ramsay MacDonald, Snowden, and indeed most Labour MPs, to demands for revolutionary socialism coming from a tiny but dedicated minority of activists.

The outlook of the labour movement was yet further complicated by the accession to the Labour Party of middle-class men and women. To them the Liberal Party seemed to have rendered itself impotent by its schism, and Toryism seemed hopelessly backward-looking or self-seeking, leaving the Labour Party as the only remaining possibility. They felt a desire to identify with those who had suffered most from the war and the peace, mingled, in some cases at least, with a judicious careerism. Such people were better educated, more articulate, and often sustained by relics of aristocratic arrogance. They complicated the life of the workers' party, increasing in numbers and authority within it. But they did not add to its clarity of thought, for they lacked the intellectual power to do so. As if these difficulties were not enough, when Labour formed governments in 1924 and 1929 it was on a minority basis, having to act within the limits of tolerance of the Liberal Party.

There was the tragic hiatus left in Britain by the lost generation of men from all classes killed or irreparably damaged by the war; the British Isles suffered 700,000 killed and many more maimed for life. No society can lose so much of its most active age group without affecting its ability to respond to new challenges.

But in spite of all the changes, for a large part of the people the old sanctities remained, though now perhaps a little self-consciously.

There was respect for goodness and for right acting and thinking, and, in spite of falling church attendances, belief in a sustaining God. Most of the population agreed in a general way with the moral and religious values imposed by John Reith on the airwaves through the state monopoly of the British Broadcasting Corporation (f.1926).[1] Though the war had brought disillusionment and hedonism in the upper reaches of British society, there remained a steadiness and decency in the general population. The empire was intact, and was still a considerable source of pride; this was coupled with a belief in a responsibility to bring elements of the empire to self-government. There was confidence in British institutions: parliamentary democracy was regarded as Britain's invaluable gift to the world – embodying a model of the ability of a nation to govern itself by consent.

The electorate who were to adjudicate between the politicians and the parties was enlarged in 1928 by the extension of the vote to all women over the age of twenty-one. Gone was the thirty-year rule; in came what the newspapers were pleased to call the 'flapper vote'. Membership of parliament was similarly extended, so that a direct women's voice could now be raised there, and, indeed, in the cabinet.

The centralising trend of British politics continued. The local and regional orientation, so powerful in the high Victorian age, had been giving place to a concentration on Westminster, and upon the great national parties centred there; by the 1920s British politics had confirmed itself in this pattern. The growing strength of the Labour Party, with its tendency to precipitate an alignment much closer to class differences, reinforced this trend. But local government could still, on occasion, challenge the centre.

2. The policy menu

In order to establish a perspective on the choices made by the British state between 1918 and 1939 it is helpful to consider conceptually what policy possibilities were available to government, both in terms of long-run objectives and in terms of short-term expedients.

At one extreme there was the collectivised model offered by the Soviet Union in the years after the 1917 revolution. For the first time

1. See chapter 18, section 3 below.

there existed a society in which revolutionary ideas had succeeded not merely in harassing or even destroying an ancien régime, but which had established and maintained its own government. It had liquidated property, seen by some as the great source of economic, social and political evil in Britain; it sought to harness the administrative revolution to the service of the state. All of this attracted a good deal of interest and admiration among those who sought an alternative mode for society.

Secondly, less radically, the British government might have continued and adapted the wartime controls, operating a system of economic management from the centre, based upon a chosen set of priorities, but pragmatically based upon experience gained under conditions of war. The view was expressed that the miracles of wartime could be repeated in peacetime if only the government had the will.

Thirdly, there were the proposals of the nationalisers – those who saw certain industries as crucial, but ill-run, and therefore requiring to be taken over and remade. Chief of such industries were the railways and the coal mines, with the miners especially strong advocates that their industry should be lifted out of private hands. There was, of course, a wider view of nationalisation as being the primary condition and instrument of socialism, to which the Labour Party, though without unanimity, was pledged from 1918. The advocates of nationalisation concerned themselves mainly with the older industries.

What of the newer? Did a growth formula offer a fourth possibility, based upon identification by the government of promising firms to be backed with government money? Could the government aid the business world in rehabilitating itself, generating conditions within which the market mechanism could regain its high Victorian vitality, doing so by identifying the growth points where new technology could be applied, and making available resources for their exploitation?

A fifth option was the long-argued one of protection, a line of policy with a strong appeal to an element of the Conservative Party and of the business world. Britain, so the argument ran, should recognise that her former dominance of world trade, with the consequent heavy dependence upon exports, was a phase now ended; selling overseas should be replaced in significant measure by a stimulus to home consumption. This would be brought about by control of imports so that home markets would be supplied by home producers. Efficiency of production would be improved by placing restrictions on the export of capital so that it would be more cheaply and plentifully available in Britain.

A sixth choice was that such protective devices should be accompanied by a radical redistribution of incomes in favour of the working classes through the taxation and wage systems. This would be a combination of socialism in the form of income redistribution and industrial regeneration made possible by protective barriers.

As a seventh possibility, should the government retain what was perhaps the most critical of controls, that of the money supply, to be used in conjunction with a more flexible budgetary policy? Instead of the pre-war system under which international gold flows determined the level of domestic credit, should the money supply, as urged by various people since the eighteenth century, together with the fiscal system, be used as a positive means of stimulus or constraint of economic activity as the needs of full employment might require? Should government thus regulate the economy from the centre, by monetary and budgetary means?

Could an eighth programme be found outside of parliament, to which it could respond? The simplest form of this notion was that governments should seek from the practical men of the business world, the traders and industrialists, or from the trade unions, a view as to what should be done. A more sophisticated version of extra-parliamentary guidance was that there should be, at the national level, an employer–worker concordat that would not only obviate the danger of a national division on class lines, but would arrive at a positive perspective and programme; this was later to become known as corporatism.

The final possibility in this conceptual list was that the government should not only dismantle its wartime system of guidance and control, but should seek fully to rehabilitate the market mechanism, with the reciprocal of minimising its own interventions in the economy, restoring a Gladstonian Britain by causing the state to wither away.

Some of these nine policies could be adopted without necessarily involving an irreversible cumulative commitment to a new form of economy and society. Selective nationalisation or growth-point policy might, for example, be carried out in areas where they seemed especially appropriate, without necessarily going any further; so too an experimental continuation of central controls would have left scope for changes of direction, as would also monetary management or a more flexible budgetary policy that included planned deficits. The same would hold of income redistribution through taxation, or the use of a tariff, for both were infinitely adjustable through the variation of incidence and rates of levy. But even where such tentativeness was possible, there remained the problem of monitoring the effects of what was being done, so as to judge whether policy was on the 'right' lines.

It is not, of course, suggested that the post-war governments tabulated the possibilities confronting them in the above manner and made a systematic and consistent choice between them. But elements of all of these ideas were to have their spokesmen in the inter-war years, and all of them played some part in the complex responses of the Conservative and Labour Parties. Conversely all of them had their limitations, both in terms of practicality and acceptability.

As to the most dramatic, that of Sovietisation, no government or party could consider it seriously. The masses in Britain lacked revolutionary fervour; in spite of a degree of sympathy, they took but a passing and sporadic interest in the evolution of the Soviet system. But a good many people found aspects to admire in the Russian confiscation of privileges and property, accompanied by an assertion of national economic and social priorities as embodied in comprehensive collectivised five-year plans. There was a growing desire among socialistically minded working men and Labour Party members (including middle-class intellectuals) to displace the profit motive among business men, and to limit among workers emulation in effort and consumption as their dominant and formative motivation. The alternative they envisaged was a compound of mutual support, co-operation and a largely egalitarian sharing. The link between effort and reward in terms of wages would be made much looser, so that the less productive and less powerful workers might enjoy a larger proportionate share. But the problems in bringing this about, and in operating such a system, were formidable.

Large-scale economic manipulation built on the base of wartime controls was alien to general inclination and impossible to retain.

There was a powerful urge among business men, trade unions and the consuming public alike to throw off vexatious authoritarian power. This was to be done, in the phrase current at the time, 'at the earliest practicable moment'. Such control smacked of bureaucracy, a German characteristic from which Europe had just been saved. The Ministry of Munitions, the central mechanism for the state's mobilisation of resources, had generated much resentment. Perhaps most important of all, there was no agreement about the aims that were to guide such a concerted policy in times of peace, when freedom of choice of consumption, investment and employment was once more released. It might have been possible, perhaps, to maintain bureaucratic guidance in particular sectors in modified form, but as a general policy control was not acceptable.

The proposal for nationalisation certainly had greater reality about it, at least in particular terms: the state could no doubt have overcome resistance from the business community and taken over the railways and the coal mines: indeed it did use coercive powers over both industries.[1] Here was an area in which choice was possible, but in which it was not politically acceptable to a sufficient degree.

The government did indeed experiment with growth points. The Trade Facilities Act of 1921 made available £25 million for this purpose. But the state's action proved incapable of generating any real new initiatives. The difficulty was, of course, to identify the firms and projects to be backed. The attempt was dropped in 1927.

A solution in terms of stimulating home consumption fenced about by import controls demanded three great associated actions. First there would have to be a major operation on the distribution of incomes, probably through taxation, in favour of those on the lower part of the scale. Such taxation would have to be borne by the wealthier, with possible consequential effects on capital accumulation and managerial incentives. Secondly, it would be necessary to change from an outward-looking attitude based on selling in world markets, to one of semi-autarky, abandoning to a great degree the traditional British belief in the theory of comparative advantage. It also required a change of view on the part of most trade unionists, who were free-traders, in part because of their hostility to proposals to tax the workers' food, a surviving vestige of their former Liberal

1. See chapter 17, sections 4 and 8 below.

creed. Thirdly, far-reaching structural changes would be needed in British industry for it to be able to supply home markets with consumer goods while it was at the same time reducing its capacity for traditional exports. The losses involved in a large-scale withdrawal from world markets would be immediate, but the structural changes would take time, and their outcome was unpredictable. As to income distribution, there were certainly advocates that the gross inequalities of pre-war years should be ended. But to act in this 'socialist' way, on the scale and at the speed required to relieve Britain of her dependence on export markets, would have produced enormous economic and political strains. As to wealth, there was indeed the suggestion that there should be a levy on capital, with which to pay off a large part of the inflated national debt (as had been proposed after the Napoleonic wars), but the practical difficulties were seen as being too great.

To have managed the currency, together with the fiscal system, and through them the general level of activity, would have been to override the most cherished beliefs of the City and the Treasury, hazarding the position of London as a money market, and foisting upon the state a function which politicians and public servants had always sought to avoid.

As to the finding of guidance outside of parliament, there were difficulties with business, union and corporatist solutions. On the business side the men of industry and commerce were in disarray, certainly to 1931, and in large measure thereafter.[1] The Trade Union movement was far from unanimous.[2] Corporatism was briefly discussed in 1928–9, but with no real success.[3]

The policy choices as they were made in the inter-war years between these nine general possibilities were dominated on the one hand by short-term configurations of electoral power generated by the parliamentary system, and on the other by emergencies arising both within the domestic economy and externally from the world economy within which it operated. The atmosphere of decision taking was therefore, at one level, a matter of extemporisation.

Yet beneath this there moved value systems, ideologies and long-

1. See chapter 19 below.
2. See chapter 20 below.
3. See section 7 below.

term goals which in some sense represented the basic views of individuals, groups and parties.

Related to this impalpable aspect was, of course, the question of consent: British society, especially under the new system of complete adult suffrage from 1928, required that for policies to be acceptable they had to enjoy a workable level of agreement as reflected in the electoral and parliamentary systems. This requirement reinforced the long British tradition of pragmatism: governments proceeded experimentally, trying partial expedients in one direction or another, in the hope that, with experience, the long-term course of action would clarify itself. Both the moderate left and the moderate right could see no other way. It is the presence of these various levels of thought and action that make an understanding of what occurred so difficult.

3. The two phases of choice

But one thing is clear: the choice from the inter-war policy menu was made, in the most general sense, in two phases, with 1931–2 as the divider. From 1918 to the beginning of the thirties there was an attempt to return to pre-war economic arrangements. The possibility of a continuation of wartime collectivism disappeared with the impetuous abandonment of universally resented controls. Nationalisation was rejected by the ruling political configuration of the day, and the tentative growth point policy failed. Purposeful protection and radical redistribution were left to one side (though there was a degree of increased redistribution through housing subsidies, unemployment benefits and welfare generally). There was a rehabilitation of older principles, especially in the monetary and budgetary fields.

When this attempt to revert to a partly imagined past collapsed in 1931 under the *force majeure* of world trade contraction, Britain, at last, began the painful task of facing the realities of a changed world and her diminished and embattled place within it. From 1931 onward the British state assumed responsibility for the monetary system, though no radical use was made of it. Government turned vigorously to tariff protection, to bilateralism and to the support of cartelisation. Though it rejected nationalisation, it sponsored the renovation of the traditional industries, using business men as the rationalisers; parts of industry were indeed forced into cartelisation.

Agriculture was brought under a system of market control.[1] These things had to be done in an atmosphere in which organised labour was moving beyond making wage claims to promoting views about the overall working of the economy.[2] In the sense of economic policy Britain entered the modern world in 1931.

It is to the chronological working out of this involved pattern that we now turn. The first great incident concerns the monetary mechanism, so basic to all else.

4. The return to gold, 1925

The misgivings that had been expressed before the war about the precariousness of the London money market were largely forgotten in the immediate post-war years, namely the inadequacy of its reserves and its vulnerability to flows both in and out of hot money. So too were the abuses of the gold standard system by countries that did not abide by the rules of the game. In large measure, indeed, the fundamental dilemma of the gold standard had faded from men's minds, namely the conflict inherent in it between the case for stable exchange rates on the one hand, and the urge by governments to try to meet the domestic needs of the economy in terms of employment and incomes on the other. It is one of the curiosities of the years following victory in 1918 that considerations such as these should have passed from men's minds.

This could happen because of certain values which had been deeply engrained in the minds of the politicians concerned, and especially in those of the City men, the Treasury and leading academics. The liberal creed had instilled a profound instinct that made it necessary, as soon as possible, to get the state clear of the money supply, committing governments once more to the 'automatic' operation of the gold standard. But not only should the money supply be self-adjusting, it should operate in conjunction with free access and egress of goods – free trade was the complementary principle to be preserved, so that here too, in the matter of markets, the state was not involved. The third in a trinity of canons of right policy was the balanced budget.

This three-part liberal economic creed, derived from the nineteenth

1. See chapter 17, section 9 below.
2. See chapter 20 below.

century, was the fundamental faith of the Liberal Party. But it was taken over, by a curious elision, by the Labour Party. It was Philip Snowden (1864–1937), as the first Labour Chancellor of the Exchequer, who in 1924 repealed the McKenna Duties, and who later fought to preserve the gold standard, free trade and the balanced budget. It was the Conservative Party, on the other hand, which was much less averse to the rise of macro-controls for the economy: indeed Stanley Baldwin (1867–1947) fought and lost the general election of 1924 to Labour on a programme proposing a return to protection in the form of a 'scientific' or selective tariff, that is, one closely adjusted to the needs of the British economy and least likely to provoke retaliatory action by other states.

And yet it was the Conservatives, with Churchill as their Chancellor, who in 1925 carried through the return to gold. This crucial step was taken with almost universal support, with only J.M. Keynes (1883–1946) and a few others objecting. This was really two actions: the restoration of the gold standard as the central monetary mechanism, and the decision to return to it at the old pre-war parity of $4.86 to the £1. To a certain extent the two issues were separable. It has been argued that had Britain returned to gold at a lower parity most if not all ill-effects would have been avoided. But the decision would still have been one which demanded that the domestic credit supply (together with employment and incomes) be made subject to the imperatives of external gold flows.

The old parity was too high, to a degree that is the subject of much dispute, perhaps by as much as 10%. This meant that foreigners wishing to buy British goods had to pay more for pounds sterling with which to pay for their purchases. The result was to damage Britain's export capacity. In part this erroneous step was due to miscalculation of the real position of the pound, and of the future course of the American price level: the pound was thought by the Treasury and the Bank to be only slightly overvalued at this parity, and it was expected that American prices would rise relative to British after 1925 bringing the currencies into line with one another; both assumptions proved to be incorrect. Moreover other countries (especially France and Belgium) returned to gold at levels which undervalued their currencies, thus giving their exports a selling advantage in world markets.

The government, having resumed payments in gold on these

terms, had three choices with which to meet the stresses thus generated: lower the parity, abandon fixed exchange rates altogether and let the pound 'float' (and thus determine its own level), or enter upon a struggle to lower costs in British industry far enough to compensate for the overvaluation of sterling. The third course was chosen: there was a sustained effort to bring down costs. The largest element in these was of course wages. Hence employers were forced into a struggle with their workers and the unions in an effort to bring money wages and the general price level down to a point at which, given the chosen fixed parity of sterling, British goods would be price-competitive abroad.

This was not a new policy, but an intensification of the pressure on wages that had been going on since the end of the post-war boom in 1920 and the collapse of prices which had followed. There had been a sustained attempt by the monetary authorities (the Treasury and the Bank of England) to act in a deflationary way, reducing both the money supply and prices (including wages). The supposed success in this earlier deflationary effort, indeed, contributed to the optimism which led to resumption at the old parity in 1925.

The stresses consequent on further deflation showed both in terms of the economy as a whole and in its component sectors. Though most of the rest of the trading world enjoyed a degree of recovery in the 1920s, Britain was less fortunate; her chosen sterling exchange rate deprived her of the power to respond to the modest growth in world trade. Moreover labour militancy was stimulated. A miners' strike had been narrowly averted in 1919, though there was a seven-day railway stoppage in that year. The Triple Alliance between miners, railway and transport workers was revived. In 1921 the miners struck from April to July: they lost, being forced to accept wage cuts. From 1925, with deflation confirmed as policy, matters were to get much worse, culminating in the nation-wide confrontation of the General Strike in 1926.[1]

In all these efforts to reduce costs and prices there was a paradox deriving from the monetary mechanism itself. It was that, because of Britain's adverse balance of payments, it was necessary to attract foreign money to London to compensate for the outflows. This could only be done by means of high interest rates: borrowing was

---

1. See chapter 20, section 2 below.

thus rendered dear in Britain, with consequent discouragement to cost-lowering through investment. Moreover the fall in the price level, together with high interest rates, made it harder for the state to service its own debt. At the same time unearned rentier incomes were favoured as against those of wage earners.

In a sense 1925 represented a climax in British public policy. It was the central action in the last attempt on the part of the state to exempt itself, in the nineteenth-century fashion, from macro-control of the economy, or, if preferred, the last attempt to implement unfettered capitalism.

5. Conspiracy, inadvertence or nostalgia?

There has been a good deal of discussion of the frame of mind in which the Conservative Party entered into the policy of returning to gold at the old parity. There are, broadly, three views: it was done as a conspiracy, it arose from ignorance and so was inadvertent or it was the result of nostalgia.

The conspiracy theory sees the Conservative Party as captured for this particular purpose by an alliance of City men and Treasury and Bank of England officials, reinforced generally by big business. The City did indeed have an interest in the policy adopted, for a return to gold, restoring London's position as the world's money market, of course favoured financial interests, at least in the short view; so too did falling prices and high interest rates. Moreover, the officials of the Treasury and the Bank represented a vested interest in terms of ideas, and were thus perhaps mentally and ideologically unresponsive to new conditions. In alliance, according to the conspiracy theory, these elements captured a befogged Conservative Party and carried it into a return to the *status quo ante*, doing so at the expense of the working classes. The climax of the conspiracy theory is that the Conservative government wilfully sought a conflict with organised labour.

The inadvertence theory rests on the assumption that the policy was so disastrous for all concerned, including its authors, that no government would have embraced it except in a state of ignorance of what it was doing, or on the basis of assumptions that were falsified in the event. The nostalgia theory is a form of the ignorance/in-advertence thesis, suggesting that the lack of objective consideration arose from ingrained preconception, together with an urge to revert to the imperfectly remembered arrangements of happier times.

It is impossible to believe that the government foresaw the conflict consequences of sustained deflation and embraced it as an opportunity to resist the growth of labour power by universal and unpredictable confrontation with the work force. Given the state of British society and politics such a policy seems hardly thinkable as the conscious choice of a party. Nor was it consistent with the Tory approach to such matters in the past.

Yet there remains a mystery. Why was there no memory of the labour troubles of pre-war years such as would be a warning against trying to exert such downward pressure on wages? Also, there had been the extensions of the franchise, which, so far as males at least were concerned, were likely to be favourable to the Labour Party. The freedom conceded to the unions from any liability for the consequences of their industrial actions had further strengthened the position of wage-earners. Such considerations as these would seem to suggest that the Conservatives, in their monetary policy in 1925, acted on assumptions that precluded, or at the least minimised, the possibility of a confrontation with labour. But when conflict came in 1926 the government's response was not to review the correctness of this basic element in its policy. Instead it had no choice in the short run but to appeal to the country against the strikers in the name of the rule of law.

The inadvertence/nostalgia thesis is supported by the part played by the Bank of England and Montague Norman (1871–1950), its Governor from 1920 to 1944. His mind was formed before 1914; it carried intact into the post-war world a body of ideas that was largely set out as long ago as the 1830s by his own grandfather. He was carried to the Governorship by a system of power that was part of the same atmosphere that had generated the prevailing banking orthodoxy, and which had evolved in empathy with it. In terms of ideas, selection and power, Norman was the creation of the institutional system and social sub-culture of the City. He was also a highly idiosyncratic man, with an immense depth of stubbornness, lonely and secretive, with an inflexible sense of duty.

After 1920 the Bank under Norman was the great centre of authority from which emanated the case for a general reversion to the pre-1914 system, its defects largely forgotten. More than this, the Bank became the paladin of gold standard central banking throughout the world; so much so that it appeared for a few years that the code developed by the Bank before 1914 had not only survived a major war, but had also been universalised over victors and vanquished alike, projecting over the world the monetary facet of British nineteenth-century liberalism. By 1925 most countries had been successful to some degree in stabilising their currencies; it was perhaps not unreasonable to think that at last there was some sort of international equilibrium between costs and prices, and that international capital movements were basically governed by calculations about real transactions rather than by speculation. The Bank had also taken the lead in the financial rehabilitation of Germany and central Europe, a series of actions which further advanced its status. Norman had formed a powerful sympathetic relationship with Benjamin Strong (1872–1928), head of the Federal Reserve Bank of New York; the world's principal central bankers met together in regular conclave. It is hardly surprising, therefore, that under such circumstances the British government in 1925 was guided, as good Conservatives should be, by tradition. But the tendency of a sound monetary policy, in prevailing conditions, was in the direction of a lowering of working-class incomes in the short run, a raising of interest rates, generalising unemployment and the provoking of protest and a further polarisation of society along class lines.

It must not, of course, be thought that domestic monetary policy was the sole villain of the piece, and that if it had been 'right' all would have been well. The other circumstances must also be recalled, namely the failure of aggregate demand on a world scale, the rise of rival producers in what were previously British markets, the increasingly archaic industrial mix in Britain, the presence of a trade union movement with its own complex views of what should be done, and a relatively negative attitude to technical education that was deeply rooted in upper- and middle-class culture.

6. Confrontation: the General Strike, 1926

The hostility of the unions to wage cuts culminated in the General Strike. It lasted nine days, from 4 to 12 May 1926. It had as its ostensible and immediate cause an attempt, by generalised sympathetic union action, to support the miners in their resistance to the owners' pressure to reduce wages. It was announced in June 1925 that the government proposed to withdraw the miners' wage subsidy it had been paying since 1920. Ernest Bevin (1881–1951) organised the Industrial Alliance of miners, railwaymen and transport workers which on 31 July ('Red Friday') forced the government into extending its subsidy for nine months. The government, of course, was anxious to escape from wage support and so had used the period of industrial peace purchased by its wage subsidy to pass the Emergency Powers Act of 1920, giving itself authority to maintain essential services in the event of strikes.

The General Council of the Trades Union Congress, the central organ of the 'federal' union structure, acted as organiser and co-ordinator of the General Strike. Throughout the strike the conditions of settlement were seen by the TUC in terms of the coal mining industry, and particularly its wages and hours. But the scale of the withdrawal of labour provoked thinking and debate at a much more general level, concerned with both economic policy and political constitutionality. The frightening question was asked, was the state being challenged by extra-parliamentary means?[1]

The TUC, in effect, surrendered without having received any undertaking whatsoever from Mr Baldwin at the head of the Conservative government. Though the miners stayed out until December, a period of eight months, the government had won. The revolutionary threat, if it had ever existed, had passed. But there followed no radical reappraisal of official deflationary policy. The challenge of the General Strike was treated by the government on an ad hoc basis, and not as a red light giving warning of a system malfunctioning at a critical point.

The General Strike showed that the unions, like the government, proceeded not in the light of consciously chosen generalised principles, but by inadvertence and response to the immediate, for the last thing the TUC wanted was to find itself suddenly, through breakdown and disturbance, placed in charge of the economy.

7. The attempt at a compact: the Mond–Turner talks, 1928–9

Though the General Strike provoked no new thinking on the part of the government, it did do so in two other important quarters. The

---

1. See chapter 20, section 2 below.

unions had to seek a new line of action in their continued struggle against wage cuts. The industrialists had long been concerned with the problem of reconciling their interests and those of labour (or, as some would say, 'socialising' or 'incorporating' labour into an acceptance of co-operation): the General Strike gave a new urgency to such attempts. Certain unions and certain industrialists, seeking a way of avoiding further hostilities, turned to one another. They were in search of common ground, both of reconciliation and in terms of a programme with which they could approach the state. A series of talks and conferences took place along these lines in 1928 and 1929. The most prominent figures were, on the union side, Ben Turner (1863–1942), chairman of the TUC General Council in 1928, and on the employers' side Sir Alfred Mond (1868–1930), chairman of Imperial Chemical Industries.

The Mond–Turner talks sought a means of lowering British industrial costs not through wage reduction, but through increased efficiency. Was it possible to rationalise whole sectors of the traditional, export-based industries, cutting away excess capacity, and concentrating on the most efficient units?[1] The unions would have to agree to accept the necessary dismissal of a proportion of the workers, to be replaced by new equipment; the employers on their side would need to agree to maintain wage levels. As the second leg of the Mond–Turner policies, there was to be, where necessary, an agreed raising of prices to support wages and profits. Such a policy was to be viewed not only in the short run, when it would mean more unemployment, in the longer run it might prove the key to recovery. The Mond–Turner conferences made strong pleas, uniting unions and employers, in urging that the beneficial effects of such a programme for efficiency be not frustrated by the restrictions involved in making the credit supply dependent upon gold. The employers, in agreeing that all workmen should belong to unions, were thinking of a system of relationships in which both sides were to have an almost corporate existence, mutually recognised, involving binding agreements.

The Mond–Turner conversations were overtaken by the major economic crisis of 1929–31. It is therefore very difficult to assess their effects. It was possible to establish contacts and even friendships

1. See chapter 17 below.

which went some way toward modifying the stereotypes held by each side of the other. Even more important, the talks could assist in generating a national discussion of the nation's economic needs at a time when official attitudes were largely sterile. They helped to provoke the appointment of the Macmillan Committee, reporting in 1931. Its chairman was a judge, Lord Macmillan (1873–1952). It was charged with an in-depth study of the monetary and financial mechanisms now being so much called into question.

The Mond–Turner incident represented the first attempt of the two great estates of the realm to define themselves against one another, coming together to arrive at policies with which to confront an apparently impotent state. But the appearance of solidarity was premature. The fissures both within the labour movement and within industry, though partially and temporarily closed for a year or two after the General Strike, were still such as to preclude any serious challenge to the state from either, or from both in combination. Moreover the participants largely passed over the danger that the consumer would be very vulnerable to such an employer–worker alliance.[1]

8. The banking response

Meanwhile the banking system had been adjusting to changing circumstances. The Bank of England, as we have seen, pursued its role as envisaged by itself and by government as the provider of the conditions for a sound currency and a stable sterling exchange rate, basing itself upon the gold standard. The currency was 'managed' to the extent that conditions propitious to the return to gold were engineered, with, of course, the objective that once this was attained further need for management would be minimal. By the same token neither the Bank of England nor the Treasury accepted any responsibility for generating conditions for industrial adjustment and growth through the monetary system.

The commercial banks, on the other hand, contrary to their tradition, did enter upon a good deal of long-term lending to the older industries, especially in cotton, steel and shipbuilding. The post-war boom of 1919–20 had brought a heavy commitment in this

1. For further discussion see chapter 20, section 3 below.

direction. It was partly the dangers involved in this kind of lending which caused the Bank of England to involve itself directly in the industrial structure, with the knowledge and sympathy of the Treasury.[1] The Bank, through its part in the economic rehabilitation of central Europe, had encountered the problems of industrial structure abroad, making its new role more acceptable.

9. *The elemental storm, 1929–32*

The second Labour government, also a minority one, took office in May 1929, elected largely as a response to heavy unemployment. Though it now had for the first time the largest number of seats in the Commons it was still dependent upon the support of the Liberal Party. In spite of its origins and expressed ideas, it fell under the constraint of responsible government, reinforced by the need to propitiate the Liberals. Also, it found itself adjudicating between workers and employers as its Liberal and Conservative predecessors had done, for it was unthinkable in industrial situations simply to enforce 'labour' solutions. In particular it had to deal with the standing challenge of the miners and their claims.

Secondly, there was the budgetary problem. The Labour Party, with Philip Snowden as its Chancellor, accepted the Treasury insistence on the duty to balance income and expenditure. The budget had become an incoherent mass of current and capital items, so that true 'balancing' in any strictly scientific sense was impossible; moreover, window-dressing in the form of ingenuity in budgetary presentation could be practised. But this could not be done on any gross scale; the idea of the balanced budget still had a considerable degree of reality.

Expenditure was of course the great threat: the cost of civil government rose from £246.4 million in 1929 to £345.7 million in 1932. Unemployment insurance payments were running far ahead of income. Accordingly, a Royal Commission on Unemployment Insurance was appointed.[2] The Liberals insisted on an inquiry into general finance: in August 1931 Sir George May's Committee reported, urging a programme of heavy retrenchment, including reductions in the social services. It seemed that the strait-jacket of

1. See chapter 17, section 2 below.
2. See chapter 21, section 6 below.

gold had its twin in the need for fiscal soundness. These two principles placed the social–democratic Labour government in a terrible dilemma.

Meanwhile world trade, on which Britain so heavily depended, was shrinking. Partly in consequence of this the system of gold parities was placed under great strain.

There was high drama as these forces worked themselves out. The New York stock exchange collapsed in October 1929: this was followed by a withdrawal of short-term credits from Europe. A breakdown of European banking seemed imminent. An agreed moratorium on demands for debt repayments, though perhaps making a short-term contribution to world stability, worsened the British position, for it made it impossible to recall assets from abroad. The traditional weapon of raising Bank Rate in London was unable to draw international money to the City on the scale necessary to ease the pressure on the pound. Distrust of the Labour government, the prospect of a huge budgetary deficit and the *Report* of the May Committee, together with a disturbance in the Navy at Invergordon over pay cuts, dealt blow after blow to confidence in sterling. In the summer of 1931 international holders of sterling, sensing its weakness, began to sell it on a large scale. The gold reserve of the Bank of England, the basis of the British credit structure, drained rapidly away.

One last expedient remained, that of borrowing from foreign bankers. But this could only be done if the British government accepted the terms imposed by them as security for their advances. One of these was that the government, in order to stabilise its finances, should cut unemployment benefits. On this the Labour cabinet split, and so ended its existence. J. Ramsay MacDonald, the Prime Minister, together with Snowden and one or two other members of the Labour cabinet, joined the Conservatives to form the National Government with MacDonald at its head. The legend was thus launched that the second Labour government had been destroyed by a combination of capitalist conspiracy and aristocratic embrace; a good many of the Labour left now moved toward Marxism or sympathy with the Communist Party.

The new government obtained the foreign loan refused to its predecessor. But the gold standard, which the National Government was formed to 'save', could not be sustained. On 21 September 1931,

301

compelled by a resumption of the selling of sterling, the government abandoned the gold standard: its instrument was the Gold Standard (Amendment) Act 1931. The Bank of England was relieved of its obligation to redeem pounds sterling in gold at a set parity. The value of the pound was thereafter determined by supply and demand. By the end of December it had declined from $4.86 to $3.40.

The result was an immense relief to the British balance of payments. Because the USA, Germany, France and other important trading countries remained on gold for some time, British exports were stimulated. The financial crisis was ended by April 1932. But unemployment reached its peak in 1932 at 2.7 million, or 22.5% of insured workers. When the United States also left the gold standard in 1933, greatly devaluing the dollar, Britain lost the advantage of her relatively undervalued currency; indeed sterling was soon close to its old parity. With the passing of the gold standard there departed the world's last hope of a virtually self-adjusting monetary system.

10. The new economic policy, 1931–9

The British formula for meeting the needs of the economy from 1931 to 1939 was arrived at by the National Government, dominated by Conservatives, overwhelming victors in a snap election in October 1931. The policy combined five main elements. These had to do with the money supply and interest rates, the control of international trade by tariffs and by treaty, the pursuit of 'sound finance' by balancing the budget and direct action in two respects – the continued though modified subsidisation of housing[1] and the sponsoring of rationalisation and market control in industry.[2]

With the abandonment of gold the currency could now, in principle, be 'managed'. But no real philosophy of how to do this developed. For some four years the break with gold was regarded as a temporary expedient, with payments in gold to be resumed when 'normal' conditions returned. There was no great debate within the Bank, partly because there was now little leadership by the Governor on internal monetary policy, and partly because of the Bank's traditional unwillingness to publish the relevant data. The manage-

1. See chapter 21, section 4 below.
2. See chapter 17 below.

ment of the money supply, interest rates and the exchanges was not therefore to become an affair of positive policy, but merely one of stabilising market conditions so far as interest rate and exchange rate policy could achieve these ends.

Insofar as low interest rates were an encouragement to investment, and through it to increased economic activity, they were available. Money tended to flow into the building societies: this made it possible for them to lend at moderate rates, thus stimulating private house building. But it is possible that the housing boom owed little to lower interest rates, and would have occurred without them. Relatively little money flowed into industrial development, as the availability of cheap loans was not able to overcome the general difficulties of industry. But cheap money allowed the government to reduce its own costs by converting much of its debt to lower rates of interest; in 1932 nearly £2,000 million of War Loan was converted from 5% to 3½%. At the same time interest rate reductions lessened the burden of debt generally in the economy and lowered the payments made to rentiers.

In order to forestall short-term fluctuations in the price of sterling due to speculative money movements, crop changes and other such destabilisers, the Exchange Equalisation Account was set up in April 1932, by the Finance Act, to be run by the Bank as agent for the Treasury. To it was transferred the Bank of England's foreign currency holdings; the Account was empowered to acquire assets to the amount of £167 million, largely by borrowing. These, with other assets provided by the government, constituted a fund on the basis of which the managers of the Account could buy and sell sterling so as to counteract excessive short-term demand or supply. In 1936 the Tripartite Agreement was made between Britain, the USA and France, under which the three countries would collaborate in the stabilisation of their currencies. But though these monetary arrangements were free of the constraint of gold, they could not obviate more deeply rooted difficulties, including the problem of the 'proper' relationship of international currencies to one another, now that a general state manipulation of parities on a world scale had begun. It was to become clear that, whatever the potential of managed currencies, the old problem of the relationship of national price levels to one another remained.

In addition to the Exchange Equalisation Account there was the

Foreign Transactions Advisory Committee set up in 1936. Its role, in co-operation with the Treasury and the Bank of England, was to control the raising of money by foreigners in the City of London through issues of securities. The Bank had for some years exercised an informal 'moral' control by establishing the custom that such issuers should obtain its permission. A general preference was given to issues within the sterling area. There was, however, no control on the buying with sterling of existing foreign securities, or those floated abroad.

British trade was now to be controlled by means of national tariffs. The verdict of the general election of 1906 was reversed: a quarter of a century after Chamberlain's defeat 'tariff reform' had come. It is true that the Conservatives, partially committed to protection since Balfour's time, had reimposed the McKenna Duties in 1926. But this was largely in order to encourage a particular range of production in which Britain was an 'infant', especially the automobile industry. There had also been the Safeguarding Act of 1925, authorising tariffs where foreigners were 'dumping' their goods in Britain (selling them at below full cost). Such protective measures, taken together, affected only some 3% of British imports. The Import Duties Act of February 1932 marked the resumption of protection as a general policy, carrying Britain back a hundred years or so to the general tariff of her pre-industrial and early industrial age. Adam Smith was at last repudiated.

At once the difficulties he had stressed reappeared. What lines of production were to be protected, and at what levels? Could there be a 'scientific' tariff, or did the tariff simply commit trade to the vagaries of the political arena? Provisional rates were set; these were revised into longer-term form in April 1932, following the recommendations of the Import Duties Advisory Committee. This was a new body set up to adjudicate on claims and needs. The government, by creating it as a pretty well autonomous agency, with little guidance, hoped to keep the tariff out of politics. There were protests at this degree of independence, but ministers insisted that they would not intervene. Thus when the free-trade principle of non-interference failed, government fell back on the second line of liberal action, namely, calling upon disinterested, Platonic adjudication by men who combined comprehension and integrity.

Foreign manufactured goods were to pay a minimum of 20% *ad valorem*, luxury goods 25% or 30% and some imports where British industry was particularly vulnerable were to pay 33⅓%. From then onward there was continuous varying of rates as proposed by the IDAC. The employers, in the new situation of tariff manipulation and currency management, found themselves in disarray, both in terms of organisation and ideas: they were required to find an identity and a direction quickly.[1]

Britain, now provided with its own protective devices, was in a position to bargain with other states. This took place generally, and, in particular terms, with the empire, or Commonwealth as it was redesignated in 1931. With the world outside the empire Britain sought to replace her old multilateral arrangements with bilateralism, bargaining directly with each trading partner on a one-to-one basis. Though she succeeded in expanding her trade with her bilateral partners, she may have lost in terms of others, possibly generating a negative outcome in net terms. At the Ottawa Conference of 1932 it seemed to some that at long last Chamberlain's dream of a system of imperial preference could come true. But the reconciliation of interests was not easy. The countries of the empire, after bitter wrangling, exchanged concessions by raising tariffs rates against others. But here, too, the long-run effect may have been one of distortion and loss, to be set against gains. It was clear, moreover, that Commonwealth sentiment was not strong enough to compensate for clashes of material interest.

In the matter of the budget there was to be no such new beginning as in monetary and trading policy. The principle of the balanced budget, so sacred to Mr Gladstone, and a major canon of the Treasury, was in principle adhered to, so that right down to 1939 relatively minor surpluses and deficits more or less cancelled one another out. Such a policy had, of course, strong implications for the social services. Snowden, the Labour Chancellor in the National Government, substantially increased both direct and indirect taxes. He also had available the revenue from the new tariff. But these devices were not enough; there had also to be economies on a massive scale. Following the proposals made by the May Committee, Snowden set about making these, at the expense of salaries in the public sector (civil servants, police, teachers). Most resented of all,

---

1. See chapter 19 below.

he cut unemployment rates by 10% (at the same time as raising contributions), as well as reducing other benefits, and this with unemployment at about 2.6 million. The local authorities behaved in the same way with their own economy committees, struggling with a drop in their revenue from rates; they too bore more heavily on the social casualties by a reduction of services. A kind of contradiction in policy was thus generated: at the very time when social need was greatest, the demands of fiscal 'soundness' led to a reduced provision.[1] The policy of budgetary balance continued to 1939, though things were eased somewhat from 1934 when the expenditure cuts of 1931 were restored.

From 1936 the rival of welfare, namely warfare, began to reassert its claims in the form of rearmament, thus posing on a much larger scale the dilemma that had confronted the reforming Liberals after 1906. Rearmament did, however, mark the beginning of the end of massive unemployment, with a general upturn in incomes, including those of governments and local authorities. But cheap money continued: Bank Rate was still 2% in August 1939.

In this range of macro-policies there was no real scope for increasing the ability of the purchasing public to buy, through the redistribution of incomes. Such proposals were certainly made, including the creation of spending power by direct monetary gift to the unemployed and the lowly paid. But to augment incomes at the lower end of the scale meant, in effect, either an increase in the money supply by the simple creation of such means of payment, or, if the thing were to be done within the balanced budget, stiff increases in direct taxes on incomes and profits. Though official ideas had moved somewhat in the direction of greater flexibility in the monetary supply, the proposal that a large addition to it should be generated by budgetary deficit was too much for ingrained caution. Such an action raised the fearful spectre of loss of control of the money supply of the kind that had taken place in post-war Germany and other parts of Europe. As for direct taxation, the rates were already progressive, bearing proportionately more heavily the higher the income. The standard rate of income tax had been 14d in the pound in 1914 (6%); it rose to a peak in 1919–22 at 72d (30%), gradually declining to 60d (25%) in 1938: the rates on super-tax and

1. The implications for welfare are further discussed in chapter 20.

surtax, together with the inheritance tax, also rose. But, partly because of the continuous generating of new fortunes, the effect on the general pattern of income and wealth was relatively slight. To go much further in a deliberate policy of redistribution in the interest of income maintenance among the less well-off could not be contemplated by governments.

Three criticisms must be made of Britain's effort to extricate herself from her difficulties when her heavy dependence upon exports was overtaken by world recession. As has been seen, Britain bore some responsibility for participating in beggar-my-neighbour policies in the trading sphere, though it should be remembered that she had held longest to free trade in the face of growing unemployment and the hostile tariffs of other nations. The basis of her former position as the exemplar of the gold standard and go-it-alone free trade having been destroyed, her governments turned to take the lead in trade manipulation. Secondly, governments made little effort to encourage new industry embodying new technology and supplying consumer goods to the domestic market. Thirdly, little was done to alter radically the distribution of income and wealth as a stimulus to demand: this meant that the losses in employment due to the shrinkage of the old export trades was insufficiently compensated for by new, home demand.

11. The reciprocal relationship between domestic and foreign policy, 1936–9

As the crisis of 1929–31 receded the concern of governments shifted away from the economy. It turned instead to foreign policy and the prospect and implications of another war; from about 1936 tension in international relationships dominated the public mind.

These two preoccupations were not, of course, independent of one another. The efforts made by competing nation states, including Britain, to relieve their internal pressures (through currency manipulation, tariffs and bilateral arrangements) could only aggravate the tensions between states. Such actions with their mercantilist implications may have helped to sponsor a revival of competitive rearmament. Such expenditure could compensate for the deficiency of effective demand in many economies, including that of Britain, and so relieve domestic stresses. But so great a weight of armaments could produce a highly unstable international pattern, with a consequent loss of world business confidence, which would act in a dampening, deflationary way.

Between 1936 and 1939 unemployment in Britain was significantly lessened, from 14.3% of the insured population to 11.7%, or from 1.7 million to 1.5 million. The price of this reduction, however, was the shadow of a second world war. The youngish Harold Macmillan (b.1894), conscious that if the war peril receded the economic recovery would probably end, asked whether there could be any escape from the relationships that linked home and foreign tensions. He pleaded in 1938 that the preoccupation with the prospect of war should not mean a neglect of the task of generating economic stability and social amelioration.

12. The search by the state for advice and consensus

The state, as it moved toward accepting responsibility for the macro-management of the economy, needed two essential facilities. First it required a means of providing itself with advice; the choice of policies ought to rest both upon systematic theory and comprehensive information concerning the performance of the economy. Secondly, labour, having entered the national policy making process, both directly through the Labour Party and indirectly through the Trades Union Congress, had become a contender for the ear of government; business too was finding a collective voice. These developments made it necessary for the government to find a means whereby a degree of working consensus between the two could be generated.

The setting up in 1930 by Prime Minister Ramsay MacDonald of the Economic Advisory Council was the culmination of a long sequence of tentative experiments in these two directions. Even before the war Labour MPs and trade union representatives had served as members of official inquiries. The various Reconstruction Committees had sought solutions to a wide range of problems, using theory and statistics to some degree, and at the same time exploring what would be acceptable to business and to the unions. There began, indeed, at this time, talk of the need for an economic general staff.

Because there had been no practice of employing professional economists in government before the war, this role had been assumed by senior civil servants who were, of course, infused with the general outlook of their kind. They were distrustful of professionalism, seeing policy as stemming from properly constituted Ministries, and hostile to any notion of intellectual overlords brought in from outside whose judgments would be dominant in the minds of the cabinet. But the first world war did bring economists into the public service, resulting in 1917 in the establishment in the Board of Trade of a General Economic Department, capable of exercising foresight about developments in commerce and industry, though only such as did not fall within the responsibility of already existing Departments. The Ministry of Reconstruction set up the Haldane Committee which was intended to take up a generalised brief for the economy. But with the loss of interest in forward planning that came with the phase of post-war dismantlement of control, the Haldane Committee, like the others, disappeared. The Geddes economies of 1921 confirmed this trend, for advisory bodies cost money: the General Economic Department of the Board of Trade was wound up. All that was left was the post of Chief Economic Adviser to the Government that had come out of the now defunct Haldane Committee. The official view continued to be hostile, rejecting a proposal from the Royal Statistical Society for a Royal Commission on the gathering of national statistics. The feeling was that data on such matters as national income and wealth did not justify their cost.

But things were happening outside the civil service, pressed on by the need to come to terms with labour. Lloyd George as Prime Minister convened in 1919 the National Industrial Conference. He intended it as an exploration of the outlook of labour and capital, with thirty representatives from each side. The Conference resolved in favour of a forty-eight hour week, and minimum rates of pay. It also recommended a National Industrial Council to have a continuous existence, meeting biannually, with a standing committee under the Minister of Labour. But the trade union members, disillusioned with the intentions of the government, resigned in 1921. So ended the high hopes placed in the National Industrial Conference.

The first Labour government in 1924 proposed a Committee of Economic Inquiry, but this went down with them in their defeat. The Conservative government that followed set up a Committee of Civil Research, but it was distracted by a concern with science and industry, and with the development of the African colonies. Though it carried out inquiries into the iron and steel industry (1925) and coal (1927), and certain other matters, it failed to become the economic general staff.

By the later 1920s it was time for organised labour to provide itself with thought machinery capable of dealing with national issues.[1] The Labour Party was divided by conflicts within itself; it could hardly expect the government bureaucracy to provide it with a radical programme, for both tradition and inclination were adverse to such an initiative. On the industrial side, the General Council of the TUC, under the influence of Citrine and Bevin, formed its Economic Committee in 1928, a step essential if the trade union movement was to find direction in terms of the economy as a whole. In a sense the Mond–Turner talks were a revival of the hopes of the National Industrial Conference, but they were different in that they took place spontaneously and directly between employers and labour. The labour participants, through the talks, learned to think generally about the economy. Citrine and Bevin agreed with Mond that the return to gold was a mistake. From this point onward the TUC had a mind and voice concerned with the macro-economy.

The general election of 1929, with its partial Labour victory, brought fresh proposals along the lines of an economic general staff, especially from the Liberals in their Yellow Book; in this kind of thinking John Maynard Keynes was a powerful element. The second Labour government, confronted by an economy in serious difficulties, and in the face of so much agitation for some kind of focus of thought, established the Economic Advisory Council. It consisted of the Prime Minister, the Chancellor, the Lord Privy Seal, the President of the Board of Trade, the Minister of Agriculture, such other ministers as might be summoned, and such other persons (some fifteen) selected 'in virtue of their special knowledge and experience of industry and economics'. This was the compromise between ministries and pundits. The Council appointed its own Committee of Economists.

The deliberations of the Council and its committees reveal much inquiry, together with dramatic differences. Every short-term formula and combination of formulae was canvassed in the search for escape

1. See chapter 20, section 6 below.

from the slump. Even between economists, with their 'objective' views as to what should be done, there was no consensus, as was revealed when MacDonald asked each member of the Committee of Economists to reply to five specific questions, intended 'to enable the Council to concentrate on large questions of public policy'. Though the perceptions of government were no doubt deepened, no grand simplifying key to the situation emerged from the Council's deliberations. Not surprisingly, in the face of conflicting advice there was a retreat from the attempt at a grand design: the Committee was replaced in 1932 with a more limited Committee on Economic Information which continued to function to 1939. The problem remained, namely how to organise the thought processes of governments presiding over a market-based economy with large semi-obsolescent sectors, together with powerful unions. But the deliberations of the Council had provided a test bed for many of the ideas that were to be synthesised in Keynes' *General Theory of Employment, Interest and Money* of 1936, the beginning of a new phase in the history of economic analysis.

17

Micro-management: the restructuring of industry and agriculture; the regions

1. *The private and the public sectors*

Micro-management, involving manipulation of units within the overall economy, chiefly its component industries, had an ancient pedigree from the mercantilist days of the seventeenth century. But micro-initiatives had largely been abandoned by the mid-nineteenth century. They had begun to revive from the 1880s, not under state initiative, however, but under the local authorities.[1] The war compelled the state into the heart of industry, making it a regulator on a grand scale. In the peace the British state, in spite of its eager dismantlement of the wartime controls, was drawn into an attempt to restructure major parts of industry and agriculture. It also took its first effective steps in the development of regional policy and spatial planning.

2. *Nationalisation versus rationalisation*

There were available to the state two general ways of restructuring the older industries: nationalisation on the one hand, and rationalisation (together with market regulation) on the other. Nationalisation meant assuming outright ownership, and with it the permanent decision-taking role within the industry. It required the formation of new administrative structures for industries, of a more or less centralised nature. Moreover the relationship between such structures and the state and the trade unions had to be defined. Rationalisation, on the other hand, meant setting the conditions for self-reorganisation within each industry, such that surplus capacity could be cut out and

---

1. See chapter 11 above.

efficiency improved, with or without arrangements for the control of markets. Such a programme would leave such industries still composed of productive units privately owned, but some would enjoy monopoly conditions, subject in some cases to control of their pricing and output policies by specially created state agencies.

Nationalisation was impossible in the conditions of the time. There was a powerful distrust of state ownership and operation, inherited from the prosperous and flexible past.[1] This negative attitude toward the state in industry was confirmed for many people by their recollections of the industrial autocracy of wartime. There was, too, the feeling that to adjust to the challenges of the new world of the peace, business men were the best judges of the needs of industry. Finally, of course, there was the configuration of power in society – the business classes were in possession and were in general not willing to surrender industry to state bureaucrats.

It is true that nationalisation had powerful advocates. Chief among them were the Labour Party, the Trades Union Congress, the unions in certain industries and the Fabians. But the strength and specificity of the commitment is difficult to judge; it also changed over time. The older Labour MPs and union leaders were not anxious to embark on hazardous experiments in public ownership, however much they might approve of such ideas in the abstract.[2] But there was one element vociferously and threateningly in favour of nationalisation, namely the coal miners.[3] They urged the displacement of the bosses on the grounds of increasing efficiency and of destroying a political power base, as well as regarding public ownership as a kind of natural right and responsibility.

Rationalisation and market control proved irresistible in certain sectors. They came by the route of improvisation. In one industry after another, as the levels and pattern of national and international demand changed, common sense seemed to suggest that there should be a slimming and a concentration on the more productive units. This was reinforced by the realisation that there was now world excess capacity in so many of the industries in which Britain had formerly excelled. Similarly, in the matter of output and prices, it seemed clear that business men in some sectors at least should no

1. See chapter 9, section 9 above.
2. But see chapter 20, section 8 below.
3. See chapter 20, section 2 below.

longer be left as autonomous units to guess about the conditions of markets and the proper response thereto in terms of output and price, but should, with governmental aid, seek by mutual agreement to arrive at formulae for regulating the relations between themselves, and thus exert a degree of market control. The resulting programme of state action in the form of the sponsorship of rationalisation schemes involved a once-and-for-all amputation, intended to remove unwanted and degenerate growth and to clear the system of accretions. In some cases this was to be followed by an ultimate return to free markets but in others there was to be a permanent market control by producers. The price mechanism still remained the general allocator of resources and rewards, but its operation was brought under a range of controls in particular sectors.

At no time was there a generalised government statement of a policy programme for industry. Instead each sector was taken up in turn as its problems reached the pitch at which action was unavoidable, just as in the field of welfare. No doubt legislators as well as business men were aware that their actions in the various sectors were beginning to produce some form of pattern, but there was no wish to make it explicit or uniform. The state in the 1930s assumed, almost by inadvertence, the role of ad hoc frame-setter for the traditional industries, treating each as a separate and distinct case. But it left ownership and production largely undisturbed.

Rationalisation and market control of course made no contribution to raising the overall level of demand – that was determined by world conditions, together with domestic macro-performance and the pattern of distribution of incomes. The remaking of the older industries was, therefore, not merely a set of improvisations, but it had no very closely planned relationship to other parts of the government's actions, themselves also largely improvised.

There were three general menus available to the state for rationalisation and market stabilisation. In terms of direct action the state could take statutory powers to compel rationalisation of capacity as it did in the case of coal and the railways. Secondly it could provide the 'opportunity' for rationalisation, by granting tariff protection, and then leave the matter to the industry, as it did in steel. Or finally it could wield its own sanctions and authority to impose the regulation of markets by producers, as with parts of agriculture.

The Bank of England, contrary to its traditional role as regulator of the money and credit supply, was drawn into the structure of industry. The very large loans made by the commercial banks to the older industries since the boom of 1919–20, in shipbuilding, steel and cotton, had become, in effect, semi-permanent. Such advances could not be called in without serious threat to the banking and industrial structures. The Bank of England's own investments in such industries had reached such a scale by 1929 that it was necessary to form the Securities Management Trust to manage them, as well as to provide experts to advise firms and industries in trouble. A more ambitious step was taken in 1930 with the setting up of the Bankers' Industrial Development Corporation (BIDCo.) to sponsor and finance industrial reorganisation. The Bank by now had apparently accepted the role of sponsor of rationalisation as a public duty; on the other hand it could be argued that the BIDCo. was intended to forestall intervention by the Labour government in industry. Certainly the Bank did not envisage more than a short-term involvement, after which industry would be autonomous again. The Governor had hoped for support from the money market, but none was forthcoming; the City did not see an acceptable return from such a venture, and so declined to help to provide the means. The notion that the Bank could sell to the money market a programme for industrial re-generation and so demonstrate the capacity of capitalism to liquidate old and damaging sectors was a non-starter. So too was the idea that state money would be forthcoming. As a result the Bank's recon-struction schemes were confined to the limits set by its own resources.

The view taken by the Bank of England in terms of the restructuring of industry is an intriguing one. The Governor saw the Bank as an autonomous entity, above both the political battle and business attitudes and intrigues. But once it descended to intervention in the lives of firms it found itself confronted with the same range of problems as had made life so difficult for the commercial bankers, namely those of management, structure, marketing and products. The Bank was obliged to accept the need for a shielding of many firms in the vulnerable sectors from immediate market forces.

The pursuit of these policies must now be observed more closely in the industries affected.

3. Energy policy

The supply of energy to Britain's industries and homes and been a matter of concern among a few perceptive men from the 1860s and 1870s.[1] The war gave the matter renewed point, inspiring the Coal Conservation Committee *Report* of 1917. It expressed a fear of exhaustion, or at least of steeply rising costs in the longer run. For coal was the basis of everything, including, of course, gas and electricity.

Gas could not be conveyed over very long distances, so that there was no question of a national system of supply. But with the new marvel of electricity such a national scheme was feasible by the 1920s, and was indeed carried out under the Central Electricity Board between 1926 and 1933.[2] But successive governments were unwilling to think in terms of an integrated energy programme. Coal was under the Department of Mines; gas, coke and oil were the concern of the Board of Trade; electricity was the responsibility of the Ministry of Transport. The private organisation, Political and Economic Planning, called for a national fuel policy in 1936, but there was no governmental response.

4. Coal: a state-created cartel

Coal mining was at the heart of both industry and politics. It became the strong point of the trade union movement.[3] From 1919 the miners pressed for nationalisation, supported by the Labour Party. In this the miners showed no signs of romantic utopianism – they intended to continue their own trade union autonomy against any new state coal owning authority. The Sankey Commission on the coal industry of 1919 produced a serious indictment of the coal masters, and was indeed almost a state trial prosecuting the business bourgeoisie. It proposed nationalisation, with a workers' say in management, together with a Ministry of Mines. The government response was the Mining Industry Act of 1920, which sought to improve relations in the industry by Pit Committees, District Committees, the Area and National Boards, a somewhat feeble concession to the miners.

The Samuel *Report* appeared in 1926. With some 1,400 separate

1. See chapter 6, section 7 above.
2. See chapter 18, section 2 below.
3. See chapter 20, section 2 below.

firms operating about 2,500 mines, many of them very small, the *Report* pointed the need for rationalisation. It stressed the failure of the industry to gain the economies of scale and to improve its management and sales methods. It rejected the nationalisation of the mines, but did propose that mineral royalties be nationalised (that is the owners of the land under which the coal seams lay should no longer own the coal, with the right to charge for its extraction, but should be bought out). The Mining Industry Act of 1926 extended the provisions of the 1920 Act facilitating amalgamation.

The government was rapidly approaching the point at which it had either to nationalise, or to impose a new pattern upon private ownership. In the Coal Mines Act of 1930 it opted to enforce rationalisation and market regulation. Under Part I competition was suppressed: the country was divided into Districts, each with a production quota and a regulated schedule of prices. Coal mining was thus removed from the market system and put in the care of a state-created cartel operated by the mine owners. Part II of the Act set up the Coal Mines Reorganisation Commission to carry through amalgamation schemes, with the approval of the Railway and Canals Commission. The intention was that Part I would provide conditions of stability for the industry, under which Part II could be carried through. The inefficiencies that might result from the ending of competition were to be more than compensated for by concentrating output on the larger mines with their lower costs. But there were immense difficulties. The colliery owners resented Part I, preferring competition. The Commission was unwilling to use enforcement: it tried hard to promote voluntary schemes. In consequence rationalisation achieved only limited success. The Coal Act of 1938 nationalised the coal royalties, paying compensation, thus ending an impost on the industry, and removing a serious obstacle to the rational exploitation of the seams.

In 1939 the nation's key industry was still in an archaic condition, with too many firms, too many pits and insufficient mechanisation. It was still composed of two powerful and intransigent interests, the colliery owners and the miners.

5. Steel: the tariff as incentive to rationalise

Iron and steel, the second great sinew of the industrial revolution, had also produced large-scale obsolescence and many firms too small to be competitive, especially as world markets shrank. The relentless advance of technology meant that a small steel works was a nonsense. The first response of the industry came in 1918 with the formation of the National Federation of Iron and Steel Manufacturers, for the purpose of collective buying and selling. This device for market control covered 97% of steel production.

The banks had become heavily involved in loans that could only be serviced if the steel producers became economic. They approached the Bank of England for advice and assistance. The Bank was worried both about the possible damage to the financial system and the possibility of state intervention in steel. It believed that governments were unable to deal with the subtle and complex problems of industrial reorganisation on the scale involved: it thought rather in terms of creating the conditions under which self-correction would take place.

The English Steel Corporation was formed in 1929 under the aegis of the Bankers Industrial Development Company; it was composed of Vickers-Armstrongs, Whitworth and Cammell Laird. The Lancashire Steel Corporation was also brought into being. There were other notable mergers in all the great steel-making areas, involving all sectors of steel making, together with certain shipbuilding and ship-owning interests. In addition a number of associations were formed to control prices.

The voluntarist principle under the sponsorship of the Bank thus made considerable progress. But it was not enough, for the difficulties of steel and its associated industries grew with the deepening of the depression. It was necessary for the industry to remake itself even more radically, on a comprehensive basis. The only way to induce this further step appeared to be to bring in the government. The means at its disposal was the tariff; its object was to bring about general reorganisation and technical redevelopment. The industry wanted protection first, to be followed by reorganisation; the Economic Advisory Council and the government preferred the reverse sequence. The dilemma was the same as that of coal: fundamental reorganisation on the basis of rationalisation required that the government provide conditions of stability and profitability, but these very conditions might serve to insulate the industry from the competition of foreigners and so permit it to continue to be slack and unresponsive. The steel companies won: protection was granted to steel from 1932 at the level of 33⅓%, on the advice of the Import Duties Advisory Committee.

Meanwhile, in 1926, the European Steel Cartel had been organised to try to operate an international system of quotas and prices. The British steel industry, in order to strengthen its bargaining position, obtained from the Import Duties Advisory Committee a rise in steel duties to 50%. Armed with this the British industry successfully pressed for a larger share in the European market, after which the tariff was returned to its former level.

A new central organisation of the steel companies was set up in 1934, the British Iron and Steel Federation, to set production quotas for firms and to regulate prices; it was also intended to carry through the reorganisation. But it concerned itself much more with the regulatory function than the renovating one, controlling competition and subsidising less efficient producers by levies on the more efficient, and failing to face up to the need to close uneconomic plants and to concentrate, integrate and modernise production. In the Federation's failure it was supported by those who saw such a programme for efficiency as likely to aggravate the already serious regional unemployment. But further amalgamations and inter-locking agreements between companies were carried out, representing piecemeal rationalisations. As rearmament proceeded in the late 1930s the urge to attack excess capacity faded. Nor could the government find the time and energy, together with the necessary conviction, to require the industry to redeem in full its undertaking to remake itself.

6. Shipbuilding: self-financed slimming

Closely interlocked with the iron and steel industry was shipbuilding. Vertical integrations in one form or another had created links of ownership and agreement from coal through steel to shipbuilding. The industrial giants of Beardmores, Vickers-Armstrongs, John Brown and Co., the Lithgow Group, Harland and Wolff, and Swan, Hunter and Wigham Richardson exemplified those connections. In bad times shipbuilders and the larger shipowners were closely linked by orders placed and the terms of payment involved. In this sense there were complex ties of indebtedness and integration. Steel and shipbuilding were in a complex empathy.

The regional employment problem in the west of Scotland and the north-east of England centred upon shipbuilding, for it was in these areas that the external economies of the past had generated heavy concentration. The post-war replacement boom after 1918 increased an already excessive capacity, in the face of fierce competition from the United States, Japan and other countries, aided in their contract bidding by state subsidies. By 1920 Britain's shipbuilding capacity stood at 3 to 4 million tons gross, something like twice the pre-war maximum output. This confronted a massive shortage in world trade. There was excess capacity to an almost incredible degree. As in steel, the banks were heavily committed. What was to be done?

Mergers were organised and much capital was written off. But some kind of collective action was clearly called for. As in steel, the Bank of England entered the picture, concerned about the threat to the banking structure. The Bank's subsidiary, the Bankers' Industrial Development Company, formed the National Shipbuilders' Security Ltd in 1930. The shipbuilding companies subscribed the shares. The programme was to buy up redundant yards and scrap them, using a levy of 1% on sales of new ships produced by the surviving yards. By 1937 about a million tons of capacity had been withdrawn. This was, of course, at the expense of further aggravating unemployment in the worst-hit regions. The scrapping programme was slowed as rearmament gained momentum in the later 1930s. In all this the state had no direct role, though approving of the Bank of England's initiatives. In a sense the industry, under the encouragement of the Bank, rationalised itself, within the framework of the National Shipbuilders' Security.

But there was a certain degree of direct state action. The Shipping (Assistance) Act of 1935 offered loans to the owners of tramp ships to undertake scrap-and-build programmes that would provide more efficient ships. By this time the working of the market in shipping services was further disturbed by subsidy schemes by various governments; the British government, placed under strong pressure by shipowners and shipbuilders, entered on this kind interference by providing a direct subsidy on freight rates. This had had the effect of making the scrapping of old ships less attractive, though it did encourage some new building. Moreover foreign governments still did much more in this direction for their shipowners than did the British. There continued to be much out-of-date equipment worked in yards now too small for modern requirements; labour costs were inflated by restrictive labour practices.

7. *Cotton: concentration and modernisation*

Cotton, like coal, was a dispersed industry, consisting of many separate firms. But it differed in that it was divided into sharply distinct elements, namely spinning, weaving, the finishing trades and merchandising, each with its organisational structure. All sections were confronted with the problems of excess capacity and technical inefficiency in the inter-war years. The war had stimulated other nations to enter the markets Britain had been obliged to starve; the post-war years saw the same perverse response as in shipbuilding, namely gross over-expansion of British capacity. All of this had a strong regional aspect; much of the collapse of British cotton was enacted in south Lancashire.

No one argued seriously for the nationalisation of the cotton industry: it was too diverse and too dependent upon foreign markets. It was almost impossible to conceive of a state organisation that could run it. This left as the only renovatory policy rationalisation by the elements of industry themselves. The weaving section by competition reduced the number of looms considerably, though a good deal of redundant plant still remained in 1939. The finishing trades, because of the combines that had been formed (there were Association of Bleachers, of Dyers and of Calico Printers), were able to scrap, modernise and concentrate on the best plant. Thus both competition and combines could contribute to the self-rationalisation of these two sectors of the industry.

But the real problem lay with spinning. The first attempts at solution came in 1927 with the formation in the coarse and medium spinning sector, the most depressed of all, of the Cotton Yarn Association. It was to fix output quotas and minimum selling prices. But it could not maintain discipline: external help was required. As in shipbuilding, it came from the Bank of England and the commercial banks, now heavily loaned to the spinners. The Bankers' Industrial Development Corporation in 1929 formed the Lancashire Cotton Corporation. It was a merger on an extraordinary scale, bringing together almost one hundred firms with a capacity of nine million spindles. By 1939 it had made striking progress in scrapping and

321

modernisation. Even so the efficiency of the industry had not been raised to the level necessary to make it internationally competitive. The government could no longer leave the matter to the Bank of England.

The government intervened directly in 1936 with the Cotton Industry Reorganisation Act. The Act set up the Spindles Board, to be financed by an annual levy on surviving capacity, as in the shipbuilding industry; by 1939 the Board had scrapped about one half of the 13.5 million spindles present in the industry when it started.

8. Transport: road and rail

In August 1919, by Act of Parliament, the Ministry of Transport was set up to provide a focus for transport policy. Powers of control over the railway companies and other forms of transport passed to the Minister.

The policy embodied in the Railways Act of 1921 was a response to four sets of problems. First there was that of ownership. The government rejected proposals for nationalisation, preferring that the railways should continue to be owned and operated under private aegis, and to be responsible for their own finance. Secondly, it was clear that restructuring was necessary: from the 120 or so existing companies the Act created four railway systems, the London and North-Eastern; the London, Midland and Scottish; the Great Western and the Southern. The intention was that the amalgamations would break down the old obstacles to standardisation of equipment and a common system of rolling stock, thus yielding economies of running costs. The third important aspect was finance: to modernise the railways the government made £60 million available to be shared equally among the four companies. Finally there was the problem of setting the rates to be charged for carriage. Because of the monopoly position of the companies now created they could not be left to set their own rates: instead the approval was required of the newly established Railway Rates Tribunal. Here was yet one more scheme of government-sponsored rationalisation, indeed it was the first of the series. Closest in similarity was the Coal Mines Act of 1930, for in the case of both railways and coal the government, by statute, caused operations to be regulated on a regional basis, setting up what were in effect regional monopolies.

The Railway Rates Tribunal had to find some sort of basis in principle. Two such were available. Charges could be according to costs, or they could be governed by what the traffic would bear, charging more than cost where this was possible, and from the extra revenue thus generated subsidising less economic services which were nevertheless of great social importance – especially heavy, low-value loads. The principle of what the traffic will bear was chosen, partly because the heavy fixed costs of the railways made the cost of production formula difficult, but also in order to affect what was really a transfer payment from one set of users to another.

The road carriers, not being responsible for the maintenance of a permanent way, charged according to cost, and so could undercut the railways for the more valuable carriage. The railways thus found themselves with the heavy loads at low rates. The poor results thus generated meant that new capital was not forthcoming from the market so that modernisation was arrested and costs raised. A Royal Commission investigated the transport problem, reporting in 1929.

The road carriers were no longer to be left largely uncontrolled. The state could not permit free entry into the haulage business; if it did so conditions of profitability might be destroyed by lorries operating on a cut-price, and, perhaps, unsafe, basis. The Road Traffic Act of 1930 dealt with the carriage of passengers, introducing a system of licensing vehicles, through which Traffic Commissioners would regulate entry into the industry. The Road and Rail Traffic Act of 1933 regulated the carriage of goods, with Licensing Authorities awarding 'A' licences for those carrying for hire, 'C' licences for those moving their own goods and 'B' licences for those that did both. The licensed operators were thus protected against the competition of others: competition was sacrificed to order and stability.

The state in this way found itself obliged both to regulate the railway and road haulage systems within themselves, and to set the terms of competition between the two by operating upon the pattern of rates charged by the railways. By the devices of rate control for the railways and licensing for the road hauliers, rather than nationalisation or directives, it was hoped that the preferences of users, under such conditions, would produce a closer approximation to an optimal division of traffic between road and rail. Market choice would thus operate within a framework of regulation set by state agencies. But this policy made great difficulties for the railways, causing them in 1939 to launch a 'Fair Deal' campaign, aimed at gaining freedom from official control of their rating structure, allowing them to compete in price terms as they saw fit.

9. Agriculture: subsidy and market control

Immediately after the war agriculture was placed under a Ministry of Agriculture and Fisheries, the first industry to be given a Minister. Yet the state sought to disengage from agricultural subsidy and wage control as soon as possible. But it could not avoid being drawn back into farming. Co-operative action among farmers was encouraged by the Agricultural Credits Act of 1923; this provision was strengthened in 1928. The rates on farms were halved in 1923 and abolished altogether in 1929. Farm workers' earnings were once more made subject to minima by the Agricultural Wages Regulation Act of 1924. In the following year the Tory government tried to promote a new beginning in terms of farm products with its Sugar Beet Act. It provided a subsidy for sugar beet, intended to encourage a new crop which would provide a domestic supply of sugar and at the same time diversify agriculture, as the Germans and others had done.

But it was the depression from the early thirties that drew governments deep into agriculture. Under the Wheat Act of 1932 a direct subsidy was given to wheat growers, financed by a levy on imports of milled wheat; protection for cereal farmers that had been ended by the repeal of the Corn Laws in 1846 had returned, though in a different form. The pastoral sector of farming was also aided: at the Ottawa Conference quotas were imposed on meat imported from empire and foreign producers, and in 1933–4 British meat imports from various countries were limited by bilateral trade agreements. By means of sugar beet and wheat subsidies and quota protection for the cattle farmers the government had at long last reversed the traditional policy of leaving the farmers fully exposed to market conditions. But this was not to be done by directly raising food prices to the consumer through tariffs, as had been the case under the corn law, but by a levy in the case of wheat, quotas in the case of meat, and in other cases subsidies the costs of which were to be met from the general tax system. The Agricultural Wages Boards were to see to it that an appropriate share of the benefits generated by such governmental action would be passed to the farm workers.

From 1936 Commodity Commissions were set up for wheat, livestock and sugar to administer the subsidies and press for more efficient production.

There was a further range of products that had by the early 1930s developed highly unstable market conditions, especially milk, eggs, bacon and potatoes. Each had its special difficulties, but all shared the problem that when supply exceeded demand, even slightly, competitive selling could be ruinous. This meant highly unstable conditions for producers and their employees. There seemed to be only one way of bringing about conditions of orderly marketing, namely to set quotas and prices. With a great many producers in each line of production only the state could bring discipline to these sub-industries. But the state was only prepared to act where a convincing majority of producers wanted it to do so. The formula arrived at was embodied in the Agricultural Marketing Acts of 1931 and 1933. Under the first a group of two-thirds of the producers of a given farm commodity might prepare a scheme for the control of prices. If approved by the government it was made binding on all. A Marketing Board was then to be set up for this product, through which all producers would sell, the producers thus becoming a national state-imposed marketing co-operative. In addition the government at its discretion could grant tariff protection for any or all of the products affected. The Milk Marketing Board came into being in 1933, together with the Bacon and Pig Board in 1933–4; the Potato Marketing Board was started in 1933. The intention was that each Board should set an overall quota of production for each year, taking account of the marketing experience of the previous year, doing so in such a way as not to generate deficits or surpluses, but to yield stable and remunerative prices to the producers as a whole without imposing unjustifiable burdens on consumers. In addition, of course, each Board had to allot shares of the quota to producers, ostensibly on the basis of efficiency. Both sets of responsibilities were difficult to discharge, generating criticisms and tensions.

Under the Sugar Industry Reorganisation Act of 1935 the government made payment of its subsidy conditional on sugar beet factories being amalgamated under a single organisation, the British Sugar Corporation.

Agricultural policy was thus an extraordinary mixture of devices. Once the policy of free trade and no subsidy or market interference was abandoned, the state found itself under pressure to act in the diverse sectors of the industry. It did so without generalised governing principles, but in terms of the specific needs of each commodity range. In so doing it behaved with the same proliferating pragmatism that it had shown in dealing with the older basic industries.

10. The state and the newer industries

What of the newer industries, relying upon new technologies, often science based? Here there was a significant growth, with the motor and aircraft manufacture, electricity, chemicals, artificial fibres, rubber and films all making their valuable contributions to the economic base of the country. But even here the state could not remain passive. Indeed by 1939 it had accepted a number of roles with respect to these newer lines of output, including helping to develop the necessary research, providing a sponsoring framework, in the form of tariff protection and quotas, and assisting in structural adjustments.

As long ago as 1900 the government had set up the National Physical Laboratory. In 1916 came the important step of founding the Department of Scientific and Industrial Research. The Medical Research Council was established in 1913 and its functions greatly extended by Royal Charter in 1920; the Agricultural Research Council began in 1931. In addition the government financed scientific research in the universities and colleges. These initiatives represented an increasing recognition by governments that scientific and technological innovation could not be left entirely to private business, though the latter had developed research and development departments of its own. Successive governments for generations had been accused of failure to provide research and education facilities of a kind that would improve Britain's economic performance.[1] The need for such a commitment was now increasingly perceived as the older basic industries faded and it became clear that the future lay with those requiring a continuous participation in the research and development race. The Balfour Committee on Industry and Trade of 1928 told industrialists that 'nothing less than a revolution is needed

---

1. See chapter 13, section 4 above.

in their general outlook on science'. The change was beginning to take place, even in the older industries, but was it fast and far-reaching enough?

The respective roles of the state and private industry in this matter left much scope for debate. So did the nature of research: how 'pure' should it be, looking into the fundamental nature of the natural world, as opposed to concerning itself with more immediate applications of science to the improvement of human life? There was, moreover, the question of the use of science in warfare, especially the production of new and more deadly weaponry. The state was becoming committed to the exploration of the physical universe with a view to its further exploitation in peace and war, but was without any general perspective to govern its role in so doing.

The state had also to concern itself with other forms of encouragement for the newer industries. The McKenna Duties of 1915 had imposed a 33⅓% tariff on a range of luxury imports, the most important of which were motor cars and cycles. The first Labour government briefly withdrew these duties in 1924–5, but otherwise they continued. The highly important new sector, the automobile industry, thus enjoyed almost continuous protection in the inter-war years. The second category of exception to free trade in the 1920s was concerned with industries that were science-based, with great potential, referred to as the 'key' industries. In these the government was aware that Britain was lagging. They included synthetic dyestuffs, drugs, scientific instruments, optical glass and electrical equipment, such as magnetos and wireless valves, in all of which British production had relatively failed. The Dyestuffs Act of 1920 prohibited imports of synthetic organic-chemical materials: behind this protection Britain made herself almost self-sufficient by 1937. The Safeguarding of Industries Act of 1921 covered a further wide range of products: it made possible a duty of 33⅓% when it could be shown that other countries were 'dumping', i.e. selling goods in Britain below cost. It was believed that, under favourable circumstances, significant gaps in industrial output that had come into being under free trade could be filled if given protection: Britain, indeed, was using the infant industries argument which she had so long condemned. When protection is extended to entertainment the outcome is not necessarily so positive: the Cinematograph Films Act of 1927 required exhibitors to present a quota of British films. The general adoption of a tariff in 1932 placed the new Import Duties Advisory Committee in the position of arbiter and adviser on protection generally.

In the case of the newer industries the Bank of England and the state had some part, though a lesser one. In 1919 the Bank took over two dyestuff firms and merged them as the British Dyestuffs Corporation. When in 1926 the giant Imperial Chemical Industries was formed by bringing together British Dyestuffs, Nobel Industries, Brunner Mond and the United Alkali Company, the government was much involved. More generally, it is clear from the Treasury and Board of Trade papers that a close watch was kept on the newer industries: there are files on the automobile industry, the chemical, the electrical and others.

11. Regional policy and spatial planning

The classic industrial revolution regions, with their dependence on exports, had become depressed areas, with frighteningly high concentrations of unemployment. On the other hand certain regions had done much better than the rest, namely London and the South-East and Birmingham and the West Midlands. Though there was considerable migration from the lagging areas to the more prosperous ones, this could not relieve the problem to any significant degree.

In the late 1920s the government began to respond to the regional problem, but very tentatively. It tried through its Industrial Transference Board, set up in 1928, to improve voluntary geographical mobility of labour by providing transfer and training schemes for workers. But these proved inadequate incentives to move. By 1934 the regional situation was much worse: unemployment rates in the north of England and Scotland averaged some 20%, and in Wales 30%, against 10 or 12% in the Midlands and the South-East. The Special Areas (Development and Improvement) Act of 1934 marked the beginning of a new state policy conceived in regional terms. It was to bring work to the workers. Two Commissioners were appointed to operate state-provided inducements to firms to locate in four newly designated Special Areas, namely the North-East, West Cumberland, South Wales and Central Scotland. The Ministry of Labour co-operated. The Bank of England took a hand in regional policy; in 1936 it set up the Special Areas Reconstruction Association to provide loans for small businesses in the Special Areas; it also succeeded in persuading one of the great steel companies to invest heavily in South Wales against its better judgment. The 1937 Special Areas (Amendments) Act introduced tax concessions to firms in the Areas, and gave the Commissioners powers to help with taxes, rent and rates. The Act also encouraged the setting up of trading estates.

Regional policy rested upon the idea that the state should attempt, to some degree at least, to preserve the nineteenth-century locational pattern of industry and population. There were compelling political reasons for doing so: in July 1936 there were 1,717,000 registered unemployed of whom over two-thirds were in Northern England, Northern Ireland and the depressed parts of Scotland and Wales. Moreover, as the prospect of war increased, the notion of industrial dispersal gained acceptance.

But there were also strong grounds for distrusting such a policy. As with other state initiatives, once begun there could be no telling how far it would be carried. There was clearly a dilemma: to what extent should the Special Areas be aided at the expense of the rest, carrying the pattern of industrial location further and further from that which business men, with their search for the most efficient point of production, would have brought about? Did the best hope for the Special Areas really lie in trying to generate employment within them by state inducements, or did it lie in the further growth of the prosperous areas? Was the problem really a macro one of inadequate aggregate demand in the economy as a whole? Should industrial location be made a political matter at all?

The attraction of the growth areas, especially the South-East, was very powerful: between 1932 and 1937 four-fifths of the new factories were established in the London area, involving two-thirds of the new jobs. Government inducements were not sufficient to cause many firms to relocate themselves contrary to their commercial judgment. Indeed it seems likely that the government had no great long-term enthusiasm for such a policy, hoping that the necessary adjustment would come about eventually through the operation of market forces.

By 1937 a new concern had arisen, namely that of spatial planning within regions. Dense slums, urban sprawl, industry spreading over prime agricultural land and ribbon building developing along the main roads had aroused serious misgivings. The Barlow Commission

329

was appointed in July of that year to consider both the inter-regional and the intra-regional problems. Its *Report* was completed in August, 1939, though not published until the following January. It was far and away the most comprehensive document of its kind to date. Barlow argued for two general sets of ideas: there should be a balanced distribution of population and industry as between the regions of Britain, and within each region there should be a planned spatial configuration. The latter would involve reducing the terrible congestion of the central slums, building new housing estates, and at the same time defining each city by a distinct perimeter surrounded by a green belt. Britain was thus to be given a set of city-regions balanced both over the country and within themselves. This was the state of spatial planning thinking when war came again in September 1939.[1]

1. See also chapter 21, section 5 below.

18

Micro-management: the public sector

1. Local and national public sectors

The public sector continued to be dominated in terms of scale of operations by local government down to 1939. Local authorities extended their provision of water, sewage disposal, gas, electricity and trams and buses. A considerable range of minor miscellaneous services was added. Some were prohibited: the municipalities were denied the right to enter banking, though Birmingham had gained such powers in 1916. The most important extension of local authority functions came after 1919 in housing,[1] and in educational provision.[2] But there was no longer the dream among socialists that the nation could be carried to socialism through a multiplicity of local socialisms.

The scale of public ownership at the national level did not greatly increase. The Forestry Commission was set up in 1919. The Post Office, telegraphs and the Pacific Cable were in the public sector before 1914. The telephone system was taken over. The government continued to own the Anglo-Persian Oil Company, involving itself deeply in the politics of Iran and the Middle East.

The state became active in four new fields. In 1926 the Central Electricity Board and the British Broadcasting Corporation were formed. In 1929 government merged four rival companies and its own Pacific Cable into the privately owned Cable and Wireless Limited. In 1939 British Overseas Airways was brought into being, a governmental merger of private companies, supported by subsidy. Each of these organisations was unique in the challenge it posed to the state. Each was placed under the control of strong-minded men

1. See chapter 21, section 4 below.
2. See chapter 21, section 3 below.

recruited by government from industry, each of whom soon established his own perspective on what should be done, following a strong managerial ethos. Such men resented the tag of socialism, just as the business men pioneers of local public utilities had done. They were entrepreneurial pragmatics who had decided that certain essential jobs could only be done by agencies in which the state played an important but not dominant part. The CEB, the BBC, C and W, and BOAC, together with the immense London Passenger Transport Board, had to seek a formula for public operation, arriving at a workable relationship with the state, generating an efficient organisational structure and establishing a system of charges appropriate to the service and capable of supporting the financial structure. All these things had to be done while keeping a tension in the system sufficient for efficiency, while operating a monopoly that could quite easily pass to the consumer the costs of its own slackness or bureaucratic ineffectualness.

2. Electricity supply

Just as the municipalities, using arguments of efficiency and public service, had wrested water, gas and the trams from the private companies before 1914, so from 1918 the central government made its challenge to the local authorities over electricity. Moreover the private companies were still important suppliers. The struggle over the generation and distribution of electricity thus became a three part one, between the companies, the municipalities and the state.

As part of the wartime reconstruction programme[1] a scheme was produced, intended to solve the problem. The Electricity (Supply) Bill provided for a national body of Electricity Commissioners to direct policy, and for the establishment of District Electricity Boards to take over and build generating capacity and to sell power wholesale at a standard price to existing undertakings, both local authorities and companies, who would distribute it to users. But the Bill, in the form of the Act of 1919, was emasculated. There was indeed to be a body of Electricity Commissioners, but their powers were limited and ambiguous; instead of District Boards there were to

---

1. See chapter 14, section 6 above.

be Joint Electricity Authorities (JEAs), voluntary in nature, combining local government and private interests. This was the compromise that emerged from the existing pattern of power and opinion. There was in consequence of it no proper central planning of generating capacity. All this was in strong contrast to the German tradition of technocratic co-operation.

Those concerned with efficiency were especially frustrated. The continuously improving technology of electricity pressed steadily toward the need for larger units, standardisation and the unification of supply. By the early 1920s there was a strong element in the Labour Party, headed by Herbert Morrison, in favour of outright nationalisation. The Weir Committee of 1925 made far-reaching proposals; these were embodied in The Electricity (Supply) Act of 1926.

They were that a new national 'gridiron' of high voltage transmission lines should be built and managed by a new state-owned agency, the Central Electricity Board. The power stations were to remain as before, under the ownership of private enterprise and the local authorities. But those that were to supply to the Grid would be under the control of the Board. The building and operation of new power stations was to be left to the companies and the municipalities, but made subject to the planning co-ordination of the Board and the control by the Board of the output of power stations contributing to the Grid. The Electricity Commissioners were to continue as the government agency directly responsible for overseeing electrical development. In particular one of their main concerns was to improve distribution on a regional and local basis, working through the JEAs. Thus no change in ownership of stations was envisaged. This was the second great compromise between state integrated operation and private and local authority enterprise. It quelled for a time the fears of general nationalisation of the industry, and yet made possible the next necessary steps in planning and execution.

The Central Electricity Board achieved a high degree of autonomy, with freedom from Treasury control, based on the government's view that the state was not competent to interfere in industrial operations. The Board proved highly effective: the national Grid as originally planned was completed in September 1933, a remarkable feat. Its construction during the slump years made a considerable contribution to employment.

3. *Broadcasting and the public mind*

The coming of the radio in the early 1920s posed an altogether new challenge to governments, and one of great complexity, involving both difficult technical and profound cultural problems. The wireless set (a boxful of wires) was the first semi-durable based upon electricity to become general in the home. The Post Office under the Wireless Telegraphy Act of 1904 controlled all wireless communication in the United Kingdom. The Marconi Company was authorised to broadcast speech and music. The problem of allocating wavelengths soon appeared. Manufacturers produced first components for amateur reception and then whole sets. By 1922 it was clear that there had to be an official policy. The Postmaster General authorised in that year the formation of a private monopoly of broadcasting, the British Broadcasting Company, with capital supplied by the manufacturers of sets. Every listener paid a ten-shilling license fee. J.C.W. Reith was appointed General Manager. By the end of 1924 most of Britain was covered by the Company's transmissions. The General Strike of 1926 demonstrated its political power. This was the first national experience simultaneously shared by all. Churchill urged the cabinet to take over the Company and use it to combat the strike, but this was refused. And yet it could hardly be said that the broadcasts were neutral.

Two committees reported on the Company, Sykes (1923) and Crawford (1926). The upshot was that broadcasting was nationalised. The British Broadcasting Corporation was given its Royal Charter in 1926. In this Reith played a powerful part, becoming Director General. A Board of Governors was to keep watch and receive complaints. Reith laid down the four sets of ideas that were to dominate the BBC in its formative years. These were independence, both of government and of advertisers (and secured by a license fee); monopoly of broadcasting; public service based upon a code of morality backed by a religious perspective; and political neutrality. The American system of private enterprise and the profit motive based on advertising was flatly rejected. The values of a Scottish Presbyterian manse were thus beamed over Britain by the most general and powerful of means.

Many battles were fought: with the Post Office on technical matters, with the press over the news (especially concerning sport), with the general public, much of whom resented the effort to raise the level of culture through music, talks and the drama, with the anti-Sabbatarians who did not accept Reith's view of the seventh day. Most difficult of all were aggrieved politicians who considered their point of view or their personality to be slighted. The main defence against this was to seek to be 'neutral'; the BBC, like many leading journalists, believed in a distinction between 'straightforward news' and comment. There was also a tendency to develop a cocoon of secrecy.

The wireless demanded for the first time that the state assume some sort of omnibus attitude toward the cultural and political diet of the nation. It was unique in that it had access to the home and to all members of the family, on a universal and instantaneous basis. To this the existing dominant news and opinion medium, the newspapers, offered no real parallel. All manner of questions of cultural control and political presentation were posed by the new technical marvel.

4. Airways, internal and external

Sir John Reith, having formed a BBC that would bear his stamp for a generation and more, left it in 1938 to become chairman of Imperial Airways. Here was a second great challenge, though of a very different kind. The government was seriously worried about British civil aviation. Down to 1938 it had left the matter to private enterprise, with a degree of subsidy, through mail contracts and directly.

One of the many wartime reconstruction inquiries had been the Civil Aerial Transport Committee of 1917 under Lord Northcliffe. It urged the government to sponsor a plan for civil aviation, but nothing was done. Four pioneering companies came into being in the peace, to fly between Britain and the continent. But by 1921 all had suspended operations. The many difficulties of building up the new and expensive mode of travel were compounded by the subsidy policies of foreign governments, especially the French. The British government, in spite of a deep aversion to subsidising business, could not stand out: subsidy support was given to the cross channel services in 1921. Government was never thereafter to be able wholly to extricate itself from aviation: it had no choice if Britain was to have an international carrying capacity.

Moreover the government had to take a hand structurally. In 1924 it sponsored the merger of four of the larger companies into Imperial Airways. It was hoped that this single large private concern, raising capital of £1 million, with state backing in the form of a subsidy that would taper away, would be able to thrive in international air carriage. While the subsidy continued Imperial Airways was effectively a monopoly, for no company not thus provided could compete. Imperial Airways did well on the empire routes, consolidating a service to India, that jewel in the imperial crown, by the later 1930s. The Empire Air Mail Scheme of 1934 assisted such expansions of services. The Atlantic air service was started in August 1938. But Imperial Airways was much less successful on the European routes: a report of 1938 was very critical in this respect, saying that Britain should have her own links with all major European capitals.

Meanwhile British internal services were in serious difficulty. There were nearly a score of companies by the mid 1930s, most of them losing money. By 1934 the railway companies had taken over a considerable share of the internal airlines; they formed Railway Air Services in that year. But their thinking was limited, seeing air links as an ancillary to rail. They, embattled in their struggle with road haulage,[1] were in no position to take a real initiative.

Once again government had to intervene. In 1935 British Airways was formed by a merger of four companies. It too was private, but became a second chosen instrument of government through subsidy. In 1938 the government took control of the internal air market: it set up an Air Transport Licensing Authority. The new body both regulated entry into the field and subsidised those companies thus licensed.

This, in general, was the situation when Reith took over Imperial Airways. Largely under his influence Imperial and British Airways were merged in the form of British Overseas Airways. This was done on the eve of the second world war, just as civil aviation was assimilated to war need.

5. Cables and empire

Communications by cable and wireless was another international area that the British government could not ignore: indeed it had

---

1. See chapter 17, section 8 above.

been drawn into it early in the century. Though empire was to pass into Commonwealth, imperial thinking was still strong here, as in airways. The Pacific Cable Board had been set up by the British government in 1901 and had created a considerable system of imperial communications. The Post Office too had acquired cables. But there was now also a complex set of rival private concerns: Eastern Telegraph, Eastern Extension, Western Telegraph and the Marconi Company. There was, indeed, the danger of chaos, and of British failure to take a full place in world communications. There was much debate as to what should be done, including the argument between private and public enterprise.

The upshot was the Imperial Telegraphs Act of 1929. It set up a comprehensive structure. This consisted of two private companies, but with identical boards. The communications company (Imperial and International Communications Ltd), with £30 million of capital provided by the Telegraph companies and Marconi, and the merger company (Cable and Wireless Ltd) that would fuse the four interests. The British government was to approve the choice of Chairman of the two Boards, as well as one member; there was also to be a Communications Advisory Committee with representatives of commonwealth governments, in the hope that a unified system could be achieved. These arrangements meant, of course, that the field was to be occupied by a private enterprise, subject to a mild degree of governmental supervision. It was hoped that in this way the economy and initiative of private management would be combined with the surveillance of public control. This latter was reinforced by the requirements that profits above a prescribed level should be used to reduce the rates charged for the service (shades of Mr Gladstone's Railway Act of 1844[1]).

The position was reviewed by the Greene Committee in 1931, largely because of criticism of the rates charged. A partial rationalisation of British communication services had been brought about by 1939, but the rates question, the nationalisation argument and the aspirations of Canada, India and Australia for their own systems, greatly complicated the picture.

1. See chapter 4, section 10 above.

6. *The public sector and science-based monopoly*

Government in each of the four cases discussed in this chapter had to seek a compromise between private and public sectors, with the exception of the BBC. In all of them the first explorations and initiatives had come from private ventures; the state had no part in this first stage of novelty and unknown potential. All of them were science based, using new and rapidly developing technologies. All were concerned with efficient delivery (respectively of energy, sound, people and messages). All had strong connotations of economies of scale and of monopoly power. For these reasons, the state, after a certain point in development had been reached in each case, had to assume a posture toward it. Moreover, though the Conservatives rejected nationalisation of the commanding heights of the economy, as envisaged by the Labour Party, refusing it even in coal, the idea of state involvement in ownership and control had gained a good deal of ground. These four areas, being new, were such that pragmatic thinking, such as had taken place earlier in the local government provision of water, gas, electricity and trams, was permissible and indeed essential. Moreover these functions involved no vast and assertive traditional labour force, and no host of embattled employers. In the case of airways and international cable and wireless communication there were Commonwealth and indeed world connotations: Britain had to be as effective as possible at these levels.

The resulting pattern was a variegated one, the outcome of technical, marketing and political considerations. In the case of electricity the state, through a statutory board, took over the distributive function at the national level, leaving generating to local government and private interests under the CEB. It was so clearly a technical challenge that the political component was minimal. Broadcasting, highly political, was passed to a corporation given monopoly control, financed by a listeners' fee, but with the Director General appointed by the government. A Board of Governors was similarly chosen, to provide surveillance: governments referred complaints to it, and so tried to depoliticise broadcasting. The state passed its interest in cable and wireless to private enterprise, but prescribed the form of organisation (the two Boards) and took a veto on the appointment of the Chairman and one member. In air travel the principal private airlines were merged by the government into a public corporation, BOAC.

In each case the government sought to minimise its responsibility and intervention, hoping that the respective bodies would perform to the public satisfaction, and hence would cease to be political.

Always there was the problem of providing leadership for these corporations. A new kind of man, of which Reith was the exemplar, had to be found. Such men had to organise on a scale and in a manner to which British industry offered no real parallel. The military mind was not drawn upon, possibly because of the need to implement whole new ranges of technology. By and large the chairmen were left to get on with the job. A new race of guardians was thus required, more Platonic and more visible than the bureaucrats, and capable of holding their own with the politicians.

19

The business response

1. Business as a component of power

British business had by 1919 established its two national bodies, the Federation of British Industries (1916) and the British Employers' Federation (1919).[1] But before they could exert their full weight upon public policy it was necessary for them to arrive at a programme capable of carrying the support of the mass of their memberships. Because of the great variety of interests represented this was very difficult. There were two great lines of cleavage. The first was between the men in command of the older staple industries and those who ran the newer more science-based (and/or consumer-oriented ones). The second was between the large firms with substantial resources and the smaller ones with slender margins, unable to sustain any prolonged contest with labour.

Nevertheless, the problem of business power in reciprocal relationship to labour power in the contest for state support, became increasingly explicit as the inter-war years succeeded one another. It had become clear well before the war that over large sectors of industry it was no longer possible to dispose of the problem of business power by dissolving it in the concept of competitive markets, each with an infinite number of buyers and sellers, none of whom could affect the price or control the supply. The war had made competitive assumptions even more implausible. For though the state made a great effort to return to them in many aspects after 1918, it soon became clear that a full revival of laissez-faire would be very difficult to implement or sustain.

The market was not a prophylactic against business power, nor was it, over a much wider range of industry and commerce, a force

1. See chapter 14, section 4 above.

for rejuvenation. The economies of scale were inducing ever larger units of production in many industries, as in chemicals, and making them necessary in others, as in railway operations and steelmaking. Major components of industry needed to be restructured, a task that was impossible without state support of one kind or another.[1] The war had seen a catastrophic loss of foreign markets, as for example the Japanese capture of Asian outlets for cotton goods: this had given rise to much competitive 'disorderly' marketing among British producers: the case could be argued that British sellers should organise their activities abroad by carefully designed co-operation or mutual regulation. There were great cyclical oscillations in the size of world markets against which, it was urged, British business should organise and evoke state aid through tariffs, subsidies and other means. Most difficult of all, threatening even the civil peace, there were the problems of wage levels and welfare costs, bringing the employers into direct confrontation with their labour forces.[2] But from the employers' point of view high wages and generous welfare could gravely endanger their ability to sell abroad.

In these many ways, therefore, business posed the irreducible problem of power. Who should wield it? Some said that the state should be the arbiter. But the state itself, under the expanding democratic formula, was in contention. Both employers and labour regarded governments with deep distrust: neither would commit the arbitrament of their differences to politicians and bureaucrats.

Should the employers continue to have the primary role in determining the shape of industry and the economy? Many, perhaps most of them, thought so. It was they who made business decisions in the boardroom and elsewhere. But how could they discharge this critical function if inhibited by the state and the trade unions? Moreover there was a strong overtone of right, namely that they had provided the capital resources (or at least they had acted for those who had done so), with the implication that this gave them a warrant for full control.

The unions, of course, rejected this kind of argument: they believed that the workers, even more than the shareholders, had an 'interest' in the business and the industry. Cuts in wages, employment and welfare should not be made without their consent, or, at the

1. See chapter 17 above.
2. See chapter 16, sections 5 and 6 above; chapter 20, section 2 below.

least, consultation. But the unions did not wish themselves to occupy the centre of business decision making.[1] Historically they had learned to define themselves not as decision takers in the boardroom, but as responding to decisions taken there by management. It is true that the syndicalists' credo involved taking over business, but it received no mass support among the workers. The formula of nationalisation seemed to provide another way out of labour's dilemma, proposing a kind of co-operation between the unions and the state. But it too, except in coal, had no great support. Could business and the unions, by direct interaction independent of the state, come to a solution? This of course was the formula sought after by the Mond–Turner conversations, but the activists on the respective sides could not win general and sustained support.[2]

Only one answer remained, namely that the business men should continue to run business, and that the state should exert itself in facilitating this task through a mixture of restructuring programmes, tariffs, subsidies, tax incentives, commercial negotiation with other countries and, where possible, diplomatic pressures. There were, however, some matters on which employers and labour could agree; business men resisted Lord Curzon's ultimatum to Russia in 1923 and helped to draw up an *entente commerciale* with the Soviets; they even gave a degree of support for the Labour government's recognition of the Soviet Union in 1924.

The state would leave wage levels, by and large, to settlement between employers and unions, though from time to time altering the rules of the contest between them, as in 1927. As to welfare, this was a state responsibility, to be discharged as governments judged social need in its many aspects, but subject to pressure from unions, philanthropists, employers and the political parties.[3]

This, in general, was the formula followed in the inter-war years: the business men ran business, the state sought to assist in this in certain sectors, while the unions followed the role of criticising, making claims and seeking to impose vetoes upon a system external to themselves. For business to need the sanctions and assistance of the state was to admit that private property and the market no longer

1. See chapter 20, section 5 below.
2. See chapter 16, section 7 above.
3. See chapter 21 below.

provided a fully self-sustaining basis for the continuous adjustment of the economy and society to change.

Under such a system the state and the employers were the only powers that had any capacity to enforce control of demand under conditions of inflation, and to impose limitations on labour costs through wage control under conditions of world market contraction. Any system of economic relations can make errors in the sense of generating excess or deficient demand; under the market system of the inter-war years the state took part in the imposing of contraction through its macro-controls, but not by direct action upon wages. It left to the employers the task of restoring due proportion in terms of wages, doing so firm by firm and sector by sector. In this way the most volatile aspect of economic control was kept out of politics. In a sense this was at the expense of business, placing it in a confrontational relationship to labour. But for the state to assume a positive wage-fixing role on any scale would have been to make politicians and bureaucrats the arbiters of the central problem of all economies, namely the distribution of the product year by year.

2. Phases and choices

The British business community in the inter-war years in policy terms, like the unions, went through two phases, though the timing was different. Down to 1931 there was a degree of weakness of organisation, together with a lack of internal cohesion based upon any real sense of direction. But from September 1931 there was a change. All trading countries became greatly concerned with their share of world markets as the great governing difficulty of the inter-war years deepened, namely the failure of demand to grow on a world scale. Business and government in Britain, as in other countries, tried a range of devices to attract as large a share of contracted demand as possible, sometimes to the further aggravation of the world's difficulties. In so doing government and business moved into a kind of alliance; the fiction that the two were distinct wore thin.

Three lines of policy were tried after 1931. Firstly, there was the revival of the tariff, together with a system of bilateral treaties.[1] By these means the state was used by business in an attempt to increase,

1. See chapter 16, section 10 above.

by close international bargaining, Britain's share of a wide range of markets. Britain, so long the great defender of the principle of free trade, reverted, with dramatic suddenness, to the mercantilism that Adam Smith had attacked a century and a half earlier. Secondly, there was the attempt to pursue the line so vigorously urged by Joseph Chamberlain of making of the empire an economic system resting on complementarity of products as between the manufactured goods of Britain and the primary outputs of the rest; indeed the thinking involved was not all that different from the ideas that had lain behind the Navigation Laws of the seventeenth century. Thirdly, there was the attempt at international cartelisation of a range of industries, with Japan and Germany as the hoped-for partners. This was a new departure, with British business, that had for so long criticised German schemes of market control, now embracing them in a kind of desperation, using the state in the attempt to bring such regulation into existence on an international basis.

3. Tariff and empire

The FBI could not at once find a stance on the tariff, or indeed on any other major commercial issue. The industries which tended to dominate it were the old heavy ones of iron and steel, shipbuilding and engineering. The coal and cotton industries, with well-developed organisations of their own, were inclined to make direct representations to government. The newer industries, especially those linked with home consumption, felt little inclination to join a centralising body. The FBI, partly because of its pattern of membership, finding questions of international trade difficult enough, was unwilling to be drawn into other issues such as industrial restructuring and the general relations between industry and the state. Thus the claim of the FBI to be a parliament of industry was a limited one, both in terms of membership and agenda. Yet when governments sought a consolidated voice speaking for industry, the FBI had no rival. It was indeed, to a large degree, pulled into many issues by the state as government sought guidance and co-operation.

The Macmillan Committee of 1931 posed a dilemma for the newly formed FBI; the Federation wished to speak for industry, but it was unwilling to make a choice between the policy possibilities that the government was offering for its consideration. The government needed the assistance of industry in order to formulate the issues for itself and for public projection. In particular there was the question of the tariff: the FBI deadlocked on this, with the cotton interest leading the resistance to protectionism. Moreover there were business radicals who regarded the tariff as a feeble palliative, contributing nothing to the need to cut British costs by restructuring and by tackling wage rigidities: real cost reduction, with its confrontational implications, became the rival programme to that of the tariff. Its leading advocate was Sir James Lithgow (1883–1952), Clydeside shipbuilder and President of the FBI. There was the danger that the FBI might disintegrate or lose any prospect of real influence. Moreover the Director of the FBI, Sir Roland Nugent, a former Foreign Office man, was anxious that the FBI not be made the capitalist end of a polarity with labour by the adoption of provocative policies.

Events clarified the position, especially the abandonment of gold. The tariff was really all that was left by way of policy; it became at long last a central element in the FBI's programme. Any belief that British business was a monolith enforcing its will upon government is wide of the mark: indeed one of the great difficulties for government was to extract a view from the business community as to what general economic policy to pursue.

September 1931 was a catalyst for the FBI not merely in terms of the tariff: it was so also with respect to empire. The FBI sought to consolidate British industry behind a programme that would delimit the industrial ambitions of the Dominions within a general imperial system. If this was to be possible at all it would be necessary to compensate the Dominions by raising the level of their commodity prices, by monetary or other means. There was failure on both fronts: the industrialists of the Dominions would not accept any real constraint on their developments, and there appeared to be no workable way of getting commodity prices up, involving dearer food for British consumers.

Throughout the negotiations at the Ottawa Conference of 1932 the FBI worked closely with government, but to little avail. The British government had a minor degree of success, but the restricted agreement achieved with the other parts of the Commonwealth provided no real basis for imperial economic integration. A basic

345

difficulty was that Britain was suffering two kinds of stagnation – of population growth and of industrial expansion. She was thus a static market, unable to buy greater quantities of primary products from the Dominions and so making it necessary for them to industrialise, thus further aggravating British difficulties.

4. *World market allocation*

The third line of policy adopted by the FBI was to seek agreements with leading foreign competitors for market sharing. This meant the creation of international cartels in various markets, co-ordinating the price and output policies of national industries on an international basis. Attempts in this direction began after 1933 as the limitations of tariff and imperial policies became apparent. The government encouraged industry in this, hoping that such market agreements would have the effect of making them raise their efficiency by reorganisation. In the Japanese case there was the hope that Britain might gain a significant share in the industrialisation of Manchuria and of China generally. But the Japanese argued that they must have an uninhibited export drive in order to save the yen from collapse, and with it the monetary system of East Asia; moreover the Japanese had too much industrial capacity still coming on stream for them to favour any limitation of their market penetration. Germany was no less a competitive threat, and one much closer to home. Although it appeared to the British business negotiators that their German counterparts were amenable to a programme of European cartelisation, the government of Germany under Hitler was pursuing political objectives that made any trading accommodation between Britain and Germany impossible, as became clear in September 1939.

20

The political and industrial
attitudes of labour

1. The Labour Party's component groups and their views

The ideas and programmes of the major political parties in Britain
have never been systematic and defined, though there has seldom
been any lack of those who would make them so. They have defeated
system and unanimity because they have been moving amalgams of
interests, aspirations and tactics, derived from a wide variety of
sources, in continuous adjustment to context, both ideologically
and practically. This had always been true of Conservatives and
Liberals.

It was even more so for the Parliamentary Labour Party from its
formal beginnings under that title in 1906. The performance of the
Party between 1918 and 1939 was a drama, the climaxes of which
were provided by the attempts, at moments of major decisions, to
reconcile the elements so that a policy might be synthesised and
group coherence maintained. Yet, though policy unanimity evaded
the Party, there continued to be, at a certain level of aspiration and
practicality, a solidarity of a kind such that the Party, in spite of its
setbacks in 1924 and 1931, was in 1939 in a stronger position than
ever.

The Labour Party had two major components, the trade union
movement and the intellectuals. The trade union movement was
rooted in the working classes, with little or no middle-class intrusion.
It was disposed to regard the Labour Party as its own political wing,
rather than as having any real independent existence. It was
necessary for unionism to express itself through the TUC in order to
find a clear policy direction that could be passed on to the Party. But
this was far from easy. The attitudes of most unionists were based on
the relationship between themselves and their jobs and their
workmates. The TUC was a loose federation of autonomous unions.

In spite of the wide-ranging debates in which it indulged on the economy, on social welfare and on foreign policy and the empire, it was no intellectual seminar. Any attempt to make it so would generate distrust at once, for discourse would pass over the heads of most participants, a clear ground for resentment. There was a tendency, too, for TUC debates to be dominated by immediate events and the mood of the moment, causing participants to search for points at which warming heart-cries could be uttered.

There was, however, a minority within the trade union movement who sought to lift the unions from their workplace perspective and to commit them to a philosophy. Among these the communists and syndicalists were the most numerous and active. They took a conflict, adversary, confrontational view of the role of organised workers. The unions thus contained within themselves two perspectives on society. The non-revolutionary one was dominant, but it was always subject to revolutionary or quasi-revolutionary pressure, tactics and challenge. It is far from clear how such working-class men arrived at the perspective and dedication needed for the revolutionary role. They could draw on continental, American and Australian ideas, or they could find or formulate such views for themselves, either taking them directly from the writings of Marx and Engels, or accepting middle-class interpreters of their system of thought.

The Independent Labour Party from its foundation in 1893 included both middle-class intellectuals and working-class seekers after a new society. It contained a large element who were clerks and shop assistants rather than manual workers; indeed the ILP was to a great extent the creation of the self-improved element among the lower middle classes, men and women with social consciences and the urge to do good (often a humanised projection of evangelicalism), accompanied by a considerable reading of literature dealing with society. The creation of the School Boards under the Education Acts of 1870 and 1872 had given them their first real opportunity for direct political participation. The reform of local government in 1888 had admitted them to the Council Chambers where they developed articulateness and confidence. The idea of the brotherhood of man was strong among them, producing a socialism that was both emotional and moral, deeply rooted in a sense of right values, demanding that both ends and means be ethically acceptable, and that the rights of the individual be respected. Such people could find

348

no wholly satisfying home in the trade union movement, though many were unionists; they needed their own organisational self-expression. Once the Labour Party had come into existence they were something of an anomaly, being both independent and in a sense assimilated.

The Communist Party of Great Britain in the late 1920s and early 1930s was largely proletarian, and isolated from the rest of the labour movement. But from 1931 it embarked upon a policy of active recruitment among the middle classes, attracting students, teachers, academics and professional persons. The Communist Party thus became, like the Labour Party, a mixture of manual workers and intellectuals. This made for a certain uneasiness of relationship between the two elements, but it brought a real accession of strategic strength to the party, making possible a dual network of Marxist intellectuals and factory militants. Though the Communist Party was rebuffed by the Labour Party, its efforts to participate in the larger body continued, both at an individual level by having common members, and by appeals for a 'United Front' between the two Parties against the capitalist enemy. But the dominant element in the Labour Party and the trade union movement, as represented by Ernest Bevin (1881–1951), Herbert Morrison (1888–1965) and Clement Attlee (1883–1967), would not have this; joint membership of the Labour and Communist Parties was later prohibited.

Syndicalist ideas found their main inter-war strength in the Minority Movement between 1924 and 1929. Its members, working men dedicated to renovation through disruption, had no hope of affecting the Labour Party by direct action within it: instead they operated at one removed, within the trade unions. They worked upon the dissatisfactions of the rank and file with the wage settlements negotiated by the union leaders. In industrial negotiation the trade union leadership had always to act in the light of an assessment of the hostages they might be giving to such men at the shop steward level. The Minority Movement was a useful weapon for the Communist Party. A considerable number of union branches and trades councils were carried into affiliation with the Movement. The union leadership had no choice but to declare war upon it. By 1929 the Minority Movement had been crushed. The Communist Party then tried to form breakaway unions, but failed disastrously. But in spite of these defeats, syndicalist and communist ideas did not die: the Labour Party was never to be free of Marxism. That hydra-headed expression of the politics of confrontation could always find new embodiment.

Middle-class syndicalism took the form of guild socialism. Its principal prophet was the Oxford don, G.D.H. Cole (1889–1959). He was hostile to the concentration of power in the large industrial and commercial units now being generated. For Cole, size and centralism were the two great enemies of freedom for the mass of men. Like the émigré Kropotkin (1842–1921), and others, he wanted a reversion to localism and to smaller-scale production. To bring this about the capitalist system had to be smashed, but gradually. Successive sectors of production would be taken over by the workers within them, to be run by local guilds, which would relate to national or international guilds. The worker having placed himself in possession, would no longer be alienated from his task, partly because he owned and controlled, and partly because of the possiblity of reversing the trend to ever larger-scale units of production. Common to syndicalists, guild socialists and a good many trade unionists was the view that somehow the worker must be put in control of his life by becoming a participant in industrial decision taking. This line of thought could, of course, lead to nationalisation.

There remained the principal manifestation of bourgeois socialism, namely Fabians. With their policy of permeation they were willing to work through Conservatives, Liberals or Labour, and indeed attempted to do so. As represented by the Webbs, they were pragmatists, gradualists and enemies of the revolutionaries; moved by a sense of moral purpose they were also believers in the scientific understanding of social institutions and the ability to improve, renovate or supersede them as occasion might demand. They were against poverty and privilege alike, but were not prepared to move against them frontally. Instead they investigated institution by institution, including local government, the poor law, municipal trading and the control and management of industry. Guided by such functional analysis, they worked for reform. In this way they combined the last phase of moralism with the new age of the social sciences. They worked always for a planned and measured outcome within each area of activity, but without any attempt at aggregation of the operation of the economy as a whole. Capitalism would disappear by being superseded at this point or that by the adoption of collectivist institutions; parliament and the constitution, far from requiring to be overthrown, would be used to renovate capitalism. The state would not, as with the Marxists, wither away, but would be run by experts, educated in the new sciences of society at the London School of Economics and elsewhere.

It is hardly surprising that within the labour movement there was confusion. It contained a highly diverse and uneasily related set of components, with chronic tension between those seeking wage settlements and those disrupting them, and between the cooly rational and the emotively millenarian.

But something of a common denominator did emerge. The labour movement was anti-capitalist, though sometimes without much conviction: there was a ritual denigration of unreformed capitalism, together with a welcoming of the prospect of capitalist collapse, accompanied by a fear of the outcome if it should occur. There was an insistence upon trade union freedom of action, with no inhibitions about union power in relation to employers, consumers or the state. It was believed that large sectors of the economy should be nationalised in the interests of efficiency, the removal of political advantage and the promotion of industrial democracy through worker participation.[1] But there was a vagueness about the new structures that should replace the old.

The poor were not responsible for their condition and so should not suffer penalties arising from it. There should be provided, through the state, a national minimum for all; this meant, of course, a policy of greater egalitarianism, brought about by redistributive taxation. Taxes on incomes should be steeply progressive, and on unearned incomes and inherited wealth almost confiscatory. There should be minimum wages prescribed by law in at least some sectors, and wage formulae should be on a national rather than a local basis. Such a programme was the result of starting from the conditions of the people in terms of their employment and incomes, and from their fulfilment while on the job. No serious consideration was given to the question whether adequate scope would be left for the operation of market forces, or, if they should be impaired to the point of breakdown, what would replace them.

1. See chapter 14, section 3 above.

This, then, was the pattern that emerged from the inter-play of forces within the labour movement. It was seldom expressed in any complete manner, and the emphasis on its component parts shifted over time. Moreover its exemplification could vary a good deal as between expressed outlook and intention when in opposition, and action when in power. At the local level some Labour Councils were not all that far removed in their attitude to the *Lumpenproletariat* from that of the Charity Organisation Society, sharing the belief in social osmosis, whereby those people who were capable of responding to assistance would move upward on the social scale as incomes, housing and education were improved by action from above.

On the employers' side, and in the Conservative Party generally, there was a pattern of fears that was the obverse of these labour aspirations. In particular there was the belief that the legal sanctioning of the strength of the unions would create conditions under which inflexible wages would destroy the viability of large parts of industry, generating unemployment of a massive and unmanageable kind.

2. The years of union assertion, 1919–26

Two sets of preoccupations were always present for labour: the industrial and the political. But their relative immediacy of course varied with changing circumstances. So too did the spirit in which they were pursued. In a crude way it is possible to distinguish a period of assertion and aggression, culminating in the General Strike of 1926, followed by one in which the tone changed, with direct strike action being replaced by a new articulateness and a new skill in manoeuvre and negotiation.

The radicalism of 1918–26 did not derive from middle-class intellectuals, though the Fabians played a significant part in it. It came rather from the working classes. It found its mass support in the general conditions of the time, of which large-scale unemployment, together with post-war disillusionment, were the most compelling. For radicalism to be sustained it was necessary that a consolidated group of workers act as its core. It was the miners, together with the railway workers and the dockers, who provided this essential coherence and continuity.

Circumstances had so converged on the miners that they could after 1918 perform this central role, and were indeed, in large measure, compelled to it. Theirs was a monster industry, such that at its peak no less than 15% of all insured men were part of it, some 1,353,000 in 1924: it was labour-intensive to an extraordinary degree. It was highly unstable in market terms, for the price and indeed saleability of coal varied greatly, with accompanying pressure on costs, of which wages were the largest component. Finally, the miners, because of the nature of their task, and because of their mode of life which largely isolated them from the rest of society, could generate an immense loyalty to one another. On the side of the coal masters there was an equally compelling ethos. They had developed and conducted a prosperous industry for several generations, following the economic philosophy of the market, so that they believed as an article of faith that free and unfettered competition was best for themselves, miners and consumers alike. Colliery owners and mine workers had thus become close prisoners of their respective cultures.

Into this situation the state was bound to be drawn. Behind the immediate conflict loomed the larger question, affecting the nature and authority of the state itself: could the miners and their allies coerce the state?

The miners' political programme had as its first objective the nationalisation of the mines.[1] As proposed in 1919, the mines were to be taken out of the owners' hands and vested in a Mining Council on which trade unionists and government representatives shared equally. This, it was hoped, would lead to greater efficiency and stability, avoiding the false profit motivation of the owners and making possible rational long-term planning. Such reorganisation, it was believed, would generate higher and more stable wages, as well as remove from political power the miners' own immediate bosses. But the trade union movement as a whole found the cry of nationalisation less compelling, especially when accompanied by the proposal for a general strike to force the government to bring it about. A special meeting of the TUC was called in December 1919 to consider the miners' demand for general strike action, but the TUC was not prepared to go beyond a political campaign to this end.

When proposals were extended beyond the mining industry to

---

1. See chapter 17, section 4 above.

some kind of generalised syndicalism, support was even more difficult to sustain. Ideas became much more diffuse, with more and more unanswered questions. The union members of the National Joint Industrial Conference of 1919 had stated flatly: 'With increasing vehemence labour is challenging the whole structure of capitalist industry . . . It demands a system of industrial control which shall be truly industrial in character.' Though the union delegates conceded that changes in this direction should be gradual, they insisted that private property in the major means of production must end. The Communist Party found one of its strongholds among the miners, offering the Soviet model of society, its appeal strengthened by wage struggles and unemployment. With the miners as a core, the Triple Alliance, revived in 1920, was the nearest thing to an effective organisational form. But the Miners' Federation would not accept a plan for concerted action that intruded upon its own independence of action.

At the same time as the mines and railways were freed from state control in 1921, the miners were confronted with wage cuts, as well as the loss of the system of wage regulation on a national basis (refused in 1912, but granted during the war). The Triple Alliance agreed to strike action and the government declared a state of emergency. The Alliance, after negotiation, postponed the strike and proposed a separate settlement of the wages question. This the miners would not accept, with the result that the Alliance collapsed, on a day to be known in labour circles as Black Friday (15 April 1921). The difficulties of concerted action, where a hard line had to be assimilated to a more flexible one, were thus dramatically demonstrated.

Even where confrontation with state or employer was not in question, there was jealous concern for the independence of unions: when the General Council of the TUC was set up in 1919 it was subject to the proviso that 'the complete autonomy' of affiliated unions was to continue.

In all this the archetypal figure was perhaps Ernest Bevin, secretary of the Dockers' Union from 1915. The dockers, indeed, had been militants when the miners were still placing their hopes in the Liberal Party. Bevin denounced the National Industrial Conference in 1919, seeing it as an attempt by government to confuse the trade union movement. He insisted that the differences between workers and employers could only be resolved by a trial of strength between them. Politics were a kind of futile game, he said; the workers should expect nothing from that quarter, but have faith only in direct action by their unions.

In 1920 Bevin led the strike threat that for the first time employed union power in the foreign policy of the state: the government's intention of intervening in the Russo-Polish war on the Polish side was stopped by the Council of Action and the Dockers' Union refusal to load the supply ships. When the government was putting through its Emergency Powers Act in the same year, giving the state extensive authority to deal with strike emergencies affecting essential services (but not affecting the right to strike), Bevin condemned the granting of such powers. He strove to create one vast union embracing transport men, miners and engineers. In 1926 he was one of the two chief organisers of the General Strike.[1]

The attitudes taken by Bevin in this phase of his career pose two questions that are personal to him, but which arise also and more importantly in terms of labour generally. Firstly there was a duality in his utterances. The public ones, especially as seized upon by hostile elements in the press, suggested a much more radical–activist stance in terms of strikes and the involvement of the state than did the private ones. Secondly, it is far from clear whether Bevin, when he used the threat of strikes, and worked to create a situation in which they could be generalised, really intended to coerce the state. Probably neither Bevin nor the trade union movement wished to attempt a revolution, but both were prepared to move in that direction, partly in order to contain the impatience of those with syndicalist ideas, and partly in order to achieve more limited gains. Bevin was far too keenly aware of the limitations of the unions and the TUC in terms of disparate aims to follow A.J. Cook in proclaiming the TUC as the parliament of the future. The same was true of most of the rank and file. Accordingly, when labour, including Bevin, after the failure of the General Strike, turned from aggression to a new kind of policy, the change was less dramatic than might appear.

The General Strike was called off by the TUC while still in its early stages. Could the strikers have won, defeating the civil power as embodied in parliament by physical action? The answer depended in

1. See chapter 16, section 6 above.

part on the reserves of resistance, as yet untapped, on the government side. There was absolutely no sign of capitulation by the cabinet – it was at least as determined as the most committed of the strikers. There was no prospect whatever of a change of government. Trade union victory therefore, if it came at all, could do so only with severe damage to the parliamentary process. If real violence had begun it is difficult to see it stopping without causing a class enmity that, if contained at all, would have lasted a generation or more.

The strike was in part a manifestation of a need for an action-cathartic, a means of releasing resentments and asserting solidarity by waging a comradely war against oppressors. And yet basically most workers accepted the parliamentary system. Moreover most working men had a horror of acting outside the law. The police, on the whole, were held in respect – this was a deeply law-abiding society; persons and property in Britain were perhaps more secure than ever before or since. There was, too, a worried unwillingness both at TUC level and among many workers to bring about a situation that could pass into the hands of the most assertive and the most violent.

3. *The years of union policy seeking, 1926–39*

There can be no doubt that the ending of the General Strike was, at least in the short and medium terms, a defeat for organised labour. It marked the end of the phase of militancy that had begun during the war: there were no further major strikes from 1926 to 1939. Ernest Bevin, like other union leaders, learned from the General Strike the limitations of union power, having been confronted with the fearful question, was organised labour prepared to challenge the organised power of the state to the point of destroying it?

A Conservative-dominated parliament took advantage of this to lay down in the Trade Disputes and Trade Union Act of 1927 four important principles. All strikes (including sympathetic ones), and lock-outs, designed or calculated to exercise pressure on the government or the community were declared illegal. But sympathetic strikes as such (that is in pursuit of industrial aims) were not forbidden. Secondly, with regard to the use of union funds for political purposes, the principle of contracting out, as adopted in the Act of 1913, was replaced by that of contracting in: this meant that union members, instead of being assumed to be agreeing to the political levy, had to certify their willingness to subscribe; in this way the workers had to go to the trouble of expressly consenting. Thirdly, no public employee, local or national, could strike if he was aware that in so doing he would cause injury or inconvenience to the community. Finally, there were tighter restrictions on the actions of pickets. There was bitter resentment against the Act, and a determination to repeal it as soon as possible. An attempt was made by the minority Labour government in 1930, but it failed. The Act, during its lifetime (1927–45), served its intended ends: it reduced Labour Party funds, and also discouraged union membership.

But the unions had already learned important lessons. The 'general' workers had been organised in a mass of small and impotent unions. The Transport and General Workers' Union was formed in 1922 under Ernest Bevin as Secretary; eighteen unions amalgamated at once to be joined by another twenty-nine by 1939. The National Union of General and Municipal Workers merged several general unions in 1924. But this increase in scale did not lead to a new aggressiveness – rather the view was now strong that the unions should set aside programmes of far-reaching change in society, and work instead for a rehabilitation of British industry, to be accompanied by firm claims for a share in the benefits. This was the mood in which so many unions entered upon the Mond–Turner conversations in 1928–9.[1]

The unions were ready to accept that business was big and should get bigger; this, however, should be matched by a parallel development on the side of labour. Under the Mond–Turner proposals there should be set up a National Industrial Council, representative of both sides of industry. It would act as a kind of industrial parliament, advising the political parliament; it would also through a Joint Conciliation Board seek to solve any industrial dispute that had otherwise been unsettled, with agreement that no lock-out or strike should take place until the Board had produced its proposals.

In a curious way these converging trends in the worlds of business and the unions could be taken as implying a new formula for exempting or excluding the state from the economy, but one quite different from that deriving from traditional laissez-faire. The two

1. See chapter 16, section 7 above.

component powers, aware of and respecting each other's potential both for productivity and warfare, would seek a continuous mutual accommodation, bargaining 'freely'. Far from the state being called upon by one of the sides to coerce the other, its presence would be largely unnecessary, except perhaps to register verdicts agreed upon between capital and labour, in order to induce conformity among the minority on each side which had refused agreement. Parliament would thus be rendered largely otiose in the industrial sphere at least, not by the market and not by syndicalism, but by a capital/labour consensus arrived at by agreement between the dominant elements in each.

Merely to outline such proposals is to convey their limitations as a general formula. In some sectors of industry such mutual accommodation might be possible, and indeed was demonstrated. From the employers' point of view there was much to be said for such an approach. But it involved, on the labour side, the recognition of the legitimacy of ownership and management; the miners and the other radical unions would accept no such position. It required, also, sustained agreement within the labour movement on such questions as differentials in wages in different jobs. So far as the general public were concerned (for the defence of whose interests parliament and the courts were responsible), they would be in a highly vulnerable position, for as consumers they would be made subject to the verdicts of converged monopolies of capital and labour.

It is hardly surprising that Mondism or what became known later as 'corporatism' was not generally acceptable to labour. But as an incident in labour's search for an institutional framework within which the unions could find a larger identity, and at the same time both define their functions and lessen the danger of blind conflict, it is of great interest. It was one set of ideas aimed at stabilising the tripod of organised labour, co-ordinated capital and the parliamentary state.

Meanwhile, in an atmosphere of mild economic recovery, some leading trade unionists, including Bevin, in looking forward to the prospect of the Labour Party forming the government, began to turn their minds to the macro-economic problems involved in the monetary and fiscal systems. Was there a range of such tools which, if intelligently employed, could be used to stabilise capitalism and raise its capacity to generate incomes and employment? From the late 1920s onward labour developed a capacity at this level to think and to propose, using the Economic Committee of the TUC, begun in 1928. Labour and capital in the Mond–Turner context agreed that the gold standard policy of 1925 had been a gross error, and that the inhibiting of the economy by monetary means should be stopped.

Labour had by the late 1920s found two outstanding leaders, Bevin and Walter Citrine (1887–1981), leader of the Electrical Trades Union and General Secretary of the TUC, 1926–46. But Bevin was the more compelling figure. As a member of the Macmillan Committee of 1930–1 he came into contact with Keynes and entered into his ideas about the need to generate an adequate level of effective demand through demand management, especially in terms of working-class incomes. He distrusted control of the money supply, especially as operated by the 'money power' that is, the City of London. In particular he attacked the use of a high Bank Rate, an important weapon for enforcing credit curtailment and for protecting the value of sterling.

Bevin and Citrine served on MacDonald's Economic Advisory Council, 1930–9,[1] providing a formidable trade union presence among the politicians, industrialists and academics, speaking there with the implied authority of the massive Transport Workers' Union and the TUC itself. Bevin favoured Britain's unilateral abandonment of gold, insisting that it was wrong that 'world commerce be harnessed to a relatively diminishing quantity of metal'. He insisted that if rationalisation of industry was to become government policy,[2] then the unions should have a voice, especially in respect of the unemployment likely to be generated at least in the short run by the suppression of less efficient plant. He urged improved unemployment statistics. If there was to be protection given to steel, then national-isation of the industry must accompany it. If a general wage cut should become necessary it must be 'undertaken as part of a wider scheme for resettling money incomes generally [including rentier incomes in particular], and not wages alone'. But the Labour Party did not formulate a general economic policy until 1937.[3]

When it came to a test of union influence over the Parliamentary Labour Party it was clear that there was a divergence of opinion. The

1. See chapter 16, section 12 above.
2. See chapter 17, section 2 above.
3. See section 7 below.

PLP asserted its independence of the trade union movement, presenting itself as governing in the name of all the people. Bevin brusquely reminded the second Labour administration of 1929–31 that 'it is essential that the Government should pay strict attention to, and consult with, the great movement from which it draws its strength and power'. For both Bevin and Citrine still based their hopes on the industrial, rather than the parliamentary–political, side of the labour movement. This did not mean that they were unconstitutional in their attitude, but rather that parliament could only be made to act rightly in terms of wages and the economy (even when Labour was in power) if the trade union movement made it do so. 'The Labour Party', Bevin proclaimed, 'grew out of the bowels of the TUC.' Herbert Morrison (1888–1965) was a leading protagonist of another view, namely that the Parliamentary Labour Party, in spite of its debt to the unions, had to arrive independently at its own decisions.

Bevin and Citrine held that the industrial system was a matter for industrialists and labour, to the exclusion of the state. From the days of the Mond–Turner talks onward the British unions and the employers' organisations exchanged views on major problems as they arose, and indeed in grave situations sometimes prepared joint submissions to the government. The state, for its part, in the matter of wages largely acquiesced in its own relegation to a minor role, at least in the direct sense. However, a government policy of wage contraction brought about by macro-economic means (chiefly curtailment of the money supply) did force the employers into the position of being the state's implementers, causing employer–union confrontation.

In carrying out this disciplinary role the employers encountered the trial by strength psychology of the unions. Workers' leaders had always to maintain a reputation for not fearing a fight, and of being effective in conducting one. This attitude arose in the nineteenth century at a time when, because of the dispersed nature of strikes and the relatively few strategic positions of strikers as against the general public, the damage, though often severe, could be borne fairly easily by the system. But by the inter-war years this was no longer so: the trial by public ordeal had arrived.

4. *The dilemma facing the unions*

In 1927 at the Edinburgh TUC Conference the trade unions set before themselves the fundamental dilemma of their role. There were indeed three general courses for them to choose from, but the debate lay between two only. The rejected possibility was that the movement should become revolutionary, seeking to overthrow existing society and to replace it with something approximating to the Soviet system. The prospect of misery, destruction and even bloodshed, followed by a dubious outcome, was unacceptable to all but a tiny minority of trade unionists.

The first of the remaining choices was to wait for capitalism to collapse, in the meantime leaving the conduct of industry to the employers, but fighting sectionally for what could be extracted from a system in decomposition. The second was to participate in an attempt to promote prosperity, at the same time demanding a voice in the conduct of industry, and in determining its future shape, as for example the carrying out of rationalisation. This would mean working for a new level of efficiency, but one which was humane and which passed a proper share of the benefits to the workers.

The General Council of the TUC chose the attempt to renovate capitalism. It did so because a war of attrition against capitalism was too negative, committing the movement to a generation or so of trying to live off a dying system. But the course that the TUC did choose involved a difficult dilemma. It meant sustaining and trying to improve the working of capitalism, regarded by a good many trade unionists as inherently evil and subject to inevitable decay.

Such a programme ran counter to many of the sustaining myths of the labour movement, and exposed it to the arguments and actions of those who held more disruptive views. Moreover a policy of renovating capitalism depended upon the willingness of industry to accept a wider role for the unions, no longer confining them to the other side of the wage-bargaining table, but accepting their participation in at least some managerial decisions. It also assumed that the state would take account of the TUC's views on general economic measures. The choice made in 1927 was to assist in making capitalism work by subjecting it to workers' control. It is difficult to see how it could have been otherwise.

But this was not the end of the role of the movement as seen by

361

Bevin and Citrine. It was to do its own thinking on problems both domestic and international. Bevin's personal pilgrimage involved looking for a 'bloc' within which Britain could be most effective. He rejected both European integration and Anglo-American affiliation in favour of the Commonwealth (1930). When the Labour government gave way to the National government in 1931 he urged the TUC to think in terms of 'planned industry', advocating this as an alternative to 'the old world economy of scramble and individualism and profit'. But the content of such planning was left vague, apart from urging that some scheme of priorities be established. The Labour left was strongly attracted by proposals made by Oswald Mosley (1896–1981) that the British economy should be reflated to prosperity behind a protective barrier of tariffs, but this was not the view of Bevin or Labour as a whole. In 1933 Bevin produced proposals to deal with unemployment (a reduction of working hours to forty per week to spread the work, raising the school-leaving age to sixteen to reduce the labour force and increasing old age pensions to stimulate purchasing power). Two years later he attacked economic nationalism, advocating an economic League of Nations where economic matters could be discussed in conference. The Commonwealth was still the international unit within which Britain should work, but it should be assimilated to a world organisation.

Bevin's thinking had a large structuralist component: it rested on the idea that national and international problems could only be solved if there were organisations at the appropriate levels capable of their solution. In this he was no doubt right, and was ahead of many of his contemporaries in saying so. But such organisations, though a necessary condition, were not a sufficient one. They would still have to deal with irreducible conflicts of interest between groups, whether of workers within a country or whether between countries.

Here was the second dilemma for a trade union leader: if such planning bodies were set up, how much authority should they have; would they involve constraints, to which unions as well as other interests would have to conform if solutions were to be found? Three possibilities arose: forbearance would be present, sufficient to reduce tensions to a manageable level; the system would revert to being governed by power struggles; or a solution would be found by reference to an agreed set of principles. These could only derive

from a theory of society, to which the eighteenth-century Enlightenment and its subsequent sons had always aspired. It would have to be
both general enough to embrace all of its contending components,
and particular enough to satisfy the specific claims of each. Even
when such principles of guidance were provided, there would follow
the need to design programmes of implementation. For Bevin the
liberal–capitalist system provided no such guidance. The socialist
spirit would be of help in inducing brotherly forbearance. But it
lacked the general theory that was needed as a guide when,
inevitably, forbearance wore thin as groups of workers compared
their position with those of others, or with some scheme of
expectations that occupied their minds. This left only the bleak
prospect of group conflicts.

There is something pathetic in the memoirs of the socialists who
held power in the inter-war years, men like MacDonald and Snowden
whose socialism was so much an aspiration and so little a programme.
Bevin wanted to move beyond this: he wanted structures. In creating
his own he had been extraordinarily successful: by 1939 he was the
direct ruler, through his own union, of some 600,000 workers;
indirectly through his union's massive block vote and his personal
stature it was difficult for the TUC to reject anything he proposed.
But his very success in structure building blinded him to the
limitations of such a formula. As a supremely powerful union official
he gave insufficient weight to the possibility that large-scale organisations can generate their own bureaucrats, becoming complacent
and conservative, unresponsive to those for whom they speak, thus
making the towering structure vulnerable to disruption from below.

5. The gains on the industrial front

Less dramatic than the striving for the grander political objectives,
but very real, were the general gains made on the industrial front in
the inter-war years.

By 1918 conditions of work were no longer a matter of serious
public contention, and, indeed, had hardly been so for a generation.
These were safeguarded by legislation and inspectorates; aggrieved
workers had ready remedies, reinforced by their unions. The
Factories Act of 1937 confirmed, defined and extended the code of
safety and working conditions. Hours of work still constituted an

important issue, but it was increasingly being merged with wages. Once the average working week was reduced to fifty hours or less, the old arguments about physical health and limited leisure were much weakened. Instead discussion and negotiation on the length of the working day or week became much concerned with the definition of overtime and the additional wages to attach thereto; in this sense the issues of hours and wages were largely merged.

A wide miscellany of legislation was passed. The Industrial Courts Act of 1919 set up a standing Court to which, with the consent of both parties, the Ministry of Labour could refer industrial disputes, a further effort to strengthen conciliation procedures. There were mining statutes in 1920, 1926, 1934 and 1939. Agricultural wages were brought under regulation again in 1924 and road haulage wages in 1938. Workmen's Compensation was further extended in 1923 and 1925. The Shops Act of 1934 improved the conditions in retail trade. The Holidays with Pay Act of 1938 gave trade boards and other statutory wage-fixing bodies power to award paid holidays of up to a week. In these many ways the state was prevailed upon to operate upon the conditions of industrial life.

But the unions still had no positive influence in industrial organisation within the firm. Indeed for the most part they did not seek to persuade the state to award them a share in the responsibilities of the boardroom, for this would mean a confusion of roles. Moreover both nationalisation and syndicalism as formulae for management left many central questions unanswered. These included, within a given firm, the following: what product mix should be planned for, in what proportions over what future period of time; what input mix, given the technological menu, and the pattern and prices of factors of production available, would be appropriate? Among the inputs was, of course, labour itself: what was the right pattern of rewards for labour, both generally and in all its different grades?

Making decisions on these matters was, of course, the classic managerial function. At a certain level of awareness in trade union circles there was a realisation that management too had its problems. But too overt a concession to this line of thought might lead to charges of softness or even betrayal.

6. *The state and the unions*

The labour movement in its industrial aspect was defeated in 1926; its militancy never really revived in the inter-war years. There were unemployment demonstrations and hunger marches, but they made only a passing impact, except perhaps upon the rising generation of sensitive younger people of the middle classes. The unemployed could scarcely avoid falling into apathy, waiting fatalistically for better times. The parties at the extremities of the political spectrum, the Communists and Fascists, gained little support; in 1933 the National Council of Labour, reflecting Labour Party and TUC opinion, published *Democracy versus Dictatorship*, which argued the similarity of fascism and communism. For those in employment there was a 15% rise in real wages. In the political sense there was defeat and humiliation in 1931; thereafter the Conservatives were the effective rulers of Britain.

From this it might perhaps be inferred that the labour movement had made no progress. This was not so. From the relations obtaining between the state and the unions by 1939, and from the events that led up to them, it is apparent that the attitudes and action of labour over the previous century comprised a pattern that followed its own logic, one of continuous and cumulative challenge.

At the same time, however, a new distinction within the field of wages had been developing. Each union continued to be much concerned with specific wage rates and earnings in the particular jobs performed by its members; indeed this was always its most important activity. But from the experiences of the first world war, from the Mond–Turner conversations of 1928–9, from the inquiries of the Macmillan Committee and from the discussions of the Economic Advisory Council, leading unionists like Citrine and Bevin were making two discoveries – that macro-economic policy could greatly affect the wages share in the general distribution of the national product, and that it was necessary for the trade union movement to seek to understand such matters from its own point of view, and arrive at an agreed policy. From 1928 the Economic Committee of the General Council of the Trade Union Congress took up just such a brief. But it did so in a loose and general way, concerning itself with altering the industrial balance in favour of the workers, and with establishing minima in certain trades, but not seeking a general theory that would indicate the optimum overall share to go to labour.

By natural extension of function the TUC had thus progressed from the argument about particular wages, to constitute itself a factor in the determination of general economic policy. Further, it had done the same with respect to welfare. The extension of the notion of the provision by the state of minimal incomes and social facilities inevitably implied union influence upon policy making at this level also. In addition, the unions supported their own MPs, and the labour movement had its own political party which had twice ruled the state.

Thus, by 1939 the trade union movement had established for itself a voice and a presence ancillary to the working of parliamentary democracy. The formula of one adult one vote yielded a House of Commons in which ostensibly resided all power, without limitation, elected on a geographical franchise. But on its flank stood the trade union movement, organised on the basis of employments or industries. Its interests both in wage bargaining and as affecting general economic policy were sectional, deriving from the working-class parts of the community, albeit in aggregate constituting the largest element. There had come into being a kind of mutated syndicalism, exercising power alongside parliament.

In this way the trade union movement had intruded into government, pushing back the limits of the freedom of action of the state. At the same time the unions, having won from the state their exemption from legal liability for their industrial actions, used this inviolability to deny to the state three important powers. The state was left with no means of improving output and efficiency by regulating restrictive practices. Secondly, it could do nothing to stop strikes or other actions intended to coerce employers. Thirdly, the state had no power to intervene in a wage struggle, except by way of conciliation and the provision of facilities for discussion. In this way a trinity of union sanctities had been established against the state. They were reinforced by the solidarity induced by the historical experience of the unions, sustained by myth, such that these three denials to the state could become absolute values, to the defence of which the entire movement would rise. Against this the state had imposed certain limits on trade union action, especially as in the Act of 1927.

But trade union loyalty and the accompanying sense of absolutes could, paradoxically, be divisive. The trade union leadership, insofar as it pursued conservative courses, and insofar as it became bureaucratised and unresponsive, was vulnerable to its more radical members. These found their natural role at the level of shop stewards on the factory and workshop floor. At the point of production the weapons of industrial action were readily accessible to men whose views could make no progress politically, and very little within the unions. Once a movement to take the workers out was begun the immensely powerful moral sanction of the charge of disloyalty to workmates and class could be used to prolong the action.

Britain's first great experience of this had come during the first world war. Throughout a large part of the inter-war years, because of the scale of unemployment and the sense of futility deriving from the General Strike, the shop stewards could do relatively little to assert their separate identity. But always trade union leaders had to act in the knowledge of their presence and potential power. Though the majority of shop stewards were non-revolutionary men, interested only in the task of obtaining better wages and terms, a significant element among them continued to hold radical or revolutionary views. In this way the trade union movement, so powerful by the late 1930s vis-à-vis the state, suffered from tension from within. Just as the state, in formulating its policies, had to take careful account of union feeling, so union leaders, in arriving at their posture, had to make an assessment of shop steward response. The nature of this tripartite relationship was not of course either uniform or constant, for circumstances differed between unions, and the balance of power between the elements in a given union could vary over time.

The state (under Conservative, Liberal or Labour governments) could use the employers, through indirect macro-action, to compel them to enforce on the workers measures of constraint. But in so doing the state weakened the position of the employers in the long run, because it made of them targets for abuse and accusations of self-seeking, setting them up as the natural enemies of the unions.

7. *The double dilemma of the Labour Party*

Because the Labour Party derived from the trade union movement it shared the great dilemma of the unions, namely whether to stand aside while capitalism succumbed (perhaps assisting in its demise),

367

or whether to attempt the amendment of at least the worst features of the market system.[1] The Labour Party, like the unions, by and large chose the ameliorating alternative. But then arose the challenge: what form should the modification of capitalism take? The highest and most accepted priority for the Labour Party was greater equality. With it went the belief that the state could and should provide the conditions of growth and stability – in short, employment. Each of these objectives posed its dilemma.

Equity ran counter to the liberal philosophy of political freedom as embodied in the rights of the individual. For there could be no doubt that a radical movement toward equity would involve the state in a continuous policing, through redistribution, of the income and wealth of individuals. Collectivism thus demanded an infringement of liberty, and on a serious scale, not only in assessment, but in deciding on how various categories of income and wealth should be treated. Moreover, because British socialism was moral rather than 'scientific' on the continental model, it was much concerned with human rights as against the state; this moralism and the elements of the liberal inheritance converged to restrain collectivist programmes. But without intruding into the life of the individual, policies for redistribution and welfare provision would be impossible.

Walter Bagehot (1826–77), that great observer of Victorian society, had argued that the British system of politics rested upon habits of acquiescence reaching back to feudal times; for the Labour Party to substitute collectivism for acquiescence, in a society in which an individualistic moralistic stance, together with liberal notions of the rights of the individual and the limitations of state action were still so strong, proved impossible. This was the first Labour Party dilemma.

Policies of economic management to promote employment provided the second. It arose directly from inherited liberal ideas. With the three great liberal macro-canons sacrosanct down to 1931, namely the gold standard (or more generally the unwillingness to involve the state in the monetary mechanism), free trade and the balanced budget, there was no possibility of significant macro-manipulation for the promotion of growth and stability. Even after 1931 monetary management and the unbalanced budget had fright-

---

1. See section 4 above.

ening connotations for the Labour Party. Nor was the adoption of the tariff and bilateralism, together with the attempt to create a system of international cartels, attractive.

8. *The Party programme of 1937*

The Labour Party by the later 1930s, aware of its two failures in government, was in search of a programme. Its younger intellectuals, including Hugh Gaitskell (1906–63), tried to find a way of reconciling the price system, on which the neo-classical economics rested, with the urge for equity and stability. They began to use the Keynesian kind of model, which envisaged an economy in which the state employed macro-economic devices, chiefly monetary and fiscal, to stabilise employment. But it was also proposed to take into direct ownership and operation (on a full compensation basis) the Bank of England, together with a range of industries. Within the latter, 'fair' wages policies could be followed, and new levels of managerial efficiency could be attained. Demand management of the Keynesian kind was thus the answer to the problem of short-term stability, while nationalisation was the longer-term structural solution as well as contributing to equity. These were the policies adopted by the Labour Party in 1937, and which were to be implemented by the first majority Labour government after 1945.

21

The welfare share:
its elements and adequacy

1. The politics of welfare

The idea of a national minimum, below which no one should fall, had taken a considerable hold before the first world war;[1] before the second it had made further progress. If there was a guiding principle in social policy it lay in the implicit belief that the state should make or make possible a basic provision available to all in the matters of health, education, housing and social security. The cost of extending the pattern of provisions was high, especially in times of serious unemployment. The strain on local authority finance obliged the government to remake the poor law and local government.

As the thirties ran their course younger men in the Conservative, Labour and Liberal Parties who possessed the necessary combination of concern, energy and intelligence to confront the challenge of unemployment began to think not only of the macro-controls necessary for growth and stability, but also of the redistributive measures necessary to meet reasonable welfare criteria, and to understand something of the relationships between the two. The TUC, through its Economic Committee, was moving in the same direction. In this way the idea of an adequate level of effective demand began to converge with that of the proper level of social provision. But no explicit model of the economy in these terms was set up by the government or anyone else. Welfare provision continued, as in the past, to be pragmatic, each aspect of need having its advocates, and each set of provisions having to fight for public and Treasury acceptance.

1. See chapter 13, section 6 above.

2. Health and hospital provision

The formation of the Ministry of Health in 1919 seemed to offer the prospect of a unified and comprehensive national health care service. But the new Ministry was also encumbered with responsibility for local government generally, together with the new housing programme.

Health insurance, begun in 1911, had by 1939 almost reached the end of its useful life, at least in its original form. The scheme made a distinction between the insured and the non-insured that was inhibitive and harmful; by 1939 it was time for a national scheme on new principles. Some 18 million people were within the provisions of the 1911 Act by 1937, leaving many still outside it. The approved societies continued as the administrators of the scheme, but their great range of size and form meant wasteful administration and differences in the benefits they paid. The Royal Commission on National Health Insurance of 1926, in spite of *Majority* and *Minority Reports*, could not resolve these difficulties.

The hospital service was out of date by the later 1920s. It had three main components, namely the philanthropically funded, the poor law provided and the municipal. The voluntarist principle had produced general hospitals (infirmaries) together with a range of specialist hospitals (for maternity, child health, tuberculosis and venereal disease, often with associated dispensaries). The poor law guardians had a range of hospitals that had grown out of their responsibilities for the poor. The cities and towns had also set up hospitals, often beginning with provision for fever patients. In all this heterogeneous growth the central government had had no part, except for its general supervision of the poor law aspect. The only tidying-up move of the inter-war years was to give local authorities power under the Local Government Act of 1929 to take over the poor law hospitals and operate them as municipal hospitals. But even this initiative, modest as it was, received a much less enthusiastic response locally than had been hoped for. For though the Act of 1929 made possible a step toward a comprehensive and integrated system through municipalisation, local authorities were not eager to assume this responsibility. But they did go on building hospitals, in this way extending the service. Hospital provision thus continued under its diversity of jurisdictions.

So it was that the reforming spirit in the inter-war years had only mild success in the fields of health insurance and hospitals. In both aspects the system, though in a sense obsolescent, was tolerable, and so failed to generate its own reform. The state was not prepared to nationalise either health insurance or the medical services. To do so would have meant offending strong interests, including the Friendly Societies, the medical profession and local authorities. But sanitation and the conditions of work were reviewed and consolidating statutes passed especially a Public Health Act in 1936 and a Factories Act in 1937.

3. *The bifurcation of education*

From the Fisher Education Act of 1918[1] down to 1944 there were no further great statutes affecting the school system of England. The Board of Education continued; education had no Ministry to rank it with Health, Pensions and Labour.[2] Yet a good deal was done, based upon two notable public inquiries.

The *Report* of the Hadow Committee of 1926 was a landmark in English education. It set as the proper objective of the system the provision of education appropriate both to the aptitudes and capabilities of the children, and to the nation's needs. It proposed that the age of eleven should mark the end of elementary education. 'A second stage should then begin', said Hadow, 'which should as far as possible be regarded as a single whole, within which there should be a variety of types of education.' These were to be of two general kinds, the grammar schools for those of 'academic' bent, and central (or secondary modern) schools for pupils suited to more directly vocational subjects. The two kinds of schools were to be different, but equal. The higher schools already established under the 1902 Act became grammar schools. An active programme of central school building was undertaken by the local authorities. Children sat the 'eleven plus' examination, on the outcome of which their future education, and to a considerable degree their life chances, depended. In this way the principle of highly selective grammar schools reserved for an upper intellectual band was confirmed and reinforced, though the conditions of entry were made less exclusive. Following

1. See chapter 14, section 6 above.
2. For Scotland see chapter 15, section 3 above.

the Spens Report of 1938 provision for technical schools was greatly improved.

Though much was achieved, the continued distinction between grammar schools (the potential gateway to the extending university system) and the secondary modern schools (with their much more limited prospects) had the affect of confirming differences between social classes. By and large, it was of course the children of the more literate families who were most likely to shine in the examinations. Conversely, it was no easy task to develop secondary education for the 'modern' children to the age of fourteen, for the level of society from which most of them came induced in them an unsettling urge to join the labour force as soon as possible.

At the university level Oxford and Cambridge continued to be strongly elitist. But the redbrick civic universities and university colleges were making real progress. With their civic and regional connections they were generating a new range of university graduates, now larger than that of the older universities, but still behind them in terms of esteem and in career opportunities.

4. Housing: the end of the subsidy barrier and the encouragement of private building

It had long been known that health and education depend in large measure upon housing.[1] If the family home was crowded, noisy and without basic facilities, then neither better health nor an educational system capable of invoking the real potential of children and adults, especially of the working classes, was possible. The inter-war years saw the first real attack by the British state on the problem of rent levels and housing supply.

Policy in these two directions could be contradictory. Rent restriction and the control of eviction, introduced in 1915, was continued, and indeed became for working-class housing, in effect, a permanent feature. Successive Acts amended it, extending the range of houses covered in some directions and reducing it in others; from 1923, for example, protection was lost where there was a change of tenancy. Newly built houses were not affected, because of the direct discouragement rent restriction was to building. This partial price

---

1. See chapter 13, section 5 above.

control on housing space offered for rent was the first direct statutory intervention in housing economics. It protected sitting tenants, but did damage to the willingness of landlords to maintain their properties, thus promoting the deterioration of an important element of the housing stock, and in the longer run reducing it.

Lloyd George in 1919 urged strong action on housing as well as other social reforms as a prophylactic against disorder and even Bolshevik revolution. Addison's Housing and Town Planning Act, the government's response to the challenge of providing houses quickly, imposed upon each local authority the duty of meeting housing need within its jurisdiction.[1] The standards set were well above those normal for working-class houses; moreover the new houses were to be provided at rents comparable to those of houses controlled under the Rent Restriction Acts, that is well below free market levels. The local authorities were to pay at a very modest level, namely to the extent of the yield of a penny on their rates. All the rest of the deficit was to come from the Treasury. On the basis of this open-ended commitment to subsidy, the British state embarked upon the age of the council house. At the same time the state became the controlling element in the provision of this principal form of social capital, involving itself deeply in one of the most complex of markets.

Addison and his staff worked with vigour to implement the Act, causing some 170,000 houses to be built. But in so doing they generated a sectoral inflation in the building trades, due to excessive pressure on limited resources of skills, materials and sites. Because most of the cost was borne by the central government, the local authorities had little concern for cost control. The extraordinary financial burdens thus generated outraged the Treasury and the Bank of England. The Geddes economy axe of 1921 fell upon the house-building programme. The state, after a frightening experience, withdrew its open-ended guarantee of housing losses, and Addison was dropped from the Ministry of Health he had founded.

But the state could not extricate itself from housing. Neville Chamberlain (1869–1940), as Conservative Minister of Health, introduced a new Housing Act in 1923. It too embodied the subsidy principle, but brought it under control, regulating the amount of

1. See chapter 14, section 6 above.

state assistance to be given per house. In addition the private sector was brought within the scope of subsidy: private builders intending to sell were made eligible for aid. Indeed they were given preference, unless the local authorities could show that they themselves were the better agency. Slum clearance received state aid for the first time under the Act, with government and local authorities dividing the costs equally. In alliance with the building societies, the Conservative government sought to encourage the working classes to own their houses, thus reinforcing their sense of citizenship. The building societies were seen as allies of the state in providing the working-class family with a home which it owned, and which was its physical and psychological base.

The Labour government that took office in 1924 placed the emphasis once more upon housing as a social service. It restored the initiative to the local authorities under its Housing Act of that year, promoted by John Wheatley (1869–1930). It raised the standards prescribed for houses, together with the grants. Private builders were eligible for subsidy only if they provided houses for letting. But there was no return to open-ended state finance. Rent increases for public sector houses were to be allowed where they were required in order to meet any shortfall not covered by the fixed Exchequer subsidies plus the contribution from the rates. The 1930 and 1935 Housing Acts further assisted slum clearance; under them some 250,000 old houses were pulled down.

Between 1919 and 1939 some 1.3 million council houses were built in Britain, all involving subsidy. More than 3 million houses were built for owner-occupation or rental, some 470,000 of them state assisted. Thus over 40% of all new housing received state help, based upon redistributive taxation. The principle of housing subsidy had become embedded in the national life, alongside rent restriction. The local authorities had become giant landlords of the working classes. This drew local government deep into the problem of social discipline through the need for principles upon which to base housing allocation. It also gave a new dimension to local politics, for housing became an important form of patronage, affecting the voting pattern. But the housing shortfall, chronic since the industrial revolution, had been eased. The default of the classic liberal, property-owning democracy had been partially repaired by state action, but with far-reaching economic and social consequences. In addition the government, by maintaining employment and incomes in the building trades, made an important contribution to supporting incomes generally.

5. Shaping the environment

Just as the state in the inter-war years took the initiative in the supply of housing, so too it involved itself deeply for the first time in spatial planning. The Town Planning Act of 1919 made the preparation of planning schemes compulsory for 249 out of the 1,798 local authorities in England and Wales. The Town Planning Act of 1925 and the Town and Country Planning Act of 1932 extended the principle, treating planning as a function in itself, making it no longer merely an extension of housing policy. In 1920 cars and lorries on British roads had totalled some 650,000; by 1939 the figure was over 3 million. In consequence the road system, together with movement within the cities, had become major problems. The new flexibility of road transport caused housing to spread along roads between cities; the Restriction of Ribbon Development Act of 1935 was an attempt to control this. There was a good deal of concern about using good agricultural land for other purposes, and with the erection of ugly buildings, badly located. Moreover the uncontrolled regional shifts continued, with increasing concentrations of population in London and the South-East and the West Midlands. The great extension of cities involved in the increase in housing was done without any real national policy of public land management, with a good deal of damage to the countryside. Between 1920 and 1939 the cities increased their physical expanse by nearly a half, from 2.2 to 3.2 million acres. The result was sprawl and ribbon building with urban tentacles spreading without control.

Local government was, of course, much involved in all this. Certain city-regions sought to find a spatial identity, drawing up regional plans, building and managing industrial estates. But the effort was not commensurate with the task: the result was that urban planning remained a fragmentary affair.[1]

One of the great difficulties had to do with land ownership. It was still in private hands, having withstood programmes for state

---

1. See chapter 17, section 11 above.

ownership or control. Taxation of land values had been dropped in 1920 because of the difficulties of evaluation and administration. The radicals still demanded action on this front, converging with the socialists. In response, holders of land joined with holders of all forms of wealth to resist attack.

6. *From poor law to limited social security*

The support of economic and social casualties continued to be the largest category of social welfare, the most diverse, and so the most difficult to deal with. In 1919 the provision was of three kinds. The state had set up old-age pensions (1908), together with unemployment insurance (1911). Both were administered from the centre, the first entirely paid for by the state and the second receiving a state contribution. The third and residual element was the poor law, run by the unions and their guardians in the localities and financed from the rates; the poor law was still the traditional catch-all of claims upon society from those with no other recourse.

With the peace unemployment re-emerged. Shortly after the Armistice in November 1918 an 'out-of-work donation' was made available to veterans, to be paid on a temporary basis, by the Treasury: a civilian counterpart soon followed. Because the government, in spite of Addison's Reconstruction Committee, had no readily adaptable scheme, this improvised mode of maintenance was generalised.

In the short run the matter did not seem too serious. The post-war boom absorbed the unemployed. Under the 1920 Unemployment Insurance Act of Lloyd George's coalition government the 1911 scheme was extended so that it included almost all workers, both manual and non-manual earning not more than £250 per year. The main exceptions were the agricultural and domestic workers. The coverage of the scheme rose from 4 to some 12 million persons. Both benefits and contributions were raised. In 1921 insurance benefits were extended to provide for the dependants of the insured. With the Fund in credit to the extent of £22 million by 1920, and the scheme almost comprehensive, all seemed well. Hope revived that unemployment could continue to be entrusted to the insurance principle.

But as unemployment rose again with the end of the boom, the

Ministry of Labour in 1921 was given authority to pay, at discretion, benefits in excess of the entitlement of the twenty-six weeks prescribed. This was a radical step, analogous to the adoption of the subsidy principle in housing. It involved the state, in times not affected by war and resettlement, in supporting the unemployed without the pretence of the insurance principle. The payments were to be known as 'extended' or 'uncovenanted' benefits. They were payable to those 'genuinely seeking work' (a relic of the idea of the 'deserving'): this was the only test applied. To these benefits the press and the public applied the term 'dole', an expression deriving from poor law usage. While the Unemployment Insurance Fund remained solvent it could bear these additional charges, and the pretext could be maintained that the insurance principle was being followed. The effect was that the workers in employment contributing to the scheme were bearing a significant part of the cost of their unemployed fellows.

Yet further scope was found for the insurance principle. In 1925 the Conservative government applied it in three new directions, on a compulsory contributory basis, involving employee and employer, together with a subsidy from the state. The new provision was integrated with the National Health Insurance scheme. Thus widows of insured men received a pension until eligible for the old age pension at the age of seventy, provision was made for orphans, and insured men became eligible for the old age pension from sixty-five.

Unemployment accelerated from 1924, reaching 1.3 million by 1926. The second Baldwin administration was unwilling to throw the many thousands of workers whose standard benefits had expired back onto the hated poor law. Instead, following the advice of the Blanesburgh Committee, it passed the Unemployment Insurance Act of 1927, which continued and extended the practice adopted in 1921 of making available extended benefits. It made a change in principle: such additional benefits were not to be a 'dole' given by favour, but were to be a statutory right. But the requirement that the recipient must demonstrate that he was 'genuinely seeking work' was continued. The government, by making such payments as of right, was recognising that unemployment was not to be blamed on the unemployed, but it still required a demonstration that the recipient was 'deserving'.

The liability for such payments still lay with the Unemployment

Insurance Fund, in the hope that when better times returned the Fund would once more become solvent. The government was obliged to borrow heavily to sustain the Fund, now loaded with what was, in effect, an open-ended liability. Some eighteen Acts of Parliament were passed in the ten years between 1920 and 1930, patching the system so that it became a maze of regulations. By 1931 the Fund was in deficit to the sum of £115 million.

The second Labour government in its brief tenure sought to escape from the confines of the Fund, and to ease the conditions of eligibility. It relieved the Fund of the cost of the additional benefits, making them a direct charge on the Treasury. Secondly, the onus was now laid on the officials of the Fund to prove that the applicant was *not* genuinely seeking work.

Meanwhile the poor law, though no longer bearing the burdens of unemployment and old age, was also in difficulties. The 600 English poor law unions as created under the 1834 Act had become hopelessly inadequate, both in terms of finance and organisation. Neville Chamberlain's Local Government Act of 1929 brought radical changes. The unions and the guardians were abolished; their functions passed to appropriate specialised local authorities as reorganised under the Act. In particular, relief to those not covered by unemployment insurance and its extended benefits, or to those who had approved needs not otherwise met, was to be paid out by new Public Assistance Committees to be set up by county and county borough authorities. The new Committees were also to take charge of institutions for the destitute. In these ways Chamberlain hoped to bring a new level of efficiency and effectiveness into the operation of relief of last resort. In 1930 the workhouse test was ended and the term 'pauper' officially abandoned.

It was with the National Insurance Fund in deep deficit, and with unemployment at 2.6 million, that the Labour government encountered the economic breakdown of 1931.[1] Foreign lenders made it a condition that the level of British unemployment relief should be reduced. This was acceded to: under the Economy Act of 1931 insurance benefits were reduced by 10%, and the period of receipt was shortened. On the other hand extended benefits continued. They were now to be known as 'transitional' benefits. They were still

---

1. See chapter 16, section 9 above.

to be wholly borne by the Treasury, but were to be administered by the local authorities through their new Public Assistance Committees.

Associated with such provision was a family means test. This, intended to confine benefits to those in genuine need, was to be the source of endless trouble and deep bitterness, replacing the workhouse as an object of working-class detestation. It was deeply humiliating to many, taking into account the incomes of all members of the family and thus requiring their disclosure. Moreover it penalised those who had practised thrift and acquired a few assets. It was the tragic and often sordid expression of the felt need of the government of the day to set limits, conceived in terms of needs and resources, and employing the concept of the family, to entitlement to state aid. The poor law had always had destitution tests; now for the first time this principle was to be applied to those out of benefit. The state had at last been forced by the demands of the balanced budget to attempt to control this drain upon itself. The payments made were enough to keep people alive, but were insufficient for full health.

The 1931 arrangements were soon seen to be in need of reform. At long last the government sought to escape from improvisation, undertaking a longer-term view. A Royal Commission reported in 1932; the Unemployment Act of 1934 embodied a solution following the lines proposed by it. The two functions of unemployment insurance and the payment of additional or transitional benefits were to be separated. Part I of the 1934 Act reorganised the insurance scheme and brought agricultural workers within it. The 'equal thirds' principle of contributions as between workers, employers and the state was adopted. Benefit was to be provided for a maximum of twenty-six weeks. The cuts of 1931 were restored. On this basis it was hoped that the insurance principle could be reinstated and the Fund kept solvent.

Part II set up a new body, the Unemployment Assistance Board, charged with providing for the able-bodied who were out of work and out of benefit. It was to be independent of the Ministry of Labour or any other governmental agency, and without connection with local government. Over 300 offices were set up throughout the country to administer the scheme. The able-bodied out of benefit were thus taken out of the care of the local authorities and their Public Assistance Committees. After some 400 years the localities were now finally relieved of all responsibility for the able-bodied. The funds of the Board were to come direct from the Treasury, £50 million annually in the first instance. The Board was to apply a common scale over the country, to be approved by parliament; it was, however, to be independent of parliament in its day-to-day working, thus taking the dole out of local politics. Appeals Tribunals were provided, though they were seldom used. The fundamental principle of welfarism, namely the entitlement of unemployed persons to state maintenance, urged by the Labour Party in 1907, having been conceded in 1927, was finally given institutional form and recognition in 1934. This came partly from the realisation that the system had failed to produce enough jobs, and partly from the danger to the civil peace of unemployed men out of benefit. In this way the insurance principle was dying its slow, stage by stage, death. But provision continued to be subject to a test of means and of a willingness to work. In spite of much bitterness, expressed in hunger marches and other forms of protest, especially over the means test, there was in the inter-war years in Britain no really serious threat to the state arising from unemployment. Such danger as there was receded as rearmament began to absorb the unemployed in the later thirties.

The poor law or, after 1929, public assistance was thus a continuously diminishing residuum. But it was still important, and indeed essential, with no less than 1,600,000 people in 1936 at one time or another in receipt of its aid. Indoor relief was given in the workhouse or 'institution', or in hospitals, infirmaries, asylums, training centres, schools, orphanages and old people's homes, many of which had evolved out of the poor law. Those catered for were a changing mass of sick, infirm, incapables, mentally defectives, deserted children, abandoned wives and so on. Outdoor or 'domiciliary' relief received much the larger share, comprising no less than 87% of public assistance. A cash allowance for the maintenance of the family in the home was its most common form. This, together with a certain amount of relief in kind, was the nation's ultimate safeguard against starvation.

By 1939 the general system of income support had thus come to include three main elements. The able-bodied unemployed had their insurance benefits, followed by their entitlement to unemployment assistance, administered by the central government's Unemployment Assistance Board. The impotent who could not be expected to support themselves were the responsibility of local authorities through their Public Assistance Committees. Certain categories of the impotent had been taken out of the general system by extensions of the pension scheme, namely the old, widows and orphans. The institutional framework would thus seem to have been comprehensive.

But two questions remained. Were the ethical principles governing eligibility for the main uncovenanted benefits right as enforced through the means test? Secondly, were the *levels* of provision in general correct, in terms of the needs of the categories of recipients, in terms of national equity and in terms of the transfer payments from rich to poor?

Those local government areas that combined low incomes and high unemployment naturally elected Labour Councils. These urged that the costs of relief should rest on central government, rather than on local. The Board of Poor Law Guardians of the London borough of Poplar, together with Gateshead on Tyneside, produced the most earnest attempts in this direction. The Poplar campaign began in 1919; because of refusal to levy a property rate of 38s in the pound George Lansbury and thirty councillors spent six weeks in prison. Later on the same guardians insisted on paying people on poor law relief amounts in excess of the pitiful scales approved by the government. The Minister of Health was alarmed that this kind of unconstitutionality would spread; 'Poplarism', he said in 1923, 'is an infectious disease.' It posed the question how was the conscientious local councillor to discharge his duty to the poor when he felt that the central government was being too restrictive?

7. The penal compromise

In spite of the attempts to humanise the prisons under the Acts of 1898 and 1899 the system continued to be harsh and insensitive, subjecting men and women to gross debasement. The inspectorate and the Commissioners reported, but had relatively little effect on public opinion because the prisons were basically working-class places. The conscientious objectors of the 1914–18 war, many of them middle-class, spoke and wrote of their experiences, generating considerable public misgiving. In 1923 at Wakefield Prison there was a series of experiments in making order and discipline the responsibility of the prisoners themselves, through their own selected leaders. In this way Elizabeth Fry's ideas of communalism and self-government tentatively re-entered the British penal system.[1] There was much educational activity, together with experiments in productive industry. In 1936 the prison without walls at Wakefield was set up, an embodiment of the principle of trust.

But given the long history of prison debasement it was difficult to extend the ideas of communalism and personal responsibility to the prison system as a whole. It was asking a lot of the middle classes, isolated as they were from working-class life, that they should think in terms of the prisons becoming communal co-operatives, housing as they did concentrations of the most depraved and violent men. There was, also, the problem of the morale of the prison officers – if they had no confidence in such a system, any attempt to implement it would simply create confusion.

The experiments of the inter-war years were done in the search for a formula which could be generalised, at an acceptable level of cost, throughout the prison service. But it was difficult to present the results of these experiments in such a way as to convince doubters. No new general formula comparable to that of Howard with his punishment of the mind emerged. The custody of criminals was as debatable a matter as ever. The advocates of punishment and deterrence still confronted those who urged redemption and re-habilitation. Moreover a paradox was present, namely that those times when an enlightened view was most needed, when criminality was at high levels, were the precise times that social fear would insist on a programme of retribution. The statistical basis of the whole matter was insecure, allowing conflicting opinions to be based on the same facts.

The prisons continued to be a system of social disposal, incarcerating those who rejected or fell foul of the rules, but governed by a set of shifting compromises and with minimal financial provision. The prisons remained a hidden world, fitfully illuminated by scandal and disturbance. For those actively concerned there was the dilemma that the more they stressed the causes of crime that derived from the basic workings of society, especially poverty in all its forms, the less

---

1. See chapter 5, section 14 above.

were the chances of reducing criminality through penal reform. So the problem continued to be a dual one, namely how to administer punishment in an urban industrial society to the intractables and the deviants, while preventing the closed societies created to contain them from becoming social cesspools polluting prisoners and their guards.

22
Public policy by 1939

1. The context

The second advanced industrial war, that of 1939–45, would see a collectivisation even more complete than that of 1914–18, from which the state would emerge explicitly committed by all political parties to two great sets of programmes, namely the generating of conditions of growth and stability in the economy, and the provision of integrated and comprehensive welfare care. The seeds of these involvements were present by 1939; so too were the attitudes towards the state, in all their complexity and inconsistency, which would condition the ability of governments to honour these undertakings.

Two great sets of practices and their associated institutions were in 1939 still central to everything else in the British economy and society. The first was the market mechanism, together with its concomitant, namely private property. Though the state in its efforts to rationalise British industry, agriculture and transport had in significant respects impaired competition, the market was still the great regulator of the economy. Secondly, there was free collective bargaining, with the state having assumed no direct authority in such matters, except to regulate the conditions of the contest; the state had thus no explicit role in the most important aspect of the distributive process. These twin pillars, namely the market plus private property, together with state-free wage bargaining between highly organised employers and unions, stood at the centre of things. Related to them was the general class configuration of British society, providing the basic conditions from which political institutions, as embodied in a democratic state, were derived. For the free market and private property were, in various forms and degrees, under challenge. But this attack was ill-defined and far from unanimous, with little developed sense of an alternative beyond greater equity in income and wealth distribution and a higher basic welfare minimum. The upper and middle classes, by and large, were of course defenders of property and the market, though some of their intellectual and political members had joined the attack upon these two central institutions. The working classes were equivocal in their attitudes.

The fact that the market economy had been in such trouble in the inter-war years, primarily because of the relative failure of aggregate demand, had caused a deep bafflement in the business community and the government, together with an almost frenetic search for solutions. But misgiving and confusion of mind had not, so far as generalised public opinion was concerned, seriously shaken the assumptions that, in spite of defects, property and the market provided the best fundamental basis for the functioning of the economy and society.

2. The eight challenges

By 1939 eight sets of challenges confronting governments had confirmed themselves. The first two were predominantly economic. There was the task of promoting stability at reasonable levels of employment in the shorter run (using monetary, fiscal and tariff techniques), together with that of inducing the structural adjustments of industry and agriculture upon which in the longer run technological adaptation to the demands of economic growth depended. The third and fourth were both economic and political, having to do with the regulation of the organisation and power of business, and of labour. The fifth and sixth were social, though with economic and political overtones; they arose from the need to promote an acceptable pattern of class or group justice, and through it, political stability. Thus the fifth aspect of government was to adjust the distribution of incomes and wealth by taxation, and the sixth was to assist social casualties, including the able-bodied, and to improve the life chances of the deprived, especially the children.[1] (By 1939 the state's

1. The sub-agenda of welfare by 1939 presented six principal challenges to the state, namely the conditions of living (sanitation, health provision and environmental control), the conditions of working (Factory and Mines Acts, compensation for injury and retiral pensions), education, housing, unemployment insurance and assistance, and, finally, the care of the residue (the paupers, the orphans, the maimed, the intemperate and the insane).

United Kingdom government expenditure by functions of all levels of government as % of GNP

Year	Total	Defence	Law, order and administration	Economic and environmental services	Social services	Public debt
1890	8.9	2.4	1.7	1.3	1.9	1.6
1938	30.0	8.9	1.9	3.9	11.3	4.0

Source: Peacock and Wiseman, 1967, p. 86.

support of a system of belief, especially religious, had sunk to the vestigial, with a nominally 'established' church and parliamentary jurisdiction over its prayer book. The BBC struggled to maintain a neutral political position, but projected a moral and religious one.) The seventh role of the state continued to involve it directly in the control of social behaviour, which related closely to the view held of the place of the family in the life of the nation and the proper means of protecting it. Finally, as an eighth and residual function of the state there were the sanctions that the state was prepared to impose on those who did not conform to the demands of its economic and social codes, namely the penal system. These eight governmental roles, with their sub-agendas, though each of them could appear to those who operated them to be distinct, constituted an interrelated pattern of governmental response.

The scale of official spending under its various functional heads had changed greatly since 1890. The increases in defence and the social services, and their dominance by 1939, taking up together one fifth of the GNP, are especially notable, as is shown in the table. The civil service concerned with central administration, having reached 54,000 in 1871, was 79,000 in 1891 and 387,000 by 1939.

3. Economic stability and growth

In the promoting of stability the government had had since 1931/2 two possibilities of initiative, namely the control of the money supply free of the constraints of the gold standard, and the capability of manipulating trade and industry through the tariff and by international trade bargaining. Little use was made of the monetary potential. The function of the Exchange Equalization Account was to dampen short-term fluctuations in sterling. There was no attempt by the Treasury or the Bank of England to use the monetary weapon to inflate the economy to induce higher levels of employment. There was still a great fear that so doing would raise British costs above those of rival exporting nations. There was also the spectre of losing control of the money supply and inducing an inflation that could threaten the fabric of the economy and society as had happened in central Europe after the war.

By contrast, the tariff weapon was being wielded with vigour, augmented by bilateralism and the attempt at an imperial economic system. British business men had abandoned the nineteenth-century pretence that commerce and the state were distinct and separate; by 1939 they were not only eager partners in the tariff system and imperial preference, they had sought, with government approval, to add a further dimension to the new British approach to markets through cartelisation in association with Japan in the Pacific and Germany in Europe. British governments, with the approval of business, had to 1939 largely eschewed monetary management, but had made market management at the international level the keystone of their economic policy.

There were, however, three respects in which government was supporting demand indirectly, doing so roughly within the constraints of the balanced budget. Two of these supportive actions stemmed from welfare, and one from the prospect of warfare. On the welfare side the state continued to supply subsidies for housing, and had by 1939 greatly increased its expenditure in the general widening range of social provisions. These actions of course generated incomes that could help to sustain the economy. To them was added government outlay on rearmament, bringing a degree of employment relief especially to the heavy industry areas where conditions were most serious. But the economic implications of housing, general welfare spending and rearmament were inadvertent: they did not stem from economic policy. Each had its own direct imperative – at home to ease social tensions, and abroad to prepare to confront a second attempt by Germany to achieve European hegemony.

4. *Industrial structure*

Behind the market strategy there lurked in 1939 two great domestic questions. Could the level of British costs in older lines of production be reduced relative to those of rivals, and could there be an improvement in the ability of British industry to supply the new range of products based upon advanced science and technology, then coming so powerfully into play? For neither task did the market seem adequate: thought had turned to the potential of the state in assisting in both the renovation of the old and the innovation of the new. Private industry, just as it had formed an alliance with the state in its struggle in international markets, also had begun to look to the government for domestic aid in terms both of costs and growth points. But it hoped that the state could assist it in pursuit of these objectives without any real intrusion of government into the managerial function, without provoking a confrontation with labour and without nationalisation.

In terms of the industrial renovation of the older industries, government had been drawn into one after another of these, just as it had been drawn piecemeal into the various aspects of welfare intervention. No general philosophy or plan of structural renovation had come into being. For this there were a number of reasons. They included the desire by government to act upon industry in as minimal a set of terms as possible, and to withdraw as soon as it could. But in spite of the lack of a general plan by government with respect to industrial renovation, the same or similar solutions had emerged in one industry after another. They involved rationalisation programmes and market control in various forms, though they left industry wholly privately owned. In essence the state by 1939 had involved itself in a function in which the market had failed, namely the amputation of excess and inefficient industrial capacity and an enforcement of concentration on the better units of production. To do this the state had been obliged in some sectors to suspend the operation of the market, though never entirely. It had done so without abrogating private property, and always in the hope that once the surgical operation was complete the market would resume its adjustive role. Over a considerable range of the older industries, government, having carried out this programme of intervention very largely by the mid-1930s, was in 1939 waiting to see if its actions had been adequate, and whether its relative withdrawal could be permanent.

It was hard enough for the state to construe its role with respect to the renovation of the older industries; the innovative role with respect to new ones was even more difficult. It was thought inappropriate for the state to engage directly in the setting up of firms. Indeed how could the state be expected to identify industrial growth points if private industry or the merchant bankers could not do so? But by 1939 the state had gone a fair way in providing infrastructural assistance. It had set up a range of scientific research bodies and provided a measure of support for pure and applied science in universities and colleges. In so doing it was augmenting the research and development activities of business firms. But both state-sponsored science and that of industry were well below the scale that was required; moreover the two had not been brought together to produce the best mutual reinforcement. The provision of scientific education, both pure and applied, had been greatly extended by institutions such as Imperial College, the notable range of new civic universities and the ancient Scottish universities, but here too there was a gap between education and industry.

The state had augmented these provisions for new industry in a number of ways. It had helped in the formation of Imperial Chemical Industries by assisting the amalgamation out of which ICI had come, and the Board of Trade maintained a surveillance of British industrial performance. The tariff had been used in some cases to assist new British enterprises. The state had concerned itself a good deal with financial provision as a necessary condition for industrial innovation. Though it had abandoned direct financial sponsorship of industrial growth points with the dropping of the Trade Facilities provision in 1927, it had inquired into business finance with the Macmillan Committee of 1931, pondering the adequacy of the range of financial institutions. More important than these actions, however, it had presided over cheap money, all the way from 1932 to 1939, with Bank Rates at 2%, a circumstance that seemed to suggest that whatever constraints there were on industrial innovation finance was not one of them.

British industry, then, with its twin challenge of renovation and innovation, had by 1939 posed problems of great difficulty and delicacy for the state. With respect to renovation the state in some sectors had been called in aid by business; in others the state had finally imposed its own will, though often after taking business advice. These two formulae had achieved some success in the older industries, but at the price of limiting market competition and so putting efficiency and the consumers' interest at risk. With respect to industrial innovation the state had largely confined itself to a fairly modest attempt to produce a seed-bed for new enterprises, hoping that the market principle would provide the vitality necessary for an adequate entrepreneurial response.

5. *Business, workers and the state*

In the promotion of conditions of economic stability and growth and in the improvement of the industrial structure the state by 1939 was deeply involved with business and with labour. Both were much regulated in their actions by the state, yet both were powerful in their influence upon the state.

The state set the rules for the business game (that is for business behaviour in the market) through the elaboration of company law, taxation law and the law of contract, together with the English common law as it related to business practice. But the British state did not oppose the concentration of industry through a control of mergers (except mildly in the case of banking); indeed the state had been busy assisting and even enforcing cartelisation, as in coal mining. Reciprocally, business had a powerful impact on the state through its views and actions concerning economic policy. Though the state had not found it easy before 1931 to extract from industry a coherent view as to what should be done concerning the monetary standard and the tariff, by 1939 business policy and that of the government had pretty well converged. Business in 1939, like the state, stood for the tariff but not for vigorous monetary management. It also stood for the attempt to regulate international markets by agreements between major national groups of producers. Both business and government took the view that the state should stay clear of wage bargaining so far as possible, and out of the ownership of industry through nationalisation. Moreover the unions should stay out of the boardroom, leaving management to manage. If the state chose to contract the economy through deflation, business was its means of doing so, through downward pressure on wages. Finally, the state (and indeed the unions) looked to business to act as the continuous regenerator of the economy by the taking of new initiatives in terms of products, production methods and marketing.

The workers on their side were regulated by the state in terms of the forms of union organisation; their powers of persuasion were set out under the law governing picketing, and their powers of coercion were defined in relation to their ability to enforce the closed shop. Any attempts to coerce the government through action on the community was expressly illegal. On the other hand the unions were free of all liability for loss or damage caused by strike action.

As to the influence the unions could exert upon the state, they certainly sought for a national economic strategy, conceived in terms of the workers' interests, that could be thrust upon the state. The unions were hostile to a constraining monetary policy, though in general, after 1932, they were in favour of the tariff. They were not opposed in principle to the growth in the size of firms, though there was always the fear of monopolistic action by industry. They agreed with the business men that the state should stay out of wage settlements. They were committed to the need to maintain a posture of potential threat. But the unions lacked a theory of wage determination: like the business world, the unions had no basis in principle that would give them guidance as to what the general wages share of the national income should be, or the relative wages appropriate to different occupations. The power of the unions was that of making demands and supporting these by imposing industrial sanctions, of an increasingly damaging kind. They, like the state, had no power to launch new industrial initiatives, or even to indicate what direction these should take. The co-operative movement was an attempt in this direction, but it did not offer a generalised alternative to the market system.

This was the context within which the unions in 1939 sought to improve the lot of their members. Short of a fundamental remodelling of society and economy (an alternative embraced by only a small minority), betterment could come in two ways – through higher levels of welfare provision financed by taxation, or larger wage packets. There was a considerable degree of distrust of government welfare, partly because it was seen as a device for buying off wage claims, and partly because of the social inquiry and personal and family manipulation it involved. On the other hand the unions also condemned policies of restricting or cutting welfare, based upon the argument that such provision was inconsistent with the market economy. Thus, though the unions did indeed press for improved welfare conditions of one kind or another, and certainly fought against cuts, their preferred outcome was higher wages; they were supporters of the market system in the sense of preferring money wages to the social wage. But a good many trade union leaders were aware of the precariousness of Britain's economic position, especially in relation to exports: too heavy an upward pressure on wages might be self-defeating in terms of employment, especially in certain sectors of industry.

There was also a constitutional question. The unions by 1939 had greatly extended the matters, both industrial and political, over which they held views, and over which they were prepared to exercise their power. Parliamentary democracy had thus sanctioned the rise of a rival. In a sense the Parliamentary Labour Party provided what seemed to be a resolution of the dilemma thus created. As the political arm of the trade union movement it could aspire to take its turn at running the parliamentary system; in doing so the Labour Party maintained a considerable degree of independence of the trade union movement, in spite of being largely financed by it. The unions, for their part, were still willing, in 1939, to accept this, though it could give rise to criticism and resentment. So long, therefore, as the trade union movement was prepared to concede the independence of the Parliamentary Labour Party, and so long as that Party sought to rule in the interests of all classes, the system of government in Britain contained no irreducible conflict of forces. It could avoid becoming a full duality in which the government of the day and indeed the parliamentary system could be challenged by the trade unions. Parliamentary democracy was still in 1939 a source of great pride, regarded not least in the trade union movement as giving the British nation its particular strength and character: this system of consent was seen as the greatest of British achievements.

The state thus stood between two powers, namely business and the unions, both of which posed difficult problems for it. Both had failed in their own organisations to arrive at structural principles that would make possible a coherent identity. Both had failed to produce a guiding theory of the economy and society. Each union continued to be intensely jealous of its complete autonomy within the TUC, strongly resisting a consolidation of power at the centre; this in turn derived from divergencies of interest and outlook as between the constituent unions. On the employers' side the FBI was subject to parallel weaknesses, arising from the fact that, because of the diversity of interests it contained, it too rested upon a loose voluntarism. The unions, on the whole, in spite of their conflict stance, were unwilling to see the market system destroyed, and were fearful of what might happen if this should occur; the employers, though ostensibly in favour of the market, had moved a long way in the direction of looking to the state to control its operation.

6. *Equity, wages, welfare and social stability*

The lines of economic policy jointly pursued by industry and the state (roughly an attempt to use the state to improve Britain's share of world markets, together with a range of measures to promote industrial restructuring and innovation) had not of course by 1939 induced a confidence that the system could generate either full employment or stability of incomes. Much less could such a policy be thought to have induced in British society a sense of well-being and equity such that the welfare functions of the state could be diminished.

On the other hand, in spite of everything, Britain was, on the whole, united and politically stable in 1939. Nothing approaching a revolutionary situation existed. To this relative stability the range of state welfare provisions, in spite of its inadequacies, was making a significant contribution. It was doing so both in terms of real benefits and in terms of a demonstration that society as a whole, through the state, had a degree of sensitivity to need, and could be brought to respond to its various forms.

Wages, by the agreement of workers, employers and the state, were governed partly by the market, and partly by the pattern of strategic advantage as between unions and employers in each sector as this operated within the constraints of trade union law as set by the state. Something might have been done by the adoption by the state of generalised minimum wage laws, but the employers were hostile to what they saw as additions to costs, and the unions were dubious about the state entering upon a policy of what would in effect become the regulation of the basic pattern of wages. The state, thus deprived of direct influence on wages as a means of operating on the pattern of incomes, was left with the possibility of redistributive taxation, the proceeds of which would be used for welfare provision in one form or another. But a policy of direct state augmentation of the lower incomes by tax-financed subsidy (e.g., a money handout) was flatly inconsistent with prevailing ideas.

This left the package of welfare services that had been evolving over the previous century. Behind these lay, in a vague form, two ideas. There was the concept of a national minimum below which no one should fall, and there was the aspiration of promoting social equity in the sense of improving life chances as they presented themselves to the lowest paid and most depressed families. The national minimum aspiration was expressed chiefly through the provision of health services, housing and unemployment insurance and benefits. As to the improvement of life chances at the nether end of society, such state operation as there was in this direction took place mainly through the educational system and through housing.

In all these welfare directions the state was confronted with the two questions – how far should it go in terms of resource provision, and what forms should the provision take? The first of these questions of course assumed an aggregate form as the Treasury made its preparations for the Chancellor's budget – at that point welfare challenged the other demands being made upon the government. Total expenditure, once arrived at, required the government to decide on the scale of the tax burdens it was prepared and able to impose on the democracy, and the distribution of these between its component classes.

Three sets of notions concerning welfare provision and organisation still played upon the minds of governments. The idea of self-help, seen in the context of the family as a unit of mutual support, was still strong. So too was the belief in the voluntarist principle, under which philanthropic men and women would provide resources either directly or by appeal to others, and would also perform important managerial functions in the operation of the various organisations thus funded. Direct state provision was to be seen, in many areas of welfare, as being in augmentation of the working-class self- and family-help, together with middle-class voluntarism. The search by the state thus continued in 1939, in many areas, for a balance between these three principles, with governmental intervention regarded as a kind of residual, to be used when self-help and voluntarism failed.

Each aspect of welfare had its long history and had provoked its peculiar governmental response. With respect to health benefits the state, though considerably involved, continued to hope to be able to leave the matter largely to the voluntarist principle and to local government, declining to take it over in order to subject it to state control on a national scale. Similarly the state was not prepared to nationalise health insurance, but had left it in the hands of the approved societies. In housing much had been achieved in meeting this basic social need among the lower income groups.

But a serious shortfall still remained. The Labour Party regarded housing provision for the needy as a social service, and was prepared to subsidise it generously. The Conservative Party, though accepting the need for a degree of subsidy, was worried at the large-scale departure from market principles that was involved, and by the assumption by local authorities of the role of major landlords; Conservatives in consequence sought for criteria that would govern such provision in the light of such considerations. Pensions for the aged and for widows and orphans had been made somewhat more generous in the inter-war years, but there remained much room for debate as to their adequacy and as to the extent that they should rest on the contributory principle. The poor law had been officially ended in 1929; its successor, public assistance, was mainly concerned with paying cash relief for the maintenance of the family in the home; here too there was argument about the scale of such payments and the terms of eligibility for them. The most publicised form of relief concerned the able-bodied unemployed: the re-organisation and extension of unemployment insurance in 1934, and the Unemployment Assistance Board set up in the same year to provide for those who had run out of benefit, were working reasonably well. But the means test, though somewhat eased, was still a deeply resented part of the system, involving the state in the most intimate and humiliating inquiry into the individual and the family. Though the state had recognised the right of the individual to aid when the market could not provide him with an income through a job, the state was still unwilling to make such aid unconditional.

What of the equalising of life chances between the children of the social classes? Here the principle of equity conflicted with that of meritocracy. A school system aimed at selecting and encouraging high standards of excellence could be inconsistent with the notion of equalising opportunity. The Hadow reforms, with their streaming of children after the 'eleven-plus' examination, had undoubtedly confirmed the class basis of English education, already deeply rooted in the public schools and the ancient universities. As a countervailing circumstance it is possible that, given the number of those wanting to be teachers, together with the widening opportunity provided for them by the civic universities, the quality and morale of teaching in schools serving working-class areas was well maintained. Moreover a good deal of the nineteenth-century optimism about the potential of education for generating both career opportunity and life fulfilment was still present. But it was sadly the case in 1939 that education was not a very powerful engine of social equity when set against the power of the class configuration of British society, with its self-confirming elements of deprivation and narrowing of horizons among the lower income groups.

7. *Thought and behaviour, women and the family*

In general Britain in 1939 enjoyed as high a level of freedom of speech, publication and assembly as any society in the world. There was no system of state spying through secret police. The state felt no serious threat against itself, either from the left or the right. The police were used to shepherd demonstrators and protestors and to hold rival groups apart on the relatively few occasions when they might have clashed. This, of course, was a reflection of the fact that no faction could offer a political programme threatening to the state, capable of carrying any degree of general support.

Nor did the state have at its disposal or take to itself any explicit means for the manipulation of minds. It is true that stage performances continued to be licensed by the Lord Chamberlain, and that the film industry, under the implied threat of state intervention, had undertaken its own system of self-surveillance. Both of these forms of control were concerned more with morality than with politics. There were also the laws of libel, defamation and slander; they, with the intention of preserving the good names of individuals, could be inhibitive on freedom of utterance. But in terms of the greatest single means of mind control available by 1939, namely the wireless, the British state had done two things in the effort to make it non-political: government had imposed a strict code of objectivity on the BBC and it had refused to permit commercial broadcasting. But the BBC was certainly on the side of moralism: it had hardly occurred to anyone that it should be otherwise.

It can be argued that the most potent form of mind control lay not in the entertainment industry, the newspapers or the radio, but in the schools system. It is certainly true that by its general values and through religious instruction in the schools the educational structure did convey a view of the proper nature of society. For example it undoubtedly backed the work ethic and promoted the sanctity of private property, together with a sense of social responsibility and self-discipline. It also promoted literacy and the widening of minds, such that a questioning of society could occur.

The principal forms of behaviour that were still under a degree of state control in 1939 were the consumption of alcohol, the taking of certain drugs, soliciting by prostitutes, obscenity and blasphemy, street betting and gaming houses, homosexuality and unnatural sexual acts and suicide. On all of these there was a pretty general national consensus as to what was fitting and proper: it was regarded as right that the state should confirm and even enforce it. The state, though it had long since in any real sense ceased to promote a religious view, had not moved out of morality. The state was seen as having a responsibility to promote the right against the wrong.

The family in 1939 was still regarded by the state as fundamental. At the working-class level steps had been taken aimed at repairing the deficiencies of the family; there were school meals and medical inspection together with the children's charter of 1908. The economic pressures on poor families had been somewhat eased by unemployment provisions and the passing of the poor law into public assistance. The family had been made somewhat less constraining upon women by 'granting' to them limited rights to hold property. A beginning had been made on easing divorce: this was carried further by the Act of 1937. But the family in the eyes of the state was still one institution under its patriarchal head. To it the women were still assimilated, perceived as wives and mothers, with no real role outside of the home. Though husband and wife had the vote on equal terms, the family was regarded by the state, through the inland revenue, as having one income, under the control of the husband.

Marriage, in the eyes of both the church and the state, was for life. Sexual relations outside of it, though not directly punished by the state (except in terms of a weakening of the position of the offending party in the case of divorce), was subject to disapproval through the law of bastardy.

8. *The ultimate sanctions*

The criminal law and penal system were not in 1939 matters of any great national concern. The courts enjoyed a high status: there was little criticism of their methods and little misgiving about the danger of miscarriage of justice. The majesty, aloofness and indeed archaism of the law continued to be emphasised by the distinctive dress of the judges and the forbidding architecture of the court houses. The adversary posture that governed court procedures, with their some-times dubious tactics, was little questioned. The death penalty was still an important part of a system of justice that was largely uninhibited by the fear of judicial mistakes. That it was the right and indeed the duty of the state, under certain conditions, to take life was not seriously questioned. The general notion was that prisoners had no rights, having forfeited these on being convicted. The theory of the 'deviant sub-culture', into which they were 'socialised' (grew up), and were thus incapable of choice concerning their way of life, had gained little ground.

Because of a relative indifference to those hidden away from society in the prisons, there was insufficient concern to generate that level of investigation and thought necessary to clarify the principles on which the whole system should rest. In the absence of a new perspective there was no possibility that the state would face the enormous cost of modernising the prison buildings and of meeting the wages bill of a staff adequate in numbers, quality and training. The ultimate residuum of society was, so far as the public was concerned, out of sight and out of mind.

Bibliography

The titles under General provide coverage for the whole book, or the greater part of it, but with varying degrees of completeness. Where a title covers more than one of the periods dealt with it appears in that chapter in which its starting date lies. Shortage of space precludes mention of articles. Unless otherwise mentioned, London is the place of publication.

General

Adamson, J.W., *English Education, 1789–1902*, 1964.
Atiyah, P.S., *The Rise and Fall of Freedom of Contract*, Oxford, 1979.
Barber, W.J., *A History of Economic Thought*, 1967.
Bienefeld, M.A., *Working Hours in British Industry: An Economic History*, 1972.
Blaug, M., *Economic Theory in Retrospect*, 3rd edn., Cambridge, 1979.
Bristow, E.J., *Vice and Vigilance: Purity Movements in Britain since 1700*, Dublin, 1977.
Bruce, M., *The Coming of the Welfare State*, 1961.
Checkland, O., *Philanthropy in Victorian Scotland*. Edinburgh, 1980.
Checkland, S.G., *Scottish Banking: A History, 1695–1973*, Glasgow and London, 1975.
Clapham, J.H., *An Economic History of Modern Britain*, 3 vols., Cambridge, 1930–2.
 The Bank of England, 2 vols., Cambridge, 1944.
Clarke, J.J., *A History of Local Government in the United Kingdom,* 1955.
Cohen, E.W., *Growth of the British Civil Service 1780–1939*, 1941.
Deane, P. and Cole, W.A., *British Economic Growth, 1688–1959: Trends and Structure*, Cambridge, 1953.
Feaveryear, A., *The Pound Sterling*, 2nd edn., Oxford, 1963.
Feinstein, C.H., *National Income, Expenditure and Output 1855–1965*, Cambridge, 1972.
Fetter, F.W., *Development of British Monetary Orthodoxy, 1797–1875*, Harvard U.P., 1965.
Fetter, F.W. and Gregory, D., *Monetary and Financial Policy: Government and Society in Nineteenth Century Britain*, Dublin, 1974.
Fraser, D., *The Evolution of the British Welfare State*, 1973.
 Urban Politics in Victorian England, 1976.

Frazer, W.M., *A History of English Public Health 1839–1939*, 1950.

Gauldie, E., *Cruel Habitations: A History of Working Class Housing 1780–1918*, 1974.

Gosden, P.H.J.H., *The Friendly Societies in England, 1815–75*, Manchester, 1961.

Self-Help Voluntary Associations in Nineteenth Century Britain, 1973.

Griffith, G., *The British Civil Service 1854–1954*, 1954.

Halévy, E., *History of the English People in the Nineteenth Century*, 6 vols., 1924–52.

Hanham, H.J., *The Reformed Electoral System in Great Britain 1832–1914*, Historical Association Pamphlet, 1968.

Hargreaves, E.L., *The National Debt*, 1930.

Hunt, E.H., *British Labour History, 1815–1914*, 1981. Esp. Part II, 'Working Class Movements'.

Mitchell, B.R. and Deane, P., *Abstract of British Historical Statistics*, Cambridge, 1962.

Morgan, E.V., *The Theory and Practice of Central Banking, 1797–1913*, 1943.

Musgrave, P.W., *Society and Education in England since 1800*, 1968.

Musson, A.E., *British Trade Unions 1800–1875*, 1972.

The Growth of British Industry, 1978.

O'Farrell, P., *England and Ireland since 1850*, 1975.

Owen, D., *English Philanthropy 1660–1960*, Oxford, 1965.

Parris, Henry, *Constitutional Bureaucracy: The Development of British Central Administration since the Eighteenth Century*, 1969.

Pelling, H., *A History of British Trade Unionism*, 1963.

Perkin, H., *The Origins of Modern English Society, 1780–1880*, 1969.

Radzinowicz, L., *A History of the English Criminal Law and its Administration since 1750*, 1948.

Raynes, H.E., *Social Security in Britain: A History*, 1967.

Roach, John, *Social Reform in England 1780–1880*, 1978.

Robson, W.A., *The Development of Local Government*, 3rd edn., 1954.

Rose, M.E., *The Relief of Poverty 1834–1914*, 1972.

Roseveare, H.G., *The Treasury*, 1969.

Sabine, B.E.V., *A History of Income Tax*, 1966.

Shehab, F., *Progressive Taxation: A Study in the Development of the Progressive Principle in the British Income Tax*, Oxford, 1953.

Silver, H. and Lawson, J., *A Social History of Education in England*, 1973.

Smellie, K.B., *A History of Local Government*, 1946.

Smith, F.B., *The People's Health, 1830–1910*, 1979.

Thompson, E.P., *The Making of the English Working Class*, 1963.

Thompson, F.M.L., *English Landed Society in the Nineteenth Century*, 1963.

Tobias, J.J., *Crime and Industrial Society in the Nineteenth Century*, 1967.

Ward, J.T., *The Factory System*, 2 vols., Newton Abbot, 1970.

Wardle, D., *English Popular Education 1780–1970*, 1970.

Williams, G., *The Coming of the Welfare State*, 1967.

Bibliography

1. The state and the proto-industrial economy of Britain

Anstey, R., *The Atlantic Slave Trade and British Abolition, 1760–1810*, 1975.

Ashton, T.S., *Economic Fluctuations in England 1700–1800*, Oxford, 1959. Chapters 3 and 4.

Chambers, J.D. and Mingay, G.E., *The Agricultural Revolution, 1750–1880*, 1966.

Chester, N., *The English Administrative System, 1780–1870*, Oxford, 1981.

Derry, J., 'Governing temperament under Pitt and Liverpool'. In Cannon, J., ed., *The Whig Ascendancy*, 1981.

Dickson, P.G.M., *The Financial Revolution in England: A Study in the Development of Public Credit 1688–1756*, 1967.

Emsley, C., *British Society and the French Wars, 1793–1815*, 1979.

Farnsworth, A., *Addington, Author of the Modern Income Tax*, 1951.

Gash, N., *Aristocracy and People: Britain 1815–1865*, 1979.

Harlow, V.T., *The Founding of the Second British Empire, 1763–1793*, vol. 1., 1952.

Harper, L.A., *The English Navigation Laws*, New York, 1939.

Heckscher, E., *Mercantilism*, 2nd edn., 1955.

Hope-Jones, A., *Income Tax in the Napoleonic Wars*, Cambridge, 1939.

Mingay, G.E., *English Landed Society in the Eighteenth Century*, 1963.

Rotwein, E., ed., *David Hume: Writings on Economics*, 1955.

Smith, A., *The Wealth of Nations,* 1776. New edn., Campbell, R.H. and Skinner, A., eds., Oxford, 1976.

Ward, W.R., *The English Land Tax in the Eighteenth Century*, Oxford, 1953.

Williams, J., *British Commercial Policy and Trade Expansion, 1750–1850*, 1972.

2. Core and periphery: England, Wales, Scotland and Ireland

Bryson, G., *Man and Society: The Scottish Inquiry of the Eighteenth Century*, Oxford, 1945.

Cage, R.A., *The Scottish Poor Law 1745–1845*, Edinburgh, 1981.

Fay, C.R., *Adam Smith and the Scotland of his Day*, Cambridge, 1956.

McDowall, R.B., *The Irish Administration, 1801–1914*, 1964.

Marshall, J.D., *The Old Poor Law, 1795–1834*, 1968.

Murdoch, A.J., *The People Above: Politics and Administration in Mid-Eighteenth Century Scotland*, Edinburgh, 1980.

Pomfret, J.E., *The Struggle for Land in Ireland*, Princeton, 1925. Reprinted New York, 1969.

Scotland, J., *The History of Scottish Education,* 1969.

3. Social values and social policy

Cowherd, R., *Political Economists and the English Poor Laws*, Athens, Ohio State University, 1977.

Hay, D., Linebaugh, P. and Thompson, E.P., *Albion's Fatal Tree: Crime and Society in Eighteenth Century England*, 1975.

Henriques, U., *Before the Welfare State: Social Administration in Early Industrial Britain,* 1979.

Horn, P., *The Rural World, 1780–1850,* 1980.

Ignatieff, N., *A Just Measure of Pain: The Penitentiary System in the Industrial Revolution 1750–1850,* 1978.

Marshall, Dorothy, *The English Poor in the Eighteenth Century,* London, 1965.

Marshall, J.D., *The Old Poor Law, 1795–1834,* London, 1968.

Poynter, J.R., *Society and Pauperism, English Ideas on Poor Relief, 1795–1834,* London, 1969.

Robertson, G., *An Account of the Obscenity Laws and their Enforcement in England and Wales,* 1979.

Rudé, G., *Protest and Punishment,* Oxford, 1978.

Thompson, E.P., *Whigs and Hunters: The Origin of the Black Act,* 1975.

4. The trend to economic laissez-faire

Black, R.D.C., *Economic Thought and the Irish Question 1817–1880,* Cambridge, 1960.

Blaug, M., *Ricardian Economics: A Historical Study,* New Haven, 1958.

Briggs, A., ed., *Chartist Studies,* 1962.

Brock, M., *The Great Reform Act,* 1973.

Brown, Lucy, *The Board of Trade and the Free Trade Movement, 1832–40,* Oxford, 1958.

Coats, A.W., ed., *The Classical Economists and Economic Policy,* 1971.

Cookson, J.E., *Lord Liverpool's Administration, 1815–1822,* 1975.

Cramp, A.B., *Opinion on Bank Rate, 1822–60,* 1962.

Gash, N., *Politics in the Age of Peel,* 1953.

  Reaction and Reconstruction in English Politics, 1832–52, Oxford, 1975.

Gordon, B., *Political Economy in Parliament, 1819–1823,* 1976.

Grampp, W.D., *The Manchester School of Economics,* Oxford, 1960.

Hilton, B., *Corn, Cash, Commerce: The Policies of the Tory Governments 1815–30,* Oxford, 1977.

Hilton, G.W., *The Truck System,* Cambridge, 1960.

Hunt, B.C., *The Development of the Business Corporation in England 1800–67,* Cambridge, Mass., 1936.

Jenkins, M., *The General Strike of 1842,* 1980.

Jones, E.L., *The Development of English Agriculture, 1815–1873,* 1973.

McCord, N., *The Anti-Corn Law League, 1838–1846,* 1958.

MacDonagh, O.O.M., *A Pattern of Government Growth 1880–1860: The Passenger Acts and their Enforcement,* 1961.

O'Brien, D.P., *The Classical Economists,* Oxford, 1975.

Parris, H., *Government and the Railways in Nineteenth Century Britain,* 1965.

Prest, J., *Politics in the Age of Cobden,* 1977.

Prouty, R., *The Transformation of the Board of Trade, 1830–55: A Study of Administrative Reorganisation in the Heyday of Laissez-Faire,* 1957.

Robbins, L., *The Theory of Economic Policy in English Classical Political Economy,* 1952.

Schuyler, R.L., *The Fall of the Old Colonial System: A Study in British Free Trade, 1770–1870*, New York, 1945.

Semmel, B., *The Rise of Free Trade Imperialism: Classical Political Economy, the Empire of Free Trade and Imperialism, 1750–1850*, Cambridge, 1970.

Shoup, C.S., *Ricardo and Taxation*, New York, 1960.

Ward, J.T., *Chartism*, 1973.

Williams, J.B., *British Commercial Policy and Trade Expansion, 1750–1850*, Oxford, 1972.

Winch, D., *Classical Political Economy and the Colonies*, 1965.

Wood, E., *English Theories of Central Banking Control, 1819–1858*, Cambridge, Mass., 1939.

5. The social action equation and the zeitgeist

Berg, M., *The Machinery Question and the making of Political Economy 1815–48*, Cambridge, 1980.

Best, G.F.A., *Lord Shaftesbury*, 1956.

Brundage, A., *The Making of the New Poor Law 1832–9*, 1978.

Chadwick, E., *Report on the Sanitary Condition of the Labouring Population*, 1842. New edn., Flinn, M., ed., 1965.

Checkland, S.G. and E.O.A., eds., *The Poor Law Report of 1834*, 1974.

Evans, E.J., ed., *Social Policy 1830–1914*, 1978.

Finer, S.E., *The Life and Times of Sir Edwin Chadwick*, 1952.

Finlayson, G.B.A.M., *The Seventh Earl of Shaftesbury 1801–1885*, 1981.

Flinn, M.W., *Public Health Reform in Great Britain*, 1968.

Harris, J.S., *British Government Inspectors*, 1955.

Hennock, E.P., *Fit and Proper Persons: Ideal and Reality in Nineteenth Century Urban Government*, 1973.

Henriques, U.R.Q., *The Early Factory Acts and their Enforcement*, 1971.

Jones, K., *Lunacy, Law and Conscience, 1744–1845*, 1955.

Lewis, R.A., *Edwin Chadwick and the Public Health Movement, 1832–1854*, 1952.

Lubenow, W.C., *The Politics of Government Growth: Early Victorian Attitudes Toward State Intervention*, 1971.

MacDonagh, O.O.M, *Early Victorian Government 1830–1870*, 1977.
Early Victorian Government 1830–1870, 1977.

Paz, D.G., *The Politics of Working Class Education in Britain 1830–50*, Manchester, 1980.

Phillips, D., *Crime and Authority in Victorian England: The Black Country 1835–1860*, 1977.

Rose, G., *The Struggle for Penal Reform*, 1961.

Silver, H., *English Education and the Radicals, 1780–1850*, 1976.

Taylor, G., *The Problem of Poverty, 1660–1834*, 1969.

Thane, P., ed., *The Origins of British Social Policy*, 1978.

West, E.G., *Education and the Industrial Revolution*, 1975.

Bibliography

6. The market triumphant

Bagehot, W., *Lombard Street,* 1873. New edn., 1919.
Burn, W.L., *The Age of Equipoise: A Study of the Mid-Victorian Generation*, 1964.
Dunham, A.L., *The Anglo-French Treaty of Commerce of 1860*, Ann Arbor, 1930.
Kieve, J., *The Electric Telegraph*, 1973.
Perkin, H., *The Origins of Modern English Society, 1780–1880*, 1969.
Smith, F.B., *The Making of the Second Reform Bill*, Melbourne, 1966.
Steele, E.D., *Irish Land and British Politics: Tenant Right and Nationality 1867–1870*, Cambridge, 1974.
Vincent, John, *The Formation of the Liberal Party*, 1965.

7. The state and the claims of labour

Jevons, W.S., *The State in Relation to Labour*, 1882.
Martin, R.M., *T.U.C. The Growth of a Pressure Group*, Oxford, 1980.
Musson, A.E., *British Trade Unions, 1800–1875*, 1972.
Roberts, B.C., *The Trades Union Congress, 1868–1921,* 1958.
Webb, S. and B., *A History of Trade Unions, 1666–1920*, 1920 edn.

8. The advance of social collectivism

Chapman, S.D., ed., *The History of Working Class Housing*, 1971.
Cruickshank, M., *Church and State in English Education*, 1963.
Dingle, A.E., *The Campaign for Prohibition in Victorian England*, 1980.
Harrison, B., *Drink and the Victorians*, 1971.
Hodgkinson, R., *The Origins of the National Health Service: The Medical Services of the New Poor Law 1834–71*, 1967.
Howard, D.L., *The English Prisons*, 1960.
Hurst, J.S., *Elementary Schooling and the Working Classes 1860–1918*, 1979.
Kelly, T., *A History of Public Libraries in Great Britain, 1845–1975*, 1977.
Lambert, Royston, *Sir John Simon, 1816–1904, and English Social Administration*, 1963.
McGregor, O.R., *Divorce in England: A Centenary Study*, 1957.
McHugh, P., *Prostitution and Victorian Social Reform*, 1980.
Petrie, G., *A Singular Iniquity: The Campaigns of Josephine Butler*, 1971.
Phillips, D., *Crime and Authority in Victorian England*, 1977.
Roach, J., *Public Examinations in England 1850–1900*, Cambridge, 1971.
Roberts, D., *Victorian Origins of the British Welfare State*, New Haven, 1968.
Roderick, G.W. and Stephens, M.D., *Education and Industry in the Nineteenth Century*, 1979.
Tompson, P., *The Charity Commission and the Age of Reform*, London, 1979.
Walkowitz, J.R., *Prostitution and Victorian Society: Women, Class and the State*, Cambridge, 1981.

405

Wohl, A.S., *The Eternal Slum, Housing and Social Policy in Victorian London*, 1977.
Wright, M., *Treasury Control of the Civil Service, 1854–1974*, 1969.

9. The continued freedom of the market mechanism; the state-induced changes in its operating conditions

Aldcroft, D.H. and Richardson, H.W., *The British Economy, 1870–1939*, 1969.
Bealey, F. and Pelling, H., *Labour and Politics, 1900–1906*, 1959.
Brown, B.H., *The Tariff Reform Movement in Great Britain, 1881–95*, 1944.
Brown, K.D., *The Labour Party and Unemployment, 1900–14*, 1971.
Cross, C., *The Liberals in Power 1905–1914*, 1963.
Dangerfield, G., *The Strange Death of Liberal England*, 1970 edn.
Fair, J.D., *British Interparty Conferences: A Study of the Procedure of Conciliation in British Politics 1867–1921*, Oxford, 1981.
Fraser, P., *Joseph Chamberlain*, 1966.
French, D., *British Economic and Strategic Planning 1905–1915*, 1982.
Grigg, J., *Lloyd George, The People's Champion, 1902–1911*, 1978.
Hamer, D., *Liberal Politics in the Age of Gladstone and Rosebery: A Study in Leadership and Policy*, 1972.
Harris, J., *Unemployment and Politics: A Study of English Social Policy 1886–1914*, Oxford, 1972.
Hicks, U.K., *British Public Finance, 1880–1952*, 1958.
Levy, H., *Monopolies, Cartels and Trusts in British Industry*, 2nd edn., 1927.
McBriar, A.M., *Fabian Socialism and English Politics, 1884–1918*, 1962.
Marsh, P., *The Discipline of Popular Government: Lord Salisbury's Domestic Statecraft 1881–1902*, 1978.
Matthew, H.C.B., *The Liberal Imperialists: The Ideas and Politics of the Post-Gladstonian Elite*, 1973.
Morgan, D., *Suffragists and Liberals: The Politics of Women Suffrage in Britain*, Oxford, 1975.
Morgan, K.O., *The Age of Lloyd George: The Liberal Party and British Politics*, 1971.
Murray, B.K., *The People's Budget 1909/10: Lloyd George and Liberal Politics*, Oxford, 1981.
Rempel, R.A., *Unionists Divided: Arthur Balfour, Joseph Chamberlain and the Unionist Free Traders*, 1972.
Sayers, R.S., *Central Banking after Bagehot*, Oxford, 1957.
The Bank of England, 3 vols., Cambridge, 1976.
Thompson, P., *Socialists, Liberals and Labour: The Struggle for London 1885–1914*, 1967.
Tomlinson, J., *Problems of British Economic Policy 1870–1945*, 1981.

10. Land and rule in England, Wales, Scotland and Ireland

Clark, S., *Social Origins of the Irish Land War*, Princeton, 1980.
Collier, A., *The Crofting Problem*, 1953.
Douglas, R., *Land, People and Politics: A History of the Land Question in the UK, 1878–1952*, 1976.
Grigg, J., *The Young Lloyd George*, 1973.
Morgan, K.O., *Wales in British Politics 1868–1922*, 1963.
  Rebirth of a Nation: Wales 1880–1980, Oxford and Cardiff, 1981.
Offer, A., *Property and Politics 1870–1914*, 1981.
Solow, B., *The Land Question and the Irish Economy, 1870–1903*, Cambridge, Mass., 1971.
Thornley, D., Historical Introduction to Chubb, B., *The Government and Politics of Ireland*, Oxford, 1974.
Webb, K., *The Growth of Scottish Nationalism*, Glasgow, 1977.
Williams, D., *A History of Modern Wales*, 1950.

11. The emergence of a public sector, chiefly at the local government level

Briggs, A., *Victorian Cities*, 1963.
Finer, H., *Municipal Trading*, 1941.
Fraser, D., *Power and Authority in the Victorian City*, 1979.
Gibbon, G. and Bell, R., *The History of the London County Council 1889–1939*, 1939.
Gill, C. and Briggs, A., *A History of Birmingham*, 2 vols., Oxford, 1952.
Hannah, L., *Electricity before Nationalisation: A Study of the Development of the Electricity Supply Industry in Britain to 1948*, 1979.
Harris, J.S., *British Government Inspection: The Local Services and the Central Authority*, 1955.
Kent, M., *Oil and Empire: British Policy and Mesopotamian Oil 1900–20*, 1976.
Robson, W.A., *The Government and Misgovernment of London*, 1938.
Schulz, M., in Wilson, C.H., ed., *Essays in Local Government*, 1948.

12. The assertion of the power of labour in industry and politics

Bealey, F. and Pelling, H., *Labour and Politics, 1900–1906*, 1959.
Beveridge, W.H., *Unemployment: A Problem of Industry*, 1909.
Brown, K.D., *Labour and Unemployment, 1900–1914*, 1971.
Bythell, D., *The Sweated Trades*, 1978.
Charles, R., *The Development of Industrial Relations in Britain, 1911–1939*, 1973.
Clegg, H.A., Fox, A. and Thompson, A.F., *A History of British Trade Unions since 1889*, vol. 1: *1889–1910*, Oxford, 1964.
Davidson, R., *Industrial Problems and Disputes*, Lord Askwith, ed., new edn., 1974.

Deakin, N., in Holmes, C., ed., *Immigrants and Minorities in British Society*, 1978.

Gainer, B., *The Alien Invasion*, 1972.

Garrard, J.A., *The English and Immigration 1880–1910*, 1971.

Gregory, R.G., *The Miners and British Politics, 1906–14*, 1968.

Harris, J., *William Beveridge: A Biography*, Oxford, 1977.

Holton, B., *British Syndicalism 1900–1914*, 1976.

Kendall, W., *The Revolutionary Movement in Britain 1900–21*, 1969.

Lovell, J., *Stevedores and Dockers*, 1969.

  British Trade Unions, 1875–1933, 1977.

Moore, R., *The Emergence of the Labour Party 1880–1924*, 1979.

Pelling, H., *Popular Politics and Society in Late Victorian Britain*, 1969.

Phelps-Brown, E.H., *The Growth of British Industrial Relations: A Study from the Standpoint of 1906–14*, 1959.

Sharp, I.G., *Industrial Conciliation and Arbitration in Great Britain*, 1950.

Turner, H.A., *Trade Union Growth, Structure and Policy*, 1962.

Wigham, E., *Strikes and the Government 1893–1974*, 1981.

13. Welfare and the social democratic urge

Allison, L.J., *Environmental Planning*, 1975.

Armytage, W.H.G., *Civic Universities*, 1955.

Banks, D., *Parity and Prestige in English Secondary Education,* 1955.

Bell, C., *The City Fathers: The Early History of Town Planning in Britain,* 1969.

Brand, J.L., *Doctors and the State: The British Medical Profession and Government Action in Public Health, 1870–1912*, Baltimore, 1965.

Brennan, E.J.T., ed., *Education for National Efficiency: The Contribution of Sidney and Beatrice Webb*, 1976.

Briggs, A., *Social Thought and Social Action: A Study of the Work of Seebohm Rowntree*, 1961.

Cherry, G.E., *The Evolution of British Town Planning*, Leighton Buzzard, 1974.

Cormack, U., *The Royal Commission on the Poor Laws and the Welfare State*, 1953.

Emy, H.V., *Liberals, Radicals and Social Politics, 1892–1914*. Cambridge, 1973.

Gilbert, B.B., *The Evolution of National Insurance in Great Britain*, 1966.

Graves, J., *Policy and Progress in Secondary Education, 1902–42*, 1943.

Hay, J.R., *The Origins of the Liberal Welfare Reforms, 1906–14*, 1975.

Kelsall, R.K., *Higher Civil Servants in Britain from 1870 to the Present Day*, 1955.

Mackintosh, J.M., *Trends of Opinion about the Public Health, 1901–51*, 1953.

Macleod, R.M., *Treasury Control and Social Administration: A Study of Establishment Growth at the Local Government Board, 1871–1905*, Occasional Papers on Social Administration, No. 23, 1968.

Morgan, D., *Suffragists and Liberals: The Politics of Women's Suffrage in Britain*, Oxford, 1975.

Mowat, C.L., *The Charity Organisation Society, 1869–1913*, 1961.

Price, S.J., *Building Societies, their Origin and History*, 1958.

Searle, G.R., *The Quest for National Efficiency*, Oxford, 1971.
Semmel, B., *Imperialism and Social Reform*, 1960.
Simey, T.S. and M.B., *Charles Booth: Social Scientist*, Oxford, 1960.
Simon, B., *Education and the Labour Movement, 1870–1920*, 1974.
Sutherland, G., *Policy Making in Elementary Education, 1870–1895*, Oxford, 1973.
Thane, P., *Old Age Pensions*, 1976.
Webb, B., *My Apprenticeship*, 1926. New edn., Harmondsworth, 1971.
Whitaker, W.B., *Victorian and Edwardian Shop Workers: The Struggle to Obtain Better Conditions and a Half-Holiday*, 1973.

14. The policy imperatives of war; the reconstruction debate and the dismantlement of control, 1914–21

Adams, R.J.Q., *Arms and the Wizard, Lloyd George and the Ministry of Munitions 1915–1916*, 1978.
Addison, G., *Four and a Half Years*, 1934.
Hinton, J., *The First Shop Stewards Movement*, 1973.
Hurwitz, S.J., *State intervention in Great Britain, 1914–19*, 1949.
Johnson, P.B., *Land Fit for Heroes: Planning for Reconstruction, 1916–19*, 1969.
Milward, A.S., *The Economic Effects of the Wars*, 1970.
Morgan, E.V., *Studies in British Financial Policy, 1914–25*, 1952.
Pribicevic, B., *The Shop Stewards' Movement and Workers' Control 1910–1922*, Oxford, 1959.
Swartz, M., *The Union of Democratic Control in British Politics during the First World War*, Oxford, 1971.
Terraine, J., *To Win a War: 1918 the Year of Victory*, 1979.
Woodward, L., *Great Britain and the War of 1914–18*, 1967.

15. The strains of nationalism: Wales, Scotland and Ireland

Bew, P., Gibbon, P. and Patterson, H., *The State in Northern Ireland, 1921–72*, Manchester, 1980.
Brown, T., *Ireland: A Social and Cultural History 1922–79*, 1981.
Milne, D., *The Scottish Office and other Scottish Departments,* 1958.

16. The advent of peacetime macro-economic management

Aldcroft, D.H., *The Inter-War Economy: Britain 1919–39*, 1970.
Alford, B.W.E., *Depression and Recovery? British Economic Growth 1918–39*, 1972.
Bentley, M., *The Liberal Mind 1914–1929*, Cambridge, 1977.
Cairncross, F., ed., *Changing Perceptions of Economic Policy: Essays in Honour of the Seventieth Birthday of Sir Alec Cairncross*, 1981.
Cowling, M., *The Impact of Labour 1920–24*, 1971.
Davison, R.C., *British Employment Policy: The Modern Phase since 1930*, 1938.

Drummond, I.M., *British Economic Policy and the Empire, 1919–1939*, 1972.
  Imperial Economic Policy 1918–39, 1974.
  The Floating Pound and the Sterling Area, 1931–1939, Cambridge, 1981.
Edelman, P., *The Decline of the Liberal Party 1910–1931*, 1981.
Glynn, S. and Oxborrow, J., *Interwar Britain: A Social and Economic History*, 1976.
Henderson, H.D., *The Inter-War Years and Other Papers*, Oxford, 1955.
Hicks, U.K., *The Finance of British Government 1920–1936*, Oxford, 1938.
Howson, S., *Domestic Monetary Management in Britain 1919–38*, 1975.
  and Winch, D., *The Economic Advisory Council 1930–39*, Cambridge, 1977.
Lyman, R.W., *The First Labour Government, 1924*, 1957.
Macmillan, H., *The Middle Way*, 1939.
Moggridge, D.E., *The Return to Gold 1925*, 1969.
  British Monetary Policy 1924–31, 1972.
Morgan, K.O., *Consensus and Disunity: The Lloyd George Government 1918–1922*, 1979.
Morris, M., *The General Strike*, 1976.
Nevin, E., *The Mechanism of Cheap Money: A Study of British Monetary Policy 1931–9*, 1955.
Peacock, A.T. and Wiseman, J., *The Growth of Public Expenditure in the United Kingdom 1898–1955*, 1967.
Peden, G.C., *British Rearmament and the Treasury, 1932–1939*, Edinburgh, 1979.
Pollard, S., ed., *The Gold Standard and Employment Policies between the Wars*, 1970.
Richardson, H.W., *The Economic Recovery in Britain 1932–39*, 1967.
Sabine, B.E.V., *British Budgets in Peace and War 1932–1945*, 1970.
Skidelsky, R., *Politicians and the Slump: The Labour Government of 1929–31*, Harmondsworth, 1970 edn.
Waight, L., *History and Mechanism of the Exchange Equalisation Account 1932–9*, Cambridge, 1939.
Wilson, T., *The Downfall of the Liberal Party 1914–35*, 1966.
Winch, D., *Economics and Policy*, 1969.
Youngson, A.J., *The British Economy, 1920–1957*, 1960.

17. Micro-management: the restructuring of industry and agriculture; the regions

Aldcroft, D.H., *British Railways in Transition: The economic problems of Britain's railways since 1914*, 1968.
Allen, G.C., *British Industries and their Organisation*, 3rd edn., 1952.
Astor, Viscount and Rowntree, B.S., *British Agriculture*, 1938.
Barker, T.C. and Collins, M.A., *History of London Transport*, 2 vols., 1963 and 1974.
Chester, D.N., *Public Control of Road Passenger Transport*, 1936.
Dennison, S.R., *The Location of Industry and the Depressed Areas*, 1939.

Duckham, B.F., *A History of the Scottish Coal Industry*, Newton Abbot, 1970.
Greenwood, H.P., *Employment and the Depressed Areas*, 1936.
Gwilliam, K.M., *Transport and Public Policy*, 1964.
Hannah, L., *The Rise of the Corporate Economy*, 1976. Pb. edn., 1979.
Hindley, B., *Industrial Merger and Public Policy,* 1970.
Jones, L., *Shipbuilding in Britain*, 1957.
Kirby, M.W., *The British Coalmining Industry 1870–1946: A Political and Economic History*, 1977.
Lucas, A.F., *Industrial Reconstruction and the Control of Competition*, 1937.
Payne, P.L., *Colvilles and the Scottish Steel Industry*, Oxford, 1979.
Political and Economic Planning, *Report on the British Iron and Steel Industry*, 1933.
Political and Economic Planning, *Report on the British Coal Industry*, 1936.
Political and Economic Planning, *The Location of Industry*, 1939.
Slaven, A., *The Development of the West of Scotland: 1750–1960*, 1975. Chapter 8.
Walker, G., *Road and Rail*, 2nd edn., 1947.

18. Micro-management: the public sector

Briggs, A., *History of Broadcasting in the United Kingdom*, vol. 1, 1961.
Byatt, I.C.R., *The British Electrical Industry 1875–1914*, Oxford, 1979.
Dyos, H.J. and Aldcroft, D.H., *British Transport*, Leicester, 1969. Chapter 3.
Gorham, M., *Broadcasting and Television since 1900*, 1952.
Higham, R., *Imperial Air Routes, 1918–39*, 1960.
Sleeman, J., *British Public Utilities*, 1953.
Wickwar, W.H., *The Public Services,* 1938.

19. The business response

Brady, R.A., *Business as a System of Power*, New York, 1943. Chapter 5.
Grant, W., *The CBI*, 1965.
Holland, R.F., 'The Federation of British Industries and the International Economy'. *Economic History Review*, 2nd ser., vol. 34 (1981).

20. The political and industrial attitudes of labour

Allen, V.L., *Trade Unions and the Government*, 1961.
Arnot, R.P., *The Miners,* 1949.
Bealey, F., ed., *The Social and Political Thought of the British Labour Party*, 1970.
Bullock, A., *Life of Ernest Bevin, 1881–1940*, vol. 1, 1960.
Challinor, R., *The Origins of British Bolshevism*, 1978.
Charles, R., *The Development of Industrial Relations in Britain, 1911–39*, 1973.
Dowse, R., *Left in the Centre: The Independent Labour Party, 1893–1940*, 1966.
Lovell, J. and Roberts, B.C., *A Short History of the TUC*, 1968.
Phillips, G.A., *The General Strike: The Politics of Industrial Conflict*, 1976.

Symons, J., *The General Strike*, 1957.
Tsuzuki, C., *H.M. Hyndman and British Socialism*, Oxford, 1961.

21. The welfare share: its elements and adequacy

Beveridge, W.H., *Unemployment: A Problem of Industry, 1909 and 1930*, 1930.
Bowley, M., *Housing and the State, 1919–1944*, 1945.
Gilbert, B.B., *British Social Policy, 1914–1939*, 1970.
Harris, A.S., *National Health Insurance in Great Britain, 1911–1946*, 1972.
Levy, H., *National Health Insurance: A Critical Study*, 1944.
Newsholme, A., *The Last Thirty Years in Public Health*, 1936.
Political and Economic Planning, *Report on Housing, England*, 1934.
Political and Economic Planning, *Report on the British Health Services,* 1937.
Swenarton, M., *Homes Fit for Heroes*, 1981.
Wilson, A. and MacKay, G.S., *Old Age Pensions*, 1941.

Index

Figures in bold type indicate whole chapter or section; *p.* means *passim*.

413

414